SHEPPARD'S BOOK DEALERS
IN NORTH AMERICA

Uniform with this volume are:

DEALERS IN BOOKS

A DIRECTORY OF DEALERS IN SECONDHAND AND
ANTIQUARIAN BOOKS IN THE BRITISH ISLES

EUROPEAN BOOKDEALERS

A DIRECTORY OF DEALERS IN SECONDHAND AND
ANTIQUARIAN BOOKS ON THE CONTINENT OF EUROPE

BOOKDEALERS IN INDIA,

PAKISTAN, SRI LANKA etc.

A DIRECTORY OF DEALERS IN SECONDHAND AND
ANTIQUARIAN BOOKS, PERIODICALS AND PRINTS
IN THE SOUTH-WEST ASIAN SUB-CONTINENT

———————————

THE BOOKDEALERS' AND COLLECTORS'
YEAR-BOOK AND DIARY

published each year in November
contains lists of additions and alterations
to all the above directories

SHEPPARD'S

BOOK DEALERS IN NORTH AMERICA

A DIRECTORY OF ANTIQUARIAN AND SECONDHAND BOOK DEALERS IN THE U.S.A. AND CANADA

1986 – 87

TENTH EDITION

LONDON: EUROPA PUBLICATIONS

First published June 1954

Tenth edition 1986

EUROPA PUBLICATIONS LIMITED
18 BEDFORD SQUARE
LONDON, WC1B 3JN, ENGLAND

I.S.S.N. 0269–1469
I.S.B.N. 0 946653 19 4
DEWEY CLASSIFICATION
655–56097058

MADE IN ENGLAND

Printed by Unwin Brothers at the Gresham Press, Old Woking, Surrey

CONTENTS

v

INTRODUCTION

THE tenth edition of this directory is the first to be published by Europa Publications, and we hope that users will continue to find it an invaluable reference work. In the thirty-two years which have elapsed since the first edition appeared, our predecessor, the Sheppard Press Limited, established a tradition of improving the book with each revision. At Europa, as long-standing specialist publishers of reference books, we shall be building on this tradition vigorously: we are particularly fortunate in having the services of T. Rendall Davies, the former editor of the Sheppard Press list, as consultant on the books and, with the resources of a larger organization and a well-developed system of distribution, we aim to attract a growing readership in the years ahead.

It goes without saying that a book of this kind must be sensitive to the needs of its users, and we are always pleased to receive comments about the book and, in particular, suggestions for ways by which it may be improved. The fact that the present edition contains about 600 new entries indicates the extent of the turnover of businesses in the antiquarian and secondhand book trade, and we should like to hear from any dealers who feel they ought to be added to the next edition of this directory.

Plan of the Directory

Miscellaneous Information. This first section is intended to fulfil some of the functions of a year-book. It contains miscellaneous information of the sort that changes from time to time and has to be kept up to date. No attempt has been made to include facts that never alter and can easily be found in one of the permanent reference books that every bookman should possess.

Geographical Directory of Dealers. The geographical section is the principal directory. It contains all the available information about every known dealer in used and antiquarian books in Canada and the United States of America. All the principal ones are certainly there, and so are all the medium and small businesses that could be traced. To these have been added some book scouts and shops that carry no used stock, but run a vigorous book-finding service, since their names and addresses are often required. There are, however, also many shops that advertise occasionally for out-of-print books. As is inevitable in a trade that can be conducted from a private residence, and needs no equipment, stock or registered qualifications, many clerks, librarians and collectors indulge in desultory dealing.

The information given in each entry should show the sort of business carried on by the dealer to whom it relates. The stock normally carried has been classified as VERY SMALL if under 2,000 volumes; SMALL if 2,000 to 5,000; MEDIUM if 5,000 to 10,000; LARGE if 10,000 to 20,000; and VERY LARGE if over 20,000. It must be emphasized, however, that these descriptions are rather arbitrary. A dealer who specializes in a particular subject and buys his stock carefully, perhaps one volume at a time, may feel justifiably proud if he can offer a choice from two thousand valuable items; on the other hand it will easily be appreciated that, by buying libraries and collections *en bloc*, a bookseller can quickly amass a vast but mediocre stock.

The arrangement of areas is simple. The first three are devoted to Canada, and the United States then follow in the usual alphabetical order with one section each, except for New York which is divided into Manhattan and Bronx, Long and Staten Islands, and Up-State addresses. At the end are American Territories, and other countries.

Americans may feel that some of the entries are a little pedantic; this is because many abbreviations that may seem quite obvious to them confuse people who do not normally speak English and who are not very familiar with the North American continent, and have therefore been carefully avoided.

There are two indexes serving the Geographical Directory of Dealers:

★ The *Alphabetical Index* is not only a complete index to the geographical entries, but a valuable "Who's Who", giving the names of the owners where these are different from the trading name.

★ The *Speciality Index* has been carefully arranged under suitable headings, and the entries indexed to the geographical areas.

A Historical Note

The present directory is not the first book of its kind. In 1885 C. N. Caspar compiled, and published at Milwaukee, Wisconsin, a "Directory of the Antiquarian Booksellers and Dealers in Second-hand Books in the United States."

The subscription price was five dollars, and the book contained details of 276 booksellers in the United States of America and Canada, arranged in three lists; first in a general alphabet, then geographically according to states and towns, and finally classified under the speciality of each dealer. Lists of the principal Jobbing Houses dealing in miscellaneous new books and of the most important News Companies, together with a few advertisements, completed the volume, which was a foolscap quarto, stoutly bound in boards.

A century later, it is interesting to read Caspar's comments about the book trade at that time:

> The Antiquarian Book-shop, which is the true preserver, and oftentime the tomb, of the books embodying the knowledge and wisdom, the errors and follies of past generations, is also a source of great delight and a treasure of information for the lover of books, the historian, the scholar, the librarian or the student . . . .

> The time is not far distant when an intelligent and discriminating public will demand of the bookseller, and especially of the dealer in old books, a thorough training and a wide knowledge of his trade, combined with a sound judgment on all matters pertaining to books and literature. Only men who have these qualifications and who possess the requisite fund of energy for one of the most ideal of the professions, the art of bookselling, will in coming days gain the patronage of bookbuyers and meet with success, **not** the underseller, bookbutcher, dry goods bazaar, etc., which today are the ruin of the honest bookseller. Every tradesman should have honest prices, and not intend to upbuild his own fortune on the ruins of his legitimate competitors. The best method of combatting these guerillas is to let them severely alone, for by so doing they will naturally exterminate one another. This does not preclude, of course, the necessity of meeting the fluctuations of the market, provided one can do so without actual loss. A bookseller should also be willing to stand the loss of a sale, if circumstances advise this. Above all every bookseller should take pride in carrying as large and well selected a stock as his means allow, suitable for his locality, and endeavour to be better versed on questions pertaining to books and their contents than his colleagues. An essential factor in the successful conduct of the bookseller's business, is a full and complete Library of Bibliographical and Literary Reference Works, Trade Catalogues, Publishers' Lists, etc. This will be more appreciated by book-buyers than any unnecessary cutting of prices on popular books.

As a final note, when addressing letters to dealers in this directory, please:

Always add to the name of the town (a) the State or Province—there are often several towns with the same name, e.g.there is, as might be expected, Kansas City in the State of Kansas, but there is Kansas City, a separate municipality, in the State of Missouri; (b) the zip-code, or postal code number, to assist speedy delivery; and (c) either CANADA or U.S.A. as the case may be—many American cities are named after places in the Old World such as Athens, Rome and London, and letters without the name of the country on them may travel to Europe first.

Do not use any abbreviations for the names of provinces or states, other than the generally recognized ones, which are shown after the name in the directory. For places in the United States the two-letter codes are to be preferred.

MISCELLANEOUS
INFORMATION

ABBREVIATIONS
USED IN DESCRIBING BOOKS

Some booksellers, and indeed some bookbuyers, use highly individualistic systems of abbreviations which, often combined with illegible writing, make their descriptions meaningless, especially to those for whom English is an acquired language. The following are sufficiently well known to be generally used, but all other words should be written in full, and the whole typed if possible.

A.D.	Autograph document	D-j., d-w.	Dust jacket, dust wrapper
A.D.s.	Autograph document, signed	E.D.L.	Edition de luxe
A.D.*	Autograph document with seal	Edn.	Edition
		Endp., e.p.	Endpaper(s)
A.e.g.	All edges gilt	Eng., engr.	Engraved, engraving
A.L.	Autograph letter, not signed	Ex-lib.	Ex-library
		Facs.	Facsimile
A.L.s.	Autograph letter, signed	Fcp.	Foolscap
		F.	Fine
a.v.	**Authorized version**	F., ff.	Folio, folios
B.A.R.	Book Auction Records	Fo., fol.	Folio (book size)
Bd.	Bound	F.O.B.	Free on board
Bdg.	Binding	Fp., front.	Frontispiece
Bds.	Boards	Free	Post free
B.L.	Black letter	G.	Good
C., ca.	Circa (approximately)	G., gt.	Gilt edges
C. & p.	Collated and perfect	G.L.	Gothic letter
Cat.	Catalogue	Hf. bd.	Half bound
Cent.	Century	Illum.	Illuminated
Cf.	Calf	Ill(s).	Illustrated, illustration(s)
C.I.F.	Cost, insurance and freight	Imp.	Imperial
Cl.	Cloth	Impft.	Imperfect
Col(d).	Colour(ed)	Inscr.	Inscribed, inscription
C.O.D.	Cash on delivery	Ital.	Italic letter
Cont.	Contemporary	Lea.	Leather
C.O.R.	Cash on receipt	Lev.	Levant morocco
Cr. 8vo.	Crown octavo	Ll.	Leaves
d.e.	Deckle edges	L.P.	Large paper
Dec.	Decorated	M.	Mint

2

Mco., mor.	Morocco	Sgd.	Signed
M.e.	Marbled edges	Sig.	Signature
M.S.(S.)	Manuscript(s)	S.N.	Sine nomine (without name of printer)
N.d.	No date		
n.ed.	new edition	Spr.	Sprinkled
n.p.	no place (of publication)	T.e.g.	Top edge gilt
		Thk.	Thick
Ob., obl.	Oblong	T.L.s.	Typed letter, signed
Oct.	Octavo	T.p.	Title-page
O.p.	Out of print	T.S.	Typescript
P.	Page	Unbd.	Unbound
P.f.	Post free	Uncut	Uncut (pages not trimmed)
Pict.	Pictorial		
Pl(s).	Plate(s)	Und.	Undated
Port.	Portrait	V.d.	Various dates
P.P.	Printed privately	V.g.	Very good
Pp.	Pages	Vol.	Volume
Prelims.	Preliminary pages	W.a.f.	With all faults
Pseud.	Pseudonym(ous)	Wraps.	Wrappers
Ptd.	Printed		
q.v.	Quod vide (which see)		
Qto.	Quarto		
Rev.	Revised		
Rom.	Roman letter		
S.L.	Sine loco (without place of publication)		

Condition is usually described in the following descending scale. — Mint — Fine — Very good — Good — Fair — Poor.

SIZES OF BOOKS

These are only approximate, as trimming varies

	Octavo (8vo)		Quarto (4to)	
	Inches	*Centimetres*	*Inches*	*Centimetres*
FOOLSCAP ..	$6\frac{3}{4} \times 4\frac{1}{2}$	$17 \cdot 1 \times 10 \cdot 7$	$8\frac{1}{2} \times 6\frac{3}{4}$	$21 \cdot 5 \times 17 \cdot 1$
CROWN ..	$7\frac{1}{2} \times 5$	$19 \cdot 0 \times 12 \cdot 7$	$10 \times 7\frac{1}{2}$	$25 \cdot 4 \times 19 \cdot 0$
LARGE POST	$8\frac{1}{4} \times 5\frac{1}{4}$	$20 \cdot 9 \times 13 \cdot 3$	$10\frac{1}{2} \times 8\frac{1}{4}$	$26 \cdot 6 \times 20 \cdot 9$
DEMY ..	$8\frac{3}{4} \times 5\frac{5}{8}$	$22 \cdot 2 \times 14 \cdot 2$	$11\frac{1}{4} \times 8\frac{3}{4}$	$28 \cdot 5 \times 22 \cdot 2$
MEDIUM ..	$9 \times 5\frac{3}{4}$	$22 \cdot 8 \times 14 \cdot 6$	$11\frac{1}{2} \times 9$	$29 \cdot 2 \times 22 \cdot 8$
ROYAL ..	$10 \times 6\frac{1}{4}$	$25 \cdot 4 \times 15 \cdot 8$	$12\frac{1}{2} \times 10$	$31 \cdot 7 \times 25 \cdot 4$
SUPER ROYAL	$10 \times 6\frac{3}{4}$	$25 \cdot 4 \times 17 \cdot 1$	$13\frac{1}{2} \times 10$	$34 \cdot 2 \times 25 \cdot 4$
IMPERIAL ..	$11 \times 7\frac{1}{2}$	$27 \cdot 9 \times 19 \cdot 0$	15×11	$38 \cdot 0 \times 27 \cdot 9$
FOOLSCAP FOLIO			$13\frac{1}{2} \times 8\frac{1}{2}$	$34 \cdot 2 \times 21 \cdot 5$
METRIC A5	$7\frac{3}{4} \times 6\frac{1}{2}$	$19 \cdot 6 \times 16 \cdot 4$		
A4	$15\frac{1}{2} \times 13$	$39 \cdot 2 \times 32 \cdot 8$		

METRIC CONVERSIONS

<table>
<tr><th colspan="4" align="center">SIZES</th><th colspan="2" align="center">WEIGHTS</th></tr>
<tr><th>inches</th><th>m.m.</th><th>inches</th><th>m.m.</th><th>lbs.</th><th>kgs.</th></tr>
<tr><td>$\frac{1}{4}$</td><td>6</td><td>$7\frac{3}{4}$</td><td>197</td><td>1</td><td>0.45</td></tr>
<tr><td>$\frac{1}{2}$</td><td>13</td><td>8</td><td>203</td><td>2</td><td>0.91</td></tr>
<tr><td>$\frac{3}{4}$</td><td>19</td><td>$8\frac{1}{4}$</td><td>210</td><td>3</td><td>1.36</td></tr>
<tr><td>1</td><td>25</td><td>$8\frac{1}{2}$</td><td>216</td><td>4</td><td>1.81</td></tr>
<tr><td>$1\frac{1}{4}$</td><td>32</td><td>$8\frac{3}{4}$</td><td>222</td><td>5</td><td>2.27</td></tr>
<tr><td>$1\frac{1}{2}$</td><td>38</td><td>9</td><td>229</td><td>6</td><td>2.72</td></tr>
<tr><td>$1\frac{3}{4}$</td><td>44</td><td>$9\frac{1}{4}$</td><td>235</td><td>7</td><td>3.18</td></tr>
<tr><td>2</td><td>51</td><td>$9\frac{1}{2}$</td><td>241</td><td>8</td><td>3.63</td></tr>
<tr><td>$2\frac{1}{4}$</td><td>57</td><td>$9\frac{3}{4}$</td><td>248</td><td>9</td><td>4.08</td></tr>
<tr><td>$2\frac{1}{2}$</td><td>64</td><td>10</td><td>254</td><td>10</td><td>4.54</td></tr>
<tr><td>$2\frac{3}{4}$</td><td>70</td><td>$10\frac{1}{4}$</td><td>260</td><td>11</td><td>4.99</td></tr>
<tr><td>3</td><td>76</td><td>$10\frac{1}{2}$</td><td>267</td><td>12</td><td>5.44</td></tr>
<tr><td>$3\frac{1}{4}$</td><td>83</td><td>$10\frac{3}{4}$</td><td>273</td><td>13</td><td>5.90</td></tr>
<tr><td>$3\frac{1}{2}$</td><td>89</td><td>11</td><td>279</td><td>14</td><td>6.35</td></tr>
<tr><td>$3\frac{3}{4}$</td><td>95</td><td>$11\frac{1}{4}$</td><td>286</td><td>15</td><td>6.80</td></tr>
<tr><td>4</td><td>102</td><td>$11\frac{1}{2}$</td><td>292</td><td>16</td><td>7.26</td></tr>
<tr><td>$4\frac{1}{4}$</td><td>108</td><td>$11\frac{3}{4}$</td><td>298</td><td>17</td><td>7.71</td></tr>
<tr><td>$4\frac{1}{2}$</td><td>114</td><td>12</td><td>305</td><td>18</td><td>8.16</td></tr>
<tr><td>$4\frac{3}{4}$</td><td>121</td><td>$12\frac{1}{4}$</td><td>311</td><td>19</td><td>8.62</td></tr>
<tr><td>5</td><td>127</td><td>$12\frac{1}{2}$</td><td>318</td><td>20</td><td>9.07</td></tr>
<tr><td>$5\frac{1}{4}$</td><td>133</td><td>$12\frac{3}{4}$</td><td>324</td><td>21</td><td>9.53</td></tr>
<tr><td>$5\frac{1}{2}$</td><td>140</td><td>13</td><td>330</td><td>22</td><td>9.98</td></tr>
<tr><td>$5\frac{3}{4}$</td><td>146</td><td>$13\frac{1}{4}$</td><td>337</td><td>23</td><td>10.43</td></tr>
<tr><td>6</td><td>152</td><td>$13\frac{1}{2}$</td><td>343</td><td>24</td><td>10.89</td></tr>
<tr><td>6¼</td><td>159</td><td>13¾</td><td>349</td><td>25</td><td>11.34</td></tr>
<tr><td>6½</td><td>165</td><td>14</td><td>356</td><td>26</td><td>11.79</td></tr>
<tr><td>6¾</td><td>171</td><td>14¼</td><td>362</td><td>27</td><td>12.25</td></tr>
<tr><td>7</td><td>178</td><td>14½</td><td>368</td><td>28</td><td>12.70</td></tr>
<tr><td>7¼</td><td>184</td><td>14¾</td><td>375</td><td>56</td><td>25.40</td></tr>
<tr><td>7½</td><td>191</td><td>15</td><td>381</td><td>112</td><td>50.80</td></tr>
</table>

To convert inches to millimetres multiply by 25.4. Millimetres to inches may be found by multiplying by .0394.

To convert pounds to kilogrammes multiply by .4536. Kilogrammes to pounds may be found by multiplying by 2.205.

BOOK-TRADE AND OTHER ORGANIZATIONS

American and Canadian

AMERICAN BOOK PUBLISHERS COUNCIL, INCORPORATED 2 WEST 46th STREET, NEW YORK 36, N.Y. TN: JUdson 2- 1313, is the trade association of publishers of general books. It was founded in 1920 to further the aims of its members through the exchange and dissemination of information, the development of widespread reading, and the extension of the use of books at home and abroad. The Council has 126 members.

AMERICAN BOOKSELLERS ASSOCIATION, INCORPORATED 800 SECOND AVENUE, NEW YORK, N.Y. 10017, TN: (212) 867–9060 TA: Ambassonew, is the only national association of retail booksellers dealing in new books. Among the services it provides for its members are a handbook giving discount schedules, returns practices and sales data, and a Basic Book List of standard, saleable stock titles. The association was founded in 1900 and has over 4,500 members.

THE AMERICAN INSTITUTE OF GRAPHIC ARTS (GUILD OF BOOKWOR-KERS) 1059 THIRD AVENUE, NEW YORK, N.Y. 10021, TN: (212) PL2–0813. Established in 1906 to establish and maintain a feeling of kinship and mutual interest among workers in the several hand book crafts: hand binders, illuminators, calligraphers and decorated paper makers.

THE AMERICAN TEXTBOOK PUBLISHERS INSTITUTE 432 PARK AVENUE SOUTH, NEW YORK 10016, is an organization of the publishers of school and college textbooks, and reference book publishers who sell to schools and colleges. It aims to produce the adequate financing of education, to encourage the wider use of printed materials of instruction in the schools, to assemble and make available significant data, to co-operate with educational authorities and others, and to provide a clearing house of ideas, suggestions and recommendations made by educators and publishers for the more effective use of books in schools. The institute was founded in 1942 and has about 130 members.

Badges of the Antiquarian Booksellers Association
of America and Canada and the International League

ANTIQUARIAN BOOKSELLERS ASSOCIATION OF AMERICA INC. 50 ROCKE-FELLER PLAZA, NEW YORK, N.Y. 10020, TN: (212) 757 9395, is the national association for dealers in secondhand and antiquarian books. It is the American section of the International League of Antiquarian Booksellers, and has more than 400 members who are organized in a number of Regional Chapters. President: Louis Weinstein. Vice-President: Edwin V. Glaser. Secretary: James Lowe. Treasurer: Raymond Wapner.

ANTIQUARIAN BOOKSELLERS ASSOCIATON OF CANADA, P.O. BOX 863, STATION F. TORONTO, ONTARIO M4Y 2N7, Canada. President: Helen Kahn.

ASTED (ASSOCIATION POUR L'AVANCEMENT DES SCIENCES ET DES TECHNIQUES DE LA DOCUMENTATION), 360 rue LE MOYNE, MONTRÉAL, QUÉ, H2Y 1Y3. Founded 1943 (transformed 1973), TN: (514) 844–8023.

BIBLIOGRAPHICAL SOCIETY OF CANADA, C/O VICTORIA COLLEGE, UNIVERSITY OF TORONTO, TORONTO, ONTARIO M5S 1K7, CANADA. Founded 1946. The principal aims of the Society are to promote bibliographical publications; to encourage the preservation and to extend the knowledge of printed works and manuscripts, particularly those relating to Canada; to facilitate the exchange of information concerning rare Canadiana; and to co-ordinate bibliographical activity and to set standards. There are 400 members. President: Prof. Desmond Neill. Secretary: Dr. William P. Stoneman.

CANADIAN LIBRARY ASSOCIATION, Association Canadienne des Bibliotheques. 151 SPARKS STREET, OTTAWA, ONTARIO, K1P 5E3. A national organization devoted to improving the quality of library and information services and developing higher standards of librarianship.

CANADIAN BOOKSELLERS ASSOCIATION, 49 LAING STREET, TORONTO, ONTARIO M4L 2N4. TN: (416) 363-3089. Established 1951. Constitutes the national booksellers' association for Canada. There are 600 members. Executive Director Serge Lavoie.

THE MANUSCRIPT SOCIETY 285 MADISON AVENUE, NEW YORK 17, N.Y. was formerly known as the National Society of Autograph Collectors. It has nearly 700 members including collectors, dealers, historical societies, colleges and libraries.

Antiquarian Booksellers' Associations outside North America

Australia and New Zealand

AUSTRALIAN AND NEW ZEALAND ASSOCIATION OF ANTIQUARIAN BOOKSELLERS P.O. BOX 356, Prahran, Victoria 3181, Australia. Founded 1977. 16 members. President: Kenneth Hince. Executive Secretary and Deputy President: Peter Arnold. Treasurer: Jack Bradstreet.

Austria
VERBAND DER ANTIQUARE OESTERREICHS, Gruen-
angergasse 4, A-1010 Wien, 1. TN: (0222) 52 15 35.

Belgium
SUNDICAT BELGE DE LA LIBRAIRIE ANCIENNE ET
MODERNE, Rue de Chêne 21, B-1000 Bruxelles. TN:
(02) 513 0525. Founded 1946. 51 members. President:
Jacques Van der Heyde. Vice-president: Louis Moor-
thamers. Secretary: J. Devroe. Treasurer: Claude Van
Loock.

Brazil
ASSOCIACAO BRASILEIRA DE LIVREIROS ANTIQUA-
RIOS, Rua Cosme Velho 800, BR-20,000, Rio de Janeiro
ZC-01 Brazil.

Denmark
DEN DANSKE ANTIKVARBOGHANDLER-FORENING,
P.O. Box 2184. DK-1017K København. TN: (01) 157044.
President: Peter Grosell. Founded 1920. 45 members.

Finland (Official languages are Finnish and Swedish)
SUOMEN ANTIKVARIAATTLYHDISTYS, Fredrikinkatu
63, SF-00100 Helsinki.
FINSKA ANTIKVARIATFÖRENINGEN, Norra.

France
SYNDICAT NATIONAL DE LA LIBRAIRIE ANCIENNE
ET MODERNE, 4 rue Gît-le-coeur F.75006 Paris. TN: 43
29 46 38. Founded 1913. 300 members. President: Mme.
Jeanne Laffitte.

Germany (Federal Republic)
VERBAND DEUTSCHER ANTIQUARE E.V. Die Vereini-
gung von Buchantiquaren, Autographen- und Graphikhänd-
lern. Unterer Anger 15, D-8000 München 2. TN: (089) 26
38 55. Founded 1949. 250 members. President: Friedrich
Zisska. Vice-President: Susanne Koppel. Treasurer: Edwin
Vömel. Chairman: Georg Sauer & Konrad Meuschel.

7

Great Britain
ANTIQUARIAN BOOKSELLERS' ASSOCIATION (INTERNATIONAL), Suite 2, 26 Charing Cross Road, London WC2H 0DG. TN: (01) 379-3041. Founded 1906. President: Clare C. Perkins. Secretary: Mrs. Bridget Cuming. Treasurer: John Wilson.

Italy
ASSOCIAZIONE LIBRAI ANTIQUARI D'ITALIA, Via Jacopo Nardi 6, 50132 Firenze. Founded 1947. 64 members. President: Vittorio Soave. Treasurer: Pietro Chellini. Periodical: GAZZETTINO LIBRARIO, 6 issues a year.

Japan
THE ANTIQUARIAN BOOKSELLERS ASSOCIATION OF JAPAN, 29 San-ei-Cho, Shin-juku-ku, Tokyo 160. TN: (357) 1411. Founded 1964, 26 members. President: Kenichiro Nakao. Vice-President: Nori Okudair. Treasurer: Keitaro Yamamoto. Secretary: Takehiko Sakai.

Netherlands
NEDERLANDSCHE VEREENIGING VAN ANTIQUAREN, Kleine Houtstraat 60, 2011-DP Haarlem. TN: (023) 323986. Founded 1935. 86 members. President: C. M. F. van der Peet-Schelfhout. Secretary: F. W. Kuyper. Treasurer: E. M. Mulder.

Norway
NORSK ANTIKVARBOKHANDLERFORENING, Ullevålsveien 1, Oslo 1. TN: (02) 20 78 05. 12 members. President: Bjørn Ringstrøm.

Sweden
SVENSKA ANTIKVARIATFÖRENINGEN, Box 22549, S-104 22, Stockholm.

Switzerland
SYNDICAT DE LA LIBRAIRIE ANCIENNE ET DU COMMERCE DE L'ESTAMPE EN SUISSE, Schloss-Str. 6, FL-9490, Vaduz, Liechtenstein. TN: (075) 2 32 61. 75 members. President: Walter Alicke. Secretary: Angela Muhrer. Treasurer: Louis Vuille.

8

PERIODICALS

Literary Magazines and Book Trade Papers

Note: magazine prices and subscriptions are given as a guide only, and are liable to change.

THE AFRICAN BOOK PUBLISHING RECORD. Covers new and forthcoming African publications. Quarterly. £48.00 per annum. Published by Hans Zell Publishers (an imprint of K. G. Saur Verlag), 14 Saint Giles, P.O. Box 56, Oxford OX1 3EL, England. TN: (0865) 512934. Telex: 946240, reference 19012715.

THE AMERICAN BOOK COLLECTOR. Monthly magazine. Editor: Anthony Fair. P.O. Box 867, Ossining, NY 10562-0867. TN: (914) 941-0409.

ABMR (ANTIQUARIAN BOOK MONTHLY REVIEW). Monthly magazine containing articles, book reviews, auction reports and catalogue news. Editor: John Kinnane. ABMR Publications Ltd., 52 St. Clement's, Oxford OX4 1AG, England. TN((0865) 721615.

AB BOOKMANS WEEKLY: ANTIQUARIAN BOOKMAN. Founded 1948. Weekly and AB Bookmans Yearbooks (two parts). Editor and publisher: Jacob L. Chernofsky, AB Weekly, P.O. Box AB, Clifton, NJ 07015, U.S.A. Telephone (021) 772-0020.

ANTIQUARIES JOURNAL. Established 1921, articles cover a wide variety of antiquarian subjects. Subscription £32.00 per annum ($69). Oxford University Press, Journals Department, Walton Street, Oxford OX2 6DP, England. TN: (0865) 56767.

APOLLO. International Magazine of Art and Antiques monthly. £4.00 a copy. Apollo, 22 Davies Street, London W1Y 1LH, England. TN: (01) 491-8752.

L'ARGUS DU LIVRE ANCIEN & MODERNE. Tous les trois mois. Description et prix des ouvrages passés en ventes publiques en France et à l'étranger. Rédaction, 18 rue Dauphine, 76006 Paris, France.

AUS DEM ANTIQUARIAT. Monthly. Editor: Dr. Karl H. Pressler. Published from Römerstrasse 7, D-8000 München 40, Federal Republic of Germany. TN: (089) 34 13 31.

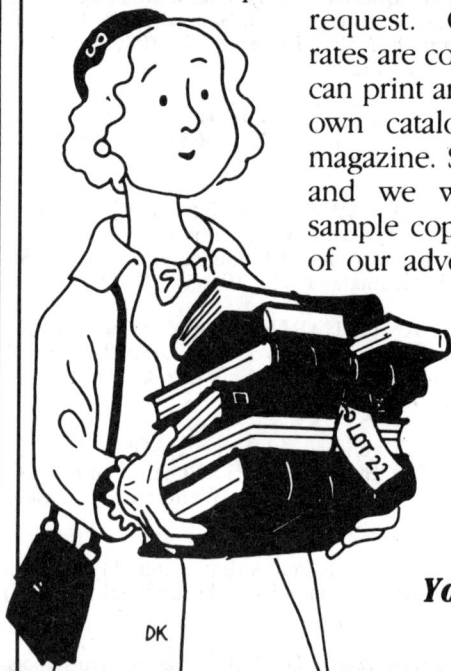

THE BIBLIOTHECK. Bibliographical articles, notes and reviews of Scottish interest. Annual supplement lists books, reviews, essays and articles on Scottish literature published in the preceding year. Published by a Scottish Group of the Library Association from Edinburgh University Library, George Square, Edinburgh EH8 9LJ, Scotland. TN: 031 667 1011 Ext: 6617.

BOOK AND MAGAZINE COLLECTOR. Monthly, lists of books for sale and wanted, £1.35 a copy, including post and packing. 45 Saint Mary's Road, Ealing, London W5 5RQ, England. TN: (01) 579-1082.

THE BOOK COLLECTOR. Established 1952. Quarterly subscription £18.00 ($35), plus post and packing £1.50 ($2.50). 90 Great Russell Street, London WC1B 3PS, England. TN: (01) 637-3029.

THE BOOKDEALER. Trade weekly for secondhand and antiquarian books for sale and wanted. Published by Werner Shaw Limited, Suite 34, 26 Charing Cross Road, London WC2H 0DH, England. TN: (01) 240-5890.

BOOK SALES & WANTS ADVERTISER. Monthly, for private and trade. Books wanted and for sale. Annual subscription, £6.50, sample free on request. Hoovey's Book Service, 10 Claremont, Hastings, Sussex TN34 1HD, England.

THE BOOKSELLER. Weekly journal of the new book trade in Britain. Subscription £43.00 per annum. Published by J. Whitaker and Sons Limited, 12 Dyott Street, London WC1A 1DF, England. TN: (01) 836-8911.

BOOKS FROM FINLAND. Quarterly English-language journal of writing from and about Finland. Subscription US$20 per annum. Published by Helsinki University Library, P.O. Box 312, SF-00171, Helsinki 17.

BOOKS OF THE MONTH AND BOOKS TO COME. Monthly list of all books published in U.K. during the month and forthcoming publications for next two months. Subscription £34.00 per annum. J. Whitaker & Sons, 12 Dyott Street, London WC1A 1DF, England. TN: (01) 836-8911.

BOOK WORLD. Monthly. Articles, reviews and advertisements of books for sale and wanted. Balmoral Publishing Works, Talcentown Road, Cheddar, Somerset, England.

BÖRSENBLATT FÜR DEN DEUTSCHEN BUCHHANDEL (Angebotene und Gesuchte Bücher). Buchhändler-Vereinigung G.m.b.H., Postfach 2404, D-6000 Frankfurt am Main, Federal Republic of Germany.

BRITISH BOOK NEWS. The British Council, 65 Davies Street, London W1Y 2AA, England. TN: (01) 499-8011. Distributed by Basil Blackwell, 108 Cowley Road, Oxford OX4 1JF, England.

BULLETIN DU BIBLIOPHILE, 18 rue Dauphine, F-75006 Paris, France.

CLASSICAL REVIEW. Established 1887 (new series 1951). Contains expert reviews of new work dealing with the literatures and civilisations of ancient Greece and Rome. Twice yearly. £19 per annum (UK), including post and packing. Oxford University Press, Journals Department, Walton Street, Oxford OX2 6DP, England. TN: (0865) 56767.

THE CLIQUE. The antiquarian booksellers weekly. Established 1890. By subscription to booksellers only. Contains advertisements and lists of books wanted and for sale in Britain and elsewhere. Subscription, including first class post and package, £17.50 per annum. Published by The Clique, c/o Stoate & Bishop (Printers), Saint James Square, Cheltenham, Glos. GL50 3PU, England. TN: (0242) 36741.

L'ESOPO, Rivista trimestrale di bibliofilia. Mario Scognamiglio, via Rovello 1, 20121 Milano, Italy.

THE FICTION MAGAZINE, 12–13 Clerkenwell Green, London EC1, England. TN: (01) 250-1504.

FINE PRINT. A Review for the Arts of the Book. Quarterly, January, April, July and October. Published by Fine Print, P.O. Box 3394, San Francisco, CA 94119, U.S.A.

GAZZETTINO LIBRARIO. Richieste ed offerte di libri antichi e moderni. Pubblicazione bimestrale. Gazzettino Librario, Via J. Nardi 6, 50132 Firenze, Italy.

INDIAN PUBLISHER AND BOOKSELLER. In English, monthly. Rs. 60 per annum. Published by Popular Book Depot, Dr Bhadkamkar Marg, Bombay 400007, India.

THE LIBRARY. Transactions of the Bibliographical Society, quarterly, £25 per annum. Oxford University Press, Journals Department, Walton Street, Oxford OX2 6DP, England. TN: (0865) 56767.

LIBRARY ASSOCIATION RARE BOOKS GROUP NEWSLETTER. Editor: Dr. Brian Hillyard, National Library of Scotland, George IV Bridge, Edinburgh EH1 1EW. Correspondence about subscriptions to Miss J. Archibald, English Antiquarian Section, British Library Reference Division, Great Russell Street, London WC1B 3DG, England. TN: (01) 636-1544.

THE LISTENER, BBC, 35 Marylebone High Street, London W1M 4AA, England. TN: (01) 927-4457. Telex 265781. Subscription, including post and packing, £36 per annum for UK; £50 per annum for North America.

LITERARY MARKET REVIEW. In English, Quarterly. U.S. $5.00 per annum. Published from Kunnuparampil Buildings, Kurichy 686549, Kottayam District, Kerala, India.

THE LITERARY REVIEW, 51 Beak Street, London W1R 3LF, England. TN: (01) 437-9392. Telex: 919034. Editor: Auberon Waugh.

THE LONDON MAGAZINE, 30 Thurlowe Place, London, SW7, England. TN: (01) 589-0618.

LONDON REVIEW OF BOOKS, Tavistock House South, Tavistock Square, London WC1H 9JZ, England. TN: (01) 388-7487. Subscription, including post and packing, £19.20 per annum for UK; £34 for North America.

NEW STATESMAN. Weekly; £37 per annum (UK); £52 per annum (U.S.A. at air mail rate). 14–16 Farringdon Lane, London EC1R 3AU, England. TN: (01) 253-2001.

NEW YORK REVIEW OF BOOKS, 250 West 57th Street, New York, NY 10107, U.S.A.

PUBLISHER'S WEEKLY. Weekly reports of new books published; promotion, market and foreign book news, etc. Enlarged Spring and Falls numbers, containing information and announcements on publishing programmes. Subscriptions: 1 year $107.00; 2 years $214.00; 3 years $321.00. Published by R. R. Bowker Co., P.O Box 1428, Riverton, NJ 08077, U.S.A.

QUILL AND QUIRE, Journal of the Canadian Book Trade, 56 The Esplanade, (Suite 213), Toronto, Ontario M5E 1A7, Canada. TN: (416) 364-3333.

RARE BOOKS AND MANUSCRIPTS LIBRARIANSHIP, half-yearly. Edited by the Association of College and Research Libraries (U.S.A.). Published by Choice, 100 Riverside Center, Middletown CT 06457-3467, U.S.A.

TAAB WEEKLY, THE LIBRARY BOOKSELLER. Founded 1944. Provides the antiquarian bookseller with a direct link to libraries and private buyers. Published by Albert Saifer, P.O. Box 239, W.O.B. West Orange, NJ 07052, U.S.A.

THE TIMES LITERARY SUPPLEMENT. Weekly journal. Subscription per annum £40 (U.K.), $75 (U.S.A.) Published by Times Newspapers Ltd., Priory House, Saint John's Lane, London EC1M 4BX, England. TN: (01) 253-3000. Telex: 264971.

WHITAKER'S CLASSIFIED MONTHLY BOOK LIST. Classified under 53 subject headings, books published during the month and forthcoming titles for the following two months, subscription £23.00 per annum. J. Whitaker and Sons Ltd., 12 Dyott Street, London WC1A 1DF, England. TN: (01) 836-8911.

THE WORLD OF BOOKS. Monthly. Poacher Publications, P.O. Box 10, Lincoln LN5 7JA, England.

CURRENT REFERENCE BOOKS

THE AFRICAN BOOK WORLD AND PRESS: A DIRECTORY, 3rd Edition, 1983. 313 pp. £46.00. Published by Hans Zell Publishers (an imprint of K. G. Saur Verlag), 14 Saint Giles, P.O. Box 56, Oxford OX1 3EL, England. TN: (0865) 512934. Telex: 946240, reference 19012715.

AFRICAN BOOKS IN PRINT, 1984. 2 vols. 1402pp. An index by author, title and subject of over 18,750 works in English, French and African languages. £85.00 the set. Edited Hans Zell. Published by Mansell, 6 All Saints' Street, London N1 9RL, England. TN: (01) 837-6676.

AMERICAN BOOK PRICES CURRENT. 35,000 entries for books, autographs and manuscripts sold at auction, U.S.A., Canada, Europe, S. Africa and Australia. 1985, Vol. 91, 1,000pp. American Book Prices Current, P.O. Box 236, Washington CT 06793, U.S.A.

AMERICAN BOOK TRADE DIRECTORY 1985. Lists every kind of book outlet, over 20,000 in 5,000 American and Canadian cities, also book wholesalers, clubs, libraries, publishers etc. 31st edition. Postpaid £117.50. R. R. Bowker Co., P.O. Box 1428, Riverton, NJ 08077, U.S.A.

AMERICAN BOOK TRADE IN INDIA: A Directory of Wholesale and Retail Booksellers, edited by Kunnuparampil P. Punnoose, $50. Published by Asian Bookmarket Information Services, 73–47–255th Street, Glen Oaks, New York 11004, U.S.A.

AMERICAN LIBRARY DIRECTORY. Lists 35,000 American and Canadian Libraries. Revised annually. £130.00. 38th edition. R. R. Bowker Co., P.O. Box 1428, Riverton, NJ 08077, U.S.A.

BANGLADESH NATIONAL BIBLIOGRAPHY. Annually. Published by National Library of Bangladesh, 106 Central Road, Dhaka 5, Bangladesh.

BOOK PUBLISHING ANNUAL 1985. 3rd edition. 252pp. (previously P.W. Yearbook). Produced annually £59.00. R. R. Bowker Co., P.O. Box 1428, Riverton, NJ 08077, U.S.A.

THE BOOK TRADE IN CANADA. Published annually. The standard reference on the Canadian book industry, includes complete listings for publishers, distributors, booksellers, etc. £12.00. Ampersand Communications Services, RR1, Caledon, Ontario L0N 1C0, Canada.

A BOOK WORLD DIRECTORY OF THE ARAB COUNTRIES, TURKEY AND IRAN. Compiled by Anthony Rudkin and Irene Butcher. Lists Newspapers, Periodicals, Publishers, Libraries and Booksellers. £30.00. Published by Mansell, 6 All Saints' Street, London N1 9RL, England. TN: (01) 837-6676.

BOOK-AUCTION RECORDS. A priced and annotated record of books sold at auction in England, Europe and North America. Vol. 82 (1984/85). £51.75. Published annually by Wm. Dawson and Sons, Cannon House, Park Farm Road, Folkestone, Kent CT19 5EE, England. TN: (0303) 57421. Telex: 96392.

BOOKDEALERS' AND COLLECTORS' YEAR-BOOK AND DIARY. Contains up-to-date information (mainly British) including additions and alterations to all the directories of dealers in secondhand and antiquarian books & desk diary. Published annually in November for the following year (1986, £8.50) by Sheppard Press, Europa Publications Ltd., 18 Bedford Square, London WC1B 3JN, England. TN: (01) 580-8236. Telex: 21540.

BOOKDEALERS IN INDIA, PAKISTAN, SRI LANKA &c. 1st edition, 1977. A directory of dealers in secondhand and antiquarian books in the Southwest Asian sub-continent. £3.50. Published by Sheppard Press, Europa Publications Ltd., 18 Bedford Square, London WC1B 3JN, England. TN: (01) 580-8236. Telex: 21540.

BOOKMAN'S GUIDE TO AMERICANA. Eighth Edition. By Norman Heard. £22.20. Published by The Scarecrow Press, Inc., Metuchen, New Jersey, U.S.A. Distributors: Bailey Bros. & Swinfen Ltd., Warner House, Folkestone, Kent CT19 6PH, England.

BOOKMAN'S PRICE INDEX. Volumes 1 through 30 in print. Edited by Daniel F. McGrath. Published by Gale Research Company, Book Tower, Detroit, Michigan 48226, U.S.A. U.S.$160.00 per volume.

BOOKS IN PRINT. 1985/86. Lists over 600,000 books in print from American publishers and distributors: Annually in October. Postpaid £215.50 for 6-volume set. R. R. Bowker Co., P.O. Box 1428, Riverton, NJ 08077, U.S.A.

BRITISH BOOKS AND LIBRARIES. A series of eight tape/slide programmes. £46.50 each. The British Council, 65 Davies Street, London W1Y 2AA, England. TN: (01) 499-8011. Distributed by Sweet and Maxwell.

BRITISH BOOKS IN PRINT. Lists books in print of British publishers. Annually in November. Post paid price in Britain £85.00. Overseas £97.00. Published by J. Whitaker and Sons Limited, 12 Dyott Street, London WC1A 1DF, England. TN: (01) 836-8911.

BRITISH NATIONAL BIBLIOGRAPHY. Records each week new and forthcoming British books with cumulations in last issue of month, two interim cumulations and annual volume. Published by the Sales and Payment Unit, the British Library Bibliographic Services Division, 2 Sheraton Street, London W1V 4BH, England. TN: (01) 636-1544.

CATALOGUE BIBLICGRAPHIQUE DES VENTES PUBLIQUES. Biennial record of book auction sales in France, Belgium, Monaco, Britain and America. Volume 10 (seasons 1980–81 and 1981–82).

Published by Editions Mayer, 224 Avenue du Maine, 75014 Paris, France. Available in the U.K. at £60.00 non-net from Europa Publications, 18 Bedford Square, London WC1B 3JN, England. TN: (01) 580-8236. Telex: 21540.

CHILDREN'S BOOKS IN PRINT. £27.00 in UK, £31.00 Export. Published by J. Whitaker & Sons, 12 Dyott Street, London WC1A 1DF, England. TN: (01) 836-8911.

COMPUTER BOOKS AND SERIALS IN PRINT, 1985. Lists over 15,000 books and 1800 serials. Revised annually £70.00. R. R. Bowker Co., P.O. Box 1428, Riverton, NJ 08077, U.S.A.

CUMULATIVE BOOK INDEX. A world list of books in the English language. Eleven issues a year including quarterly cumulations and permanent bound annual cumulation. Bound four, five or six year cumulations through 1956; two years cumulations 1957 through 1968. Published by the H. W. Wilson Company, 950 University Avenue, Bronx, New York 10452, U.S.A.

DICTIONARY OF BRITISH BOOK ILLUSTRATORS: THE TWENTIETH CENTURY, compiled by Brigid Peppin and Lucy Micklethwait. Covers mainly illustrators of fiction and poetry between 1900 and 1975, over 800 artists and 400 specimens of their work. £30.00. John Murray, 50 Albemarle Street, London W1X 4BD, England. TN: (01) 493-4361.

DIRECTORY OF AMERICAN BOOK SPECIALISTS, 4th edition 1981. Published by Continental Publishing Co., 1261 Broadway, New York, NY 10001, U.S.A.

DIRECTORY OF AMERICAN BOOK WORKERS. Compiled by Renée Roff. $20.95 including postage. Published by Nicholas T. Smith, P.O. Box 66, Bronxville, NY 10708, U.S.A.

A DIRECTORY OF LITERARY TERMS. By J. A. Cuddon. £25.00. Published by Basil Blackwell (in association with André Deutsch) 108 Cowley Road, Oxford OX4 1JF, England. TN: (0865) 724041.

CASSELL & PUBLISHERS' ASSOCIATION DIRECTORY OF PUBLISHING, in Great Britain, the Commonwealth, Ireland, South Africa and Pakistan 1985. £17.95. Customer Services Department, 1 St. Anne's Road, Eastbourne, Sussex BN21 3UN. TN: (0323) 638221.

DIRECTORY OF PUBLISHING AND BOOKSELLING IN BRAZIL. £11.50. Published by the British Council, 65 Davies Street, London W1Y 2AA, England. TN: (01) 499-8011. (Design, production and publications department).

DIRECTORY OF SPECIALIST BOOKDEALERS IN THE UNITED KINGDOM HANDLING MAINLY NEW BOOKS. Third edition. 1985. £8.50. Peter Marcan Publications, 31 Rowcliff Road, High Wycombe, Buckinghamshire, England.

DIRECTORY OF SPECIALIZED AMERICAN BOOKDEALERS. 350pp. £10.25. Published by the Moretus Press, 274 Madison Avenue, New York, N.Y. 10016, U.S.A.

DIRECTORY OF THE INDIAN BOOK INDUSTRY. Edited by Dinkar Trivedi. Rs. 50. Published by New Order Book Co., Ellis Bridge, Ahmedabad 380006, India.

EIGHTEENTH CENTURY BRITISH BOOKS, an author union catalogue extracted from the British Museum, Bodleian Library and University Library Cambridge Catalogues, by F. J. G. Robinson, G. Averley, D. R. Esslemont and P. J. Wallis. 1981. 5 vols. £1,250.00. Published by Wm. Dawson & Sons, Cannon House, Folkestone, Kent, England. TN: (0303) 57721.

EUROPEAN BOOKDEALERS. A directory of dealers in secondhand and antiquarian books on the continent of Europe. 6th edition (1985-87) £12.00 ($21). Published by Sheppard Press, Europa Publications Ltd., 18 Bedford Square, London WC1B 3JN, England. TN: (01) 580-8236. Telex: 21540.

FIRST EDITIONS: A GUIDE TO IDENTIFICATION. Published by the Spoon River Press, P.O. Box 3635, Peoria IL 61614, U.S.A.

FIRST PRINTINGS OF AMERICAN AUTHORS: Contributions Towards Descriptive Checklists. Four volumes. Matthew J. Bruccoli, Series Editor. C. E. Frazer Clark, Jr., Managing Editor. Richard Layman, Project Editor. Benjamin Franklin V, Associate Editor. 1,648 pages. Annotations; Author portraits; Reproductions of 3,000 title pages, dust jackets, and bindings; Cumulative index to volumes 1-4 in Vol. 4. £335.00 set. Published by Gale Research Co., Detroit, MI 48226.

GUIDE DES LIBRAIRIES D'OCCASION par Denis Basane, donne l'adresse de 273 librairies. Editions Hubschmid et Bouret, Paris.

INTERNATIONAL BIBLIOGRAPHY OF REPRINTS/ INTERNATIONALE BIBLIOGRAPHIE DER PRINTS. Band I, Books and Serials, 1976, DM 360,-; Band II, Annuals and Periodicals, 1980, DM 240,-. Published by K. G. Saur Verlag, Pössenbacherstr. 2ᴮ, Postfach 711009, D-8000 München 71, Federal Republic of Germany. TN: (089) 798901. Telex: 5212067.

INTERNATIONAL BIBLIOGRAPHY OF THE BOOK TRADE AND LIBRARIANSHIP. 1981. DM 168,-. K. G. Saur Verlag. Pössenbacherstr. 2ᴮ, Postfach 711009, D-8000 München 71, Federal Republic of Germany. TN: (089) 798901. Telex: 5212067.

INTERNATIONAL BOOK COLLECTORS DIRECTORY, $35.00. Pegasus Press, P.O. Box 1350, Vashon, WA 98070, U.S.A.

INTERNATIONAL BOOKS IN PRINT. 4th edition, 1985. English language titles published outside the U.S.A. and U.K. 2 parts, each of 2 vols, 3,294pp, each part DM 498,-. K. G. Saur Verlag, Pössenbacherstr. 2^B, Postfach 711009, D-8000 München 71, Federal Republic of Germany. TN: (089) 798901. Telex: 5212067.

INTERNATIONAL DIRECTORY OF ANTIQUARIAN BOOKSELLERS. Published by I.L.A.B. A world list of members of organisations belonging to the International League of Antiquarian Booksellers. 8th edition. 1984.

INTERNATIONAL DIRECTORY OF ARTS. 1985/86. Art Address 17th edition, £109.00. R. R. Bowker Co., P.O. Box 1428, Riverton, NJ 08077, U.S.A.

INTERNATIONAL DIRECTORY OF BOOK COLLECTORS. 4th edition, £18.50. Published by the Trigon Press, 117 Kent House Road, Beckenham, Kent BR3 1JJ, England.

INTERNATIONAL LITERARY MARKET PLACE 1985/86. 500pp. £76.75 Revised annually. R. R. Bowker Co., P.O. Box 1428, Riverton, NJ 08077, U.S.A.

INTERNATIONAL MAPS AND ATLASES IN PRINT. ed. Kenneth Winch. £17.50. R. R. Bowker Co., P.O. Box 1428, Riverton, NJ 08077, U.S.A.

IRREGULAR SERIALS AND ANNUALS 1986, 11th edition. Lists over 37,000 publications worldwide. Revised annually. £147.50. R. R. Bowker Co., P.O. Box 1428, Riverton, NJ 08077, U.S.A.

JAHRBUCH DER AUKTIONSPREISE für Bücher, Handschriften und Autographen. Veröffentl. bei Dr. Ernst Hauswedell & Co., Rosenbergstrasse 113, D-7000 Stuttgart 1, Federal Republic of Germany. Bericht über Bücher, Handschriften und Manuskripte, die auf Auktionen in Deutschland, Holland, Österreich und der Schweiz im Laufe eines Jahres gehandelt werden. Im Anhang eine Liste wichtiger Händler und ihrer Spezialitäten.

LIBRARIES IN THE UNITED KINGDOM AND THE REPUBLIC OF IRELAND. 11th edition, £9.95. Library Association Publishing, 7 Ridgmount Street, London WC1E 7AE, England. TN: (01) 636-7543.

LES LIVRES DISPONIBLES. Index of French books in print. 6,210pp. listing 261,289 French language books. Cercle de la Librairie, 35 rue Grégorie de Tours, F-75279, Paris, France, Cedex 06.

MEDICAL AND HEALTH CARE BOOKS AND SERIALS IN PRINT 1985. Lists over 60,500 books and 14,400 serials. Revised annually, £106.50. 2 volume set. R. R. Bowker Co., P.O. Box 1428, Riverton, NJ 08077, U.S.A.

THE PRELIMS TO BRITISH BOOKS IN PRINT 1984. Lists 10,000 U.K. publishers and their addresses. 10,000 U.K. series ISBN prefixes, and Book Trade Bibliography. £3.25. Published by J. Whitaker & Sons, 12 Dyott Street, London WC1A 1DF, England. TN: (01) 836-8911.

PUBLISHERS IN THE UNITED KINGDOM AND THEIR ADDRESSES. A list of over 2,000 publishers. U.K. £3.50, outside Europe £5.00. Published by J. Whitaker & Sons Limited, 12 Dyott Street, London WC1A 1DF, England. TN: (01) 836-8911.

PUBLISHERS' INTERNATIONAL DIRECTORY, 12th edition, 1985, 2 vols, DM348,-. Published by K. G. Saur Verlag. Pössenbacherstr. 2^B, Postfach 711009, D-8000 München 71, Federal Republic of Germany. TN: (089) 798901. Telex: 5212067.

PUBLISHERS WEEKLY YEARBOOK. 252pp. £46.50. 1984 edition. R. R. Bowker Co., P.O. Box 1428, Riverton, NJ 08077, U.S.A.

RELIGIOUS BOOKS IN PRINT. £19.50 in U.K. Export £22.00. Published by J. Whitaker & Sons, 12 Dyott Street, London WC1A 1DF, England. TN: (01) 836-8911.

SCIENTIFIC ENGINEERING AND MEDICAL SOCIETIES PUBLICATIONS IN PRINT 1980/81. 4th edition £76.75. R. R. Bowker Co., P.O. Box 1428, Riverton, NJ 08077, U.S.A.

SHEPPARD'S BOOK DEALERS IN THE BRITISH ISLES: A DIRECTORY OF ANTIQUARIAN AND SECONDHAND BOOK DEALERS IN THE UNITED KINGDOM AND IRELAND. Annual; 12th edition (1987), October 1986. Published by Sheppard Press, Europa Publications Ltd., 18 Bedford Square, London WC1B 3JN, England. TN: (01) 580-8236. Telex: 21540.

A SHORT-TITLE CATALOGUE OF BOOKS PRINTED IN ENGLAND, SCOTLAND & IRELAND AND OF ENGLISH BOOKS PRINTED ABROAD. 1475–1640 by A. W. Pollard and G. R. Redgrave. Second edition, revised and enlarged by W. A. Jackson, F. S. Ferguson and Katharine F. Pantzer. Vol. 1 £125.00, Vol. 2 £75.00. Published for the Bibliographical Society by Oxford University Press, Walton Street, Oxford OX2 6AD, England. TN: (0865) 512201.

SUBJECT GUIDE TO BOOKS IN PRINT 1985/86. Classifies more than 575,000 non-fiction titles in-print of almost every American publisher under 62,500 subject headings. Issued annually, £147.50 for 4 volume set. R. R. Bowker Co., P.O. Box 1428, Riverton, NJ 08077, U.S.A.

TASCHENBUCH DER AUKTIONSPREISE ALTER BÜCHER. Annual record of auction prices of old books in Germany, Austria and Switzerland. Volume 10 (Season 1984). Published by S. Radtke, 5100 Aachen, Postfach 1756, Federal Republic of Germany. Available in the U.K. at £36.00 non-net from Europa Publications, 18 Bedford Square, London WC1B 3JN, England. TN: (01) 580-8236. Telex: 21540.

TITLES OF ENGLISH BOOKS AND OF FOREIGN BOOKS PRINTED IN ENGLAND. By A. F. Allison and V. F. Goldsmith. Vol. 1: 1475–1640. £10.00, Vol. 2: 1641–1700, £20.00. Published by Wm. Dawson & Sons Ltd., Cannon House, Folkestone, Kent, England. TN: (0303) 57721.

ULRICH'S INTERNATIONAL PERIODICALS DIRECTORY 1985 (24th edition). A guide to over 69,000 world periodicals under 557 subject headings. Each entry tells where magazine is published, price, frequency of issue, where indexed or abstracted, whether it carries advertisements, book reviews, or any of twenty descriptive characteristics. 2 vols. £147.50. R. R. Bowker Co., P.O. Box 1428, Riverton, NJ 08077, U.S.A.

UNIVERSITY LIBRARIES IN INDIA: A Guide for Direct Mail Promotion, edited by Kunnuparampil P. Punnoose, $25. Published by Asia Bookmarket Information Service, 73–47–255th Street, Glen Oaks, New York 11044, U.S.A. Available from Kunnuparampil Buildings, Kurichy 686549, India.

USED BOOK PRICE GUIDE. Standard reference work for pricing rare, scarce and used books. 5-year edition, hard cover. $79.00. Price Guide Publishers, P.O. Box 525, Kenmore, WA 98028, U.S.A.

VERZEICHNIS LIEFERBARER BÜCHER (German Books in Print) 1985/86. Author-Title-Catchword Catalogue, 4 vols., DM 480; ISBN Register, DM 212; Subject Guide, 4 vols., DM 354; Spring Supplement 1986, DM 108; ISBN Index to Spring Supplement 1986, DM 48. K. G. Saur Verlag, Pössenbacherstr. 2B, Postfach 711009, D-8000 München 71, Federal Republic of Germany. TN: (089) 798901. Telex 5212067.

WHITAKER'S CUMULATIVE BOOK LIST. A complete record of British book production. Annual volume UK £28.00, Export £31.50. Published by J. Whitaker & Sons Limited, 12 Dyott Street, London WC1A 1DF, England. TN: (01) 836-8911.

WILLINGS PRESS GUIDE 1986. Facts on over 20,000 newspapers, periodicals and annuals, world wide. £44.00. Published by Thomas Skinner Directories, Windsor Court, East Grinstead House, East Grinstead, West Sussex RH19 1XE, England. TN: (0342) 26972.

WRITER'S MARKET. Published by Writer's Digest, 9933 Alliance Road, Cincinnati, OH 45242. 55th annual edition, 1985. 1,056pp. $19.95.

WORLD GUIDE TO SPECIAL LIBRARIES, 1983. DM 298,-. Edited by Helga Lengenfelder. Published by K. G. Saur Verlag, Pössenbacherstr. 2B, Postfach 711009, D-8000 München 71, Federal Republic of Germany. TN: (089) 798901. Telex 5212067.

WORLD OF LEARNING. Standard reference work on the world's educational, scientific and cultural institutions. Published annually; 36th edition, 1986, U.K. £72.00, Export US $170.00. Published by Europa Publications, 18 Bedford Square, London WC1B 3JN, England. TN: (01) 580-8236. Telex: 21540.

SUPPLIES AND SERVICES

for the antiquarian book trade, in Canada and the U.S.A.

APPRAISERS, AUCTIONEERS, CATALOG PRINTERS, REPAIRING,
CLEANING AND BINDING BY HAND

APPRAISERS

LEE ASH, 66 Humiston Drive, Bethany, CT 06515. TN: (203) 393-2723.
MARY BETH BEAL, 3919 North Vlaremont Avenue, Chicago IL 60618.
TN: (312) 539-0105.—*rare books, manuscripts, prints.*
RICHARD BOULIND, 52 Lorimer Avenue, Providence, RI 02906. TN:
(401) 831-3268.
CROSSON DANNIS INC., Fine Arts Appraisal Group, 8848 Greenville
Avenue, Dallas TB 75243. TN: (214) 340-0309.
WILLIAM A. LONGO ASSOCIATES, 14 West Natick Road, Warwick,
RI 02886.
SOTHEBY'S, 1334 York Avenue, New York NY 10021. TN: (212) 606-
7000. TA: Parkgal New York. Telex 232643.
SWANN GALLERIES INC., 104 East 25th Street, New York, NY 10010.
TN: (212) 254-4710.

AUCTIONEERS

CALIFORNIA BOOK AUCTION GALLERIES, 358 Golden Gate
Avenue, San Francisco CA 94102. TN: (415) 775-0424.
CANADA BOOK AUCTIONS, Beardmore Buildings, 35 Front Street
East, Toronto, Ontario M5E 1B3, Canada. TN: (416) 368-4326.
CHRISTIE, MANSON & WOODS INTERNATIONAL INC., 502 Park
Avenue, New York, NY 10022. TN: (212) 546-1000. TA: Chriswoods
New York. Telex: 620721.
ROBERT C. ELDRED CO., INC. P.O Box 796B , East Dennis, MA
02641. TN: (617) 385-3116.
EMERY'S BOOK AUCTIONS, Route 2, Duston Road, Contoocook, NH
03229. Monthly mail auctions.
SAMUEL T. FREEMAN & COMPANY, 1808-10 Chestnut Street, Phila-
delphia, PA 19103. TN: (215) 563-9275.
CHARLES HAMILTON GALLERIES INC., 200 West 57th Street, New
York, NY 10019. TN: (212) 245-7313.
HARRIS AUCTION GALLERIES, 875 North Howard Street, Baltimore
MD 21201. TN: (301) 728-7040.
HENSEY INC., Book Department, Epping, NH 03042. TN: (603) 679-
2428.

LESLIE HINDMAN AUCTIONEERS, 215 West Ohio Street, Chicago IL 60610 TN: (312) 67-0010.
WAYNE MOCK INC., P.O. Box 37, Tamworth, NH 03886. TN: (603) 323-8749.
OINONEN BOOK AUCTIONS, P.O. Box 470, Sunderland, MA 01375. TN: (413) 665-3253.
PHILLIPS, SON & NEALE INC., 406 East 79th Street, New York, NY 10021. TN: (212) 570-4830. Telex: 126380.
CHARLES ROBINSON & JAMES D. JULIA, AUCTIONEERS, Rt. 201, Skowhegan Road, Fairfield, ME 04937. TN: (207) 453-9725.
SOTHEBY'S, 1334 York Avenue, New York, NY 10021. TN: (212) 606-7000. TA: Parkgal New York. Telex: 232643.
SWANN GALLERIES INC., 104 East 25th Street, New York, NY 10010. TN: (212) 254-4710.
WAVERLY AUCTIONS, 7649 Old Georgetown Road, Bethesda, MD 20814. TN: (301) 951-0919.

CATALOG PRINTERS
DINNER AND KLEIN, 600 South Spokane Street, (P.O. Box 3814-N), Seattle, WA 98124. TN: (206) 682-2494.
K. N. A. PRESS INC., 107 North Union Street, Kennett Square, PA 19348. TN: (215) 444-3678.—*catalogs and general printing by offset.*
STANDARD PRINTING COMPANY, P.O. Box 1736, Louisville, KY.—*catalogs printed by photo-offset from typed copy.*

REPAIRING, CLEANING, BINDING BY HAND,
CALLIGRAPHY, ILLUMINATING
ARCHIVAL CONSERVATION CENTER, INC., 8225 Daly Road, Cincinnati, OH 45231. TN: (513) 521-9858.—*binding, repairs, deacidification of paper etc.*
BENNETT BOOK STUDIO, 920 Broadway, New York, NY 10010. TN: (212) 674-8520. Est: 1899.—*fine binding, repairs, cases.*
STANLEY CLIFFORD, at the Sign of the Cast Iron Press, King Row, Deer Isle, ME 04627.—*hand bookbinding, rare book repairs.*

Miss FLORENCE BROOKS, P.O. Box 51, Lenox, MA 01240.—*calligrapher, illuminator*.

Miss JEAN L. CHAPMAN, 149 Barksdale Drive North East, Atlanta, GA 30309.—*hand bookbinding, designer, illuminator*.

Mrs. FREDERICKA B. CHILD, Star Route, Lumberville, PA 18933.—*hand bookbinding*.

COMSTOCK BINDERY, 7903 Rainier Avenue, Seattle, WA 98118.—*hand bookbinding and restoration*.

JOHN E. CRAIB, Jr. Mechanic Street, Upton, MA 01568.—*hand book binding, restoration and conservation*.

Capt. GEORGE M. CUNHA, 33 High Street, Topsfield, MA 01983.—*hand bookbinding, restoration*.

CUNNINGHAM PRESS BINDERY, 3036 West Main Street, Alhambra, CA 91801. TN: 283-2085. Est: 1947.—*restoration of rare volumes, binding etc*.

WILLIAM H. DIERKES, Jr., DIERKES BINDERY, P.O. Box 509, Eureka Springs, AR 72632.—*hand bookbinding, restoration, Designer*.

HAZEL DREIS, 1020 Benito Avenue, Pacific Grove, CA. Est: 1928.—*hand binding*.

MARVIN EISENBERG, P.O. Box 53, Rifton, NY 12471.—*hand binding and restoration*.

KURT GAEBEL & SONS, 833 Holland Road, Holland, Bucks County, PA 18966. TN: (215) 357-6739.—*hand bookbinding.*

Mrs. KATHRYN GERLACH, The Old Mill, Shaftsbury, VT 05262.—*hand binding, restoration.*

B. GIMELSON, 96 South Limekiln Pike, Chalfont, PA 18914. TN: (215) 822-1393.—*paper restoration laboratory.*

Mrs. MARY E. GREENFIELD, 26 Perkins Road, Woodbridge, CT 06525.—*hand binding, restoration, designer.*

THE HARCOURT BINDERY INC., 9–11 Harcourt Street, Boston, MA 02116.—*bookbinding.*

SUSAN R. HARRIS, 2000 East Roger Road, NBU 115, Box 141, Tucson, AZ 85719. TN: (602) 795-2833.—*colourist, prints watercoloured.*

Mrs. CAROLYN HORTON, 430 West 22nd Street, New York, NY 10011.—*book and manuscript repair and restoration, hand binding.*

JOHANNES H. HYLTOFT, 251 Knight Lane, Herndon, VA 22070.—*hand binding, repair and restoration, designer.*

Mrs. JOANNE ISAAC, R.D.4., Quakertown, PA 18951.—*book designer and artist.*

Mrs. ANNETTE J. LAUER, 5116 Fairglen Lane, Chevy Chase, MD 20015.—*hand binding, restoration.*

Mrs. MARGARET LECKY, 7029 Senalda Road, Los Angeles, CA 90068.—*hand binding, restoration.*

LO GATTO BOOKBINDING INC., Medo Lo Gatto, 390 Paterson Avenue, East Rutherford, NJ 07073. TN: (201) 438-4344.—*binding and repairs.*

Miss FRANCES MANOLA, 345 West 55th Street, New York, NY 10019.—*hand binding, calligraphy, illuminating, repair and restoration.*

Miss ROSALIND MEYER, 2513 North Stowell Avenue (Apt. 16) Milwaukee, WI 53211.—*hand binding, restoration, designer.*

RICHARD P. MINSKY, 115–25 Metropolitan Avenue, Kew Gardens, NY 11418.—*hand binding and restoration, designer.*

THE MONASTERY HILL BINDERY, 1751 Belmont Avenue, Chicago, Il 60657. TN: (312) 525-4126.

Miss MARGARET L. MULLER, THE MEDUSA STUDIO, 806 Fremont, Menlo Park, CA 94025.—*calligrapher, designer, illuminator.*

Mrs. INEZ PENNYBACKER, P.O. Box 513, Georgetown, CT 06829.—*hand binding, restoration.*

Miss MARIANA K. ROACH, 5722 Farquhar Lane, Dallas, TX 75209.—*hand binding, calligraphy, designing.*

NATHAN O. ROGERS, 422 8th Street, Hermosa Beach, CA 90254.—*rebinding.*

IVAN J. RUZICKA, 2981 South Webber Place, Sarasota, FL 33580.—*hand binding, restoration, designing.*

Rev. JAMES F. S. SCHNIEPP, 204 East 6th Street, New York, NY 10003.—*hand binding.*

FRED H. SHIHADEH, 106 East Athens Avenue, Ardmore, PA 19003.—*hand binding, restoration.*
NORMAN L. SPELMAN, 116 Warren Avenue, Plymouth, MA 02360.—*Makers of boxes and slip cases for rare books.*
Mrs. NANCY M. STORM, Drawer L. Sedona, AZ 86336.—*hand binding, restoration, designer.*
TREASURED BOOKS BINDERY, P.O. Box 24158, Dayton, OH 45424.—*handbinding and repairs.*
Miss CHARLOTTE M. ULLMAN, Whittlesey Road, New Preston, CT 06777.—*hand binding, restoration.*
Mrs. KATHLEEN L. WICK, 35 West Cedar Street, Boston, MA 02114.—*hand binding.*
Mrs. LAURA S. YOUNG, 21 Claremont Avenue (Apt. 81), New York, NY 10027.—*hand binding. restoration.*

SUPPLIES AND MATERIALS FOR BINDERS AND REPAIRERS
REBECCA B. DESMARAIS, GARGOYLE PRESS AND PAPER WORKS, 1 Nixon Road, P.O. Box 2286, Framingham, MA 01701.—*hand-made papers for fine editions etc.*
PEACOCK PAPERS, P.O. Box 533, Fairview, NJ 07022.—*marbled papers.*

SUPPLIES AND SERVICES

———— ♦ ————

Entry in this directory is free at the discretion of the Editor who invites names for inclusion in the next edition from those specializing in supplies and services for the antiquarian book trade. Full details should be sent, including samples, catalogs or other descriptive matter, or the names of dealers for whom similar work has already been done.

CABLE ADDRESSES

REGISTERED TELEGRAPHIC ADDRESSES

AUTOGRAPHS,	NEWTON, MA	— The Rendells.
BENMARBOOK,	LOS ANGELES, CA	— Bennett & Marshall.
BIBLIOPOLE,	CHICAGO, IL	— James M. W. Borg.
BOOKJOHNS,	NORWOOD, NJ	— Walter J. Johnson Inc.
BOOKMAN,	SAN-FRANCISCO, CA	— John Howell.
BROMSENBOOKS,	BOSTON, MA	— Maurey A. Bromsen.
CANNBOOKS.	BOSTON, MA	— J. S. Canner & Co. Inc.
CELLARBOOK,	DETROIT, MI	— Cellar Book Shop.
COLCENT,	DENVER, CO	— Collectors' Center.
DAWBOOK,	LOS-ANGELES, CA	— Dawson Book Shop.
EDGRENART,	CARMEL, CA	— J. S. Edgren.
ELLSONBOOK,	LANSING, MI	— Ellison Bookshop.
EXPERIMENT,	NEW YORK, NY	— Bruce Ramer.
FINDALL,	NEW-YORK, NY	— Mary S. Rosenberg.
GOODBOOKS,	NEW-YORK, NY	— Philip Duschnes.
GULLIVER,	LOS ANGELES, CA	— Tollivers Books.
HALEBOOKS,	WASHINGTON, DC	— William F. Hale.
HALEVINSON,	BEVERLEY-HILLS, CA	— Harry A. Levinson.
HILLSTONE,	NEW-HAVEN, CN	— C. A. Stonehill Inc.
HYSONS,	LOS ANGELES, CA	— Hyman & Sons.
INCIPIT,	SOUTHPORT, CT	— Lawrence Witten.
INTERSERV,	BREWER, ME	— International House Books.
JABBERWOCK,	LOS-ANGELES, CA	— Zeitlin & Ver Brugge.

KINDERBOOK,	NEW-YORK, NY	— Justin G. Schiller.
KRAUSBOOKS,	NEW-YORK, NY	— Kraus Periodicals Inc. & H. P. Kraus.
LACTAGE,	NEW-YORK, NY	— Lathrop C. Harper Inc.
LIVRORARO,	NEW-YORK, NY	— Richard C. Ramer.
LOGOS,	SAN FRANCISCO, CA	— Jeremy Norman.
MONTOWESE,	BRANFORD, CT	— Branford Rare Books.
MINKOFF BOOKS,	GREAT BARRINGTON, MA	— George Robert Minkoff.
NATURUM,	WOODLAND HILLS, CA	— Rudolf Wm. Sabbot.
NEBENBOOKS,	CHICAGO, IL	— Kenneth Nebenzahl.
PARAGALERY,	NEW-YORK, NY	— Paragon Book Gallery.
PEGACYCLE,	LOS ANGELES, CA	— William & Victoria Dailey.
PICKWICK,	PHILADELPHIA, PA	— Charles Sessler.
PIGLET,	WASHINGTON, DC	— Booked Up.
PRINTSMITH,	NEW-YORK, NY	— Lucien Goldschmidt.
PROBKS,	DAYTON, OH	— Professional Books Service.
PUBWEEK,	NEW-YORK, NY	— R. R. Bowker Co.
RAREBOOKS,	FULLERTON, CA	— Book Cellar.
ROOTBOOKS,	SHERMAN OAKS, CA	— B. & L. Rootenberg.
RUBOOKS,	STOUGHTON, MA	— Robert H. Rubin.
RUSHBOOKS,	BALTIMORE, MD	— Cecil A. Rush.
SCHNASBOOK,	SCARSDALE, NY	— Annemarie Schnase.
SHARONBOOKS,	STOUGHTON, MA	— Western Hemisphere.
TOMEHELLER,	SWARTHMORE, PA	— F. Thomas Heller.
TUTTBOOKS,	RUTLAND, VT	— Chas E. Tuttle Co.
UNISCO,	MONTREAL, P.Q.	— University Book & Supply Co.

VOYCARTE,	GILROY, CA	— Roy V. Boswell.
WHITMANACK,	LONDON	— J. Whitaker & Sons Ltd. (*The Bookseller*).
WILFOL,	CHICAGO, IL	— Follett College Book Co.
WREDENBOOK,	PALO-ALTO, CA	— William P. Wreden.
YOUNGSOLO,	BERMUDA	— The Bookmart.

29

GEOGRAPHICAL DIRECTORY
OF DEALERS

EXPLANATORY NOTE

The information given, if available, for each entry is:

Name of business and postal address, and then street address if P.O. box is used.

Name of proprietor if different from foregoing (Prop:).

Telephone exchange and number (TN:), telegraphic address (Cables:) and telex number (Telex:).

Date of Establishment (Est:).

Type of premises occupied. If described as a shop or store they are, unless otherwise stated, open to the public and members of the trade without appointment during normal business hours. If described as a storeroom or private premises, information as to whether an appointment is necessary or not is added.

Type and size of business. Whether the firm deals in new books, and the size of the normal stock of secondhand (used) or antiquarian (antiq.) books; and also if any other business is carried on.

The subjects, if any, in which the business specializes (Spec:). Whether catalogs are issued, and if so, on what subjects, how often, and if a charge is made for them (Cata:).

If the business is a member of any of the following associations—
    American Booksellers' Association—ABA.
    Antiquarian Booksellers' Association of America—ABAA.
    British Antiquarian Booksellers' Association Int.—ABA (Int.)
    Canadian Booksellers' Association—CBA.
    International League of Antiquarian Booksellers—ILAB.
    Manuscript Society of America—MS.
    National Association of College Stores—NACS.

GEOGRAPHICAL AREAS
into which the Directory is divided

The Directory of Dealers has been arranged geographically in areas numbered as under. The first three cover Canada; then follow the United States in the usual alphabetical order, New York having three areas. Territories and possessions are at the end. The recognized abbreviations are shown in front of the name below; please use no other form of abbreviation.

CANADA
1. THE ATLANTIC
   PROVINCES
2. ONTARIO
3. THE WESTERN
   PROVINCES

UNITED STATES
4. AL ALABAMA
5. AK ALASKA
6. AZ ARIZONA
7. AR ARKANSAS
8. CA CALIFORNIA
9. CO COLORADO
10. CT CONNECTICUT
11. DE DELAWARE
12. DC DISTRICT OF COLUMBIA
    Federal Territory
13. FL FLORIDA
14. GA GEORGIA
15. HI HAWAII
16. ID IDAHO
17. IL ILLINOIS
18. IN INDIANA
19. IA IOWA
20. KS KANSAS
21. KY KENTUCKY
22. LA LOUISIANA
23. ME MAINE
24. MD MARYLAND
25. MA MASSACHUSETTS
26. MI MICHIGAN
27. MN MINNESOTA
28. MS MISSISSIPPI
29. MO MISSOURI
30. MT MONTANA
31. NE NEBRASKA
32. NV NEVADA
33. NH NEW HAMPSHIRE
34. NJ NEW JERSEY
35. NM NEW MEXICO
36. NY NEW YORK
    MANHATTAN &
    BRONX
37. NY NEW YORK
    LONG ISLAND &
    STATEN ISLAND
38. NY NEW YORK
    STATE
39. NC NORTH CAROLINA
40. ND NORTH DAKOTA
41. OH OHIO
42. OK OKLAHOMA
43. OR OREGON
44. PA PENNSYLVANIA
45. RI RHODE ISLAND
46. SC SOUTH CAROLINA
47. SD SOUTH DAKOTA
48. TN TENNESSEE
49. TX TEXAS
50. UT UTAH
51. VT VERMONT
52. VA VIRGINIA
53. WA WASHINGTON
54. WV WEST VIRGINIA
55. WI WISCONSIN
56. WY WYOMING
57. **UNITED STATES
    EXTERNAL
    TERRITORIES**
58. **OTHER COUNTRIES**

CANADA

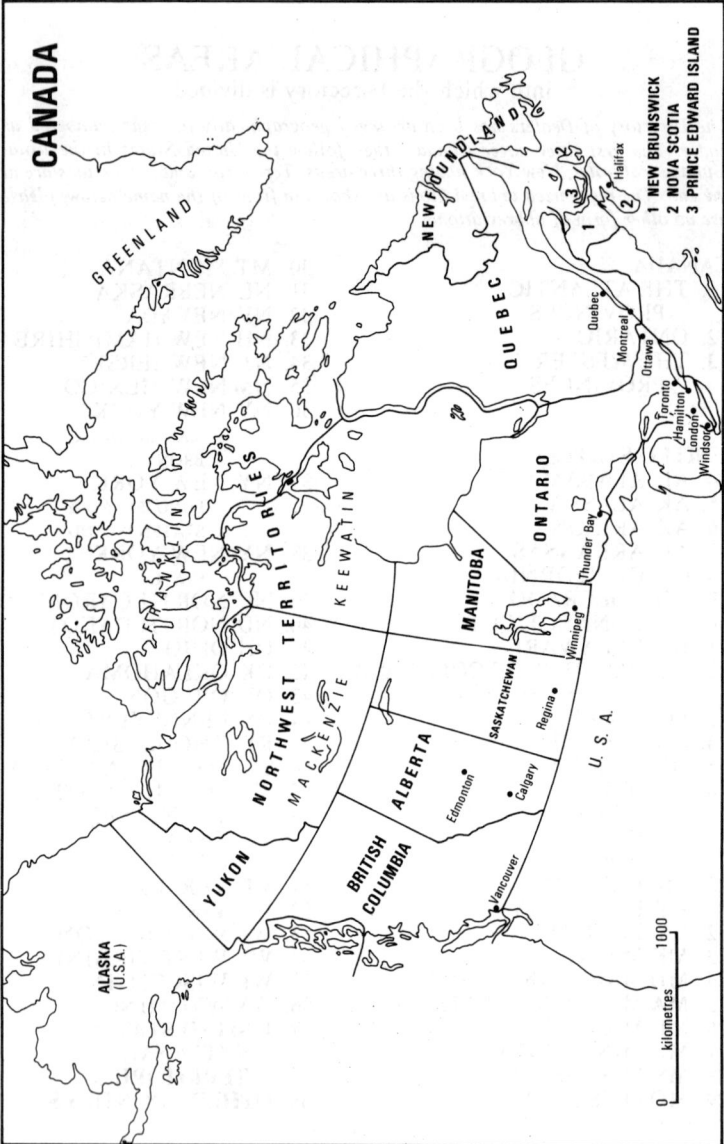

GREENLAND

YUKON

NORTHWEST TERRITORIES

MACKENZIE

FRANKLIN

KEEWATIN

ALASKA (U.S.A.)

BRITISH COLUMBIA

ALBERTA

SASKATCHEWAN

MANITOBA

ONTARIO

QUEBEC

NEWFOUNDLAND

Vancouver

Edmonton

Calgary

Regina

Winnipeg

Thunder Bay

Toronto

Hamilton

London

Windsor

Ottawa

Montreal

Quebec

Halifax

U.S.A.

1 NEW BRUNSWICK
2 NOVA SCOTIA
3 PRINCE EDWARD ISLAND

0   1000

kilometres

UNITED STATES OF AMERICA

CANADA

WASHINGTON
Seattle

OREGON

IDAHO

MONTANA

NORTH DAKOTA

SOUTH DAKOTA

MINNESOTA

WISCONSIN

MICHIGAN

Detroit
Cleveland
Milwaukee
Chicago

NEW YORK
Buffalo

VERMONT
NEW YORK
Boston
New York

PENNSYLVANIA
Pittsburgh
Philadelphia
Baltimore
Washington D.C.

OHIO
Cincinnati
WEST VIRGINIA

VIRGINIA

NORTH CAROLINA

SOUTH CAROLINA

GEORGIA
Atlanta

FLORIDA
Miami

NEVADA

UTAH

WYOMING

COLORADO
Denver

NEBRASKA

IOWA

ILLINOIS

INDIANA

KENTUCKY

TENNESSEE

ALABAMA

MISSISSIPPI

ARKANSAS

MISSOURI
St. Louis
Kansas City

KANSAS

OKLAHOMA

LOUISIANA
New Orleans

CALIFORNIA
San Francisco
Los Angeles
San Diego

ARIZONA
Phoenix

NEW MEXICO

TEXAS
Dallas
Houston
San Antonio

MEXICO

1 VERMONT
2 NEW HAMPSHIRE
3 MASSACHUSETTS
4 CONNECTICUT
5 RHODE ISLAND
6 NEW JERSEY
7 DELAWARE
8 MARYLAND

kilometres

0   1000

35

A DIRECTORY OF DEALERS IN
ANTIQUARIAN AND SECONDHAND BOOKS

CANADA

01. ATLANTIC PROVINCES AND QUEBEC

NEW BRUNSWICK (N.B.)
    FREDERICTON,
    SAINT ANDREWS
NOVA SCOTIA (N.S.)
    HALIFAX, WINDSOR

QUEBEC (P.Q.)
    MONTREAL,
    POINTE CLAIRE,
    SAINT BRUNO

ARCTICIAN BOOKS, P.O. Box 691, FREDERICTON, N.B. E3B 5B4. Prop: Harry E. Bagley. TN: (506) 457-0544. Est: 1966. Private premises, appointment necessary. Small stock. Spec: Canadiana, Americana, Arctic. B: The Royal Bank of Canada, Queen Street, Fredericton, N.B.

ART 45, 1460 SHERBROOKE STREET WEST (3RD FLOOR), MONTREAL, P.Q. H3G 1K4. Prop: Serge Vaisman. TN: (514) 843-5024. Spec: Art, illustrated.

MICHEL BRISEBOIS, C.P. 246. STATION B, MONTREAL, P.Q. H3B 3J7. TN: (514) 931-7033. Private premises; appointment necessary. Spec: first editions; illustrated, autographs.

WILFRED M. DeFREITAS, P.O. Box 883, STOCK EXCHANGE TOWER, MONTREAL, P.Q. H4Z 1K2. TN: (514) 935 9581. Shop: appointment advisable. Large stock sec. and antiq. Spec: Conan Doyle, Somerset Maugham, Gilbert and Sullivan.

DIAMOND BOOK STORE, 5035 SHERBROOKE STREET WEST, MONTREAL 260, P.Q. Prop: A. Handel. TN: (514) 482-2641. Est: 1914. Shop. Large stock used, also new.

PAUL DUCHOW RARE BOOKS, 5422 JEANNE MANCE, MONTREAL, P.Q. H2V 4K4.

EVERYMAN'S BOOKSHOP LIMITED, 5027 GLENCAIRN AVENUE, MONTREAL 248, P.Q. Prop: Mrs. Esther Handel. TN: (514) 481-1028. Est: 1937. Private premises, appointment necessary. Small stock used. Spec: Canadiana, history. C.B.A.

LIBRAIRIE JEAN GAGNON, B.P. 653 HV, 764 RUE SAINT JOSEPH (E), SALLE 402, P.Q. G1R 4S2. Prop: Jean Gagnon. TN: 523-6760. Est: 1955. Shop. Spec: Canadiana and French books. Cata: 10 per year. M: A.B.A.C.

LIBRAIRIE GUÉRIN, 4440 RUE SAINT DENIS, MONTREAL, P.Q. Prop Marc Guérin. TN: 843-6241. Est: 1926. Shop. Very large stock used, also new. Spec: Canadiana (French). Cata: Canadiana. A.B.A.C., C.B.A.

NIGEL AUBREY JONES, 4170 DECARIE BOULEVARD, MONTREAL, P.Q. H4A 3KT. TN: 488-6279.

HELEN R. KAHN, P.O. Box 323, VICTORIA STATION, MONTREAL, P.Q., H3Z 2V8. TN: (514) 844-5344. Est: 1977. Private premises; appointment necessary. Small stock used. Spec: rare Canadiana and Americana; Arctica; travel and explorations. M: A.B.A.C.

KATHLEEN AND MICHAEL LAZARE, 59 CARLETON STREET, SAINT ANDREWS, N.B. E0G 2X0. TN: (506) 529-3834. Shop open seven days a week. Large stock used. Spec: children's books; illustrated; also original wood engravings, oil painting, graphics etc. (At this address May to September only: October to May at Sherman, Conn. U.S.A., q.v.).

L.S. LOOMER, BOX 878, WINDSOR, NOVA SCOTIA B0N 2T0 (17 Water Street). Est: 1966. Shop. Medium stock used and antiq. Largest stock of antiquarian in the Maritime Provinces, books, pamphlets, prints, maps.

PHILIP LOZINSKI, 1175 WOLFE STREET, SAINT BRUNO, P.Q. J3V 3K7. Prop: Mrs. Helena Zamovski. TN: (514) 653-8890. Est: 1960. Private premises; appointment necessary. Medium stock used. Spec: Slavica, Russica; linguistics, bibliography. Cata: 5 or 6 a year. (Also a Branch in U.S.A.).

MANSFIELD BOOK MART, 2065 MANSFIELD STREET, MONTREAL 110, P.Q. Prop: H.E. Heinemann. TN: 845-1846. Shop. Very large stock used, also new. Spec: Canadiana, first editions, rare. A.B.A.C.

NAUTICA BOOKSELLERS, 1579 DRESDEN ROW, HALIFAX, N.S. B3J 2K4. Prop: John Holland. TN: (902) 429-2741. Est: 1975. Shop, appointment desirable. Stock of about 8,000 volumes used; also a few new and remainders. Spec: exclusively books on the sea and Arctica. Cata: 3 a year. C.B.A.

RUSSELL BOOKS, 275 SAINT ANTOINE STREET WEST, MONTREAL, P.Q. H2Z 1H5. TN: (514) 866-0564.

SCHOONER BOOKS LIMITED, 5378 INGLIS STREET, HALIFAX, N.S. B3H 1J5. Prop: John D. Townsend & Mary Lee MacDonald. TN: (902) 423-8419. Est: 1975. Shop. Very large stock used. Spec: Canadian Atlantic Provinces. M: A.B.A.C.

LIBRAIRIE STRYKER'S BOOKS, 5947, AVENUE DU PARC, MONTREAL, P.Q. H2V 4H4. Prop: M. Friedland, TN: 485-1723. Est: 1968. Private house; no stock carried. Mail order only. Search service only. Spec: Dr. Herbert M. Shelton, Natural Hygiene. B: Barclays Bank (London) Acc. No: 90386553. Montreal City & District Bank. Acc. No: 1827-0.

TALLY-HO BOOK STORE, 764 ST PIERRE, MONTREAL, P.Q. Prop: D. Turkington. TN: (514) 842-6393. Est: 1943. Shop. Large stock used. A.B.A.C.

UNIVERSITY BOOK & SUPPLY COMPANY, 417 SAINT PETER STREET, MONTREAL 1, P.Q. Prop: Richard Sair. TN: VI 5-6993. Cables: Unisco Montreal. Est: 1943. Store. Large stock used, also new. Spec: Canadiana, magic, numismatics.

WESTMOUNT PHOENIX, 320 VICTORIA AVENUE, MONTREAL, P.Q. M3Z 2M8. Prop: Robert North, Judith Knight & Ruth Portner. TN: (514) 482-4428.

WILLIAM P. WOLFE INC., P.O. BOX 1190, POINTE CLAIRE, P.Q. H9S 5K7. Prop: Patricia Brown. TN: (514) 697-1630. Est: 1958. Shop. Large stock used. Spec: Canadiana. Cata: Americana, Canadiana and general, 2 a year. Also art gallery featuring early Canadian art. A.B.A.A. A.B.A.C.

GRANT WOOLMER, 4823 SHERBROOKE STREET WEST, MONTREAL, P.Q. H3Z 1G7. TN: (514) 933-3968. Est: 1954. Office, open usual business hours. Medium stock used. Spec: Canadiana, Arctica. Cata: on foregoing, 6 a year. A.B.A.C. I.L.A.B.

02.   ONTARIO (ONT.)

ALLISTON	NORTH BAY
BEWDLEY	OTTAWA
COBALT	PARIS
FORT ERIE	PETERBOROUGH
GEORGETOWN	SAINT CATHERINES
GUELPH	SIX NATIONS RESERVE
HAMILTON	THORNHILL
HENSALL	TORONTO
KINGSTON	UXBRIDGE
LONDON	WATERDOWN
MANOTICK	

ABELARD BOOKS, 519 QUEEN STREET WEST, TORONTO, ONT. M5V 2B4. Prop: Paul Lockwood & Joyce Blair. TN: (416) 366-0021. Spec: theology, philosophy, social sciences. M: ABAC.

ABOUT BOOKS, 280 QUEEN STREET WEST, TORONTO, ONT. M5V 2A1. Prop: L. A. Wallrich & A. Greenwood. TN: (416) 593-0792. Shop, open daily. Large stock used. Spec: modern first editions; mountaineering; older dog books. Cata: occasionally. M: A.B.A., A.B.A.C.

BEN ABRAHAM BOOKS, 97 DONNAMORA CRESCENT, THORNHILL, ONT. L3T 4K6. TN: (416) 886-0534. Spec: Occult.

ACADIA BOOK STORE, 232 QUEEN STREET EAST, TORONTO, ONT. M5A 1S3. Prop: Asher Joram. TN: (416) 364-7638. Est: 1931. Shop. Large stock used and rare. Spec: Canadiana, rare, travel and art books. M: A.B.A.C.

ALLISON THE BOOKMAN, 342 MAIN STREET EAST, NORTH BAY, ONT. P1B 1B4.

ALPHABET BOOKSHOP, 656 SPADINA AVENUE, TORONTO, ONT. M5T 2H9. Prop: Richard Shuh & Linda Woolley. TN: (416) 924-4926. Spec: Canadian Literature.

ANN'S BOOKS, 225 CARLTON STREET WEST, TORONTO, ONT. M5T 2W1. TN: (416) 964-6470. Shop, open afternoons Tuesdays to Fridays and all day Saturdays, closed Mondays.

HUGH ANSON-CARTWRIGHT, 229 COLLEGE STREET, TORONTO, ONT. M5T 1R4. TN: (416) 979-2441. Est: 1966. Shop, closed Sundays and by appointment. Large stock used. Spec: Canadiana, modern literature, juveniles. Cata: various subject lists, periodically. A.B.A.C. I.L.A.B.

DIANA ARMOUR, 473 BESSERER STREET, OTTAWA K1N 6C2.

ATTIC BOOKS, 388 CLARENCE STREET, LONDON, ONT. N6A 3M7. Prop: Marvin Post. TN: (519) 432-6636. Spec: Canadiana, True Crime.

ATTICUS BOOKS, 84 HARBORD STREET, TORONTO, ONT. M5S 1G5. Prop: Michael Freedman. TN: (416) 922-6045. Est: 1979. Shop. Very large stock used. Spec: philosophy: classics, linguistics; history of science. Corresp: Français, Deutsch. B: Canadian Imperial Bank of Commerce, Toronto. M: A.B.A.C. *Also at* 589 MARKHAM STREET, TORONTO. Shop, open Sundays.

BAKKA: A SCIENCE FICTION BOOK SHOPPE, 282-286 QUEEN STREET WEST, TORONTO, ONT. M5V 2A1. Prop: Charles P. McKee & Raymond Alexander. TN: (416) 596-8161. Est: 1972. Shop. Very large stock used; also new books. Spec: science fiction, fantasy; comics; children's illustrated; astronomy.

NELSON BALL, 31 WILLOW STREET, PARIS, ONT. N3L 2K7. TN: (519) 442-6113. ABAC.

BARCLAY'S BOOKS, 98 HAWTHORNE AVENUE, OTTAWA, ONT. K1S 0B1. TN: (613) 238-7509. Est: 1985. Shop, closed Mondays. Medium stock used. Spec: Canadiana and Military.

BATTA BOOK STORE, 710 THE QUEENSWAY, TORONTO, ONT. M8Y 1L3. Prop: Bela Batta. TN: 259-2618. Est 1965. Shop (open 14.00 to 19.00 daily). Stock of 50,000 volumes. Spec: Fiction, Canadiana, literature also History, Biography, General used books. A.B.A.C.

BERRY & PETERSON, 225 Princess Street, Kingston, Ont. K7L 1B3. TN: (613) 548-4871. Spec: travel & exploration. Canadiana.

THE BOOK BAZAAR, 755 Bank Street, Ottawa, Ont. K1S 3V3, Canada. Prop: Beryl McLeod. TN: (613) 233-4380. Est: 1974. Shop. Medium stock used; also some remainders. Music and Books on Music.

THE BOOK BIN, 225 Princess Street, Kingston, Ont. K7L 1B3. Prop: Richard Peterson & John Berry. TN: (613) 548-4871. Est: 1972. Shop. Very large stock. Spec: Canadiana, Art, 1st edition literature. Cata: 1 or 2 a year. B: Bank of Montreal, King St. Kingston. Acc.No: 1014-278.

BOOK MART OF HAMILTON, LTD., 54 James Street North, Hamilton 11, Ont. Prop: Mrs. F. Beverley Moore. TN: (416) 528-1752. Est. 1963. Shop. Medium stock used. Also new. Cata: occasionally. N.A.C.S. A.B.A. C.B.A.

THE BOOK STORE, 228 Charlotte Street, Peterborough, Ont. Prop: A.R. Stewart. TN: (705) 743-5132. Est: 1967. Shop. Medium stock used, some new. Spec: Canadiana. Cata: general, occasionally. A.B.A.C. I.L.A.B. C.B.A.

BOUDICCA BOOKS, P.O. Box 901, Station K, Toronto, Ont. M4P 2H2. Prop: Elizabeth F. Nuse. TN: (416) 483-2431. Est: 1982. Private premises, appointment necessary. Small stock sec. and antiq. Spec: books by and about women. Cata: 3-4 a year. B: Canada Imperial Bank of Commerce, Young & Bloor, Toronto.

DYMENT BOOKS, 319 Wilbrod Street, Ottawa, Ont. K1N 6MA. Prop: J. Paul and Margaret S. Dyment. TN: (613) 235-0565. Est: 1967. Shop. Large stock used; academic, mail order search service. Spec: philosophy, literature, sociology, political science, history. Cata: on foregoing, monthly. *Also Shop at* 54½ George Street, Ottawa, Ontario, K1N 5V9.

GLENN'S BOOKS, 2130, Queen Street, East, Toronto, Ont. TN: 698-7408. Spec: children's and illustrated.

D.W. GOUDY BOOKS, 264 Indian Road, Toronto Ont. M6K 2X2. Est: 1976. Private premises, appointment necessary. Very small stock. Spec: Napoleon Bonaparte. Cata: Every 4 months. Also new books. B: Royal Bank — Main Branch, Guelph, Ontario. Acct.No: 112.595.4.

GREAT NORTHWEST BOOK COMPANY, 338 JARVIS STREET, TORONTO, ONT. M4Y 2G6. Prop: D. V. Baker & T. Antonov. TN: 964-2089. Est: 1977. Shop, open noon to 18.00 hrs. Large stock used, also new books. Spec: Canadiana.

NORMAN HART BOOKS LTD., 66 DUNDAS STREET EAST, TORONTO, ONT. M5B 1C7. Prop: Norman Hart. TN: (416) 362-7610. Est: 1973. Shop. Medium stock. Spec: Social History & Canadiana. Cata: Periodically. B: Royal Bank of Canada, Sherbourne & Queen Street, Toronto, Ont. M: A.B.A.C. I.L.A.B.

HANNELORE HEADLEY, 71 QUEEN STREET, SAINT CATHARINES, ONT. L2R 5G9. TN: 684 6145. Est: 1972. Shop, closed on Mondays. Medium stock. M: A.B.A.C. A.L.A.C.

HIGHWAY BOOK SHOP, COBALT, ONT. Prop: Douglas C. Pollard. TN: (705) 679-8375. Est: 1957. Shop. Very large stock used, also new. C.B.A.

HORTULUS, 101 SCOLLARD STREET, TORONTO, ONT. M5R 1G4. Prop: Linda & Bruce Marshall. TN: (416) 960-1775. Est: 1978. Shop. Very small stock used, and a few new books. Spec: horticulture; architecture and related subjects.

HURONIA CANADIANA BOOKS, BOX 685, ALLISTON, ONT. Prop: H.I. Wray. TN: (705) 435-7255. Est: 1970. Private premises, appointment necessary. Small stock used. Spec: Canadiana, arctica material. Cata: on foregoing, 10 a year.

IROQRAFTS LIMITED, RR2, OHSWEKEN, SIX NATIONS RESERVE, ONT. N0A 1M0. Spec: books on the Iroquois North American Indians.

THE IRWIN COMPANY, 413 BROCK AVENUE, TORONTO 4, ONT. Prop: I.L. Honsberger. Est: 1946. Private premises, open normal business hours. Small stock used, a few new. Cata: lists, regularly.

PETER L. JACKSON, 23, CASTLE GREEN CRESCENT, TORONTO, ONT. M9R 1N5. TN: (416) 249-4796. Est: 1970. Private premises; appointment necessary. Small stock used. Spec: Military Books, Regimental histories, Uniforms and Campaigns—all countries and Eras. Cata: 2 per year.

D. & E. LAKE LIMITED, 106 BERKELEY STREET, TORONTO, ONT. M5A 2W7. Prop: Don & Elaine Lake. TN: (416) 863-9930. TA: Lakebooks Toronto. Est: 1977. Storeroom. Large general stock. Spec: Americana, Canadiana, travel. Cata. M: A.B.A.C. (I.L.A.B.)

PATRICK McGAHERN BOOKS INC., 783 BANK STREET, OTTAWA, ONT. K1S 3V5. Prop: Pat. McGahern. TN: (613) 233-2215. Est: 1969. Shop; closed on Mondays. Large stock used. Spec: Canadiana, Arctica: Irish history and literature. Used and rare. Cata: on Arctica, and general antiquaria, 6 per year. M: A.B.A.C.

DAVID MASON, 342 QUEEN STREET WEST, TORONTO, ONT. M5V 2A2. TN: (416) 598-1015. Est: 1967. Shop. Medium stock used. Spec: modern first editions, 19th century literature, Canadiana. Cata: on foregoing, 2-4 a year. A.B.A.C. I.L.A.B.

WILLIAM MATTHEWS, 16 JARVIS STREET, FORT ERIE, ONT. Prop: William Matthews and Ann Hall. TN: (416) 871-8484. Est: 1976. Shop. Medium stock used. Spec: 19th and 20th Century first editions; fantasy and science fiction. M: A.B.A.C.

MONTGOMERY BOOKSTORE, 384 QUEEN STREET EAST, TORONTO, ONT. M5A 1T1. Prop: Morton A. Montgomery. TN: (416) 363-7648. Est: 1939. Shop. Small stock used, also new books and back number magazines. Spec: business and technical. Cata: Canadiana, rare, occasionally. C.B.A.

GORDON NORMAN, BOX 247, STATION "F", TORONTO 5, ONT. TN: (416) 922-2833. Est: 1963. Private premises, appointment necessary. Medium stock used and rare. Spec: literature, private press books, literary criticism, biography, Canadiana. Cata: on foregoing, 6 a year. A.B.A.C. I.L.A.B.

NOSTALGIA BOOKS, P.O. BOX 1442, GUELPH, ONT. N1H 6N9. Prop: William Roberts. Est: 1977. Private premises, mail order only. Small stock used. Spec: Canadiana; fine arts; Johnsoniana. Cata: 4 per year.

OLD FAVORITES BOOK SHOP LIMITED, 250 ADELAIDE STREET WEST, TORONTO, ONT. M5H 1X8. Prop: Ken Saunders. TN: (416) 977-2944. Est: 1954. Shop. Stock of over 300,000 items. Spec: Canadiana, horses and coaching. Book auctions. Cata: general, 1 a year. A.B.A.C. I.L.A.B.

OXBOW BOOKS, 102 MAIN STREET SOUTH, GEORGETOWN, ONT. L7G 3E4. TN: Georgetown 877-8861

JOSEPH PATRICK BOOKS, 1600 BLOOR STREET WEST, TORONTO, ONT. M6P 1A7 Prop: Joseph G. Sherlock. TN: (416) 531-1891. Est: 1954. Very large stock used. Spec: Canadiana, Catholica, first editions, scholarly, maps and prints. Cata: Canadiana monthly. A.B.A.C. I.L.A.B.

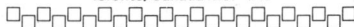

FRANK POLLARD BOOKS, RR4, Uxbridge, Ont. L0C 1K0. Prop: Frank Pollard. TN: (416) 649-2079. Est: 1974. Private premises, appointment necessary. Small stock used. Spec: World travel & history. Cata: Yearly. B: Bank of Nova Scotia, Brock Road, Pickering, Ontario 3055-062.

POMONA BOOK EXCHANGE, Highway 52, Rockton P.O., Ont. L0R 1X0. Props: Frederic & Walda Janson. TN: (519) 621-8897. Est: 1951. Private premises, appointment necessary. Small stock used. Spec: Horticulture, pomology and botany (none other). Cata: 3 per year. Also new books. B: Bank of Montreal (Canada), Lloyds (England), Marine Midland (U.S.A.)

ST. NICHOLAS BOOKS, P.O. Box 863, Station F., Toronto, Ont. M4Y 2N7. Prop: Yvonne Knight. TN: (416) 922-9640. Est: 1974. Private premises, appointment necessary. Small stock. Spec: Printed ephemera, juvenile and related bibliography. Cata: 3 or 4 per year. M: A.B.A.C.

SCHOLARS' BOOKSTORE, 1126 Bank St., Ottawa, K1S 3X6, Canada. Prop: Paul & Margaret Dyment. TN: (613) 235-0565. Est: 1978. Shop. Large stock used, some new. Spec: Philosophy, Sociology, Political Science. Open Tues-Sat. 10-6, Friday 10-9.

SEVEN SEAS BOOK SERVICE REGISTERED, Oak Street, Bewdley, Ont. K0L 1E0. Prop: Charlotte Clay. TN: (416) 797-2281. Est: 1950. Shop. Very small stock used, also new. Spec: natural history, outdoors, animal husbandry. Cata: on foregoing, occasionally.

JOHN W. SMITH BOOKS, R.R.1., Hensall, Ont. N0M 1X0. TN: (519) 262-5122. Est: 1966. Storeroom: appointment necessary. Small stock used catalogues. Spec: Manufacturers', agricultural and trade catalogues, pre-1960.

SPECIALTY BOOK CONCERN, 11 Dundas Street East, Waterdown, Ont. L0R 2H0. Prop: Craig Fraser. TN: (416) 689-8436. Est: 1937. Large stock used. Spec: Canadiana. Cata: old and rare, Canadiana, 5 a year. A.B.A.A.

THE SPORTSMAN'S CABINET, P.O. Box 15, Manotick, Ont. K0A 2N0. Props: William & Kathryn McClure. TN: (613) 692-3618. Private premises, no appointment necessary. Small stock used. Spec: Shooting, angling and dog books. Cata: 4 times per year. Also new books. B: Bank of Nova Scotia, Ottawa, South branch.

STARLIGHT BOOK CO., 994 LEMAR ROAD, NEWMARKET, ONT. L3Y 1S1, CANADA. (475 PENROSE STREET, NEWMARKET, ONT. L3Y 5L5.) Prop: Roma & Hugh Waignein. TN: Residence, (416) 898-7906; shop (416) 898-7179. Shop, open Tuesday-Saturday. Stock of sec. and antiq.

STEVEN TEMPLE, 483 QUEEN STREET WEST, TORONTO, ONT. M5V 2A9. Spec: fiction, poetry, drama. M: A.B.A.C.

VILLAGE BOOK STORE, 239 QUEEN STREET WEST, TORONTO, ONT. Prop: Martin Ahvenus. TN: (416) 363-6816. Est: 1961. Shop. Small stock used, also new. Spec: books for collectors, modern Canadian poetry. Cata: on foregoing and small press publications. A.B.A.C. I.L.A.B.

ARTHUR WHARTON BOOKS, 652 QUEEN STREET WEST, TORONTO, ONT. M6J 1E5. TN: (416) 865-9907. Spec: science fiction. ABAC.

GAIL WILSON BOOKSELLER INC., 355 QUEEN STREET WEST, TORONTO, ONT. M5V 2A4. TN: (416) 598-2024. Shop. Very large stock used. Spec: agriculture; books on books; domestic science; technology. M: A.B.A.C.

03. CENTRAL AND WESTERN PROVINCES

ALBERTA	MANITOBA
CALGARY, EDMONTON	WINNIPEG
BRITISH COLUMBIA (B.C.)	SASKATCHEWAN (SASK.)
NEW WESTMINSTER	REGINA,
QUEEN CHARLOTTE CITY	SASKATOON
VANCOUVER, VICTORIA	

A TO ZEE BOOKS, 1820-22 GOVERNMENT STREET, VICTORIA, B.C. V8T 4N5. Prop: Paul Manhas. TN: (604) 368-1534.

THE ADELPHI BOOK SHOP LTD., 822½, FORT STREET, VICTORIA, B.C. President: R.D. Hilton-Smith. TN: (604) 385-1746. Est: 1956. Shop. Very large stock used, some new. Spec: Canadiana, early children's books, 18th century. Cata: on foregoing and general. A.B.A.C.

BISHOP-WILLIAMS ANTIQUE PRINTS, MAPS & BOOKS, 346 WEST PENDER, VANCOUVER, B.C. Prop: Louis Bishop and Joyce Williams. TN: (607) 688 7434. Est: 1982. Store, closed Mondays. Very small stock sec. and antiq. books, also prints and maps. Cata: 2 a year.

BJARNE'S BOOKS, 10005 82ND AVENUE, EDMONTON, ALBERTA T6B 1Z2.

BOND'S BOOK SHOP, 319 WEST HASTINGS STREET, BOX 3166, VANCOUVER, B.C. V6B 3X6. Prop: E.R. Bowes. TN: (604) 688-5227. Est: 1932. Shop. Very large stock used. Spec: Western Canada, arctic, Alaska, travel, art. Cata: on foregoing, occasionally. A.B.A.C.

COLOPHON BOOKS, 407 WEST CORDOVA STREET, (UPSTAIRS), VANCOUVER, B.C. James F. McIntosh. TN: (604) 685-4138. Cata.

BILL ELLIS BOOKS, BOX 436, QUEEN CHARLOTTE CITY, B.C., V0T 1S0. TN: (604) 559-4681. Private premises; appointment necessary. Very small stock used; also new books. Spec: Indians of the Northwest Coast.

THE HAUNTED BOOKSHOP, 13-560 JOHNSON STREET, VICTORIA, B.C. V8W 1H6. Prop: Howard & Marina Gerwing. TN: (604) 382-1427. Cata: occasionally.

WILLIAM HOFFER, 58 AND 60 POWELL STREET, VANCOUVER, B.C. V6A 1E7. TN: (604) 683-3022. Est: 1969. Shop. Large stock used. Spec: Canadian literature, modern first editions, Pacifica.

JULIANTIQUARIAN BOOKS, 927 SECOND, NEW WESTMINSTER, B.C. Prop: Terry Julian. TN: (604) 521-0378. Est: 1984. Private house, appointment necessary. Very small stock sec. and antiq. Spec: theology, Bibles.

S.C. LUNSFORD BOOKS, P.O. BOX 86773, NORTH VANCOUVER, B.C. V7L 4L3. Prop: Stephen Lunsford. TN: (604) 681-6537. Est: 1977. Private premises; appointment necessary. Small stock used. Spec: Western Americana, Ethnology, Arctic. Cata: Quarterly. B: Bank of Montreal.

BURTON LYSECKI BOOKS, 527 OSBORNE STREET, WINNIPEG, MAN. R3L 2B2. Prop: Burton J. Lysecki. TN: (204) 284-4546. Est: 1971. Shop. Large stock. Spec: Canadiana, general out of print books.

MacLEOD'S BOOKS, 455 WEST PENDER STREET, VANCOUVER, B.C. V6B
1V2. Prop: Don Stewart. TN: (604) 681-7654. Shop. Very large stock
used. Spec: Canadiana; radical and labour history. M: A.B.A.C.

NORTHLAND BOOKS, 813 BROADWAY AVENUE, SASKATOON, SASK.
S7N 1B5. Prop: Garry & Janice Shoquist. TN: (306) 242-9466. Est:
1968. Shop. Very large stock used. Spec: North and West Canada.
Cata: occasionally.

OAK BAY BOOKS, 1964 OAK BAY AVENUE, VICTORIA, B.C.

PACIFIC BOOKS, 1135 LONSDALE, NORTH VANCOUVER, B.C. V7M 2H4.
Prop: George Carroll. TN: (604) 980-2121.

POOR RICHARD'S BOOKS LIMITED, 968 BALMORAL ROAD, VICTORIA,
B.C. V8T 1A8. Prop: Barney & Joanna Hagar. TN: (604) 384-4411.
Shop. Large sec. and antiq. stock. M: A.B.A.C.

RED RIVER BOOKSHOP, 346 CUMBERLAND AVENUE, WINNIPEG,
MANITOBA, R3B 1T3. TN: 943-9788.

TERRY RUTHERFORD, P.O. Box 1684 STATION A, VANCOUVER, B.C.
V6C 2P7. TN: (604) 687-3097. Spec: Mystery & detective fiction.

RICHARD W. SPAFFORD, 3036 13TH AVENUE, REGINA,
SASKATCHEWAN, S4T 1N9. TN: (306) 527-0844.

CHARLES H. TUPPER, BOOKSELLER, 756 DAVIE STREET,
VANCOUVER, B.C. V6Z 1B5. Prop: Charles H. Tupper. TN: (604)
683-2014. Shop. Stock of about 30,000 volumes used. Libraries
appraised.

TOM WILLIAMS—BOOKS, Box 4126C, CALGARY, ALBERTA, T2T 5M9.
TN: 264-0184. Est: 1959. Storeroom: By appointment only. Large
stock. Spec: Canadiana, mountaineering, polar regions, fur trade.
Cata: occasionally. M: A.B.A.C.

WINDHOVER BOOKS, 4432 CROWN STREET, VANCOUVER, B.C. V6S
2K5. Prop: R. Klarenbach. TN: (604) 224-7532. Est: 1979. Private
premises; appointment necessary. Very small stock used. Spec: modern
literary first editions.

UNITED STATES OF AMERICA

04. ALABAMA (AL.)

AUBURN	HUNTSVILLE
BIRMINGHAM	MOBILE
FORT PAYNE	MONTGOMERY

ACKERMAN & THOMPSON, 610, FLORENCE DRIVE, AUBURN, AL 36830.

AMSTEL BOOKS, P.O. Box 2022, HUNTSVILLE, AL 35804. Prop: Billy Garrison. TN: (205) 534-8490.

THE BOOKMONGER, 3 NORTH GOLDTHWAITE STREET, MONTGOMERY, AL. Prop: Julian Godwin. TN: (205) 834-5238. Shop.

WILLIAM M. BOULTON, 4003 MEDFORD DRIVE S.E., HUNTSVILLE, AL 35802 TN: 881-5021.

CATHER & BROWN BOOKS, 3109 7TH AVENUE SOUTH, BIRMINGHAM, AL. TN: (205) 591-7284. Private premises, appointment necessary.

CHILTON'S INC., 938-944 CONTI STREET, MOBILE, AL 36604. Prop: Chilton R. Powell, Jr. TN: (205) 432-3036. Spec: natural history, old prints and maps, Americana. A.B.A.A.

THE HAUNTED BOOK SHOP, 150 GOVERNMENT STREET, MOBILE, AL. TN: (205) 432-6606. Est: 1941. Shop. Very large stock used, also new. Spec: Alabama and Gulf Coast of U.S. Also stamps, coins and bottles.

MARCIA'S RARE BOOKS, 2364 WHITESBURG DRIVE, HUNTSVILLE, AL 35802. TN: (205) 534-1708. Shop.

R.E. PUBLICATIONS, P.O. Box 66212, MOBILE, AL. Prop: Rhoades Enterprise Publications. TN: (205) 433-1213. Private premises, appointment necessary. *Also at:* 210 SOUTH GEORGIA AVENUE.

REED BOOKS, P.O. Box 55293, BIRMINGHAM, AL 35255. Prop: Jim Reed. Full-time search service provided.

RHODDES ENTERPRISE PUBLICATIONS, 210 SOUTH GEORGIA AVENUE, P.O. Box 66212, MOBILE, AL. TN: 433-0213.

04. ALABAMA (AL.)

DAVID L. STONE, 522 JORDAN LANE N.W., HUNTSVILLE, AL 38502. TN: (205) 539-5547. Shop.

GARY WAYNER, ROUTE 3, BOX 13, FORT PAYNE, AL. TN: (205) 845-5866. Private premises, appointment necessary.

05. ALASKA (AK.)

ANCHORAGE   SITKA
JUNEAU

ALASKA BOOK SEARCH, 6402 BLACKBERRY STREET, ANCHORAGE, AK. Prop: David L. Beale.

ALASKANA, 4617 ARCTIC BLVD., ANCHORAGE, AK 99503. Prop: Eugene Short. TN: (907) 277-8113. Est: 1968. Shop, closed on Mondays. Open Tuesdays-Saturdays 1-6 p.m. Small stock used. Spec: Alaska, Arctic, Northwest Passage, hunting, fishing, mountaineering. New books on Alaska only.

MICHAEL LESH, BOOKFINDER, 124 BEHRENDS AVENUE, JUNEAU, AK. Prop: Michael Lesh.

THE OBSERVATORY, P.O.BOX 1770, 212 KATLIAN STREET, SITKA, AK 99835. Prop: Dee Longenbaugh. TN: (907) 747-3033. Est: 1977. Shop. Medium stock used. Spec: Alaskana, Polar regions.

WILDWOOD BOOKS AND PRINTS, 1972 WILDWOOD LANE, ANCHORAGE, AK 99503. Spec: Alaska, Arctic.

06.   ARIZONA (AZ.)

ALPINE	PRESCOTT
BISBEE	SCOTTSDALE
CAVE CREEK	TEMPE
COTTONWOOD	TOMBSTONE
FLAGSTAFF	TUCSON
PHOENIX	WICKENBURG

ARIZONA BOOKSHOP, P.O. Box 4093, TUCSON, AZ 85717 (803 East Helen Street). Prop: Irving Schaeffer. TN: (602) MAin 2-1963. Shop. Medium stock used, also antiques. Spec: topography, Arizona and Western States.

BISBEE BOOK STALL, P.O. Box 73, 8, BREWERY GULCH, BISBEE, AZ 85603. Prop: John W. Kuehn. TN: (602) 432-4249. Est: 1957. Shop. Medium stock. Spec: Arizona, South-Western Americana, Military history. Cata: Monthly. B: 1st National Bank of Arizona. M: A.B.A.A.

THE BOOKSTOP, 2504 NORTH CAMPBELL AVENUE, TUCSON, AZ 85719. Prop: L. Allen. TN: (602) 326-6661. Est: 1967. Shop, open 10 to 23 hours daily, Sundays noon to 23 hrs. Stock of almost 80,000 volumes used. Spec: Arizona and Southwest.

VAN ALLEN BRADLEY INC., P.O. Box 4130, HOPI STATION, SCOTTSDALE, AZ 85258. TN: (602) 991-8633. Est: 1964. Private premises, appointment necessary. Small stock used. Spec: Americana, Literary First Editions. Cata: 3-5 per year. B: Valley National Bank. M: A.B.A.A.

BRADSTREET PRESS, 7500 EAST McCORMICK PARKWAY NO. 14, SCOTTSDALE, AZ 85258.

CAMPBELL'S BOOKS, 4602 E. PALO VERDE, PHOENIX, AZ 85018.

R.F. CARSON, P.O. Box 686, BISBEE, AZ 85603.

DUCK'S BOOKS, 1800 SOUTH MILTON, FLAGSTAFF, AZ. TN: (602) 779-5365. Shop.

L.E. GAY, SOUTHWEST BOOKS, Box 319, ALPINE COUNTRY CLUB, ALPINE, AZ 85920. TN: (602) 339-4341. Est: 1950. Shop. Very large stock of used and antiq. also new books. Spec: out of print and rare Arizona, New Mexico and Southwest; limited and de-luxe editions. Cata: 8 a year.

GUIDON BOOKS, 7117 MAIN STREET, SCOTTSDALE, AZ 85251. Prop: Aaron L. and Ruth K. Cohen. TN: (602) 945-8811. Est: 1964. Shop. Medium stock used, also new. Spec: Western Americana, Civil War. Cata: Western Americana. A.B.A.

DONALD E. HAHN, NATURAL HISTORY BOOKS, P.O. Box 1004, 512 WEST GILA STREET, COTTONWOOD, AZ. Prop: Donald Hahn. TN: (1-602) 634-5016. Est: 1979. Private premises; appointment necessary. Very large stock. Spec: Natural history. Cata: 4 a year. B: First Interstate Bank of Arizona, Cottonwood, AZ 86326. M: Guild of Arizona Antiquarian Bookdealers.

JANUS BOOKS LIMITED, P.O. Box 40787, TUCSON, AZ 85717. Prop: Michael S. Greenbaum. TN: (602) 881-8192. Est: 1979. Private premises; appointment necessary. Very small stock used. Spec: detective, mystery and suspense fiction; bibliography and criticism related to mystery fiction.

JOE'S BOOKS, 3652 EAST FORT LOWELL ROAD, TUCSON, AZ 85716, (in Shopping Center). Prop: Joe Patterson. TN: (602) 325-4114. Est: 1963. Shop. Medium stock used; also new books. Spec: Southwest Americana, Arizona Highways; Bibles, reference; art; periodicals. Cata: occasionally.

RUBY D. KAUFMAN, 518 EAST LOMA VISTA DRIVE, TEMPE, AZ 85282. TN: (602) 968-9517. —Private premises; appointment necessary.

FRED. LUDWIG, PERIODICA, 3801 EAST KLEINDALE ROAD, TUCSON, AZ 85716. TN: (602) 326-2513. Est: 1963. Shop and storeroom, appointment necessary. Very large stock of back-issues, serials and periodicals. Cata: 4 a year.

McGINNS BOOKS AND GIFTS, 121 NORTH MOUNT VERNON, PRESCOTT, AZ 86301. Prop: John & Barbara McGinn. TN: (602) 778-0493. Est: 1976. Private premises; appointment necessary. Medium stock. Spec: Circus, Lighthouse, South West. Some new books on medical and nursing. B: Valley National Bank, Miller Valley Road, Prescott, AZ 86301-18032991. Acc. No: 1155-2187-7047. M: A.B.A.

McLAUGHLIN'S BOOKS, P.O. BOX 2106, WICKENBURG, AZ 85358. Prop: Robert F. McLaughlin. TN: (602) 684-5824. Est: 1946. Shop. Small stock used. Spec: Desert Flora and Fauna, Dogs, Southwestern Americana, Horses, Gold Mining. New books also stocked. B: Valley National, Community Bank, Bank of America, Wells Fargo Bank.

MORGAN PARK TRADING CO, 1150 NORTH ELDORADO PLAZA (APT. 158), TUCSON, AZ 85712. TN: (602) 886-4653. Private premises, appointment necessary.

NIE BOOKSELLERS, 5828 EAST LINDEN, TUCSON, AZ 85712. Prop: Joseph and Trudy Nie. TN: (602) 885-8164. By appointment only.

OLD TOWN BOOKS, 10 WEST 7 STREET, TEMPE, AZ 85282. TN: (602) 968-9881. Shop.

OVERLAND BOOKSHOP, 903 EAST HENDRICK DRIVE, TUCSON, AZ 85719. Prop: Mrs. Dorothy McNamee. TN: (602) 623-5092. Private premises, appointment preferred but not essential. Small stock used. Spec: topography, Western States. Cata: occasionally. A.B.A.A.

BONITA PORTER, 2011 WEST BETHANY HOME, PHOENIX, AZ 85018. TN: (602) 242-9442. Shop.

ROSE TREE INN BOOKSHOP, P.O. BOX 7, TOMBSTONE, AZ 85638. Prop: Mrs. Burton Devere. TN: (602) 457-3326. Est: 1966. Shop; appointment desirable. Small stock used; also a few new books and antiques. Spec: Western Americana only. Cata: 2 a year.

BEN SACKHEIM, 5425 EAST FORT LOWELL ROAD, TUCSON, AZ 85712. TN: (602) 327-4285. Est: 1969. Private premises; appointment necessary. Medium stock used: also new books and fine art and original prints. Spec: 20th century first editions and art books. Cata: first editions, occasionally.

53

06.

R.M. SCHRAMM, 7101 East 34th Street, Tucson, AZ 85716. TN: (602) 885-4839. Shop.

RUSS TODD BOOKS, 28605 North 63rd Street, Star Route 2, Box 872F, Cave Creek, AZ 85331. TN: (602) 585-0070. Private premises, appointment necessary. Spec: Arizona & New Mexico.

GENE S. VINK, 2213 East Copper Street, Tucson, AZ 85716. TN: (602) 323-7188. Bookfinding service. Private premises, appointment necessary.

WILKE'S BOOK CORRAL, P.O. Box 1445, Wickenburg, AZ 85358 (51 South Kerkes Street). Prop: Al and Margi Wilke. TN: (602) 684-7748. Est: 1955. Shop, open 12.30 p.m. to 8 p.m. Medium stock used, a few new. Spec: Western Americana and fiction. Cata: general, occasionally. Also publishers.

07.   ARKANSAS (AR.)

FAYETTEVILLE	SPRINGDALE
HOT SPRINGS	

JACK BAILES BOOKS, P.O. Box 150, Eureka Springs, AR. TN: (501) 253-9131. Est: 1937. Mail order only. Medium stock sec. and antiq.

CENTAURI BOOKS, 1906 Lowell Road, Springdale, AR 72764. TN: (501) 756-2002. Spec: teleology.

DICKSON STREET BOOKSHOP, 318 West Dickson Street, Fayetteville, AR. TN: (501) 442-8182.

YESTERDAY'S BOOKS, ETC., 258 Whittington Avenue, P.O. Box 1728, Hot Springs, AR 71901. Prop: Rose Edwards. TN: (501) 624-6300. Est: 1974. Private premises: postal business only. Medium Stock. Lists on request. B: First National Bank. Garland County Antique Dealers Assoc.

08.   CALIFORNIA (CA.)

ALBANY	ANAHEIM
ALPINE	APTOS
ALTADENA	ARROYA GRANDE

ATHERTON
AUBURN
BAKERSFIELD
BALBOA
BELLFLOWER
BERKELEY
BEVERLY HILLS
BISHOP
BUELLTON
BURBANK
BURLINGAME
CAMPBELL
CARLSBAD
CARMEL
CHULA VISTA
CLAREMONT
CONCORD
COSTA MESA
CRESTLINE
CUPERTINO
CYPRESS
DALY CITY
DANA POINT
DANVILLE
DEL MAR
DIXON
EL CAJON
EL CERRITO
ELK GROVE
ENCINITAS
ENCINO
ESCONDIDO
FAIROAKS
FALLBROOK
FARMERSVILLE
FERNDALE
FRESNO
FULLERTON
GARBERVILLE
GARDEN GROVE
GEORGETOWN
GILROY

GLENDALE
GLEN ELLEN
GOLETA
HAYWARD
HOLLYWOOD
ISLA VISTA
JULIAN
LA CANADA
LAFAYETTE
LAGUNA BEACH
LA JOLLA
LAKESIDE
LA MESA
LANCASTER
LEUCADIA
LONG BEACH
LOS ALTOS
LOS ANGELES
LOS OSOS
MALIBU
MARTINEZ
MENLO PARK
MILLBRAE
MILL VALLEY
MODESTO
MOKELUMME HILL
MONTCLAIR
MONTEREY
MORRO BAY
MOUNTAIN VIEW
NATIONAL CITY
NEVADA CITY
NORTH HOLLYWOOD
NORTHRIDGE
NORWALK
OAKLAND
OJAI
ORANGE
PACHECO
PACIFIC GROVE
PACIFIC PALISADES
PALM DESERT

PALO ALTO	SANTA CRUZ
PANORAMA CITY	SANTA MONICA
PASADENA	SANTA ROSA
PINE GROVE	SAUSALITO
QUINCY	SCOTTS VALLEY
RAMONA	SEBASTOPOL
RANCHO SANTO FE	SEPULVEDA
REDDING	SHERMAN OAKS
REDLANDS	SOLANA BEACH
REDONDO BEACH	SOLVANG
REDWOOD CITY	SOUTH GATE
RESEDA	SPRING VALLEY
RIVERSIDE	STOCKTON
SACRAMENTO	STUDIO CITY
SAINT HELENA	SUN VALLEY
SAN BERNARDINO	TEMPLE CITY
SAN BRUNO	TOPANGA
SAN CARLOS	TORRANCE
SAN DIEGO	TURLOCK
SAN FERNANDO	TWENTY-NINE PINES
SAN FRANCISCO	UNIVERSAL CITY
SAN GABRIEL	VAN NUYS
SAN JOSE	VENTURA
SAN LUIS OBISPO	VISTA
SAN PEDRO	WHITTIER
SAN RAFAEL	WOODLAND HILLS
SANTA ANA	YUCAIPA
SANTA BARBARA	

ABBEY BOOKSHOP, P.O. Box 64384, Los ANGELES, CA 90064. (2701 Westwood Boulevard, Los Angeles, CA.) TN: (213) 470-2296. Store-room; appointment necessary. Large stock used. Spec: economic history, literature, anthropology, military: hunting, Latin America. Cata: general, 6 a year.

A B I BOOKS, P.O. Box 30564, SANTA BARBARA, CA 93130. Prop: Jeffrey Akard and Nancy Isakson. TN: (805) 682-9686. Private premises; appointment necessary. Small stock used. Spec: English, American and European Modernism; illustrated books; the artist and the book. Cata: 3 a year.

ACADEMIC LIBRARY SERVICE, 6489 SOUTH LAND PARK DRIVE, SACRAMENTO, CA 95831. Prop: Philip & Ramelle Onstott. TN: (916) 428-2863. Est: 1950. Private premises, but open normal business hours. Medium stock. Spec: anthropology, archaeology, pre-history; folklore; primitive art; children's books. Cata: 4 a year.

A-C-H BOOKSHOP, 1919 WEST 7TH STREET, LOS ANGELES, CA 90057. Prop: Carl C. Harris. TN: (213) 483-8413. Est: 1946. Shop. Large stock used; also new books. Spec: metaphysics, art, language, photography. Also stereo records and art prints; Auto manuals; Bibles and Bible Commentaries; Technical.

ACOMA BOOKS, P.O. BOX 4, RAMONA, CA 92065. Prop: Robert Neutrelle. TN: (619) 789-1288. Est: 1957. Private premises, appointment necessary. Large stock used books, also new. Spec: archaeology, anthropology, ethnology, Western Americana. Cata: on foregoing, quarterly.

ACORN BOOKS, 510 O'FARRELL STREET, SAN FRANCISCO, CA 94102. (BETWEEN JONES AND LEAVENWORK STREETS, DOWNTOWN). Prop: Mr. & Mrs. Joel M. Chapman. TN: (415) 563-1736. Est. 1980. Shop. Very large stock used and rare books.

ACRES OF BOOKS INC., 240 LONG BEACH BLVD., LONG BEACH, CA 90802. Prop: E.P. Smith. TN: (213) 437-6980. Est: 1934. Shop, closed Sunday and Monday. Very large general stock used; also remainders.

STEPHEN ACRONICO, SUITE 207, 903 STATE STREET, SANTA BARBARA, CA 93101. Private premises, appointment necessary.

ADA'S, 1624 WEST LEWIS STREET, SAN DIEGO, CA 92103. Prop: Ada Greer. TN: (619) 291-4736. Shop, closed Mondays. Spec: Children's Books.

ADAMS AVENUE BOOK STORE, 3502 ADAMS AVENUE, SAN DIEGO, CA 92116. Prop: Laura & Irvin Weiss & Barbara Oaks. TN: (619) 281-3330. Store. Spec: out of print fiction.

AGAIN BOOKS, 16A HELENA STREET, SANTA BARBARA, CA 93101. Shop.

AIDE-BOOKPOST, P.O. BOX 666, 962 GLENLAKE COURT, CARDIFF BY THE SEA, CA 92007. Prop: Ted Rogers. TN: (714) 753-3392. Est: 1954. Storeroom: business by mail and telephone only. Specializing in search service.

ALADDIN BOOKS AND MEMORABILIA, 122 WEST COMMONWEALTH AVENUE, FULLERTON, CA 92632. Prop: John T. Cannon. TN: (714) 738-6115. Est: 1982. Shop. Selected new and used. Spec: Modern first editions, popular fiction, cinema and performing arts. Want lists accepted.

ALBATROSS BOOK STORE, 166 EDDY STREET, SAN FRANCISCO, CA 94102. Owners: Rose H. & Donald W. Sharp. TN: (415) 885-6501. Est: 1954. Very large stock of used. Spec: Western Americana; fine children's; science fiction; well illustrated books. A.B.A.A., I.L.A.B.

ALBION FINE PRINTS, 1751 SAN LORENZO AVENUE, BERKELEY, CA 94707. Prop: Albert M. Shapiro. TN: (415) 527-0103. Spec: Art reference, drawings, philosophy, prints, psychiatry, psychology. M: A.B.A.A.

ALCOVE BOOK SHOP, 1226½ BROOKHURST, ANAHEIM, CA 92804.

ALDINE BOOKS, 4663 HOLLYWOOD BOULEVARD, LOS ANGELES, CA 90027. Prop: Alfred Kronfeld. TN: (213) 666-2690. Est: 1968. Shop. Large stock used. A.B.A.

ALICAT GALLERY, 1027 D.N. COAST HIGHWAY, LAGUNA BEACH, CA 92651. Prop: Florenz Baron. TN: (714) 497-2707.

ROBERT ALLEN, 1555 EAST HOMEWOOD DRIVE, ALTADENA, CA. TN: (818) 794-4210. Private premises, appointment necessary.

ALTA CALIFORNIA BOOKSTORE, P.O. BOX 296, LAGUNA BEACH, CA 92652. Prop: John Swingle. TN: (714) 494-5252. Est: 1961. Shop, appointment necessary. Small stock used. Cata: general, 3-4 a year, and lists. A.B.A.A. I.L.A.B.

AMERICAN BOOK STORE, 608 EAST OLIVE, FRESNO, CA 93728. TN: (209) 264-2648. Very large stock sec. and antiq. Spec: California; 19th and 20th century literature; World War II, history; religion. Cata.

AMERICAN FRAGMENTS, P.O. Box 271369, ESCONDIDO, CA 92027. Prop: Jim Lance. TN: (619) 747-8327. Est: 1964. Private premises; appointment necessary. Small stock used. Spec: illustrated books; bindings; prints.

AMES' SOUTH CALIFORNIA BOOKS, 6742 GREENLEAF AVENUE, WHITTIER, CA 90609. TN: (213) 696-3417. Very large stock sec. and antiq.

ANTIQUUS BIBLIOPOLE, 4147 24th STREET, SAN FRANCISCO, CA 94114. Prop: Pauline A. Grosch. TN: (415) 285-2322. Est: 1973. Medium stock used. Spec: Americana, the West; children's; nature; travel; biography; history; cookery. Hours: Tues.-Sat. 11 to 5.

APOLLO BOOK SHOP, 545 WEST 18th STREET, COSTA MESA, CA. Prop: James L. Currie. TN: (714) MIdway 6-7045. Est: 1961. Store. Medium stock used.

W. GRAHAM ARADER III, 560 SUTTER STREET, SUITE 201 SAN FRANCISCO, CA 94102. TN: (415) 788 5115.

ARCHAEOLOGIA, 707 CARLSTON AVENUE, OAKLAND, CA 94610. Prop: Arthur Richter. TN: (415) 832-1405. Spec: Archaeology of Egypt, Rome, Greece and central America; early travel. M: A.B.A.A.

ARGONAUT BOOK SHOP, 786-792 SUTTER STREET, SAN FRANCISCO, CA 94109. Prop: Robert D. Haines, Jr. TN: (415) 474-9067. Est: 1941. Shop. Very large stock. Spec: Californian and Western American History; Early American Exploration; Voyages of Discovery (Americas or South Pacific), etc. Cata: 6 per year devoted to fine and rare books. M: A.B.A.A. I.L.A.B.

ARGUS BOOKS, 1714 CAPITOL AVENUE, SACRAMENTO, CA 95818. Prop: Herb Caplan. TN: (916) 443-2223. Est: 1967. Shop. Large stock used. Spec: Western Americana, social sciences. Cata. A.B.A.A.

ARK BOOK SEARCHES, P.O. Box 9656, NORTH BERKELEY STATION, BERKELEY, CA 94709. Prop: Edith F. & Louis Laub. TN: (415) 524-7668.

ARKADYAN BOOKS AND PRINTS, 926 IRVING STREET, SAN FRANCISCO, CA 94122. Prop: Gerald L. Webb. TN: (415) 664-6212. Spec: fine original prints; 16-19th century maps; children's books; books on China and Japan. M: A.B.A.A.

ART & LETTERS BOOKSHOP, 555 SUTTER STREET, SAN FRANCISCO, CA 94102. Prop: Kenneth Starosciak. TN: (415) 982-3384. Est: 1978. Shop. Closed Tuesdays and Thursdays. Medium Stock available. Spec: Art, Architecture, First Editions. Cata: 10 per year.

ASUCLA BOOKSTORE, 308 WESTWOOD PLAZA, LOS ANGELES, CA 90024. (ground floor Ackerman Union, UCLA). TN: (213) 825-7711 ext. 251. Trade & Technical books. Open: Mondays-Thursdays, 7.45 a.m.-7.30 p.m. Fridays, 7.45 a.m.-6 p.m., Saturdays, 10.00-5 p.m., Sundays, 12-5 p.m.

ATLANTIS BOOKS, P.O. BOX 38387, HOLLYWOOD, CA 90028. (6513 Hollywood Boulevard.) Prop: H.E. Burroughs. TN: (213) 461-4491. Est: 1969. Shop. Very large stock used. Spec: social, political and economic history; World War II; Russian and European history. Cata: 4 a year. A.B.A.A.

ATTICUS BOOKS, P.O. BOX 26668, SAN DIEGO, CA 92126. (728 BROADWAY, SAN DIEGO, CA 92101.) Prop: Ralph & Deborah Cook. TN: (619) 566-8208. Shop, closed Tuesdays & Thursdays. Spec: modern first editions.

AUTHORS TODAY BOOKS, SUITE 111, 1 WEST CALIFORNIA BOULEVARD, PASADENA, CA 91105. TN: 441-1690.

AVONS RESEARCH, P.O. BOX 40, LA CANADA, CA 91011. TN: (213) 790-5370.

CALVIN AXFORD, 133 WARREN DRIVE, SAN FRANCISCO, CA 94131.

B. AND G. FINE BOOKS, P.O. BOX 8895, UNIVERSAL CITY, CA 91608. TN: (818) 848-0389. Private premises, appointment only. Spec: Western Americana; magicians, circus, clowns, cinemas; military; detective fiction.

BAILEY SEARCH SERVICE, P.O. BOX 326, REDONDO BEACH, CA 90277. Prop: Bill Bailey. Est: 1954. Storeroom, mail order only. Large stock used. Spec: science fiction, fantasy, occult, mystery, Edgar Rice Burroughs; Aleister Crowley detective mystery, pulps 1930s and 1940s (spider).

BARGAIN BOOK STORE, 1053 8TH AVENUE, SAN DIEGO, CA 92101. Prop: James Lindstrom. TN: (714) 234-5380. Est: 1950. Shop. Very large stock used. Spec: Americana, Illustrated, Art.

BAROQUE BOOK STORE, 1643 NORTH LAS PALMAS AVENUE, HOLLYWOOD, CA 90028. Prop: Sholom Stodolsky. TN: (213) 466-1880. Est: 1972. Shop. Medium stock. Spec: Modern Literature and Poetry, Music and Theatre. B: City National Bank, Los Angeles.

BART'S CORNER, 302 WEST MATILIJA STREET, OJAI, CA 93023. Prop: Gary Schlichter. TN: (805) 646-3755. Est: 1964. Shop, closed Mondays. Stock of 85,000 used books, paperbacks and some magazines; also about 1% new books. Spec: Krishnamurti.

BAY CITY BOOKS, SUITE 215, 629 STATE STREET, SANTA BARBARA, CA 93101. Private premises, appointment necessary.

BEAVER BOOKS, P.O. BOX 974, DALY CITY, CA 94017. Prop: Edgar L. Weber. TN: (415) 584-1302. Est: 1971. Mail order only. Spec: North American fur trade and related materials.

BEERS BOOK CENTER, 1013 14TH STREET, SACRAMENTO, CA 95815. TN: (916) 443-9148.

BELL'S BOOK STORE, 536 EMERSON STREET, PALO ALTO, CA 94301. Prop: Herbert Bell. TN: (415) 323-7822. Est: 1935. Shop. Very large stock used and out-of-print; also new books, especially horticultural. M: A.B.A.

CARLOS E. BENEMANN, FERNDALE BOOKS, 405 MAIN STREET, FERNDALE, CA 95536. Prop: Carlos and Marilyn Benemann. TN: (707) 786-9135. Est: 1980. Shop. Large stock used books. Spec: Latin Americana; natural history; travellers; California. M: A.B.A.

BENNETT & MARSHALL, 8214 MELROSE AVENUE, LOS ANGELES, CA 90046. Prop: George Allen. TN: (213) 653-7040. TA: Benmarbook. Est: 1941. Shop. Medium stock used. Spec: Americana (North and South), early printing, Pacific voyages, early science and medicine, old maps and atlases, literature. Private presses. Cata: rare Americana and general, 1-2 a year. A.B.A.A. I.L.A.B.

J. AND J. BERGER, 3905 MACARTHUR BOULEVARD, OAKLAND, CA 94619.

FRED A. BERK, P.O. Box 1367, STUDIO CITY, CA 91604. TN: (818) 789-4372. Est: 1968. Private premises, appointment necessary. Very small stock of used. Spec: Californiana, Americana, Travel. Cata: 2 to 4 times a year.

BERKELOUW, P.O. Box 1900, SANTA MONICA, CA 90406. Prop: Isidoor Berkelouw. TN: (213) 393-2116. Spec: topography.

WILLIAM BERNER, Box 31175, SAN FRANCISCO, CA 94131. TN: (415) 564-6297. Est: 1963. Private premises, appointment necessary. Small stock used, also new. Spec: detective fiction. Cata: detective fiction, 3 a year. A.B.A.

BIBLE COMMENTARY HOUSE, P.O. Box 2485, EL CAJON, CA 92021-0485. (1262 CAMILLO WAY.) Prop: Arnold D. Ehlert. TN: (619) 440-5871. Est: 1953. Private premises; appointment necessary. Very small stock used. Spec: Bible translations; Plymouth Brethren authors. Cata: occasionally.

BIBLIOCTOPUS, P.O. Box 309, IDYLLWILD, CA 92349. Prop: Mark J. Hime. TN: (714) 659-5188. Spec: fiction.

BIBLIOMANIA, 2556 TELEGRAPH AVENUE, BERKELEY, CA 94704.

BLACK OAK BOOKS, 1491 SHATTUCK AVENUE, BERKELEY, CA 94707. TN: (415) 486-0698. Shop.

BLAKESLEY & REED, BORREGO STAR ROUTE, JULIAN, CA 92036.

ROY BLEIWEISS — FINE BOOKS, 92 NORTHGATE AVENUE, BERKELEY, CA 94708. TN: (415) 548-1624. Spec: Fine printing and private presses, literary first editions, books about books; early law; tobacco and smoking. M: A.B.A.A.

BLUE JAY BOOKS, 4415 LONG BRANCH AVENUE, SAN DIEGO, CA 92107. Prop: Alice & Robert DeBow. TN: (619) 222-1991. Private premises, postal business only. Spec: rare & out of print.

JAMES M. BLUME, 125 ELM AVENUE, SAN BRUNO, CA 94066.

BOLERIUM BOOKS, SUITE 300, 2141 MISSION STREET, SAN FRANCISCO, CA 94110. Prop: John R. Durham. TN: (415) 863-6353. Private premises; appointment necessary. Spec: scholarly books; women's studies; labor history; classical studies; linguistics.

J.C. BONNETTE, 5525 DEWEY DRIVE (SUITE 104), FAIROAKS, CA 95628. TN: (916) 966-5780.

THE BOOK BARON, 1236 SOUTH MAGNOLIA AVENUE, ANAHEIM, CA 92804. Prop: Bob Weinstein. TN: (714) 522-2022. Shop. Very large stock used; also new books.

THE BOOK BARREL, 6937 (REAR), LA TIJERA BOULEVARD, LOS ANGELES, CA 90045. Prop: George Thomson. TN: (213) 641-6889. Est: 1980. Shop, closed Mondays. Medium stock sec. and antiq. B: Hughes Credit Union, Manhattan Beach Calif.

BOOK BUDDY, 1328 SARTORI AVENUE, TORRANCE, CA 90501. Prop: Bud Gobler. TN: (213) 328-1134. Est: 1977. Shop. Large stock of general books used. B: U.C.B. Torrance, Acc. No: 165626586.

BOOK CARNIVAL, 840 NORTH TUSTIN, ORANGE, CA 92667. Prop: Ed. Thomas. TN: (714) 538-3210. Est: 1981. Shop. Very large stock used; also new books. Spec: modern first editions; literature mystery, science fiction.

BOOK CASE BOOKS, 461 NORTH LAKE AVENUE, PASADENA, CA 91101. Prop: Alice Lee. TN: (213) 793-6527. Shop. Large stock used. Spec: illustrated children's books; detective, mystery fiction; cookbooks.

BOOK CELLAR, 124 ORANGEFAIR MALL, FULLERTON, CA 92632. (Three miles north of Disneyland.) Prop: David Cormany. TN: (714) 879-9420. TA: Rarebooks. Est: 1975. Shop. Very large stock. Spec: Influential books, scholarly works, literature, Literary criticism, Women, Philosophy, Erotica, Art, Cookery, Wine, Books about books. Cata: 2 illustrated per year. B: Bank of America, South Fullerton Main Branch. M: A.B.A.A.

THE BOOK CENTER, P.O. Box 11402, SANTA ANA, CA 92711. Prop: David L. Henson. TN: (714) 542-8839. Large stock used.

THE BOOK COMPANY, 1328 NORTH LAKE AVENUE, PASADENA, CA 91104. TN: 798-4630. Shop, open afternoons, closed Mondays.

THE BOOK CONDUCTOR, P.O. Box 2231D, PASADENA, CA 91105. Est: 1968. Private premises, appointment necessary. Very small stock used. Spec: United States railroads. Cata: on foregoing, occasionally.

BOOK CORNER, 995 EAST GREEN STREET, PASADENA, CA 91106.

THE BOOK DEN, P.O. Box 733, SANTA BARBARA, CA 93102. (15 East Anapamu Street, Santa Barbara, CA 93101.) Prop: Eric Kelley. TN: (805) 962-3321. Est: 1928. Shop. Very large stock.

BOOKFINDERS OF SAN GABRIEL, 217 SOUTH SAINT FRANCIS STREET, SAN GABRIEL, CA 91776. Prop: Herbert G. Williams. TN: (213) 287-5846. Est: 1951. Private premises, appointment necessary. Very large stock used, also antiques, coins and stamps.

BOOKHAVEN, 1037 CHORRO STREET, SAN LUIS OBISPO, CA 93401. Prop: James R. & Virginia V. Shober. TN: (805) 544-7551. Shop. Very large stock used; also new books on local and California history. M: Central California Antiquarian Booksellers.

THE BOOKIE JOINT, 7246 Reseda Boulevard, Reseda, CA 91335.
Prop: Jerry Blaz. TN: (213) 343-1055. Est: 1975. Shop and storeroom.
Very large stock.

A BOOKMARK, P.O. Box 1967, Rancho Santa Fe, CA 92067.

THE BOOK NEST, 366 Second Street, Los Altos, CA 94022. Prop:
Edwin Schmitz. TN: (415) 948-3446. Est: 1978. Shop, closed on
Mondays. Medium stock used. Spec: Steinbeck. B: Bank of America.
Acc.No: 820-2-1019.

BOOK PEDDLER, 842 Main Street, Morro Bay, CA 93442. Prop:
Kathleen Muhs. TN: (805) 772 3810.

THE BOOK RACK, 13330 Highway 8, Business Route, Lakeside, CA
92040. Prop: Beth Holderbach & Phyllis Connolly. TN: (619)
461-2297. Shop. Large stock used books, also new books and cards.

BOOKS AGAIN, 3341 Adams Avenue, San Diego, CA 92116. Prop: Jan
Mager. TN: (619) 280-6014. Shop. Spec: science fiction, mysteries.

THE BOOK SAIL, P.O. Box 5728, Orange, CA 92667. Prop: John
McLaughlin. TN: (714) 997-9511. By appointment only. Spec:
Literary manuscripts; original book and magazine art and illustration;
early television and cinema memorabilia. M: A.B.A.A.

THE BOOK SELLER, 1732 West Hammer Way, Stockton, CA 95209.
Prop: Paul Gauthier. TN: (209) 951-5530. Est: 1963. Shop, closed
Monday. Very large stock. Spec: fiction; history; occult; flora and
fauna. Also book-binding, restoration and repair.

BOOK SERVICE OF SANTA CRUZ, P.O. Box 511, Santa Cruz, CA
95061. (510 Errett Circle.) Prop: Milton T. (Bill) Belec. TN: (408)
426-3486. Est: 1952. Shop. Medium stock used. Spec: humanities.
Cata: on English and American literature, history and religion, 2 a
year.

BOOKS ETC., 3212 Greyling Drive, San Diego, CA 92123. TN: (619)
569-7509. Shop.

THE BOOK STALKER, 4907 Yaple Avenue, Santa Barbara, CA
93111. Private premises, appointment necessary.

THE BOOK STALL, 931 NORTH BLACKSTONE AVENUE, FRESNO, CA 93701.

THE BOOKSTALL, 708 SUTTER STREET, SAN FRANCISCO, CA 94109. Prop: Henry & Louise Moises. TN: (415) 673-5446. Est: 1975. Shop. Medium stock. Spec: Children's Collectibles, Maths, Physics. Mountaineering, Cookbooks. Cata: 2 a year on children's books, mountaineering.

THE BOOK STOP, 3369 MOUNT DIABLO BOULEVARD, LAFAYETTE, CA. TN: (415) 284-2665. Shop.

THE BOOK TREASURY, P.O. BOX 20033, LONG BEACH, CA 90801. Prop: Jon Gentilman. TN: (213) 435-7383. Est: 1974. Shop. Large used and antiq. stock, some new. Spec: science fiction; illustrated books. Cata: on foregoing and general, 4 a year.

BOOK WORLD, 1141B SOUTH SARATOGA, SUNNYVALE ROAD, SAN JOSE, CA. Prop: Robert Whitehead. TN: (408) 996-2384. Est: 1982. Shop. Large stock sec. and antiq. books. Spec: history of technology. M: A.B.A.

ROY V. BOSWELL, P.O. BOX 278, GILROY, CA 95020. TN: (408) 842-9702. Cables: Voycarte. Est: 1952. Private premises; appointment necessary. Spec: rare voyages and travel; early atlases and maps; History of cartography. Cata: on foregoing, occasionally. A.B.A.A., A.B.A.(Int.).

BOULEVARD BOOKS, P.O. BOX 89, TOPANGA, CA 90290. Prop: Clifford McCarty. TN: (213) 455-1036. Private premises: postal business only. Very large stock used. Spec: Mystery and Detective Fiction. Plays and Screenplays.

BOUND FOR PLEASURE, (EDWINA B. EVERS), 3451 JACKSON STREET, SAN FRANCISCO, CA 94118.

BRANNAN BOOKS, 879 SUNNYBANK LANE, P.O. BOX 475, GARBERVILLE, CA 95440. Prop: Paul Brannan. TN: (707) 923-3552. Est: 1980. Private premises; appointment necessary. Medium stock used. Spec: European, American and Oriental art and artists.

VERNON AND ZONA BRAUN, 9004 ROSEWOOD DRIVE, SACRAMENTO, CA 95826. TN: (916) 363-3862. Private premises, appointment necessary. Spec: Western & regional Americana.

JIM BREEN BOOKS, P.O. BOX 7764, CAVALERAS STATION, STOCKTON, CA 95207. Prop: Edna B. Breen. Est: 1959. Private premises; catalog sales by mail only. Very small stock. Books on horses only incl. some new books (bloodlines, pedigrees, training, etc.). Cata: 4 a year.

BRENTANO'S, 10918 LE CONTE AVE., LOS ANGELES, CA 90024. TN: (213) 477-1291. New and used books bought and sold. Open: Mondays to Saturdays 10 a.m.-9.30 p.m. Sundays, 12-6 p.m.

BRICK ROW BOOK SHOP, 278 POST STREET (ROOM 303), SAN FRANCISCO, CA 94108-5071. Prop. John Crichton & Matt Lowman. TN: (415) 398-0414. Est: 1915. Shop. Medium stock used, also manuscripts and prints. Spec: English and American literature; bibliography; fine printing. Cata: on foregoing occasionally. M: A.B.A.A.

THE BROWSERS' BOOKSHOP, 1539 EAST HOWARD STREET, PASADENA, CA 91104. TN: 798-8689. Shop, open afternoons. Very large stock sec. and antiq.

BUCCANEER BOOKS, INC., P.O. BOX 518, LAGUNA BEACH, CA 92652. President: J.C. Vincent. Medium stock. Antiquarian. Search Service. Spec: L.F. Baum, Ruth P. Thompson, Oz Books & related items. Mail order only.

BUCKABEST BOOKS & BINDERY, 247 FULTON STREET, PALO ALTO, CA 94301. Prop: Margaret A. Simmons. TN: (415) 325-2965. Est: 1972. Private premises: appointment necessary. Small stock, also new books. Spec: Wales; unicorns. Cata: general, 1 a year.

BUNKER BOOKS, 704 SAFFORD AVENUE, SPRING VALLEY, CA 92077. Prop: M.C. Hill. TN: (619) 469-3296. Private premises, appointment necessary.

WILLIAM J. B. BURGER, P.O. BOX 832, PINE GROVE, CA 95665. TN: (209) 296-7970. Spec: autographs and early manuscripts on America, California; also prints and painting. A.B.A.A.

VIRGINIA BURGMAN, 8057 EL MANOR AVENUE, LOS ANGELES, CA 90045. TN: (213) 776-1360. Est: 1968. Storeroom, appointment necessary. Medium stock used, large stock magazines. Spec: regional fiction, history, art, little magazines.

BYRON'S BOOKS, 1328 CAMINO DEL MAR, DEL MAR, CA 92014. Prop: Byron Weege. TN: (714) 755-3111. Est: 1966. Shop and storeroom, open 10 a.m. to 8 p.m. Large stock used, some new. Also custom made leather goods.

DIRK CABLE, 350 SOUTH LAKE AVENUE, PASADENA, CA 91101. TN: 449-7001. Shop.

JOHN W. CALER, P.O. BOX 1426, 7506 CLYBOURN AVENUE, SUN VALLEY, CA 91352. TN: (818) 765-1210. Est: 1960. Shop, open 10 a.m. to 5 p.m. Monday to Saturday. Medium stock used, very large stock back issue periodicals, also new books. Spec: back sets of periodicals in all subjects, aviation, history, art. A.B.A. A.B.A.A. I.L.A.B.

JOHN P. CAMPBELL, 690 FIRST AVENUE, CHULA VISTA, CA 92010.

CAMPBELL BOOK SHOPPE, 428 EAST CAMPBELL AVENUE, CAMPBELL, CA 95008.

CAPE COD CLUTTER, 3523 FIFTH AVENUE, SAN DIEGO, CA 92103. Prop: Sandee Gillis. TN: (619) 291-8088. Shop. Spec: Travel, cookery.

CARAVAN BOOKSTORE, 550 SOUTH GRAND AVENUE, LOS ANGELES, CA 90071. Prop: Lillian E. Bernstein. TN: (213) 626-9944. Est: 1954. Store. Very large stock used. Spec: Americana, art, antiques, exploration, children's books, cookery, railroads, Civil War and Confederacy, Californian Gold Rush. A.B.A.A. I.L.A.B.

CARLOS CANTERBURY BOOK STORE, 1107-1117 SAN CARLOS AVENUE, SAN CARLOS, CA 94070. Prop: Donna Lee Houtchens. TN: 593-3392 and 593-7466. Est: 1958. Shop. Large stock used. Spec: California and the West, fore-edge paintings. A.B.A. A.B.A.A.

BARRY CASSIDY RARE BOOKS, 2003 T STREET, SACRAMENTO, CA 95814. TN: (916) 456-6307. Est: 1974. Shop. Small stock used of literary first editions, Western Americana, Western fine press books. and autographs. Cata: 4 to 6 times per year. B: River City Bank, 825 K Street, Sacramento, CA 95814. Acc.No: 01-60651-4. M: A.B.A.A.

CELESTIAL BOOKS, P.O. Box 1066, LA CANADA, CA 91011. Prop: Dr. D.K. Yeomans. TN: (213) 790-4984. Est: 1974. Private premises, appointments only or mail order. Very small stock used. Spec: Astronomy, optics, physics, mathematics. Cata: 2 per year.

A CHANGE OF HOBBIT, 1371 WESTWOOD BOULEVARD, LOS ANGELES, CA 90024. Prop: Sherry Gottlieb. TN: (213) 473-2873. Est: 1972. Shop and storeroom. Small stock used. Spec: Science fiction, fantasy, horror. B: Crocker National Bank 335. Acct.No: 191941.

CHEROKEE BOOK SHOP INC., P.O. Box 3427, HOLLYWOOD, CA 90028. (6607 Hollywood Boulevard.) TN: (213) 463-6090. Est: 1950. Shop. Very large stock used; also some new. Spec: Americana; military; literature; folklore; business; art and music; educational; biography; comic. Cata: 4 to 6 a year. A.B.A.A.

CHIMAERA BOOKS, 405 KIPLING STREET, PALO ALTO, CA 94301. Prop: Walter Martin. TN: (415) 329-9217. Est: 1970. Shop on two floors. Large stock used. Out of print and antiq. Spec: arts, classics, humanities, literature, scholarly. editions, literature in translation.

CHLOE'S BOOKSTORE, 3600 MCKINLEY BLVD., SACRAMENTO, CA 95816.

PEGGY CHRISTIAN, 110 SOUTH LA BREA AVENUE, LOS ANGELES, CA 90036.

CHULA VISTA BOOKSTORE, 265½ THIRD AVENUE, CHULA VISTA, CA 92010. Prop: Robert D. Blatchley. TN: (619) 427-9518. Shop, open seven days. Spec: Wales, Scotland, medical.

CIPRIANO'S BOOKS, 402½ MENDOCINO AVENUE, SANTA ROSA, CA 95401. Prop: Charles Cipriano. TN: (707) 542-1986. Est: 1954. Shop. Large stock used, also remainders.

LA CITE DES LIVRES, 2306 WESTWOOD BLVD., LOS ANGELES, CA 90064. TN: 475-0658. French books, Records, Magazines. Open: Tuesday-Saturday, 10.00-6 p.m.

CLAREMONT BOOKS AND PRINTS, 126 YALE AVENUE (UPSTAIRS), CLAREMONT, CA. TN: (714) 624-0757. Shop.

THE ARTHUR H. CLARK COMPANY, P.O. Box 230, GLENDALE, CA 91209. TN: (213) 245-9119. Est: 1902. Shop; by appointment only. Very large stock used, also new books and publishing. Spec: American history and travel, periodical sets and journals. Cata: bi-monthly.

JOHN COLE'S BOOK SHOP, 780 PROSPECT STREET, LA JOLLA, CA 92038. Prop: Barbara T. Cole. TN: (619) 454-4766 & 454-0814. Shop. Spec: California, Mexico, Art, Childrens.

COLLEGE BOOK STORE, 3413 SOUTH HOOVER BOULEVARD, LOS ANGELES 7, CA. Prop: The Missouri Store Company. TN: (213) RIchmond 9-7329. Shop. Large stock used, also new books, stationery, college novelties, etc. Spec: Law books. Cata: 3 a year for college students. N.A.C.S.

LOUIS COLLINS BOOKS, 1083 MISSION STREET, SAN FRANCISCO, CA 94103. Prop: Louis B. Collins, Jr. TN: (415) 431-5134. Est: 1968. Shop; appointment preferable. Medium stock used; also a few new books. Spec: native American anthropology; modern literature. Cata: on foregoing, 2 to 4 a year.

CONNOLLY & WADE, 777 WEST VISTA WAY, VISTA, CA 92083. Prop: Glory Wade & Daniel Connolly. TN: (619) 758-2488. Shop, open 7 days. Spec: mystery, occult.

CONTROVERSIAL BOOK STORE, 3021 UNIVERSITY AVENUE, SAN DIEGO, CA 92104. TN: (619) 296-1560. Store. Spec: metaphysics, holistic health; music.

CORNHILL BOOKS, P.O. Box 870, BUELLTON, CA 93427-0870.

COSMOPOLITAN BOOK SHOP, 7007 MELROSE AVENUE, LOS ANGELES, CA 90038. Prop: Eli Goodman. TN: 938-7119. Est: 1958. Shop. Very large stock used; also new books. Spec: psychology; show business.

CRAWFORD-PETERS AERONAUTICA, 3702 NASSAU DRIVE, SAN DIEGO, CA 92115. Prop: Mike Crawford & Jim Peters. TN: (619) 287-3933 & 461-3514.

JOHN PARKE CUSTIS, 2125 P2, SACRAMENTO, CA 95816. TN: (916) 941-3184. Est 1960. Private premises, postal business only. Large stock sec. and antiq. Spec: modern British Literature and fiction.

JUDITH DABBS, 6091 DELOR COURT, SAN DIEGO, CA 92120. TN: (619) 284-3148. Private premises, appointment necessary. Spec: suspense & mystery. Cata: occasionally.

WILLIAM AND VICTORIA DAILEY, 8216 MELROSE AVENUE, P.O. BOX 69812, LOS ANGELES, CA 90069. TN: (213) 658-8515. TA: Pegacycle, Los Angeles. Est: 1974. Shop, closed on Mondays. Medium stock used. Spec: Art, typography, science, literature, fine prints. Cata: 3 or 4 times yearly. B: Sumitomo Bank of California. M: A.B.A.A.

DAISY BOOKS, 3878 VAN DYKE AVENUE, SAN DIEGO, CA 92105. Prop: Daisy Lamberti. TN: (619) 281-4528. Private premises, appointment necessary. Spec: Astrology: occult.

B. DALTON, BOOKSELLER, 904 WESTWOOD BLVD., LOS ANGELES, CA 90024. TN: 477-9573. Open: Mondays-Saturdays, 9.30 a.m.-9.30 p.m. Sundays, 12-5 p.m.

DANVILLE BOOKS, 176 S. HARTZ AVENUE, DANVILLE, CA 94526. Prop: James E. Sherriff. TN: (415) 837-4200. Est: 1977. Shop, closed on Mondays. Medium stock used. Spec: American Civil War, Chinese in America, First Editions especially Eugene O'Neill and Californian authors, Western Americana. B: United Californian Bank.

ROSALIE DAVIDSON, 6315 CONNIE DRIVE, SAN DIEGO, CA 92115. TN: (619) 582-0894. Private premises, appointment necessary. Spec: California, Southwest; birds.

DAVIS AND SCHORR ART BOOKS, MAILING ADDRESS: 14755 VENTURA BOULEVARD, SUITE 1-747, SHERMAN OAKS, CA 91403. 1547 Westwood Blvd., Los Angeles, CA 90024. TN: (213) 477-6636. Out of Print and some new Art books, Exhibit Catalogues. M: A.B.A.A.

DAWSON'S BOOK SHOP, 535 NORTH LARCHMONT BOULEVARD, LOS ANGELES, CA 90004. Prop: Glen & Muir Dawson, & Stephen Tabor. TN: (213) 469-2186. Est: 1905. Shop. Very large stock used and rare, also a few new. Spec: rare books, typography, Western States, Oriental art, history of books. Cata: general, about monthly. A.B.A.A. A.B.A.(Int.).

DAY'S ARMS AND ANTIQUES, P.O. Box 1846, 2163 EAST MAIN, QUINCY, CA 95971. Prop: Rod and Pat Day. TN: (916) 283-3291. Est: 1979. Shop. Medium stock sec. and antiq. B: Plumas Bank, Quincy, CA 95971.

GENE DECHENE, 11556 SANTA MONICA BOULEVARD, LOS ANGELES, CA 90025. Prop: Eugene Dechene. TN: (213) 477-8734. Est: 1968. Shop. Very large stock used. Spec: psychology, psychiatry.

GEORGE DEEDS BOOK FINDER, 1025 SOUTH GOODHOPE AVENUE, SAN PEDRO, CA 90732. TN: (213) 831-3700. Private premises; appointment necessary. Small stock used. Spec: Americana; illustrated books; modern first editions; civil war; juvenile. M: A.B.A.A.

R. AND G. DESMARAIS, FINE BOOKS, 210 POST STREET, SUITE 206, SAN FRANCISCO, CA 94108. Prop: Rebecca B. Desmarais. TN: (415) 781-2252. Shop, open Monday to Saturday, 10-4. Spec: History of ideas; press books; bibliography. M: A.B.A.A.

HAROLD B. DIAMOND, P.O. Box 1193, BURBANK, CA 91507. (707 NORTH KENWOOD STREET.) TN: (818) 846-0342. Est: 1964. Mail order and by appointment. Large stock used. Spec: American and English literature, Literary criticism, Shakespeariana, Dickensiana, Omar Khayyam; classical world; Latin America; science; technology; natural history; medicine. Cata: on foregoing.

CAROL DOCHEFF, BOOKSELLER, 1605 SPRUCE STREET, BERKELEY, CA 94709. TN: (415) 841-0770. Est: 1979. Private premises; appointment necessary. Small stock used. Spec: children's and young adults' literature; original art by children's book illustrators.

H. & L. DODD, P.O. Box 7494, SAN DIEGO, CA 92107. TN: (619) 222-4491. Private premises, appointment necessary. Spec: California, travel, American Indians.

JAMES M. DOURGARIAN, 205 RILEY DRIVE, PACHECO, CA 94553. TN: 680 8010. Spec: Modern First Editions.

DRAMA BOOKS, 511 GEARY, SAN FRANCISCO, CA 94102. Prop: Andrew De Shong. TN: (415) 441-5343. Est: 1975. Shop. Medium stock used; also new books. Spec: film, theatre, dance, only.

DREWS BOOKSHOP, P.O. Box 163, SANTA BARBARA, CA 93101. (31 EAST CANON PERDIDO.) Prop: Warren E. Drew. TN: (805) 966-3311. Est: 1950. Shop and storeroom. Large stock of used and antiq. Spec: Americana, literature, scarce and rare. Cata: on foregoing, 2 to 6 a year. A.B.A.A.

LOUISE DUICH, P.O. Box 1231, WHITTIER, CA 90609. TN: (213) 694-3443.

VIRGINIA DUNBAR, 19904 MERRITT DRIVE, CUPERTINO, CA 95014. TN: (408) 257-2026. Private premises, appointment necessary. Books and Antiques. Spec: Books about Books: Books and Collectors by Maurice Dunbar.

DUSTY TOMES, 322 CHESTER AVENUE, BAKERSFIELD, CA 93301. Prop: Clara B. & William G. Marr. TN: (805) 322-4814. Est: 1961. Shop. Large stock used, also new books on antiques and collecting.

EARTHLING BOOKSHOP, 1236 STATE STREET, SANTA BARBARA, CA 93101. Prop: Penelope Davies. TN: (805) 965-0926. Est: 1972. Shop, open seven days a week. Small stock used and rare; also large stock new books. Spec: modern first editions and detective fiction. M: A.B.A.

THE ECLECTIC GALLERY, P.O. Box 1581, SAUSALITO, CA 94965. Prop: Dick Rykkon & Robert Scull. TN: (415) 383-1125. Est: 1974. Private premises, appointment necessary. Small stock used. Spec: illustrated; press books, art books. Edward & Curtis Photogravures. B: Wells Fargo Bank.

J.S. EDGREN, 5225 WILSHIRE BOULEVARD, SUITE 604, LOS ANGELES, CA 90036. TN: (213) 933-4251. Est: 1977. Office, appointment necessary. Medium stock. Spec: China, Japan, Korea; especially art and archaeology. Cata: on foregoing 1 or 2 a year.

LARRY EDMUNDS BOOKSHOP, 6658 HOLLYWOOD BOULEVARD, HOLLYWOOD, CA 90028. Prop: Milton Luboviski. TN: (213) 463-3273. Est: 1938. Shop. Large stock used, also new. Spec: cinema and theatre. A.B.A.A.

ELL DEE BOOK FINDERS, P.O. Box 1231, WHITTIER, CA 90609. Prop: Louise Duich. TN: (213) 694-3443. Book Search Service.

L'ESTAMPE ORIGINALE, P.O. Box 3117, SARATOGA, CA 95070. Prop: Sandra A. Sofris. TN: (408) 867-0833. Spec: Illustrated books, art reference, 19th and 20th century prints, old master prints, drawings. M: A.B.A.A.

ETHNOGRAPHIC ARTS PUBLICATIONS, 1040 ERICA ROAD, MILL VALLEY, CA 94941. TN: (415) 383-2998. Appointment necessary. Large stock sec. and antiq. Spec: Primitive and Tribal Arts.

EVERYBODY'S MAGAZINES, P.O. Box 338, LA VERNE, CA 91750 (2241 1st Street, suite A, La Verne, CA 91750). Prop: Al Regalado, Drake Jasso, Joe Horchak, Louise Klaber. TN: (714) 596-6247. Est: 1928. Shop. Medium stock used. Spec: racing books; back-issue magazines. Cata: back-issue magazines only.

FANTASY ILLUSTRATED, 12531 HARBOR BOULEVARD, GARDEN GROVE, CA 92641. TN: (714) 537-0087. Shop.

PETER R. FELTUS, P.O. Box 5339, BERKELEY, CA 94705. TN: (415) 658-9627. Est: 1970. Private premises, appointment necessary. Very small stock used. Spec: Old Travel Guides, Egyptian Philatelic literature. Cata: occasionally issued but unscheduled. New books on Egyptian philately.

H. LAWRENCE FERGUSON, 8321 LINCOLN BOULEVARD, LOS ANGELES, CA 90045. Near Lax. TN: (213) 670-0300. Est: 1974. Shop. Large stock. Spec: Botany, Military, Literature and Poetry. Some new books. M: A.B.A.

FIFTH AVENUE BOOK STORE, 3921 FIFTH AVENUE, SAN DIEGO, CA 92103. Prop: Don & Linda Baker. TN: (619) 299-8238. Store.

50,000 BOOKS, 116 EAST MAIN, EL CAJON, CA 92020. Prop: Tom Chambers. TN: (619) 444-6191. Shop, open daily.

FINE ART SOURCE MATERIAL, P.O. Box 4841, PANORAMA CITY, CA 91412. (4347 Van Nuys Boulevard, Sherman Oaks, CA.) Prop: John Alan Walker. TN: (213) 990-5572. Est: 1970. Shop, open 11.00 to 16.00 Tuesday through Saturday, or by appointment. Small stock used; also some new. Spec: out of print art books; autographs, all fields; books on books. Cata: art books, 2 or 3 a year.

FIRST EDITIONS BOOKSHOP, 693 AMALFI DRIVE, PACIFIC PALISADES, CA 90272.

A.S. FISCHLER, 604 SOUTH 15TH STREET, SAN JOSE, CA 95112.

DONALD L. FOLEY—BOOKS, 1050 MARIPOSA AVENUE, BERKELEY, CA 94707. TN: (415) 525-6983.

T.T. & JEAN FOLEY, P.O. BOX 111, SOLVANG, CA 93463. TN: (805) 688-3598. Est: 1945. Shop and storeroom; appointment necessary. Very small stock used; also new books, art and antiques. Spec: arts, applied arts, antiques.

FOX BOOK AND PUBLISHING COMPANY, P.O. BOX 1683, TWENTY-NINE PALMS, CA 92277. TN: (619) 367-1303.

LEE FREESON—THEATRE BOOKS, P.O. BOX 922, HOLLYWOOD, CA 90028. TN: (213) HOllywood 3-6090. Spec: theatre. A.B.A.A.

PALMER D. FRENCH, P.O. Box 2704, OAKLAND, CA 94602. TN: (415) 530-1648. Private premises; appointment necessary, mainly business by mail. Spec: History, Americana, Exploration. A.B.A.A.

FRONTIER-PIONEER BOOKS, 6014 BURWOOD AVENUE, LOS ANGELES, CA 90042. Prop: Phil & Mary Davidson. TN: (213) 256-2321. Est: 1979. Shop. Very large stock used. Spec: Alaska, Arctic, Canada, automotive, cookbooks, camping. Cata: on foregoing 2 a year.

THEODORE FRONT MUSICAL LITERATURE, 16122 COHASSET STREET, VAN NUYS, CA 91406. Prop: T. Front. TN: (818) 994-1902. Est: 1961. Shop. Large stock. Spec: Music. Cata: 2 per year. New books are also stocked, mostly music and dance books and music editions. M: A.B.A.A., I.L.A.B., A.B.A.

GAMUT BOOK SHOP, 723 CALIFORNIA DRIVE, BURLINGAME, CA 94010. Prop: Vernon Howard. TN: (415) 343-7428. Est: 1940. Shop. Very large stock used, 'Alpha to Zulu'. Spec: mountaineering; Western U.S.A.; literature. Cata: rarely. A.B.A.A.

GARCIA GARST, BOOKSELLERS, 334 NORTH CENTER (SUITE L), TURLOCK, CA 95380. Prop: Kenneth M. Garst. TN: (209) 632-5054. Est: 1978. Shop. Stock of 45000 volumes, used out-of-print and rare. Spec: Illustrated children's, juvenile, Americana, Californiana. Cata: Lists twice a year. B: Golden Valley Bank, 301 East Main Street, Turlock, CA 95380. Acct.No: 1-06772-2.

GARVIN'S BOOK SHOP, 321 NO. GOLDEN MALL, BURBANK, CA 91502. Prop: Jack Garvin. TN: (818) 848-2132. Spec: Mining and minerology, geology and geological surveys, paleontology and fossils; jewelry and gemstones; general Americana. M: A.B.A.A.

GEOSCIENCE BOOKS, P.O. Box 487, YUCAIPA, CA 92399. Prop: Russell Filer. TN: (714) 797-1650. Private premises, mail order only. Small stock. Spec: mining, minerals, gems; fossils. Cata: 1-2 a year.

LOIS GEREGHTY—BOOKS, 9521 ORION AVENUE, SEPULVEDA, CA 91343. TN: (818) 892-1053, Est: 1970. Private premises; appointment necessary. Small stock used. Spec: General, with search service. B: Great Western Sav & Loan Assn., 10233 Sepulveda Boulevard, Mission Hills, CA 91345. A.B.A.

BENNETT GILBERT, P.O.Box 46056, Los Angeles, CA 90046. TN: (213) 876-8677. Private premises; appointment necessary. Very small stock rare. Spec: philosophy, theology; science; early printed books.

EDWIN V. GLASER RARE BOOKS, P.O. Box 1765, Sausalito, CA 94965. (Suite 1, 25 Rodeo Avenue, Sausalito, CA 94965.) TN: (415) 332-1194. Est: 1964. Private premises; appointment necessary. Small stock used. Spec: Early Science and Medicine. Cata: twice yearly. B: Bank of America, Sausalito Branch. M: A.B.A.A., I.L.A.B.

THE GLOBE BOOKSTORE, P.O. Box 69218, Los Angeles, CA 90069. (8934 Keith Avenue). Prop: Michael R. Goth. Spec: rare, early science, alchemy, medicine. A.B.A.A.

GOLDEN LEGEND INC., 8586 Melrose Avenue, Los Angeles, CA 90069. Prop: Gordon Hollis. TN: (213) 657-4446. Shop. Select stock rare. Spec: Fine illustrated books; fine bindings; literature; performing arts.

MARIAN L. GORE, P.O. Box 433, San Gabriel, CA 91778. TN: (818) 287-2946. Private premises, appointment necessary. Medium stock used on everything relating to food and drink, cookery, wine, beverages, menus, etc. Cata: on foregoing 2 a year. A.B.A.A.

GRADY'S BOOKS, 142 Rutherford Avenue, Redwood City, CA 94061.

GREEN RIVER BOOKSHOP, 6509 Wandermere Road, Malibu, CA 90265. Prop: Robert H. & Maryhope Weir. TN: (273) 457-2066. Est: 1965. Private premises; appointment necessary. Medium stock of used.

RON GREENWOOD, P.O. Box 1618, Costa Mesa, CA 92626.

DANIEL E. GUICE, BOOKSELLER, 8568 1/2 Melrose Avenue, Los Angeles, CA 90069. TN: (213) 854-0753. Spec: Science, medicine; early printed books; illustrated books. M: A.B.A.A.

G.F. GUSTIN, 56 East Colorado Blvd., Pasadena, CA 91105.

THE HABITAT BOOKSHOP, 4711 Third Street, La Mesa, CA 92041. Prop: Audrey Ali. TN: (619) 697-7922. Shop. Medium sec. and antique stock; also coffee shop. Spec: science fiction, poetry.

HELEN HALBACH, P.O. BOX 613, SANTA BARBARA, CA 93101. (116 East De La Guerra Street, Studio 3.) TN: (805) 965-6432. Est: 1968. Studio, open noon to 9 p.m. every day. Small stock used. Spec: Sherlock Holmes, heraldry, Lafcadio Hearn, Rubaiyats. Cata: Sherlockiana.

BERNARD H. HAMEL—SPANISH BOOKS. 2326 WESTWOOD BLVD., LOS ANGELES, CA 90064. TN: 475-0453. Books and Records from Spain & Latin America.

MILTON HAMMER, SUITE 125, EL PASEO, SANTA BARBARA, CA 93101. TN: (805) 965-8901. Est: 1969. Shop. Stock of rare books, maps and prints. Spec: literature, art, Americana. M: A.B.A.A.

JIM HANSEN, 3514 HIGHLAND DRIVE, CARLSBAD, CA 92008. TN: (619) 729-3383. Private premises, appointment necessary.

RICHARD HANSEN, 11245 DRY CREEK ROAD, AUBURN, CA 95603.

THE HAPPY BOOKER, 4096 NORTH SIERRA WAY, SAN BERNARDINO, CA 92407. Prop: Breck & Ruth Petersen. TN: (714) 883-6110. Shop. Very large stock used; also new books.

DORIS HARRIS AUTOGRAPHS, 5410 WILSHIRE BOULEVARD (ROOM 907), LOS ANGELES, CA 90036. TN: (213) 939-4500. Est: 1966. Suite in office building, open normal business hours. Autographs in all fields (historical, literary, scientific, music, etc.). M: A.B.A.A.

HELEN HARTE, 2249 GLENDON AVENUE, LOS ANGELES, CA 90064. TN: (213) 474-0181. Spec: Ireland.

HARVARD BOOKSTORE, 338 EAST MARKET ST., STOCKTON, CA 95202.

HENNESSEY & INGALLS INC., 1254 SANTA MONICA MALL, SANTA MONICA, CA 90401. Pres: R.G. Hennessey, Vice-Pres: D.K. Ingalls. TN: (213) 474-2541. Est: 1964. Shop. Large stock of used and new. Spec: art, architecture, original graphics. Cata: monthly. A.B.A.

HERITAGE BOOKSHOP INC., 8540 MELROSE AVENUE, LOS ANGELES, CA 90069. Prop: Benjamin and Louis Weinstein. TN: (213) 659-3674. Est: 1964. Shop. Medium stock used; also selected new books, fine bindings and book repairing. Spec: modern literature, fine printing and general antiquarian. Cata: on foregoing, 6 a year. A.B.A.A.

JOE HERWEG, 958 FIFTH AVENUE, SAN DIEGO, CA 92101. TN: (619) 233-0880. Shop. Large stock sec. and antiq. also new books.

RICHARD HILKERT BOOKSELLER LIMITED, 434 PACIFIC AVENUE, SAN FRANCISCO, CA 94133.

MICHAEL S. HOLLANDER, 1433 SANTA MONICA BOULEVARD, SANTA MONICA, CA 90404. TN: (213) 828-0773. Est: 1973. Private premises; appointment necessary. Medium stock. Spec: Colour plate, Asian Travel, illuminated Mss., Photography (19th century). Cata: 1 per year. B: Santa Monica Bank, Santa Monica, CA. Acc.No: 02971119. M: A.B.A.A., I.L.A.B.

HOLLYWOOD BOOK CITY, 6625-31 HOLLYWOOD BOULEVARD, HOLLYWOOD, CA 90028. Prop: Alan & Frances Siegel. TN: (213) 466-2525 or 466-1049. Est: 1973. 3 Stores. Very large stock of second-hand books. Spec: Cinema, photography, art, illustrated, occult.

HOLLYWOOD BOOK SERVICE, 1654 CHEROKEE AVENUE, HOLLYWOOD, CA 90028. TN: (213) 464-4164. Est: 1961. Shop. Large stock used. Spec: political and social sciencs, law, economics.

HOLLYWOOD BOOK SHOP, 6613 HOLLYWOOD BLVD., HOLLYWOOD, CA 90028. A.B.A.A.

THE HOLMES BOOK COMPANY, P.O. BOX 858, OAKLAND, CA 94604. (274 14th Street, Oakland, Calif. 94612.) Pres: Craig H. Keyston. TN: (415) 893-6860. Est: 1894. Shop. Stock of 300,000 volumes used, also new. Spec: Western American, general antiquarian. Cata: general, 3 or 4 a year. A.B.A.A., I.L.A.B., A.B.A.

BETSY HOOK, BOOKFINDER, 7345 HEALDSBURG AVENUE, SEBASTOPOL, CA 95472. Prop: Betsy Hook. TN: (707) 829-0916. Est: 1981. No stock. Book search service only. B: Imperial Savings and Loan, Sebastopol.

GEORGE HOULE—RARE BOOKS, 7260 BEVERLY BOULEVARD, LOS ANGELES, CA 90036-2537. TN: (213) 937-5858. Shop. Medium stock used and rare. Spec: First Editions; Art & Antiques refs.; leather bindings; Autographs; signed photographs. M: A.B.A.A.

HOURGLASS ANTIQUES AND BOOKS, ANTIQUE WAREHOUSE 82 AND 45, 212 S. CEDROS AVENUE, SOLANA BEACH, CA 92075. Stand, closed Tuesdays. Spec: children's, California.

J. AND J. HOUSE, 682 BROADWAY, SAN DIEGO, CA 92101. Prop: Jonathan G. House. TN: (619) 232-8331. Shop. Medium stock sec. and antiq. Spec: science; natural history; rare books. Cata. M: A.B.A.A.

HOUSEHOLD WORDS, 284 PURDUE AVENUE, BERKELEY, CA 94707. Prop: Kay Caughren. TN: (415) 524-8859. Private premises, appointment necessary.

HOUSE OF BOOKS, 1758 GARDENAIRE LANE, ANAHEIM, CA 92804. Prop: Marilyn O. Bennett. TN: (714) 778-6406. Est: 1981. Private premises, appointment necessary. Very small stock used and antiquarian. Spec: Scotland, Ireland and Wales only. Cata: 2 per year. B: Security Pacific, Garden Grove, CA.

THE HOUSE OF FICTION, 663 EAST COLORADO BOULEVARD, PASADENA, CA 91101. TN: 449-9861. Shop, open afternoons.

HOUSE-WOLFORD BOOKSELLERS, 1959 GARNET AVENUE, SAN DIEGO, CA 92109. TN: (714) 270-9120. Est: 1978. Shop, closed on Fridays. Very large stock. Spec: Press books and Fine printing, Western Americana, Illustrated, Modern first editions. Cata: 6 per year. B: San Diego Trust & Savings. Acc.No: 170115821.

VERNON HOWARD, P.O. BOX 693, MILLBRAE, CA 94030. TN: (415) 343-7428. Est: 1940. Shop. Large stock used. Spec: mountaineering, U.S. West, literature. Cata: subject lists in all fields, occasionally. A.B.A.A.

JOHN HOWELL BOOKS, 434 POST STREET, SAN FRANCISCO, CA 94102. TN: (415) 781-7795. Cables: Bookman SanFrancisco. Est: 1912. Very large stock rare books, also prints and paintings. Spec: Western Americana, voyages, literature, fine press books, Bibles. Cata: Western Americana and general rare books. A.B.A.A., A.B.A.

MAXWELL HUNLEY, 634 MISSION STREET, SOUTH PASADENA, CA. TN: (213) CRestview 5-7466. Est: 1930. Shop. Large stock used. Spec: Western Americana, juveniles (rare), English and American first editions. Cata: 2 to 3 a year. A.B.A.A.

HUNTER'S BOOKS, 1002 WESTWOOD BOULEVARD, LOS ANGELES, CA 90024. TN: 477-1966. General stock and Children's books. Open: Sundays-Thursdays, 10 a.m.-10 p.m., Fridays and Saturdays, 10 a.m.-midnight.

HUTCHINS ORIENTAL BOOKS, P.O. BOX 177, SOUTH PASADENA, CA 91030.

HYMAN AND SONS RARE BOOKS, 2341 WESTWOOD BOULEVARD, SUITES 2 AND 3, LOS ANGELES, CA 90064. Prop: V. Lee Blackburn, Ph.D. TN: (213) 474-8023 or 559-7275. TA: Hysons. Est: 1977. Appointment necessary. Medium stock used. Spec: Egyptology and Archaeology. Cata: Yearly. B: Sumitomo Bank of California.

IMAGE WEAVERS USED BOOKS, 1612 BROADWAY, SACRAMENTO, CA 95818.

L'IMAGERIE, 15030 VENTURA BLVD., SHERMAN OAKS, CA 91403.

INTERNATIONAL BOOKFINDERS, P.O. BOX 1, PACIFIC PALISADES, CA 90272. Prop: Richard Mohr. Est: 1950. Mail order only. Cata: Americana, irregularly. A.B.A.A. I.L.A.B.

THE INVISIBLE BOOKMAN, 97 FRANCISCAN WAY, BERKELEY, CA 94707. Prop: Allan Covici. TN: (415) 524-7823. Private premises; appointment necessary. Small stock used. Spec: modern first editions, poetry, first books.

IAN JACKSON, P.O. BOX 9075, BERKELEY, CA 94709. TN: (415) 548-1431. Private premises, appointment necessary. Very small stock used. Spec: Botany and Gardening. Cata: Quarterly. B: Wells Fargo Bank. Acc.No. 0125 411 280

PAULINE JENKINS, 13313 VAN NUYS, PACOIMA, CA 91331. TN: (213) 899-2153. Est: 1965. Shop. Large stock used; also new books.

JAMES H. JOHNSON, 3548 GREENFIELD PLACE, CARMEL, CA 93921.

SAM. JOHNSON'S BOOKSHOP, 11552 SANTA MONICA BOULEVARD, LOS ANGELES, CA 90025. Props: R.E. Klein & L. Myers. TN: (213) 477-9247. Est. 1977. Shop. Medium stock available.

JOSEPH THE PROVIDER BOOKS, 903 STATE STREET, SANTA BARBARA, CA 93101. Prop: Ralph B. Sipper. TN: (805) 962-6862. Est: 1970. Shop. Large stock used. Spec: modern Literature, first editions. Cata: 2 or 3 a year. A.B.A.A.

THE JOYCE BOOK SHOPS, P.O. Box 310, MARTINEZ, CA 94553. Prop: Everett V. Cunningham & Donna R. Rankin. TN: (415) 228-4462. Spec: rare, out-of-print; periodicals. A.B.A.A. *Also at* 1116 FRANKLIN STREET, OAKLAND, CA 94612. TN: (415) 452-2571, and 538 15th STREET, OAKLAND, CA 94612. TN: (415) 834-8108.

JUST BOOKS and. . ., 3630 LA HABRA WAY, SACRAMENTO, CA 95825. Prop: Frank Just. TN: (916) 482-7493. Private premises; appointment necessary. Small stock used. Spec: Western Americana; military; arts and crafts.

L.S. KAISER, 1820 GRAHAM HILL ROAD, SANTA CRUZ, CA 95060. Est: 1970. Shop. Small stock. Spec: Western Americana; religious; old juveniles. Cata: 1 a year.

KALEIDOSCOPE BOOKS, 625 CONNELL AVENUE, ALBANY, CA. Prop: Stuart A. Teitler. TN: (415) 528-1017. Est: 1966. Shop open noon to 17.00 hours. Medium stock. Spec: science fiction, fantasy, utopias, 19th century mystery fiction. Cata: occasionally, lists monthly.

VICTOR KAMKIN BOOKSTORE, 2320 WESTWOOD BOULEVARD, LOS ANGELES, CA 90064. TN: 474-4034. Russian Books, Records, Folk Arts. Open: Tuesday-Saturday 10.00-6 p.m. Sundays, by appointment.

GEORGE ROBERT KANE, BOOKS, 252 THIRD AVENUE, SANTA CRUZ, CA 95062. TN: (408) 426-4133. By appointment only. Spec: Children's books; illustrated books; costume; typography; press books. M: A.B.A.A.

CAROLYN KAPLAN, P.O. Box 201, LAGUNA BEACH, CA 92652. TN: (714) 497-1098. Private premises, appointment necessary. Medium stock used. Spec: plays, theatre. Cata: on foregoing, 2-3 a year. A.B.A.A. I.L.A.B.

KENNETH KARMIOLE, BOOKSELLER, INC., P.O. Box 464, SANTA MONICA, CA 90406. (2255, WESTWOOD BOULEVARD, LOS ANGELES, CA 90064.) TN: (213) 474-7305. Est: 1976. Shop. Medium stock available. Spec: Antiquarian (General), Fine Printing, Travel, Art. Cata: Monthly, City National Bank. A.B.A.A. (I.L.A.B.)

HOWARD KARNO BOOKS, P.O. Box 431, SANTA MONICA, CA 90406. (1703 Ocean Front Walk.) Prop: Howard Karno. TN: (213) 458-1619. Est: 1978. Large stock. Spec: Latin Americana—all languages, most subjects. Cata: Approx 40 lists per year. M: A.B.A.A.

SAMUEL W. KATZ, 10845 LINDBROOK DRIVE, LOS ANGELES, CA 90024. TN: (213) 208-7934. Rare and unusual books and prints. Appointment necessary. M: A.B.A.A.

KISCH BOOK SHOP, 25½ WEST CANON PERDIDO STREET, SANTA BARBARA, CA 93101. Shop.

GAIL KLEMM — BOOKSELLER, P.O. Box 518, APPLE VALLEY, CA 92307. TN: (619) 242-5921. Spec: Early and contemporary children's books; Western Americana; Randolph Caldecott; printing and papermaking. M: A.B.A.A.

GEORGE FREDERICK KOLBE, P.O. DRAWER 1610A, CRESTLINE, CA 92325. TN: (714) 338-6527. Est: 1967. Office; appointment recommended. Small stock used. Spec: Numismatics in all its aspects. Cata: 2 per year. B: California First Bank. Acc. No. 0691214795. M: A.B.A.A., American Numismatic Association, American Numismatic Society, Royal Numismatic Society.

VALERIE KRAFT, FINE BOOKS, 41-617 ARMANAC COURT, PALM DESERT, CA 92260. TN: (619) 340-4674.

KROWN & SPELLMAN, BOOKSELLERS, 2283 WESTWOOD BOULEVARD, LOS ANGELES, CA 90025. Prop: Franklin V. Spellman. TN: (213) 474-1745. Est: 1977. Shop, closed on Mondays. Medium stock. Spec: Classical antiquity, Middle Ages, Renaissance. Cata: 2 per year. B: Western Bank of Commerce. Acc. No: 691 626784. M: Westwood Booksellers Assoc.

DONALD LaCHANCE, 1032 BAY OAKS DRIVE, LOS OSOS, CA 93402. TN: (805) 927-4145. Est: 1950. Shop. Small stock used. Spec: English and American first editions. Cata: rarely. A.B.A.A.

LAKE LAW BOOKS, 138 MCALLISTER STREET, SAN FRANCISCO, CA 94102. TN: (415) 863-2900. Est: 1920 at Harry B. Lake. Shop. Very large stock used; also new books. Spec: law books for the attorney, general legal and political. Cata: annual.

LAVOIE'S WORLD OF BOOKS, 803 PARK WAY, ARROYO GRANDE, CA 93420. Prop: Raymond J. Lavoie. TN: (805) 489-2662. Est: 1974. Private premises; appointment necessary. Very small stock used. Spec: First editions, Poetry, Children's books.

LENNIE'S BOOK NOOK, 8124 MELROSE AVENUE, LOS ANGELES, CA 90046. Prop: Leonard & Abraham Weinrib. TN: (213) 651-5584. Spec: literature, biography, cinema, theatre, Americana, fine editions.

LEON'S BOOK STORE, 659 HIGUERA STREET, SAN LUIS OBISPO, CA 93401. Prop: Jack, Jim and Cathy Dyer. TN: (805) 543-5039. Est: 1969. Shop. Very large stock used. Spec: biography.

BARRY R. LEVIN, 2265 WESTWOOD BOULEVARD, ROOM 669, LOS ANGELES, CA 90064. TN: (213) 474-5611. Est: 1973. Medium size stock. Spec: rare, scarce and out-of-print first editions of science fiction & fantasy. (Consultants for colleges etc. building collections in these fields, and science fiction film consultants.) Cata: 1 or 2 detailed cata. every year in specialities. New Books in science fiction and fantasy. M: A.B.A.A. A.B.A.

HARRY A. LEVINSON—RARE BOOKS, P.O. BOX 534, BEVERLY HILLS, CA 90213. TN: (213) 276-9311. Private premises; appointment necessary. Medium stock of fine and rare books and manuscripts. Spec: books in Wing and Short Title Catalogue, incunabula, early printed continental books (1500 to 1700); early science and medicine; early illustrated books; English literature. Cata: infrequently. A.B.A. (Int.), manuscript society. A.B.A.A.

R.E. LEWIS, INC., P.O. BOX 1108, SAN RAFAEL, CA 94915. Prop: E. Raymond. TN: (415) 461-4161. Est: 1952. Private premises: appointment necessary. Spec: old master and modern original prints, Japanese prints; Indian miniatures. A.B.A.A.

LIBROS LATINOS, P.O. Box 1103, 418 NORTH FIFTH STREET, REDLANDS, CA 92373. Prop: George F. Elmendorf. TN: (714) 793-8423. Est: 1973. Storeroom, appointment necessary. Very large stock. Spec: Antiquarian and scholarly Latin Americana and Iberian Peninsular. Cata: 10 per year. B: Bank of America. Acc.No: 6306-03805.

ROBERT LOREN LINK, 1855 WISCONSIN AVENUE, REDDING, CA 96001. TN: (916) 243 8125. Cata.

LION BOOK SHOP, 3422 BALBOA STREET, SAN FRANCISCO, CA 94121. Prop: Marion Pietsch. TN: (415) 221-5522. Est: 1958. Shop, appointment necessary. Large stock used. Spec: Americana, 1920's, California. B: Crocker National Bank. Acc.No: 0341-77732-3333

LITTLE OLD BOOK STORE, 12918 EAST PHILADELPHIA STREET, WHITTIER, CA 90609.

LIVE OAK BOOKSELLERS, Box 853, TEMPLE CITY, CA 91780. Prop: Mr. & Mrs. Paul DiBiase. TN: (213) 442-1151. Est: 1981. Private premises; appointment necessary. Small stock used. Spec: Western Americana; fine printers; mountaineering.

LOGOS OF WESTWOOD, 10884 WEYBURN AVENUE, LOS ANGELES, CA 90024. TN: (213) 208-5432. Christian Literature, Bibles, Cards, Gifts, Music. Open: Mondays-Saturdays, 10 a.m.-11 p.m., Sundays: 2 p.m.-6 p.m.

JACK LONDON BOOKSTORE, Box 337, 14300 ARNOLD DRIVE, GLEN ELLEN, CA 95772. Prop: Winnie & Russ Kingman. TN: (707) 996-2888. Est. 1971. Shop, sometimes closed Mondays and Tuesdays. Large stock available. Spec: Jack London, California, Alaska, Hawaii. B: United California 689-2-00921.

LORSON'S BOOKS AND PRINTS, VILLA DEL SOL, (SUITE A-9) 305 NORTH HARBOR BLVD., FULLERTON, CA 92632. Prop: James Lorson. TN: (714) 526-2523. Spec: Western Americana; Civil War; first editions, miniature books. M: A.B.A.A.

LOST HORIZON BOOKSTORE, 703 ANACAPA STREET, SANTA BARBARA, CA 93101. Shop.

CARLTON LOWENBERG, 451 SIXTH STREET, SAN FRANCISCO, CA 94103.

ERNEST LUBBE, BOOKS, 280 GOLDEN GATE AVENUE, SAN FRANCISCO, CA 94102. TN: (415) 441-5682. Spec: Western American. A.B.A.A.

JIM LYONS, Box 608, MOUNTAIN VIEW, CA 94042. TN: (415) 494-0790. Spec: historical newspapers.

LAURENCE McGILVERY, P.O. BOX 852, LA JOLLA, CA 92038. TN: (619) 454-4443. Est: 1960. Office and showroom, appointment necessary. Medium stock used and antiquarian art books and exhibition catalogues; very large stock of art periodicals. Spec: visual arts. Cata: irregular. M: A.B.A.A.

MARY MACKENSEN, 12040 HIERBA PLACE, SAN DIEGO, CA 92128.

JOHN MAKAREWICH, BOOKS, P.O. Box 7032, VAN NUYS, CA 91409. Est: 1946. Mail order only. Large stock used. Spec: The Humanities, Literature, Fine Press, books on books, medical history, sciences, Americana, art & architecture. Cata: on foregoing and general: 6-8 a year.

MANNINGS BOOKS & PRINTS, 1255 POST STREET, SAN FRANCISCO CA 94109. Prop: Kathleen Manning. TN: (415) 621-3565. Est: 1973. Private premises, appointment necessary. Medium stock used. Spec: Prints and Maps. Cata: issued but not at set times. B: Wells Fargo. Acc.No: 6-358-246. M: A.B.A.A., American Historical Print Collectors Society, Autograph Collectors Club, Map Society of California.

MARCELLUS BOOKERY, P.O. Box 255, RIVERSIDE, CA 92502. Est: 1957. Storeroom, appointment necessary. Medium stock used. Spec: Western Americana, modern first editions; illustrated books. Cata: on foregoing and sporting books, furniture, glass, decorative arts.

MARLOW'S BOOKSHOP, 6609 HOLLYWOOD BOULEVARD, HOLLYWOOD, CA 90028.

MARSH FARMS PUBLICATIONS, 7171 PATTERSON AVENUE, GARDEN GROVE, CA 92641. Prop: Dietrich Gerlach. TN: (714) 891-5871. Est: 1965. Shop and Storeroom. Open 5 days per week 8a.m.-5p.m. Very large stock. Spec: Birds and Nature subjects. Cata: 1 per year. New books also available. B: Western Commercial Bank, Los Angeles, CA 92640. No: 004 043146.

LEO MARTYN, P.O. BOX 49263, LOS ANGELES, CA 90049. TN: (231) 476-2608.

MERLIN'S BOOKSHOP, 6543 PARDALL AVENUE, ISLA VISTA, CA 93117. TN: (805) 968-7946. Shop.

KATHLEEN MERO, BOX 272, CONCORD, CA 94522. TN: (415) 825 5876.

MEYER BOSWELL BOOKS, 982 HAYES STREET, SAN FRANCISCO, CA 94117. Prop: Jordan D. Luttrell. TN: (415) 346-1839. Est: 1976. Private premises, appointment necessary. Small stock used. Spec: Law, legal history, constitutional history. Cata: on foregoing every three to six months. A few new books. B: Barclay's. Acc.No: 18–60422.

MIL-AIR PHOTOS AND BOOKS, 11809 SOUTH ALBURTIS AVENUE, NORWALK, CA 90650. Prop: Harold N. Miller. TN: (213) 632-8081 and 863-5028. Est: 1960. Three hangar end-rooms and showroom; appointment necessary. Medium stock used; also new books, photos, prints, stamps, jewelry, pilot supplies. Spec: aviation, military, naval, automotive, rail. Cata: occasionally.

GARY MILAN, 9401 WILSHIRE (SUITE 1140), BEVERLY HILLS, CA 90212. TN: (213) 273-5272.

MITCHELL BOOKS, 926 EAST WASHINGTON BOULEVARD, PASADENA, CA 91104. TN: 798-4438. Shop, closed Mondays, open Tuesday to Friday evenings and Saturday afternoons. Spec: modern first editions; mysteries.

MITHRAS BOOKS, 7458 LA JOLLA BOULEVARD, LA JOLLA, CA 92037. Prop: Harold Darling. Est: 1953. Shop. Medium stock used, also new. Spec: metaphysical, occult, illustrated, children's books.

BRONISLAW MLYNARSKI, P.O. Box 367, BEVERLY HILLS, CA 90213. TN: (213) 275-6130. Est: 1956. Private premises, appointment necessary. Medium stock used and new. Spec: rare books about music (not sheet music). Cata: musicology, 1 a year.

MOE'S BOOKS, 2476 TELEGRAPH AVENUE, BERKELEY, CA 94704. Prop: M. Moskowitz. TN: (415) 849-2087. Est: 1960. Shop. Very large stock used; also new books. Spec: Art, scholarly, fine editions. Cata: art; photography; architecture (every two or three years).

H.J. MOLLOY, P.O. Box 5267, SAN FRANCISCO, CA 94101. Est: 1965. Mail order only. Small stock used, also new. Spec: Anglo Mediaevalism.

MONROE BOOKS, 809 EAST OLIVE, FRESNO, CA 93728. Prop: John M. Perz. TN: (209) 441 1282. Est: 1979. Shop, open business hours or by appointment. Very large stock. Spec: archaeology, western Americana; modern first editions; English and American fiction. Also new books. Cata: one a month. M: A.B.A., Central Valley Antiquarian Booksellers, Central California Antiquarian Booksellers Assoc.

MOUNTAIN HOUSE BOOKS, P.O. Box 831, NEVADA CITY, CA 95959. TN: (916) 265-2647. Spec: California and the American West. Cata. *Also at*: 519 COYOTE STREET.

MOUNT EDEN BOOKS & BINDERY, 2315 BERMUDA LANE, HAYWARD, CA 94541. TN: (415) 782-7723. Private premises, appointment necessary.

P.F. MULLINS, 109 BEECHTREE DRIVE, ENCINITAS, CA 92024. TN: (619) 436-7810. Private premises, appointment necessary. Spec: first editions. Cata.

J.B. MUNS, FINE ARTS BOOKS, 1162 SHATTUCK AVE., BERKELEY, CA 94707. TN: (415) 525-2420. Est: 1964. Private premises, appointment necessary. Medium stock, also some remainders. Spec: art, architecture; photography (20th century); music and musical autographs. Cata: irregularly. M: A.B.A.A.

NEEDHAM BOOKFINDERS, P.O. Box 491040, LOS ANGELES, CA 90049. Prop: Stanley & Eleanor Kurman. TN: (213) 475-9553. Spec: Judaica; cookery.

MAURICE F. NEVILLE RARE BOOKS, 835 LAGUNA STREET, SANTA BARBARA, CA 93101. Prop: Maurice F. Neville. TN: (805) 963-1908. Est: 1977. Shop. Large stock. Spec: 19th & 20th Century American & English Literature. Autograph letters and manuscripts. Cata: 3 or 4 per year. M: A.B.A.A.

NEW AGE WORLD SERVICES AND BOOKS, 8416 STATE STREET, SOUTH GATE, CA 90280. Prop: Victoria E. Vandertuin. TN: (213) 588-4323. Est: 1974. Shop. Closed Saturdays after 3 pm. Medium stock. Spec: occult, metaphysical, mystical astrology, oriental mysteries, UFO, spiritualism. Also romance fiction and health and beauty. Stock of periodicals and back-numbers of journals. Cata: every year. Corresp: Deutsch and Español. M: The International Women's Writing Guild, Academy of Science Fiction, The Ancient Astronaut Society.

NILES & SILVER, P.O. Box 3662, BEVERLY HILLS, CA 90212. Prop: Joel Silver & William Niles. TN: (213) 474-5050. Est: 1976. Storeroom, appointment necessary. Very small stock used. Spec: British and American Law to 1800. Cata: Annually.

JOHN B. NOMLAND, 404 SOUTH BENTON WAY, LOS ANGELES, CA 90057. TN: (213) 389-9745. Est: 1963. Storeroom; appointment necessary. Medium stock used. Spec: modern literature, Mexico. Cata: on foregoing, once a year.

JEREMY NORMAN & CO. INC., 442 POST STREET, SAN FRANCISCO, CA 94102. TN: (415) 781-6402. Cables: Logos San Francisco. Est: 1970. Shop. Spec: History of medicine, science and technology; history of ideas and scholarship; history of art and illustrated books; voyages and travel, maps and prints; natural history; manuscripts. Cata: on foregoing, two a year. A.B.A.A., A.B.A.

JAMES NORMILE, BOOKS, 6888 ALTA LOMA TERRACE, LOS ANGELES, CA 90068. TN: (213) 874-8434. Private premises; appointment necessary. Spec: arts of Africa, Asia, Oceana, ancient Americas, first editions; also drawings and prints. A.B.A.A.

NORTHWEST BOOKS, 3814 LYON AVENUE, OAKLAND, CA 94601. Prop: Don McKinney. TN: (415) 532-5227. Store, appointment advisable. Spec: prints, engravings, colourplate books.

NORTHWOODS BOOKS, P.O. Box 23435, Santa Barbara, CA 93121. TN: (805) 962-2812.

THE NOVEL EXPERIENCE, 778 Marsh Street, San Luis Obispo, CA 93401. Prop: Margaret Nybak & Jo Mott. TN: (805) 544-1549. Est: 1976. Shop, closed on Mondays. Appointments can be made outside business hours. Medium stock. Spec: Belles Lettres. B: Security Pacific National Bank, 1144 Morro St., San Luis Obispo, CA 93401 Acc.No: 039-562.

JUNE O'SHEA BOOKS, 1206 South Roxbury Drive, Los Angeles, CA 90035. TN: (213) 553-0678. Est: 1960. Private premises; appointment necessary. Very large stock used; also some new books. Spec: psychology, psychiatry; criminology. Cata: on foregoing, 2 a year. A.B.A.A.

OLD BOOK SHOP, 1104 Sutter Street, San Francisco, CA 94109. Prop: Miriam McGrail & Sydney Engelberg. TN: (415) 776-3417. Est: 1952. Shop. Medium stock used, also old prints and antiques.

OLD MONTEREY BOOK CO., 136 Bonifacio Place, Monterey, CA 93940. Prop: Cecil & Todd Wahle. TN: (408) 372-3111. Est: 1976. Shop. Medium stock. B: Crocker, Monterey. M: A.B.A.A., I.L.A.B.

RAMELLE ONSTOTT, 6489 South Land Park Drive, Sacramento, CA 95831. TN: (916) 428-2863. Spec: Children's; illustrated; Cata.

GEORGE K. OPPENHEIM, 51 Vallejo Street, Berkeley, CA 94707. TN: (415) 527-5169. By appointment only. Spec: Fine arts, illustrated books, decorative prints; foreign languages. M: A.B.A.A.

THE ORIENTAL BOOKSTORE, 630 East Colorado Boulevard, Pasadena, CA 91101. Prop: Frank Mosher. TN: (818) 577-2413. Est: 1937. Shop, open Monday to Friday 15.30-17.30 hrs. Saturday 11.00-17.30. Very large stock sec. and antiq. Also new books. Spec: the Orient, South Pacific and Asia.

OSTBY'S AMERICANA, 8758 Park Avenue, P.O. Box 89, Bellflower, CA 90706. Prop: Duane Ostby. TN: (213) 925-7767. Est: 1960. Storeroom, appointment necessary. Small stock used, also new. Spec: U.S. Civil War, 1861-1865, soldier genealogy. Cata: Americana, 1 a year.

OTENTO BOOKS, 3817 FIFTH AVENUE, SAN DIEGO, CA 92108. Prop: Robert J Gelink. TN: (619) 296-1424. Est: 1963. Shop. Medium stock sec. and antiq. Spec: nautical and voyages of discovery. B: Bank of America. M: A.B.A.A.

OTHER TIME BOOKS, 10617 PICO BOULEVARD, LOS ANGELES, CA 90064. TN: 475-2547. Spec: Popular Culture and Modern Fiction. Open Tuesdays-Saturdays 12-6 p.m.

OUT-OF-PRINT BOOKS, 5038 HAZELTINE AVENUE, SHERMAN OAKS, CA 91423. Prop: Arnold Jacobs. TN: (818) 789-6431. Est: 1951. Private premises; appointment necessary. Very small stock used. Spec: World War II. B: Bank of America.

PACIFIC BOOK SUPPLY COMPANY, P.O. BOX 337, FARMERSVILLE, CA 93223. Prop: Anna S. Tornow. Est: 1952. Mail order only. Large stock used, also new. Spec: college text and reference books. Cata: frequently.

PAPERBACK ALLEY USED BOOKS, 5840 HOLLISTER AVENUE, GOLETA, CA 93101. Shop.

PAPERBACK PLACE, 1994 CLIFF DRIVE, SANTA BARBARA, CA 93101. Shop.

PARTRIDGE BOOKSTORE, 6739 HOLLYWOOD BOULEVARD, HOLLYWOOD, CA 90028. Prop: James I. Hubler. TN: (213) HO 6-1477. Est: 1961. Shop. Medium stock used, also new. Spec: paperbacks.

THE PATCHY FOG, 142 WEST MAIN, EL CAJON, CA 92020. Prop: Ray P. & May Clare Reynolds. TN: (619) 579-8640. Medium stock sec. and antiq. Also ephemera and original small art.

PENINSULA ANTIQUARIAN BOOKSELLERS, 506½ WEST BALBOA BOULEVARD, BALBOA, CA 92661. Prop: Dorothy Beek & Joan Spangler. TN: (714) 675-1990. Est: 1978. Shop, closed on Mondays. Small stock used. Spec: Illustrated, Children's Illustrated, Nautical, California, Fine Bindings. B: Bank of America, 615E, Balboa Boulevard, Balboa, CA. 00372-00218

08. CALIFORNIA (CA.)

PEPPER AND STERN RARE BOOKS INC., P.O. Box 2711, SANTA
BARBARA, CA 93120. Prop: James Pepper & Deborah Sanford. TN:
(805) 569-0735.

ROBERT PERATA — BOOKS, 3170 ROBINSON DRIVE, OAKLAND, CA
94602. TN: (415) 482-0101. By appointment only. Spec: Press books
and fine printing; printing and printing history; western Americana;
books about books, ephemera. M: A.B.A.A.

PERI LITHON BOOKS, P.O. Box 9996, SAN DIEGO, CA 92109 (5372
Van Nuys Court). Prop: John & Marjorie Sinkankas. TN: (714)
488-6904. Est: 1971. Private premises, appointment necessary. Small
stock. Spec: geology, mineralogy, gemology, mining, jewelry. Cata: on
foregoing, 6 a year and lists. A.B.A.A.

PERRY'S ANTIQUES AND BOOKS, 1863 WEST SAN CARLOS, SAN JOSE,
CA 95128. Prop: Frank D. Perry. TN: (408) 286-0426. Est: 1949.
Shop. Stock of over 100,000 volumes used books; also art, prints and
antiques. Spec: Jack London, Edgar Rice Burroughs and Western
Americana. Cata: Western Americana and Californiana, once a year.

DIANE PETERSON—BOOKLADY, P.O. Box 2544, 27 WALNUT
AVENUE, ATHERTON, CA 94025. TN: (415) 324-1201. Private
premises: appointment necessary. Small stock used. Spec: Steinbeck,
John Muir; Jack London. Wallace Stegner; modern fantasy first
editions; miniature books.

PETTLER AND LIEBERMAN, BOOKSELLERS, 2345 WESTWOOD
BOULEVARD, ROOM 3, LOS ANGELES, CA 90064. Prop: Robert Pettler
and Victor Lieberman. TN: (213) 474-2479. Est: 1978. Shop. Medium
stock used; also some new books. Spec: contemporary literature.

THE PHOENIX BOOKSTORE, 514 SANTA MONICA BOULEVARD, SANTA
MONICA, CA 90401. Prop: Michael R. Groth. TN: (213) 395-9516.
Spec: Astrology, occult; religion, theology; folklore; magic. M:
A.B.A.A.

W. H. PINCKARD, JR., 6130 ACACIA AVENUE, OAKLAND, CA 94618.
TN: (415) 653-9466. Est: 1977. Private premises; appointment
necessary. Very small stock used. Spec: fine Japanese prints and
illustrated books, 17th to 20th century. M: Ukiyo-e Print Dealers'
Association of Japan.

KEN PRAG, PAPER AMERICANA, P.O. Box 531, Burlingame, CA 94011. TN: (415) 566-6400.

PRUFROCK BOOKS ETC., 55 West Colorado Boulevard, Pasadena, CA 91105. TN: 795-3558. Shop, open afternoons, closed Mondays.

RAIR LITERATURE, P.O. Box 2488, Leucadia, CA 92024. Prop: B.L. Gerard. Est: 1960. Storeroom, appointment necessary. Small stock used. Spec: air warfare, aviation of the Services; al, unit and ship combat histories, World War II to date. Cata: on foregoing, occasionally.

RANCHO BOOKS INC., P.O. Box 2040, Santa Monica, CA 90406. (3008 Santa Monica Boulevard, Santa Monica.) Prop: Ralph S. Dahl & John C. Jones. TN: (213) 828-7167. Est: 1960. Office premises; appointment necessary. Medium stock used; also new books. Spec: historic and scholarly items on California and the Old West. Cata: occasionally.

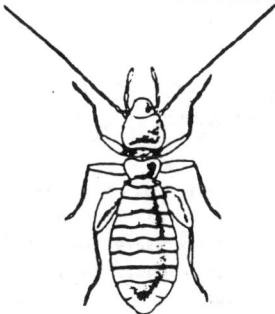

RANDALL HOUSE, 185 POST STREET, SAN FRANCISCO, CA 94108. Prop: Ronald R. Randall, President. TN: (415) 781-2218. Est: 1975. Shop. Large stock. Spec: Fine & Rare books in all fields, Autographs, Prints & Paintings of American interest. Cata: 4 per year. B: Bank of America San Francisco Main Office. M: A.B.A.A.

RARE ORIENTAL BOOK COMPANY, P.O. Box 1599, APTOS, CA 95001. President: Jerrold G. Stanoff. TN: (408) 724-4911. Est: 1966. Private premises, appointment necessary. Medium stock. Spec: Buddhism, China, Japan, Mount Everest, Himalayas, Tibet, Lafcadio Hearn; Japanese woodblock printing, science & natural history of Japan, China and Far East; missionaries in China and Japan; Japanese and Chinese in America, Japanese and Chinese art reference books. Cata and lists issued. Also Japanese objets d'art Ukiyoe, antique maps of Japan and China. M: A.B.A.A., I.L.A.B.

REGENT HOUSE, 108 NORTH ROSELAKE AVENUE, LOS ANGELES, CA 90026. TN: (213) 389-0687. Est: 1951. Storeroom, appointment necessary. Large stock used, also new. Cata: fiction, international affairs, history, literature, 2 a year on each subject. A.B.A.A.

REGENT STREET BOOKS, 2747 REGENT STREET, BERKELEY, CA. TN: (415) 548-8459. Shop.

J.E. REYNOLDS, 16031 SHERMAN WAY, VAN NUYS, CA 94106. TN: (213) 785-6934. Shop, appointment necessary. Small stock used. Spec: Western Americana, California.

JOHN ROBY, 3703 NASSAU DRIVE, SAN DIEGO, CA 92115. TN: (714) 583-4264. Est: 1960. Private premises, appointment necessary. Medium stock used and out-of-print, also new. Spec: aviation, nautical, technical. Cata: on foregoing.

DICK RONGSTAD, P.O. BOX 787, LAKESIDE, CA 92040. TN: (619) 291-6094. Private premises, appointment necessary. Spec: Paranormal, UFO, ESP, occult.

B & L ROOTENBERG RARE BOOKS, P.O. Box 5049 SHERMAN OAKS, CA 91403. Prop: Barbara Rootenberg. TN: (818) 788-7765. Cables: Rootbooks. Private premises; appointment necessary. Medium stock. Rare books and manuscripts. History of science, medicine; early illustrated; natural history; technology. Cata: 1 per year. M: A.B.A.A. I.L.A.B.

BERNARD M. ROSENTHAL INC., 251 POST STREET, SAN FRANCISCO, CA 94108. TN: (415) 982-2219. Spec: manuscripts before 1600, early printed books, history from AD 500 to 1650, paleography, bibliography. Cata: on foregoing. A.B.A.A., I.L.A.B. A.B.A.

ROBERT ROSS AND CO., 6101 EL ESCORPION ROAD, WOODLAND HILLS, CA 91367. Prop: Robert and Marilyn Ross. TN: (818) 346-6152. Est: 1980. Private premises; appointment necessary. Small stock used. Spec: illustrated; antique maps and prints; old and rare geography, history and map books. M: American Historical Print Collectors' Society.

THE ROSS VALLEY BOOK CO. INC., 1407 SOLANO AVENUE, ALBANY, CA 94706. Prop: Robert L. Hawley. TN: (415) 526-6400. Est. 1978. Shop, closed on Mondays. Small stock. Spec: Western Americana, Western Literature. Cata: 1 a year: lists several times yearly. B: Security Pacific National Bank 570 069303. M: A.B.A.

M.J. ROYER, 441 NORTH KINGS ROAD, LOS ANGELES, CA 90048. TN: (213) 651-3280. Est: 1946. Shop. Medium stock used, some new. Spec: art and illustrated books. Cata: art, annually. A.B.A.A.

S. & J. USED BOOKS, 113 WEST COLLEGE STREET, FALLBROOK, CA 92028. Prop: Stephen & Jennie Spears. TN: (619) 728-9668. Shop, closed Mondays. Spec: Children's; history; first editions.

RUDOLPH WM. SABBOT, P.O. BOX 772, WOODLAND HILLS, CA 91364. (5239 Tendilla Avenue.) TN: (818) 346-7164. Cables: Naturum. Est: 1965. Storeroom and private house; appointment necessary. Medium stock used; also new books to order. Spec: Natural History (excluding flora and earth sciences). Cata: specialized, mammals, birds, reptiles, etc., 3 a year. A.B.A.A.

GEORGE SAND, BOOKS, 9011 MELROSE AVENUE, LOS ANGELES, CA 90069. Props: Charlotte Gusay. TN: (213) 858-1648. Est: 1976. Shop. Medium stock of new books only. Spec: Dance, Music, Performing & Media Arts and George Sand titles in English. Cata: Occasionally. M: A.B.A.A.

SAND DOLLAR BOOKS, P.O. BOX 7400, LANDSCAPE STATION, BERKELEY, CA 94707. Prop: Jack Shoemaker. TN: (415) 527-1931. Spec: Modern poetry; modern first editions, literary magazines; letters and manuscripts; dance. M: A.B.A.A.

SAND HILL BOOKS, 500 SAND HILL ROAD, SCOTTS VALLEY, CA 95066.

SAN FERNANDO BOOK CO., P.O. BOX 447, SAN FERNANDO, CA 91341. (Westchester Faire Antique Mall, 8655 South Sepulveda Boulevard, Los Angeles, CA 90045.) Prop: Emil N. Eusanio TN: (818) 362-2173. Est: 1973. Shop, open daily. Medium stock used; also new books. Spec: numismatics; treasure-hunting; money and banking histories; gold and silver rushes; antiques and collectibles.

SAN FRANCISCIANA SHOP, CLIFF HOUSE, 1090 POINT LOBOS AVENUE, SAN FRANCISCO, CA 94121. Prop: Marilyn Blaisdell. TN: (415) 751-7222 and 661-7399. Spec: Pictorial material on California and San Francisco (photos, postcards, prints, maps). A.B.A.A.

SANTA BARBARA BOOKFINDERS, P.O. BOX 21252, SANTA BARBARA, CA 93121. Private premises, appointment necessary.

SCENE OF THE CRIME BOOKSHOP, 13636 VENTURA BOULEVARD, SHERMAN OAKS, CA 91423. Spec: crime, mystery, detection.

WILLIAM SCHNEIDER, 212 17th STREET, PACIFIC GROVE, CA 93950.

BERNARD SCHMIDT, 808 N. MAYFAIR AVENUE, DALY CITY, CA 94015.

KURT L. SCHWARZ, 738 SOUTH BRISTOL AVENUE, LOS ANGELES, CA 90049. Prop: Mrs. Martha Schwarz. TN: (213) 828-7927. Est: Vienna 1917, California 1947. Private premises; appointment necessary. Medium stock used and antiq. also some new art books. Spec: art, architecture, foreign literature, sociology. Cata: art, history, sociology, orientalia, 5 or 6 a year. A.B.A. (int.), A.B.A.A., A.B.A.

JOHN SCOPAZZI, 278 POST STREET (SUITE 305), SAN FRANCISCO, CA 94108. TN: (415) 362-5708. Est: 1969. Suite, 3rd floor of a commercial building, open normal business hours. Small stock antiq.; also antique maps. Spec: fine bindings, private press books; voyages; literature. Cata: irregularly. M: A.B.A.A.

SCOTS BOOKS – JOHN W. McCONNELL, 1370 FAIRBANKS COURT, DIXON, CA 95620. TN: (916) 678-1172. Est: 1979. Private premises; appointment necessary. Medium stock used; also some new. Spec: Scottish interest; British Heraldry.

THE SCRIPTORIUM, 427 NORTH CANON DRIVE, BEVERLY HILLS, CA
90210. Prop: Charles Sachs. TN: (213) 275-6060. Est: 1966. Shop.
Spec: autograph letters, manuscripts, documents, signed photographs
and books. MS.

SEBASTOPOL BOOK SHOP, 133 NORTH MAIN STREET, SEBASTOPOL,
CA 95472. TN: (707) 823-9788. Spec: Japanese Art & Culture. M:
A.B.A.A.

THE SECOND TIME AROUND, 391 EAST MAIN STREET, VENTURA, CA
93003. TN: (805) 643-3154. Store. Very large stock sec. and antiq.
also magazines and comics. Spec: Rare, First editions.

SERENDIPITY BOOKS, 1790 SHATTUCK AVENUE, BERKELEY, CA 94709.
Prop: Peter B. Howard. TN: (415) 841-7455. Est: 1963. Shop. Small
stock used, a few new. Spec: modern first editions, literary
manuscripts; fine printing; little magazines. Cata: modern literature,
one a year. A.B.A.A.

SERGIO OLD PRINTS, 50 MAIDEN LANE, SAN FRANCISCO, CA 94108.
Prop: Sergio L. Domeyko. TN: (415) 434-3314. Spec: General
Americana; botanicals; maps; Hawaiiana. M: A.B.A.A.

SEVEN ROADS BOOK SEARCHES, 2611 LAKE STREET, SAN
FRANCISCO, CA 94121. Prop: Robert Baker & Olympia Trésmontan
Stitt. TN: (415) 751-7427. Spec: Americana, philosophy, music. Cata.

SHARP AND HAFFNER BOOKS, 5043 LANKERSHIM BOULEVARD,
NORTH HOLLYWOOD, CA 91602. Prop: Elisabeth Shart & Gerda
Haffner. TN: 980-6980. Est: 1976. Shop. Medium stock used; also new
books, bookbinding and Xerox service. Spec: genealogy, history;
historical novels.

FLORIAN J. SHASKY, 1901 OLD MIDDLEFIELD WAY (SUITE 19),
MOUNTAIN VIEW, CA 94043. TN: (415) 967-5330. Store.

MICHAEL J. SHERICK, P.O. BOX 91915, SANTA BARBARA, CA 93101.
TN: (805) 966-5819. Est: 1982. Private premises, appointment
necessary. Very small stock sec. and antiq. Spec: poetry; fiction;
literary criticism; letters, manuscripts. Cata: 6 a year. *Also at*: 1512
DE LA VINA STREET.

THE SHTETL, 7603, BEVERLY BLVD., (BOX 480058) LOS ANGELES, CA 90048.

SHUEY BOOK SEARCH, 8886 SHARKEY AVENUE, ELK GROVE, CA 95624. Prop: C. R. Shuey. TN: (916) 685-3044. Est: 1979. Private premises; postal business only. Very small stock used. Spec: general non-fiction.

FRANCES AND ALAN SIEGEL, 308 NORTH GOLDEN MALL, BURBANK CITY, CA. TN: 848-4417. Est 1980. Large stock used; also new books.

SIGN OF THE SUN BOOKSTORE, 2357 ALPINE BOULEVARD, ALPINE, CA 92001. Prop: Elizabeth Rattisseau & Benjamin Darling. Store.

THE SILVER DOOR, P.O. BOX 3208, REDONDO BEACH, CA 90277. Prop: Karen La Porte. TN: (213) 379-6005. Est: 1977. Private premises; appointment necessary. Very large stock new and out-of-print detective/mystery fiction and related items. Cata: 2 per year. B: Bank of America/Marina Del Rey. 09142-00850.

S. RICHARD SIMMONS, P.O. BOX 1072, RESEDA, CA 91335. TN: (213) 885-7704. Est: 1974. Private premises, appointment necessary. Small stock used. Spec: Art, Mysteries, Scholarly. B: Crocker, Tarzana.

SISTERHOOD BOOKSTORE, 1351 WESTWOOD BOULEVARD, LOS ANGELES, CA 90024. TN: (213) 477-7300. Shop, open daily. Feminist Books, Non-sexist Children's books.

SLIGHTLY READ BOOKS, 9829 MIRA MESA BOULEVARD, SAN DIEGO, CA 92131. Prop: Deanna Simpson & Faye Kob. TN: (619) 695-0750. Shop.

STANLEY S. SLOTKIN, 2220 AVENUE OF THE STARS, LOS ANGELES, CA 90067. TN: (213) HO 9-0100. Est: 1951. Storeroom, appointment necessary. Very large stock used. Spec: religious works, medicine.

R. SORSKY, 3845, NORTH BLACKSTONE, FRESNO, CA 93726. TN: (209) 227-2901. Est: 1976. Stockroom, open normal business hours, closed Saturdays, open other days. Very small stock used; also new books. Spec: woodworking only. M: A.B.A.

SOUTH BAY BOOKSTORE, 1489 PLAZA BOULEVARD, NATIONAL CITY, CA 92050. Prop: Debra Reed. TN: (619) 474-4444. Shop, open 7 days.

KENNETH STAROSCIAK, 117 WILMOT PLACE, SAN FRANCISCO, CA 94115. TN: (415) 346-0650. Est: 1968. Private House—mail order only. Medium stock. Spec: Art, Architecture, First editions. Cata: 10 per year. M: A.B.A.A.

SUN DANCE BOOKS, 1520 NORTH CRESCENT HEIGHTS, HOLLYWOOD, CA 90046. Prop: Allan Adrian. TN: (213) 654-2383. Est: 1967. Private premises; appointment necessary. Small stock used. Spec: utopian literature; Pacific Ocean voyages; imaginary voyages, imaginary travel to the planets; Latin America, Western United States. M: A.B.A.A., I.L.A.B.

SUNSET BOOKSTORE, 2161 IRVING STREET, SAN FRANCISCO, CA 94122.

SYLO ANTIQUES, P.O. BOX 126366, SAN DIEGO, CA 92112. Prop: Robert O Denison. TN: (619) 231-4477. Shop. Spec: early California books, maps, magazines and newspapers. Shop at 719 East Street.

JOSEPH TABLER, 5650 RILEY STREET, SAN DIEGO, CA 92110. TN: (619) 291-6399. Private premises, appointment necessary. Spec: fine, juveniles, mysteries.

THE TALISMAN PRESS, P.O. BOX 455, GEORGETOWN, CA 95634. TN: (916) 333-4486. A.B.A.A.

TECHNICAL BOOK CO., 2056 WESTWOOD BOULEVARD, LOS ANGELES, CA 90025. TN: 475-5711, 879-9411. Professional, Scientific, Medical, Law. Open: Mondays to Saturdays: 9.30 a.m.-5.30 p.m.

TED'S USED BOOKS, DE LA VINA STREET, CA 93101. Shop.

TEN O'CLOCK BOOKS, 8786 CLING COURT, ELK GROVE, CA 95624-1837. Prop: J.A. Grenzeback. TN: (916) 685-8219. Est: 1973. Private premises, stock not able to be seen. Search service only, supplying books on demand to university and college libraries. Out-of-print and current publications bought. Inventory not available to dealers or general public.

THIS OLD HOUSE BOOK SHOP, 5399 WEST HOLT BOULEVARD, MONTCLAIR, CA 91763. Prop: Thomas H. Guthormsen. TN: (714) 624-5144. Est: 1956. Shop. Very large stock used; also new and antiq. Spec: fiction, mystery; Christian religion; first editions.

JEFFREY THOMAS, 49 GEARY STREET (SUITE 230), SAN FRANCISCO, CA 94102. TN: (415) 956-3272. Est: 1982. Shop, closed Saturday. Large stock used and rare. Spec: literature, Western and other Americana; fine press; illustrated books. Cata: occasionally.

TOLLIVER'S BOOKS 1634 & 1636, STEARNS DRIVE, LOS ANGELES, CA 90035. Props: James & Evelyn Tolliver. TN: 939-6054. Cables: Gulliver, Los Angeles. Est: 1969. Shop, office and 2 houses. Shop open every day, Sats: 10.00-16.00, Suns: 12.00-16.00. Large stock. Spec: Natural history, Marine science, Mathematics, Engineering, Mexico & Meso America. Cata: 4-6 times yearly. B: Bank of America, Hollywood Main Office, Hollywood, CA. Acc: 373-4-06411. M: A.B.A.A.

TRANSITION BOOKS, 445 STOCKTON STREET, SAN FRANCISCO, CA 94108 Prop: Richard Q. Praeger. TN: (415) 391-5161. Spec: 20th century first editions, art; surrealism and Dada; French literature; photography. M: A.B.A.A.

TROPHY ROOM BOOKS, 4858 DEMPSEY AVENUE, ENCINO, CA 91436. Prop: Ellen Enzler-Herring. TN: (818) 784-3801. Est: 1977. Private premises; appointment necessary. Large stock used; also a few new books. Spec: worldwide big game hunting; Asian travel and exploration; Richard Burton first editions. M: A.B.A.A.

THE TRUTH SEEKER COMPANY, INC., P.O. BOX 2832, SAN DIEGO, CA 92112. Prop: James Hervey Johnson. TN: (714) 291-2297. Est: 1873. Offices, open normal business hours. Small stock used, also new. Spec: atheism, freethought, philosophy. Cata: 3 a year.

UCLA HEALTH SCIENCES STORE, UCLA MEDICAL CENTER, 1st FLOOR ROOM 13-126, LOS ANGELES, CA. TN: 825-7721. Open: Mondays-Thursdays 08.00-18.00, Fridays 08.00-17.00, Saturdays 10.00-17.00.

UNISON BOOKS, 3930 FIFTH AVENUE, SAN DIEGO, CA 921030. Prop: Cutty & Diane Hyde. TN: (619) 299-1237. Store. Medium stock sec. and antiq. also new books. Spec: metaphysics, psychology.

URBAN BOOKS, 295 GRIZZLY PEAK BOULEVARD, BERKELEY, CA 94708. Prop: James W. McCreary. TN: (415) 524-3315. Est: 1960. Private premises, appointment necessary. Small stock used. Spec: social sciences, Californiana, business history, Urbanism. Cata: on economics and foregoing, irregularly.

VAGABOND BOOKS, 2076 WESTWOOD BOULEVARD, LOS ANGELES, CA 90025. Prop: Craig Graham. TN: 475-2700. Modern Fiction, Cinema, Theatre & Art. Open: Mondays-Saturdays, 12.00-18.00.

R. VALDEZ, 7232A SOUTH GREENLEAF AVENUE, WHITTIER, CA 90609. TN: (213) 693-6648.

VALLEY BOOK CITY, 5249 LANKERSHIM BOULEVARD, NORTH HOLLYWOOD, CA 91601. Prop: Mark J. Marlow. TN: (213) 985-6911. Est: 1975. Shop—open 7 days per week. Very large stock. Spec: Literary 1st editions, Art, Cinema, Science Fiction, Occult, Metaphysics. Cata: twice yearly. New books also. B: Bank of America. Acc. No: 1051-1-6055. M: A.B.A.A.

VALLEY BOOK STORE, 120 West Main Street, El Cajon, CA 92020. Prop: Clifford Lloyd Trittipo. TN: (619) 447-9068. Store, open 7 days.

GRAEME VANDERSTOEL, P.O. Box 599, El Cerrito, CA 94530. TN: (415) 527-2882. Est: 1962. Private premises; appointment necessary. Medium stock used; also some new books. Spec: Asia, Africa, Australia and the Pacific; especially art, music, dance, theatre, religion, anthropology and travel. Cata: on foregoing; 5 a year. A.B.A.A.

VAN NORMAN BOOKSELLERS, 4047 Bay View Court, San Diego, CA 92103. Prop: Allen & Grace Van Norman. TN: (619) 296-6451. Private premises, appointment necessary. Spec: Americana; art; children's.

ICART VENDOR, 8111 Melrose Avenue, Los Angeles, CA 90046. Prop: Sandy Verrin. TN: 653-3190. Est: 1978. Shop. Closed Mondays. Small stock. Spec: Art Deco & Art Nouveau only. Antique Illustrations turn of Century to 1940's. P.P.F.A. A.S.I.D.

VILLAGE CAMERA SHOP—MORMON BOOKS, 1417 Westwood Boulevard, Los Angeles, CA 90024. TN: 477-5791. Genealogical Supplies, Photo copies, L.D.S. books. Open: Mondays-Saturdays, 08.00-17.30 hrs.

VIRGINIA'S BOOK LOFT, 5096 Brunswick Drive, Cypress, CA 90630.

VOICES WW II BOOKSHOP, Box 6397, Los Osos, CA 93402. TN: (805) 528-6792. Spec: World War II Books.

VOLKOFF & VON HOHENLOHE, 1514 La Coronilla Drive, Santa Barbara, CA 93109. Prop: A.A. von Hohenlohe & Ivan Volkoff. TN: (805) 966-2100. Est: 1953. Storeroom; appointment necessary. Spec: rare and scholarly books and manuscripts. Cata: occasionally. Specializing in institutional collection development. A.B.A.A., Verband deutscher Antiquare.

MARIETTA VOORHEES, 1108 Adams Street, Saint Helena, CA 94574.

VROMANS, 695 East Colorado, Pasadena, CA 91101.

WAHRENBROCK'S BOOK HOUSE, 726-728 BROADWAY, SAN DIEGO, CA 92101. Props: C.A. Valverde & L.S. Stowe. TN: (619) 239-8604. Est: 1935. Shop. Stock of 200,000 used, also new books. Spec: Americana, Californiana. A.B.A.A.

JOHN ALAN WALKER, P.O. Box 516, BISHOP, CA 93514. TN: (619) 872-1680. Spec: art.

LOIS WARD—BOOKS, Box 1564, TORRANCE, CA 90505. Prop: Lois H. Ward. TN: (213) 539-5725. Est: 1972. Private premises, appointment necessary. Small stock used. Spec: Religion and Theology. Mail order search service. Cata: 4-6 per year. Also a few new books. M: A.B.A.

WESSEX BOOKS, 558 SANTA CRUZ AVENUE, MENO PARK, CA 94025. Prop: Thomas Haydon. TN: (415) 321-1333. Est: 1975. Shop. Open seven days a week. Large stock. Spec: Fiction, Literature, University Press and Scholarly books. B: Eureka Federal Savings.

WESTWOOD BOOK STORE, 1121 GAYLEY AVENUE, LOS ANGELES, CA 90024. TN: 473-4644. Est: 1936. General trade books. Open: Mondays-Thursdays: 09.00-23.00, Fridays and Saturdays: 09.00-midnight. Sundays, 13.00-21.00.

WEST COAST BOOKERY, P.O. Box 724, GLENDALE, CA 91209. Prop: Jack Berlin. Est: 1959. Storeroom appointment necessary. Medium stock used. Spec: magic lanterns, pipes, tobacco, Alaska, heraldry.

WEST COAST LIBRARY SERVICE, Box 242, S.V.R.S., SANTA CRUZ, CA 95060. (130 South Navarra Drive, Scotts Valley.) Prop: Geoffrey Mazer. TN: 438-2382. Est: 1929. Private premises, appointment necessary. Medium stock used, also remainders. Spec: books for college libraries. Cata: American and English literature, 1 a year.

WESTERN PERIODICALS COMPANY, 13000 RAYMER STREET, NORTH HOLLYWOOD, CA 91605. Prop: Sol. Grossman. TN: (213) 875-0555. Est: 1958. Storeroom, open normal business hours. Spec: the sciences.

STEPHEN WHITE GALLERY OF PHOTOGRAPHY INC., 752 N. LA CIENGA BOULEVARD, LOS ANGELES, CA 90069. TN: (213) 657-6995.

R.G. WILBORN, P.O. Box 70, MOKELUMME HILL, CA 95245.

DENNIS G. WILLS, 7527 LA JOLLA BOULEVARD, LA JOLLA, CA 92037. TN: (619) 456-1800. Shop, open 7 days. Spec: science, military, politics.

WILSHIRE BOOK COMPANY, 12015 SHERMAN ROAD, NORTH HOLLYWOOD, CA 91605. Prop: Melvin Powers. TN: (213) 875-1711. Est: 1942. Shop. Stock of over 50,000 used, also new. Spec: hypnotism and psychology. Cata: on foregoing, occasionally.

WINDSOR HOUSE, P.O. Box 145, DANA POINT, CA 92629. Prop: Mary Lou Powell. TN: (714) 240-3242. Est: 1977. Private premises, appointment necessary. Very small stock used. Spec: Americana; fiction.

CAROL J. WINSLOW, P.O. Box 709, LANCASTER, CA 93534. Est: 1971. Business by mail only. Spec: first editions, juvenile, illustrated, technical.

ALAN WOFSY, FINE ARTS, 150 GREEN STREET, SAN FRANCISCO, CA 94111. TN: (415) 986-3030. Spec: illustrated books with original graphics; also old and modern prints. A.B.A.A.

WORDS & MUSIC, 3806 FOURTH AVENUE, SAN DIEGO, CA 92103. Prop: Ann Marik & Victor Margolis. TN: (619) 298-4011. Store, open 7 days. Medium stock sec. also new books. Spec: cookbooks, biography, art.

WORLD WIDE HUNTING BOOKS, P.O. Box 3095, LONG BEACH, CA 90803. Prop: Ludo J. Wurfbain. TN: (213) 430-3693. Private premises, appointment necessary. Small stock sec. and antiq. Spec: big game hunting and exploration only. Corresp: Français, Deutsch, Dutch. B: Bank of America, Los Angeles; Lloyds Bank, London.

WILLIAM P. WREDEN, BOOKS AND MANUSCRIPTS, 200 HAMILTON AVENUE, P.O. BOX 56, PALO ALTO, CA 94302. TN: (415) 325-6851. TA: Wredenbook. Est: 1937. Shop: closed on Mondays. Stock can be seen 10.00-17.00 hours Tuesday-Saturday and by appointment. Large stock. Spec: general antiquarian books; English and American literature; Western Americana; fine printing; trade catalogues. Cata: Annually. M: A.B.A.A. A.B.A.

HERB YELLIN, 19073 Los Alimos Street, Northridge, CA 91326. TN: (818) 363-6621. Est: 1970. Private premises; appointment necessary. Medium stock used. Spec: modern first editions and collectibles. M: A.B.A.

YERBA BUENA BOOKS, 882 Bush Street (at Taylor), San Francisco, CA 94108. Prop: Jennifer S. Larson. TN: (415) 474-2788. Spec: Californiana, California authors; books about books; pacific voyages; prints. M: A.B.A.A.

YESTERDAY'S BOOKS, Highway 99, Modesto, CA 90004. Prop: Philip G. Mason. TN: HO 2-3851. Est: 1960. Store, open 12 noon to 6 p.m. Stock of 45,000 used.

YESTERDAY'S BOOKS, 2859 University Avenue, San Diego, CA 92104. Prop: Kenneth E. Baker. TN: (619) 298-4503. Store, medium stock sec. and antiq. Spec: photography, religion, aviation.

ZEITLIN & VERBRUGGE, 815 North La Cienega Boulevard, P.O. Box 69600, Los Angeles, CA 90069. Prop: Jacob & Josephine Zeitlin. TN: (213) 652-0784. Cables: Jabberwock Los Angeles. Est: 1927. Shop. Very large stock used; also new books, maps, prints, photography, drawings and paintings. Spec: rare history of science and medicine; fine art; fine printings; classics; A.E. Housman (literature); bibliography; horology; Californiana. Cata: on foregoing, 6 a year. A.B.A.A.

ZEITLIN PERIODICALS COMPANY, INC., 817 South La Brea Avenue, Los Angeles, CA 90036. Prop: Stanley L. Zeitlin. TN: (213) 933-7175. Est: 1925. Shop and storeroom, appointment necessary. Spec: back issue periodicals, over 2 million issues in stock. Cata: periodically. A.B.A.A.

MURRAY ZUCKERMANN, 1037 10th Street, Santa Monica, CA 90403. Very large stock used. Spec: social sciences and humanities.

09.   COLORADO (CO.)

BEULAH BOULDER	FORT COLLINS
COLORADO SPRINGS	LITTLETON
DENVER	LOVELAND
ENGLEWOOD	

THE BOOK HOME, INC., P.O. Box 825, COLORADO SPRINGS, CO 80901. Prop: Leo Mohl. TN: (303) 632-0555. Est: 1942. Shop. Very large stock. Spec: Natural Science. Cata: 4 per year. B: Exchange National Bank. M: A.B.A.A.

BOOK HOUSE, 5154 SOUTH BROADWAY, ENGLEWOOD, CO 80110.

THE CACHE, 7157 WEST U.S.34, LOVELAND, CO 80537. Prop: M. Anderson. TN: (303) 667-1081. Est: 1973. Shop. Medium stock used; also a few new books. Spec: Zane Grey.

CHINOOK BOOKSHOP, 210 N. TEJON STREET, COLORADO SPRINGS, CO 80902.

HENRY A. CLAUSEN BOOKS, 224½ NORTH TEJON STREET, COLORADO SPRINGS, CO 80902. TN: (303) 634-1193. Est: 1946. Shop and storeroom. Large stock used; also a few new books, old maps and photographs of Colorado mining towns. Spec: Western history; Chinese art; railroads.

COLLECTORS' BOOKS, 1707 COUNTRY CLUB ROAD, FORT COLLINS, CO 80524. Prop: Harry & Eleanor Deines. Est: 1972. Private premises, appointment necessary. Small stock. Spec: Western American history; modern American literature; illustrated children's books. Cata: on foregoing, 1 a year.

COLLECTORS' CENTER, 654 EMERSON STREET, DENVER, CO 80218. Prop: Don Bloch. TN: (303) 832-7512. Cables: Colcent, Denver. Est: 1952. Premises: mail order or by appointment. Denver's largest, oldest antiquarian book store: 10,000 out-of-print titles. Spec: Americana, art, almanacs, entertainment, juveniles, London-iana, old sheet music, periodicals, sports, transportation, etc.

COURT PLACE BOOKSHOP AND GALLERY, 3827 WEST 32ND AVENUE, DENVER, CO 80211. Prop: Alan & Mary Culpin. TN: (303) 455-0317 and 5477. Est: 1978. Shop. Very large stock used. Spec: Americana (Western); geology and mining; travel.

THE HERMITAGE BOOKSHOP, 2817 EAST THIRD AVENUE, DENVER, CO 80206. TN: (303) 388-6811. Large stock. Spec: Western Americana; travels; first editions; military. M: A.B.A.A.

KUGELMAN & BENT, 5924 East Colfax Avenue, Denver, CO 80220. TN: (303) 333-1269.

LOIS NEWMAN, BOOKS, INC., 1428 Pearl Street, Boulder, CO 80302. Prop: Miss Lois E. Newman. TN: (303) 442-5302. Est: 1974. Shop. Small stock used; also new books. Spec: science-fiction. Cata: 1 or 2 a year. A.B.A.

FRED A. ROSENSTOCK, 1228 East Colfax Avenue, Denver, CO 80218. TN: (303) 832-7190. Spec: Western history; art; autographs; Civil War.

FRED. B. ROTHMAN & CO., 10368 West Centennial Road, Littleton, CO 80127. Prop: Paul A. Rothman. Manager: Richard J. Spinelli. TN: (303) 979-5657. TA: Rothlaw Littletonco. Est: 1945. Shop, closed Saturday and Sunday. Very large stock used; also back-numbers of journals, new books and periodicals. Spec: law and related fields. Cata. B: Colorado National Bank, P.O. Box 17047, Denver, CO 80217.

RONALD S. SIMPSON, 222 Linden Street, Fort Collins, CO 80521.

STAGE HOUSE II, 1039 Pearl Street, Boulder, CO 80302. Prop: Karl R. Gaee & Richard K. Schwarz. TN: (303) 447-1433. Est: 1962. Shop. Large stock used, also antiques, furniture, china, glass, silver. Spec: Western Americana, first editions, leather bindings.

SUN CIRCLE BOOKS, 107 E. Laurel Street, Fort Collins, CO 80521.

TATTERED COVER BOOK STORE, 2823 E. 2nd Avenue, Denver, CO 80206.

BARRIE D. WATSON, P.O. Box 38, 8760 Grand Beulah, CO 81023. TN: (303) 485-3136. Est: 1969. Storeroom, appointment necessary. Very large stock used and antiq. Spec: old law; natural history; facolnry.

10. CONNECTICUT (CT.)

BETHANY	BRIDGEPORT
BRANFORD	BRISTOL

BROOKFIELD
CANAAN
CANTERBURY
COLEBROOK
COLLINSVILLE
COS COB
COVENTRY
DANBURY
DANIELSON
DARIEN
DERBY
EAST HADDAM
EAST HAMPTON
EAST WOODSTOCK
ESSEX
FAIRFIELD
FALLS VILLAGE
GOSHEN
GRANBY
HADDAM
HAMDEN
HARTFORD
HARWINTON
KENSINGTON
MADISON
MANSFIELD CENTER
MERIDEN
MIDDLEBURY
MIDDLETOWN
MILLDALE
NEW BRITAIN
NEW CANAAN
NEW HAVEN

NEW LONDON
NEW PRESTON
NEWTOWN
NORFOLK
NORTHFORD
NORWALK
OLD MYSTIC
OXFORD
POMFRET
SALISBURY
SANDY HOOK
SHERMAN
SOUTH WILLINGTON
SOUTH WOODSTOCK
SOUTHPORT
STAMFORD
STERLING
STONINGTON
STRATFORD
TORRINGTON
VERNON
WALLINGFORD
WATERTOWN
WEST CORNWALL
WEST REDDING
WESTPORT
WHITNEY VILLE
WILTON
WINDHAM
WINDSOR
WINSTED
WOODBURY

SHEILA D. AMDUR, P.O. Box 151, MANSFIELD CENTER, CT 06250. TN: (203) 423-3176. Private premises, appointment necessary. Small stock sec. and antiq. Spec: medicine; psychiatry; New England.

AMERICAN WORLD BOOKS, Box 6305, WHITNEYVILLE STATION, HAMDEN, CT 06517. Prop: Nolan E. Smith. TN: (203) 776-3558. Est: 1975. Private premises: postal business only. Stock of over 10,000 volumes used. Spec: American Studies (literature, fiction, criticism, poetry, cultural history).

ANGLER'S & SHOOTER'S BOOKSHELF, GOSHEN, CT 06756. Prop: Col. Henry A. Siegel. TN: (203) 491-2500. Est: 1966. Private premises, appointment necessary. Over 75,000 volumes used, some new. Spec: hunting, fishing, sporting dogs, sporting art. Cata: on foregoing, 1 a year (in two parts, 6 months apart). A.B.A.A.

THE ANTIQUARIUM, 66 HUMISTON DRIVE, BETHANY, CT 06525. Props: Lee & Marian Ash. TN: (203) 393-2723. Est: 1959. Private premises, appointment necessary. Medium stock. Spec: Books about Books, Natural history, Bibliography, History of medicine, Icelandica, Haitiana, Witchcraft. Cata: Annually.

ANTIQUE BOOKS, 3651 WHITNEY AVENUE (ROUTE 10), HAMDEN, CT 06518. Prop: Willis O. Underwood. TN: (203) 281-6606. Private premises, appointment necessary. Large stock sec. and antiq. Spec: History; Civil War; Americana. Cata.

ARCHIVES HISTORICAL AUTOGRAPHS, 119 CHESTNUT HILL ROAD, WILTON, CT 06897. Prop: Warren P. Weitman. TN: (203) 226-3920. Private premises, appointment necessary. Spec: autograph letters, documents, manuscripts.

BANCROFT BOOK MEWS, 86 SUGAR LANE, NEWTOWN, CT 06470. Prop: Eleanor Bancroft. TN: (203) 426-6338. Private premises, appointment necessary. Small stock sec. and antiq. Spec: music, theatre, dance.

DEBORAH BENSON, RIVER ROAD, WEST CORNWALL, CT 06796. Prop: Deborah Covington. TN: (203) 672-6614. Appointment advisable. Large stock sec. and antiq. Spec: early medical; books about books.

BEST BOOKS LIMITED, BOX 648, LOVERS LANE, NORFOLK, CT 06058. Spec: Philippines. Cata.

PRESTON BEYER, 752A, PONTIAC LANE, STRATFORD, CT 06497. TN: (203) 375-9073. Spec: books about books; fine press books, modern first editions.

BIBLIOLATREE, COUNTRY STORE (ROUTE 66), EAST HAMPTON, CT 06424. Prop: Paul O. Clark. TN: (203) 267-8222. Appointment advisable. Large stock sec. and antiq.

WARREN BLAKE, 131 SIGWIN DRIVE, FAIRFIELD, CT 06430. TN: (203) 259-3278. Appointment advisable. Very small stock sec. and antiq. Spec: Americana.

P. AND H. BLISS CO., P.O. BOX 1079, 215 EAST MAIN STREET, MIDDLETOWN, CT 06457. TN: (203) 347-2255. Est: 1931. Three warehouses; postal business only. Stock of over four million magazines, journals and periodicals on all subjects, no bound books. Cata: occasionally.

BO AND CO., P.O. BOX 162, POMFRET, CT 06258. Prop: Elizabeth B. Wood. TN: (203) 928-3939. Private premises, appointment necessary. Small stock sec. and antiq. Spec: social history; technology.

THE BOOK BARN, P.O. BOX 108, RT.183, COLEBROOK, CT 06021. Prop: Robert Seymour. TN: (203) 379-3185. Est: 1953. Shop, open from May 1st-November 1st but appointment advised. Large stock. Spec: Americana, History and Literature. Cata: Occasionally—1 or two per year.

THE BOOK BLOCK, 8 LOUGHLIN AVENUE, COS COB, CT 06807. Prop: David Block TN: (203) 629-2990. Est: 1979. Private premises, appointment necessary. Small stock sec. and antiq. Spec: Early and fine printing; rare and illustrated; private press books, fine bindings; Americana, travel and voyages. Cata: 5 or 6 a year. M: A.B.A.A., I.L.A.B.

BOOK REPOSITORY, BOX 424, SOUTHPORT, CT 06490. Prop: Carolyn R. Vogel. TN: (203) 255-2277 Shop. Small stock sec. and antiq. books. Spec: Children's; sport; military. Cata.

BOOKCELL BOOKS, 90 ROBINWOOD ROAD, HAMDEN, CT 06517. Prop: Dorothy & Louis Kuslan. TN: (203) 248-0010. Private premises; by appointment only. Medium stock sec. and antiq. books. Spec: Science; technology; children's; illustrated.

BOOKS AND BIRDS, 375 HARTFORD TURNPIKE (ROUTE 30), VERNON, CT 06066. Prop: Gil Salk. TN: (203) 875-1876, evenings (203) 643-0380. Shop, open Tues. and Wed. 11-4.30; Thurs. 11-8; Fri. and Sat. 11-5; or by appointment. Large stock sec. and antiq. books. Spec: Connecticut; birds and nature.

BOOKS BY THE FALLS, 253 Roosevelt Drive, Derby, CT 06418. Prop: R. Paulus Knox. TN: (203) 734-6112. Shop. Small stock sec. and antiq. books. Spec: Poetry; philosophy; classics; religion. Cata: occasionally.

BERT AND PHYLLIS BOYSON, 23 Cove Road, Brookfield, CT 06804. TN: (203) 775-0176. Private premises; by appointment only. Small stock sec. and antiq. books. Spec: Illustrated; science, technology.

BRANFORD RARE BOOK & ART GALLERY, 221 Montowese Street, Branford, CT 06405. Prop: John R. Elliott. TN: (203) 4885-882. TA: Montowese, Branford, Conn. Est: 1978. Shop, closed Mondays. Small stock used. Spec: Travel, Cartography, Voyages. Cata: twice a year.

BRITANNIA BOOKSHOP, Main Street, New Preston, CT 06777. Prop: Barbara Corey Tippin & Sarah Stock. TN: (203) 868-0368. Shop, open Wed. to Sun., 11 to 5. Medium stock sec. and antiq. books. Spec: Old British and Irish books; old prints and paintings. Cata: occasionally.

PAUL BROWN—BOOKS, 577 Bank Street, New London, CT 06320. TN: (203) 443-6608, evenings (203) 848-7310. Shop, open Wed. to Sat., 12-5. Large stock sec. and antiq. books. Spec: Nautical; history of eastern Connecticut. Cata: occasionally.

BRYN MAWR BOOK SHOP, 56½ Whitney Avenue, New Haven, CT 06510. Prop: Meigs and Carter. TN: (203) 562-4217, or (203) 787-2714 out of business hours. Shop, open winter, Wed., Thurs., Fri. 12-3, Sat. 10-1, and summer, Wed. and Thurs. 12-3; by appointment for dealers. Very large stock. Spec: Art; biography; children's.

A CABINET OF BOOKS, P.O. Box 195, Watertown, CT 06795. Prop: Leland & Suzanne H. Kirk. TN: (203) 274-4825. Private premises; postal business only. Small stock used. Spec: hunting, fishing, natural history; ice skating (not hockey). Cata: annually.

BARBARA CHARRETT, 567 Roosevelt Drive (RT.34), Oxford, CT 06483.

CHISWICK BOOK SHOP, INC., 98 WALNUT TREE HILL ROAD, SANDY HOOK, CT 06482. Prop: Aveve & Herman Cohen. TN: (203) 426-3220. Est: 1935. Storeroom, appointment necessary. Medium stock. Spec: private press books, history of printing, paper-making, calligraphy, first editions. Cata: on foregoing, occasionally. A.B.A.A., A.B.A. (Int.).

THE CLIPPER SHIP BOOK SHOP, 12 No. MAIN STREET, ESSEX, CT 06426. Prop: Frank T. Crohn, Jr. TN: (203) 767-1666. Shop, open Mon. to Sat. 9-6; Sun 12-5 (May-Sept. only). Medium stock. Spec: Nautical, maritime; hunting, fishing; modern American fiction; biography, autobiography; New England.

COLEBROOK BOOK BARN, ROUTE 183, COLEBROOK, CT 06021. Prop: Bob Seymour. TN: (203) 379 3185. Appointment advisable. Large stock. Open daily May to October only. Spec: American history and literature; fine books. Cat: occasionally.

COUNTRY LANE BOOKS, P.O. BOX 47, COLLINSVILLE, CT 06022 (Country Lane). Prop: Edward & Judith Myers. TN: (203) 489-8852. Est: 1966. Private premises; appointment desirable. Medium stock used. Cata: Western Americana and general, quarterly. A.B.A.A.

COVENTRY BOOKSHOP, 1159 MAIN STREET (ROUTE 31), P.O. BOX 36, COVENTRY, CT 06238. Prop: John R. Gambino. TN: (203) 742-9875. Shop, open Tues. to Sat., 12-5. Large stock sec. and antiq. books.

BOB COWELL BOOKSELLER, 15 PEARSDALL WAY, BRIDGEPORT, CT 06605. Prop: Robert P. Cowell. TN: (203) 334-3025. By appointment only. Medium stock. Spec: dogs. Also shop at 2720 Fairfield Avenue, Bridgeport, CT 06605. Open Mon. to Tues., Thurs. to Sat. 11-4. Very small stock general sec. and antiq. books.

JOHN DOBRAN—PHOTOGRAPHICA, 20 STONE BOAT ROAD, WESTPORT, CT 06880. Spec: photography 1830-1930; all books illustrated with tipped-in photographs; illustrated travel and biography.

MICHAEL C. DOOLING, 72 NORTH STREET, P.O. BOX 1047, MIDDLEBURY, CT 06762. Prop: Michael & Jean Dooling. TN: (203) 758-8130. Private premises; by appointment only, evenings and weekends. Very small stock sec. and antiq. books. Spec: Americana; architecture; art; bindings; travel.

ANN DUMLER BOOKS, 67 Westway Road, Southport, CT 06490. TN: (203) 255-9094. Est: 1979. Private premises, appointment necessary. Small stock. Spec: children's books; illustrated. Cata: occasionally. Corresp: Français. B: Connecticut National Bank, Southport, CT 06490.

DUNN'S MYSTERIES OF CHOICE, 251 Baldwin Avenue, Meriden, CT 06450. Prop: William Dunn. TN: (203) 235-0480. —Appointment necessary. Medium stock. Spec: detective fiction; Ayn Rand; H.L. Mencken. Cata.

EAST AND WEST SHOP INC., 4 Appleblossom Lane, Newtown, CT 06470. Prop: Thelma Ziemer. TN: (203) 426-0661. Est: 1954. Appointment necessary. Medium stock used, also new. Spec: Orientalia, Far and Middle and Near East, Africa. Cata: on foregoing and India, China, Japan. A.B.A.A. I.L.A.B.

WILLIAM H. EDGERTON, 241 Long Neck Point Road, Darien, CT 06820. TN: (203) 655-9510. Spec: Mechanical Music.

ELLIOT'S BOOKS, Box 6, Northford, CT 06472. Prop: E.M. Ephraim. TN: (203) 484-2184. Est: 1957. Storeroom; postal business only. Stock of 400,000 used. Spec: Yale, Harvard University Press books, University presses, scholarly, history, social sciences, literature, science. Lists on foregoing, regularly, free search service.

R. AND D. EMERSON, The Old Church, Main Street, Falls Village, CT 06031. TN: (203) 824-0442 Est: 1957, Shop, but appointment is advised. Medium stock sec. and antiq. Spec: fine books. Cata: occasionally. B: Salisbury Bank and Trust Co., Lakeville, Conn. M: A.B.A.A., I.L.A.B.

EXTENSIVE SEARCH SERVICE, Squaw Rock Road, Danielson, CT 06239. Prop: David Haveles. TN: (203) 774-1203 and 774-1829. Storeroom; appointment necessary. Medium stock used. Spec: Derrydale Press; Walt Kelly, Little Lulu, Disney, Baum Oz and non-Oz items, Beatles, comics. Cata: on foregoing, 4 a year.

BARBARA FARNSWORTH, BOOKSELLER, Route 128, West Cornwall, CT 06796. TN: (203) 672-6571. Private premises; appointment necessary. Very large stock sec. and antiq. books. Spec: Horticulture; art; fine printing.

113

FELIX PAWS, 2 STONECROP ROAD, NORWALK, CT 06851. Prop: Sonja Bay. TN: (203) 846-3095. Private premises; viewing at weekends by appointment only. Very small stock sec. and antiq. books. Spec: Children's books of the 1920s and 1930s.

FLEUR DE LYS BOOKS, P.O. Box 1081, NEW CANAAN, CT 06840. Prop: De Lys & Dick Brown. TN: (203) 966-5162. By appointment only. Medium stock sec. and antiq. books. Spec: Children's; illustrated, prints; maps; ocean liners.

AVIS & ROCKWELL GARDINER, 60 MILL ROAD, STAMFORD, CT 06903. TN: (203) 322-1129. Appointment necessary. Large stock. Spec: trade catalogues; early newspapers; ephemera.

GASTRONOMIC BOOK SHOP, P.O. Box 631, BRISTOL, CT 06010. Prop: Normand J. Boulanger. TN: (203) 584-0312. By appointment only. Very small stock. Spec: Cookbooks, winebooks, baking books, gastronomic literature.

GEOLOGICAL BOOK CENTER, BOX 235, FALLS VILLAGE, CT 06031. Prop: Robert & Dorothy Emerson. TN: (203) 824-0442. Private premises, appointment necessary. Large stock used. Spec: geology, mining and petroleum exclusively. Cata: geology, occasionally.

GILANN BOOKS, 301 WEST AVENUE, DARIEN, CT 06820. TN: (203) 655-4532. Shop open seven days a week. Stock of used books, also maps, prints and original art.

LAWRENCE F. GOLDER, P.O. Box 144, COLLINSVILLE, CT 06022. TN: (203) 693-8110 and 693-8631. Est: 1967. Private premises, appointment necessary. Small stock used. Spec: Scarce and rare Americana (North and South). Cata: Americana, 1 per year.

GUTHMAN AMERICANA, P.O. Box 392, WESTPORT, CT 06881. TN: (203) 259-9763. Private premises, appointment necessary. Spec: American Revolution, Indian Wars.

WALTER HALLBERG, 16 HAWTHORN STREET, HARTFORD, CT 06105. TN: (203) 524-1618.

HARRINGTON'S, 333 COGNEWAUG ROAD, COS COB, CT 06807. Prop: Alton Ketchum. Spec: historic newspapers, newspapers before 1870.

HAYLOFT BOOK & PRINT SHOP, INDIAN LANE (off ROUTE 43), WEST CORNWALL, CT 06796. Prop: John A. Nuese. TN: (203) 672-6246. Est: 1945. Shop. Large stock old and rare.

THE JOHN STEELE BOOK SHOP, 107 MAIN STREET, COLLINSVILLE, CT 06022. Prop: Bill Keifer. TN: (203) 693-2343, or (203) 693-8017 (home). Shop, open Tues. to Sat. 11-5.30; Sun. 1-5. Very large stock sec. and antiq. books. Spec: Connecticut history; science; medicine.

THE JUMPING FROG, 161 SOUTH WHITNEY STREET, HARTFORD, CT 06105. Prop: Bill McBride. TN: (203) 523-7707. Shop, open Wed. to Fri. 11.30-5.30; Thurs. until 9; Sat. 10-5.30; Sun. 1-5.30; or by appointment. Large stock. Spec: Modern fiction; automobiles.

KINGSMILL BOOK SHOP, ROUTE 32, HALL COMPLEX, SOUTH WILLINGTON, CT 06265. Prop: William & Eleanor Peters. TN: (203) 429-6694. Shop, open Thurs. and Fri. 1-5; Sat. 12-5. Medium stock sec. and antiq. books. Spec: Literary criticism; theology; philosophy; modern fiction.

DAVID LADNER, P.O. BOX 6179, WHITNEYVILLE, CT 06517. TN: (203) 288-6575. Est: 1970. Private premises, appointment necessary. Small stock sec. and antiq. also new books. Spec: Slavica, bibliography, history of printing & art and architecture. Cata: 2 a year. Français, Deutsch, Polish. B: Colonial Bank, Waterbury CT. *Also at* 34 WAKEFIELD STREET.

LANGHAMMER SHOP, RT. 9A, HADDAM, CT 06438. Prop: Rose and Otto Langhammer. TN: (203) 345-2675. Est: 1960. Shop, closed Wednesdays. Very large stock used; also new books. M: Antiquarian Booksellers of Connecticut.

KATHLEEN AND MICHAEL LAZARE, P.O. BOX 117, SHERMAN, CT 06784. TN: (203) 354-4181. Est: 1971. Private premises; appointment necessary. Large stock used. Spec: children's books, illustrated; also original wood engravings, oil paintings, graphics etc. (At this address October to May only: May to September at Saint Andrews, N. B. Canada, q.v.)

LION'S HEAD BOOKS, ACADEMY STREET, SALISBURY, CT 06068. Prop: Spalding McCabe. TN: (203) 435-9328. Shop, open Mon. to Sat., 10-5. Small stock sec. and antiq. books, also medium stock new. Spec: Gardening; natural history.

A. LUCAS, BOOKS, 89 ROUND HILL ROAD, FAIRFIELD, CT 06430. Prop: Alexander & Kathleen Lucas. TN: (203) 259-2572. By appointment only. Large stock sec. and antiq. books. Spec: 19th and 20th century first editions.

McBLAIN BOOKS, P.O. BOX 5062, HAMDEN, CT 06518. Prop: Philip & Sharon McBlain. TN: (203) 281-0400. Est: 1970. Private premises, appointment necessary. Large stock sec. and antiq. Spec: Africa, Asia and the Pacific; Latin America; Russia & East Europe. Cata: on foregoing, 6-8 a year. M: A.B.A.A. *Also at* 2348 WHITNEY AVENUE.

BERNIE McMANUS—WOODBURY HOUSE, 494 MAIN STREET SO. (ROUTE 6), WOODBURY, CT 06798. Prop: Bernie McManus. TN: (203) 263-3407. Shop, open Thurs. to Sun., 10-5, or by appointment. Small stock sec. and antiq. books.

WILLIAM MADDEN, CARLTON ROAD, HARWINTON, CT 06790.

MAGIC HORN, LTD., 95 RAY HILL ROAD, EAST HADDAM, CT 06423. Prop: Fred & Kathy Miller. TN: (203) 873-1346. Open Sat. and Sun., 11-6, or by appointment. Small stock sec. and antiq. books. Spec: Children's; illustrated; ephemera.

JAN & LARRY MALIS, P.O. BOX 211, NORTH WILTON ROAD, NEW CANAAN, CT 06840. TN: (203) 966-8510. Est: 1965. Private premises, appointment necessary. Small stock. Spec: general; also ephemera and manuscripts. M: A.B.A.A., Manuscript Society, Ephemera Society.

TIMOTHY MAWSON BOOKS AND PRINTS, MAIN STREET, NEW PRESTON, CT 06777. TN: (203) 868-0732. Shop, open Thurs. to Sat., 11-5.30, or by appointment. Medium stock. Spec: Gardening; food and wine; 18th and 19th century prints.

FRISBEE MILL BOOKS, 1260 SCARD ROAD, WALLINGFORD, CT 06492. Prop: Dr. F.J. Mill and Jos. Riotte. TN: (203) 269-4374. Est: 1972. Stockroom; appointment necessary. Very small stock used. Spec: Connecticut; America literature 1800-1850; Civil War; Egyptology.

MINERVA BOOKS, 136 BABCOCK STREET, HARTFORD, CT 06106. Prop: Melissa & Ralph Coury. TN: (203) 246-8355. By appointment only. Small stock sec. and antiq. books. Spec: Middle Eastern history, politics, culture; scholarly; first editions.

ELIZABETH MOODY, Box 327, WINDHAM, CT 06280. TN: (203) 423-3275. Private premises; appointment necessary. Small stock sec. and antiq. Spec: Children's.

MURRAY'S BOOKFINDING SERVICE, 292 JACKSON AVENUE, BRIDGEPORT, CT 06606. Prop: Murray Novick. TN: (203) 335 5598. By mail only. Very large stock used. Spec: fiction.

MUSEUM GALLERY BOOK SHOP, 360 MINE HILL ROAD, FAIRFIELD, CT 06430. Prop: Henry B. Caldwell. TN: (203) 259-7114. By appointment only. Large stock sec. and antiq. books. Spec: Fine arts.

JULIAN J. NADOLNY, NATURAL HISTORY BOOKSELLERS, 121 HICKORY HILL ROAD, KENSINGTON, CT 06037. Mail order only. Est: 1967. Medium stock used; also new. Spec: natural history, especially entomology and other zoology. Cata: on zoology, geology, palaeontology, 2 a year.

RUSSELL NORTON, Box 1070, NEW HAVEN, CT 06504-1070. TN: (203) 562-7800. Est: 1974. Private premises; appointment necessary. Very small stock used. Spec: history of photography; a leading dealer in 19th century stereoscopic cards.

NUTMEG BOOKS, 354 NEW LITCHFIELD STREET, TORRINGTON, CT 06790. Prop: William & Debby Goring. TN: (203) 482-9696. Est: 1977. Shop, open daily. Large stock used.

OLD MYSTIC BOOKSHOP, 58 MAIN STREET, OLD MYSTIC, CT 06372. Prop: Charles B. Vincent. TN: (203) 536-6932. Est: 1940. Shop on first floor. Large stock used, a few new. Spec: marine, Americana, manuscripts. Cata: on foregoing and general 4 a year, plus lists. A.B.A.A.

ORDNANCE CHEST, P.O. Box 905, MADISON, CT 06443. Prop: B.R. Williams. TN: (203) 245-2387. Est: 1976. Private premises; appointment necessary. Very small stock used. Spec: military history, ordnance, sporting; also prints, guns, swords, uniforms etc. Cata: 3 a year. M: Collector Arms Dealers Association.

THE PAGES OF YESTERYEAR, OLD HAWLEYVILLE ROAD, NEWTOWN, CT 06470 Prop: John Renjilian. TN: (203) 426-0864. By appointment only. Small stock sec. and antiq. books.

PHAROS BOOKS, P.O. BOX 17, FAIR HAVEN STATION, NEW HAVEN, CT 06513. Props: Sheila & Matthew Jennett. TN: (203) 562-0085. Est: 1973. Shop and Storeroom, appointment necessary. Very large stock. Spec: Modern first editions; literature 18th-20th century; modern and Byzantine Greek; illustrated; travel; photography. Cata: Quarterly. Monthly short lists. New books also.

WILLIAM AND LOIS PINKNEY, 240 NORTH GRANBY ROAD, GRANBY, CT 06035. TN: (1-203) 653-7710. Est: 1960. Open Monday to Friday; appointment necessary at weekends. Large stock used. Spec: New York State, Americana, the West; first editions. M: A.B.A.A., Limited Editions Club.

POMFRET BOOK SHOP, P.O. BOX 214 (ROUTES 44 AND 169), POMFRET CENTER, CT 06259. Prop: Roger & Judith Black. TN: (203) 928-2862. By appointment only. Medium stock sec. and antiq. books. Spec: New England books and town maps; atlases.

POOR FARM, ROUTE 128, WEST CORNWALL, CT 06796. Prop: Dick & Charlotte Lindsey. TN: (203) 672-6567. Shop; appointment advisable. Medium stock sec. and antiq. books. Spec: Regional Americana; decorative arts; automobiles. *Also at:* RIVER ROAD, WEST CORNWALL.

STEPHEN POWELL, BOX 871, TORRINGTON, CT 06790. Spec: gambling. Cata.

PRINTER'S DEVIL BOOKSHOP, 1660 MERIDEN-WATERBURY ROAD, MILLDALE, CT 16467. Prop: Robert W. Thompson. TN: (1-203) 621-4770. Est: 1969. Shop. Very large stock. Spec: out of print paperbacks, science fiction. New books also. M: A.B.A.

THE READER'S ROOM, 938 STATE STREET, NEW HAVEN, CT 06511. Prop: Ann Burke. TN: (203) 624-6804. Shop, open Tues. to Sat. 10-5; Sun. 12-5. Large stock general sec. and antiq. books.

WILLIAM REESE COMPANY, 409 TEMPLE STREET, NEW HAVEN, CT 06511. TN: (203) 789-8081. Private premises: appointment necessary. Spec: rare Americana and literature; bibliography. Cata: 8 per year.

RINHART GALLERIES INC., UPPER GREY, COLEBROOK, CT 06021. TN: (203) 379-9773. Private premises, appointment necessary. Spec: 19th and 20th century photographs.

CEDRIC L. ROBINSON, 597 PALISADO AVENUE (RT. 159), WINDSOR, CT 06095. TN: (203) 688-2582. Est: 1946. Private premises; appointment necessary. Very large stock used. Spec: Americana, American literature, Connecticut. Cata: on foregoing, occasionally. A.B.A.A.

ROOSTER HILL BOOKBARN, R.R.1. BOX 88, MARGARET HENRY ROAD, STERLING, CT.

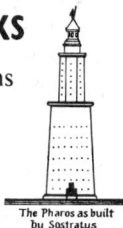

SCARLET LETTER BOOKS AND PRINTS, P.O. Box 117, SHERMAN, CT. Prop: Kathleen A. Lazare. TN: (203) 354-4181. Est: 1972. Private premises, appointment necessary. Very small stock sec. and antiq. Spec: children's and illustrated. Cata: occasionally. M: A.B.A.A.

WOLFGANG SCHIEFER BOOKS, P.O. Box 474, NEW HAVEN CT 06502. Also in New York, 10010, q.v.

BARRY SCOTT, P.O. Box 207, STONINGTON, CT 06378. TN: (203) 535-2643. Est: 1970. Bookroom; appointment necessary. Spec: first editions, illustrated manuscripts, fine printing. M: A.B.A.A.

JOHN SKUTEL GALLERIES, 251 CARROLL ROAD, FAIRFIELD, CT 06430. TN: (203) 259-1997. Est: 1954. Mail order only. Also auctioneers as the Connecticut Book Auction Gallery.

R.W. SMITH, BOOKSELLER, 51 TRUMBULL STREET, NEW HAVEN, CT 06510. TN: (203) 776-5564. Est: 1975. Private premises, appointment necessary. Medium stock used. Spec: Strictly specialist stock in American art and architecture, American decorative arts, photography, 19th Century European painting. Cata: 2 or 3 per year. B: Colonial Bank (New Haven). Acc: 1-18636-8.

PAULA STERNE, BOOKS, HUCKLEBERRY ROAD, R.F.D.2., WEST REDDING, CT 06896. Prop: George B. & Janice E. Burgeson. TN: (203) 938-2756. Spec: Sporting, dogs, guns; Americana. A.B.A.A.

STONE OF SCONE ANTIQUES /BOOKS/FIREARMS, ROUTE 14 WEST, CORNER WATER STREET AND BINGHAM ROAD, CANTERBURY, CT 06331. Prop: Tom & Jan Stratton. TN: (203) 546-9917. Shop, open seven days, 10-8. Small stock general sec. and antiq. books. Spec: New England, Connecticut, Americana. Cata: occasionally.

C.A. STONEHILL, INC., 282 YORK STREET, NEW HAVEN, CT 06511. TN: (203) 865-5141. Spec: incunabula and manuscripts, English literature through the 19th century, 20th century American and English first editions. A.B.A.A.

ROBERT O. STUART, P.O. BOX 636, CANAAN, CT 06018. (Railroad Street.) TN: (203) 824-5637. Spec: Military history. Cata: general, occasionally.

KATHLEEN SULLIVAN—CHILDREN'S BOOKS, 861 MAIN STREET, COVENTRY, CT 06238. Prop: Kathleen & Andrew Sullivan. TN: (203) 742-7073. By appointment only. Small stock sec. and antiq. books. Spec: 19th and 20th century children's and illustrated books.

ANTHONY MORETTI TUFTS—BOOKSELLER, 1786 JENNINGS ROAD, FAIRFIELD, CT 06430. Prop: Anthony Moretti Tufts. TN: (203) 259-8626. By appointment only. Small stock sec. and antiq. books. Spec: Scottish books; horticulture.

TURKEY HILL BOOKS, 46 TURKEY HILL ROAD SOUTH, WESTPORT, CT 06880. Prop: Jack & Marilyn Grogins. TN: (203) 255-0041. By appointment only. Large stock sec. and antiq. books. Spec: First editions; fiction; children's; limited editions; autographs.

VERDE ANTIQUES AND BOOKS, 64 MAIN STREET, WINSTED, CT 06098. Prop: Ginny & Ray Dethy. TN: (203) 379-3135. Shop, open Wed. to Sun. afternoons, May 15th to Sep. 1st, and Nov. 15th to Dec. 24th; rest of year open Fri. and Sat. 11-5. Very small stock. Spec: First editions; children's; illustrated ephemera.

BARBARA WEINDLING, 69 BALL POND ROAD, DANBURY, CT 06810. TN: (203) 746-2514. Est: 1970. Private premises. Large stock used. Spec: cookbooks; children's. Cata: once a year.

WHITLOCK FARM BOOKSELLERS, 20 SPERRY ROAD, BETHANY, CT 06525. Prop: Gilbert Whitlock. Gen. Mgr.: Everett Whitlock. TN: (203) 393-1240. Est. 1932. Two large barns. Very large stock used & rare; also prints, maps and small collectables. Cata: general bi-monthly. A.B.A.A.

WHITLOCK'S INCORPORATED, 17 BROADWAY, NEW HAVEN, CT 06511. TN: (203) 562-9841. Est: 1900. Shop. Large stock used rare and out-of-print; also new books. Spec: Connecticut history, Americana.

THE WINDSOR BOOK STORE, 99 POQUONOCK AVENUE, WINDSOR, CT 06095. Prop: Amy & Arthur Wyllie. TN: (203) 688-2159. Shop, open Mon. to Fri. 11-6; Sat. 9-5; Sun. by appointment. Very large stock sec. and antiq. books. Spec: Science fiction; mystery; history; military history; Golden Age comics.

LAURENCE WITTEN, P.O. BOX 490, 181 OLD POST ROAD, SOUTHPORT, CT 06490. TN: (203) 225-3474. Cables: Incipit Southport-Connecticut. Private premises; appointment necessary. Small stock of rare books and manuscripts. Spec: incunabula, 16th century, early manuscripts and bindings, classics, Middle Ages, Renaissance, music. Cata: rare books, bindings, manuscripts, music, annually. A.B.A.A. I.L.A.B.

YESTERDAY'S GALLERY, P.O. BOX 154, EAST WOODSTOCK, CT 06244.

YOUNG AND OLD BOOKS, 530 NEWFIELD STREET (ROUTE 27), MIDDLETOWN, CT 06457. Prop: Les & Gloria Young. TN: (203) 346-1637. Shop, open Tues. to Sat. 10-5.30, Thurs. until 7. Very large stock sec. and antiq. books. Spec: Mystery, science fiction, fiction; technical; cooking; nature.

HENRY ZEMBKO, 80 KNOLLWOOD DRIVE, NEW BRITAIN, CT 06052. TN: (203) 225-3032. Est: 1973. Private premises—mail business. Small stock used. Spec: Elbert Hubbard and Roycrofter publications. Cata: yearly.

11.   DELAWARE (DE.)

NEWARK	REHOBOTH BEACH
NEWCASTLE	WILMINGTON

ATTIC BOOKS, 1175 PLEASANT HILL ROAD, NEWARK, DE 19711.

STEVEN D. BEARE, 7 EAST BROOKLAND AVENUE, WILMINGTON, DE 19805.

THE BOOKPRESS LIMITED, P.O. BOX 272, THE OLD COURTHOUSE ON MARKET PLAIN, NEWCASTLE, DE 19720. Prop: John & Emily Ballinger. TN: (302) 322-8188. Spec: applied arts, bibliography, Americana.

EDWIN C. BUXBAUM, P.O. BOX 465, WILMINGTON, DE 19899. Appointment necessary. Spec: National Geographic Magazines. Cata: 1 a year.

DORSEY BOOKS, 811 WEST 19TH STREET, WILMINGTON, DE 19802. TN: (302) 655-5781.

HOLLY OAK BOOK SHOP, 306 WEST 7TH STREET, WILMINGTON, DE 19801. TN: (302) 429 0894.

OAK KNOLL BOOKS, 214 DELAWARE STREET, NEWCASTLE, DE 19720. TN: (302) 328-7232. Shop. Large stock sec. and antiq. Spec: books on books, bibiography, history of printing.

PALMA BOOK SERVICE, P.O. BOX 602, 120 WEST 19th STREET, WILMINGTON, DE 19899. Prop: Harry M. Stuart. TN: (1-302) 656-8629. Est: 1962. Private premises, appointment necessary. Medium stock. Cata: Monthly.

NICHOLAS PAPANTINAS, 303 STOCKLEY STREET, REHOBOTH BEACH, DE 19971. TN: (302) 227-7459. Spec: 20th century, photographic literature.

12. DISTRICT OF COLUMBIA (DC.)

WASHINGTON

BOOKED UP, 1209 31ST STREET NORTH WEST, WASHINGTON, DC 20007. TN: (202) 965-3244. Cables: Piglet Washington. Est: 1971. Shop. Large stock used. Spec: modern first editions. Cata: 2 a year.

THE BOOKINIST, 2820 38TH STREET N.W., WASHINGTON, DC 20007. TN: (202) 338-9474.

Q.M. DABNEY & CO., P.O. BOX 42026 WASHINGTON, DC 20015. TN: (301) 881-1470. Est: 1968. Very large stock. Spec: history, military, social sciences, law, Government general. Also bindery. A.B.A.A.

EAST-WEST FEATURES SERVICE, P.O. BOX 8867, WASHINGTON, DC 20003. Manager, Antiquarian Books department: Igor G. Kozak. Spec: Russica (mainly pre-revolutionary and emigrę) and Slavica. Cata: occasionally.

ESTATE BOOK SALES, 2824 PENNSYLVANIA AVENUE NORTHWEST, WASHINGTON, DC 20007. Prop: Howard Wilcox & Christopher Cooper. TN: (202) 965-4274. Est: 1948. Shop. Very large stock used. Open every day, including Sunday 13.00 to 18.50 hrs. B: Union First, Washington, DC. and National Savings and Trust, Washington.

GEORGETOWN BOOK SHOP, 3144 DUMBARTON STREET, N.W., WASHINGTON DC. TN: (202) 965 6086. Shop.

DUFF & M.E. GILFOND, 1722 19th STREET, N.W., WASHINGTON, DC 20009.

WILLIAM F. HALE BOOKS, 1208 THIRTY-FIRST STREET N.W. WASHINGTON, DC 20007. TN: (202) 338-8272. TA: Halebooks Wash. DC. Est: 1975. Shop. Small stock used. Spec: Art, travel & exploration, Intellectual history. Cata: Monthly lists and several single-subject catalogues per year.

LLOYDS BOOKS, 1346 CONNECTICUT AVENUE N.W. (SUITE 719), WASHINGTON, DC 20036. TN: (202) 785-3826. Shop, closed on Saturdays. Spec: fine and rare 18th and 19th centuries.

THE OLD PRINT GALLERY, 1220 31st Street N.W., Washington, DC 20007. Prop: James C. Blakely, James R. von Ruster & Judith Blakely. TN: (202) 965-1818. Est: 1971. Shop. Spec: antique prints and maps, American and European. M: A.B.A.A., American Appraisers Association.

PARK REIFSCHNEIDER'S BOOK GALLERY, 1310 19th Street N.W., Washington, DC 20036.

SECOND STORY BOOKS, 2000 P Street North-West, Washington, DC 20036. TN: (202) 659-8884. *Also at* 7730 Old Georgetown Road, Bethesda, MD 20814; and at 3322 Greenmount Avenue, Baltimore, MD 21218.

OSCAR SHAPIRO, 3726 Connecticut Avenue North West, Washington, DC 20008. TN: (202) 244-4446. Postal business only. Spec: music (autographs, books, scores, violin) chess. A.B.A.A.

WAYWARD BOOKS, 1002-B Pennsylvania Avenue S.E., Washington, DC 2003. Prop: Sybil Ake and Doris Grombach. TN: (202) 546-2719. Shop. closed Mondays. Medium stock used. Spec: modern first editions; books on books; arts; civil liberties.

YESTERDAY'S BOOKS, 4702 Wisconsin Avenue, Washington, DC 20016.

13. FLORIDA (FL.)

ATLANTIC BEACH
BOCA RATON
CHULUOTA
CLEARWATER BEACH
CORAL GABLES
EUSTIS
FERN PARK
FORT LAUDERDALE
GAINESVILLE
HOLMES BEACH
JACKSONVILLE
LAKE WORTH
MIAMI
MIAMI BEACH
NAPLES
NEWBERRY
NORTH FORT MYERS
ORLANDO
OSPREY
PALM BEACH
PENSACOLA
SAINT AUGUSTINE
SAINT PETERSBURG
SARASOTA
TALLAHASSEE
TAMPA
TITUSVILLE
TREASURE ISLAND
WINTER HAVEN

AARDVARKS BOOKSELLERS, P.O. Box 15070, ORLANDO, FL 32858.

ACETO BOOKMEN, 5721 ANTIETAM DRIVE, SARASOTA, FL 33581. Prop: Charles D. Townsend. TN: (813) 924-9170. Est: 1960. Private premises; appointment necessary. Very small stock used; also a few new books. Spec: genealogy; town and county history.

CHRISTOPHER ACKERMAN, 180 EAST INLET DRIVE, PALM BEACH, FL 33480. Est: 1969. Private premises, business by mail only. Small stock used. Free Search service for out-of-print books. Send titles required or mention areas of specific interest. Spec: Collections formed, Virginiana, Classical Antiquity. Cata: On foregoing spec. bi-monthly. B: Messrs. Coutts & Co. London, First National Bank in Palm Beach, Florida. M: B.S.A., Society for the Bibliography of Natural History (British Museum), Virginia Historical Society.

ALL BOOKS AND PRINTS STORE, 4329 SOUTH WEST 8th STREET, MIAMI, FL 33134. Prop: Albert H. Ledoux. Est: 1949. Shop. Very large stock used. Spec: art, occult, religious history, philosophy, technical, fiction, biography, rare, old medicine, Civil War, juvenile, illustrated books, Bibles.

AMERICANA BOOKSHOP, 1719 PONCE DE LEON BOULEVARD, CORAL GABLES, FL 33134. Prop: John Detrick. TN: (305) 442-1776. Est: 1982. Shop, open Mon. to Sat. 10-5.30. Small stock sec. and antiq. Spec: Cuba, Florida, treasure diving, Napoleonic Wars, military. B: Sun Bank, Ponce de Leon Blvd, Coral Gables, FL 33134. M: Florida Antiquarian Booksellers Association.

APPLETREE BOOKS, 4035 38th AVENUE NORTH, SAINT PETERSBURG, FL 33713. Prop: Margaret M. Hudspith. TN: (813) 527-4819. Est: 1968. Private premises. Small stock used. Spec: poetry, gardening. Cata: 1 a year. A.B.A.

A TO Z BOOK SERVICE, P.O. Box 610813, NORTH MIAMI, FL 33161. Prop: Lucile Coleman. Est: 1961. Mail order only. Spec: poetry; fiction; biography; juvenile. Cata: rarely. M: A.B.A.A., I.L.A.B.

CARL J. BEGEMANN, 10701 SOUTH WEST 63rd AVENUE, MIAMI, FL 33156. TN: (305) 666-8755. Est: 1968. Private premises, appointment necessary. Small stock used. Spec: West Indies, Latin America, rare atlases, voyages, geographies, illustrators.

BEST BOOKS, 2016 EUCLID STREET, JACKSONVILLE, FL 32210.

THE BOOKFINDERS, INC., P.O. BOX 2021, MIAMI BEACH, FL 33140. Prop: Leon & Sylvia Cooke. TN: (305) 538-4795. Est: 1939. Mail order only. Very large stock used. Spec: educational and reference, college texts, art & music; architecture.

THE BOOK GALLERY, 1150 NORTH MAIN STREET, GAINESVILLE, FL 32601. Prop: Dan Morgan and Kaye Henderson. TN: (904) 378-9117. Est: 1972. Shop. Stock of 100,000 used, also some new books. Spec: Floridiana; metaphysical; cookbooks.

BOOKS & THINGS, 473 20th STREET N.E., BOCA RATON, FL 33431. Prop: E.Z. & D.J. SeGall. TN: (305) 395-2227. Shop. Medium used and antiq. stock.

BOOKS 'N THINGS, 1826 E. SUNRISE BLVD., FORT LAUDERDALE, FL 33304.

BOOKSTRADERS, INC. P.O. BOX 9403, 355 THIRD STREET N.W., WINTER HAVEN, FL 33880. Prop: Frank J. Ujlaki. TN: (813) 299-4904. Est: 1977. Shop, open daily and Sundays 13.00 to 18.00 hours. Spec: Used, rare, comics, records and tapes. Cata: Monthly. B: S.E. Bank of Winter Haven, 135-9197.

THE BOOK SCOUT, P.O. BOX 583, FERN PARK, FL 32730. Prop: Tracy Catledge. TN: AC 305/831-3794. Est: 1972. Private premises, appointment necessary. Medium stock. Spec: Scouting, Lord Baden-Powell, Siege of Mafeking, Boys Series Juveniles. Cata: twice a year. B: Barnett Bank, Winter Park, FL 1:15 378 8, Bank of New South Wales, London, 00220407.

BOOK WAREHOUSE, 2010 PONCE DE LEON BOULEVARD, CORAL GABLES, FL 33301. TN: (305) 448-3223.

CLIVE A. BURDEN INC., P.O. BOX 2792, NAPLES, FL 33939. Prop: Eileen Burden. TN: (813) 261-1978. Est 1981. Private premises, appointment necessary. Very small stock of antiquarian prints and maps. P.P.F.A., A.H.P.C.

CULLAR'S BOOKSTORE, 3425 THOMASVILLE ROAD, TALLAHASSEE, FL 32308.

JOHN C. DAUB, 316 4TH AVENUE, ST PETERSBURG, FL 33701. TN: (813) 577-4124. Est: 1944. Private premises, appointment necessary. Very small stock used. Spec: Americana and military. Cata: on foregoing and general, several a year.

JEFF DAVIS, RAINTREE BOOKS, 432 NORTH EUSTIS STREET, EUSTIS, FL 32726. TN: (904) 357-4275. Est: 1963. Large stock sec. and antiq. Cata.

ROBERT C. DEMAREST, (MYCOPHILE BOOKS), 1166 ROYAL PALM DRIVE, NAPLES, FL 33940. TN: (813) 262-3363. Est: 1979. Private premises; appointment necessary. Very small stock used, and some specialist new. Spec: Hallucinogenic plant or drug books and journals. M: Florida Antiquarian Booksellers Association.

FLORIDA BOOK STORE INC., P.O. Box 14076, GAINESVILLE, FL 32601.

ALLA T. FORD, 114 SOUTH PALMWAY, LAKE WORTH, FL 33460. TN: (305) 585-1442. Est: 1955. Private premises; appointment necessary. Medium stock used; also a few new. Spec: children's books; metaphysics, occult, science fiction; miniatures. Cata: occasional small lists.

GALVEZ BOOKS AND SILVER INC., 208 SOUTH FLORIDA BLANCA STREET, PENSACOLA, FL 32501. Manager: Lana Services. TN: (904) 432-2874. Est: 1979. Shop, closed Mondays. Medium stock used, also some new books. Spec: regional (southern U.S.)

WM. W. GAUNT AND SONS INC., GAUNT BUILDING, 3011 GULF DRIVE, HOLMES BEACH, FL 33510-2199. TN: (813) 778-5211 or 4832. Est: 1968. Stockroom open normal business hours, closed Saturday. Small stock used, also new books. Spec: law.

GLOBE AND ANCHOR BOOK COMPANY, P.O. Box 1173, SAINT AUGUSTINE, FL 32084. Prop: Charles R. Sanders, Jr. TN: (904) 824-4617. Private premises; by appointment only. Medium stock used. Spec: history and literature of Southeastern U.S.A.

HASLAM'S BOOK STORE, 2025 CENTRAL AVENUE, ST. PETERSBURG, FL 33713. TN: (813) 822-8616.

S. HAUBEN INC., 1410 20th STREET (ROOM 205), MIAMI BEACH, FL 33139.

ROBERT A. HITTEL, BOOKSELLER, 3020 North Federal Highway, Suite 6, Fort Lauderdale, FL 33306. Prop: Robert A. Hittel. TN: (305) 563-1752. Est: 1965. Shop, open Tuesday to Saturday, 9-6, or by appointment. Very large stock sec. and antiq. books. Spec: sporting; science fiction. B: Florida National, 3300 North Federal Highway, Fort Lauderdale, FL 33306. M: Florida Antiquarian Booksellers Association.

HYDE PARK BOOK SHOP, 1109 Swann Avenue, Tampa, FL 33606. Prop: James & Vivian Shelton. TN: (813) 259-1432. Est: 1980. Shop. Small stock used, also new books. Spec: literature; children's. M: A.B.A.

ISLAND BOOK COMPANY, P.O. Box 389, Saint Augustine, FL 32084. Prop: Nancy Sparkes Sanders. TN: (904) 829-2117. Private premises, appointment necessary. Very small stock. Spec: History & Literature of South Eastern U.S.A.

HORST K. JOOST, 11014 Forest Hills Drive, Tampa, FL 33612. By mail only. Very large stock sec. and antiq. books. Spec: early western Americana. Cata: regularly.

CAPT. KIT S. KAPP, P.O. Box 64, Osprey, FL 33559. Est: 1965. Storeroom: appointment necessary. Medium stock used: also a few new about maps, and publishers of hydrographic charts and cartobibliography studies. Spec: antique maps and prints, atlases, travel and voyages. Cata: annually. M: A.B.A., F.B.A.

KEEGAN'S BOOK SERVICE, 1416 Bell Terrace, Titusville, FL 32780. Prop: Norman R. Keegan. TN: (305) 267-1580. Est: 1967. Storeroom, appointment necessary. Large stock used. Cata.

LIGHTHOUSE BOOKS, 1735 FIRST AVENUE NORTH, SAINT PETERSBURG, FL 33713. Prop: Michael Slicker. TN: (813) 822-3278. Est: 1977. Shop. Large stock used. Spec: Florida and Caribbean material, Americana (Southern States). Cata: on foregoing, 3 to 4 a year. Also maps and prints. A.B.A.A. I.L.A.B.

LONGS BOOKS, 711 WEST LAKEVIEW, PENSACOLA, FL 32501. Prop: James Long. TN: 438-1956. Est: 1954. Storeroom open normal business hours. Medium stock used. Spec: Civil War; The South, Confederacy etc. Cata: occasionally.

McQUERRY ORCHID BOOKS, 5700 WEST SALERNO ROAD, JACKSONVILLE, FL 32244. Prop: Jack & Mary Noble McQuerry. TN: (904) 387-5044. Office premises, mail order only. Spec: orchids only (books and magazines). Cata: one a year and newsletters. B: Florida First National Bank, Jacksonville.

MICKLER'S ANTIQUARIAN BOOKS, P.O. BOX 38, 154 LAKE DRIVE, CHULUOTA, FL 32766. Prop: Mr. & Mrs. Thomas Mickler. TN: (305) 365-3636. Est: 1960. Storeroom, appointment necessary. Large stock used, also new. Spec: Florida related books, maps and memorabilia. Cata: on foregoing, 1 a year.

ARTHUR L. MITTELL, 11180 FOURTH STREET EAST, TREASURE ISLAND, FL 33706. Est: 1950. Shop. Large stock used and antiquarian. Spec: out-of-print, first editions, American authors, rare books.

OARHOUSE MARINE ANTIQUES, 600 MANDALAY AVENUE, CLEARWATER BEACH, FL 33515. TN: (813) 441-8288. Spec: Marine.

THE OLD BOOK SHOP, 108 EAST ADAMS STREET, JACKSONVILLE, FL 32202. Prop: Bob L. Gavilan. TN: (904) 355-6159. Est: 1970. Shop. Large stock used (15,000 paperbacks, 5,000 hardbacks) in all fields.

OLD BOOK SHOP, 3110 COMMODORE PLAZA, COCONUT GROVE (MIAMI), FL 33133. Prop: Margaret Donovan DuPriest. Est: 1961. Shop. Large stock used; also antique prints. Spec: Floridiana. Cata: general, 2 a year. A.B.A.A.

JACK OWEN OLD BOOK SHOP, P.O. BOX 447, PALM BEACH, FL 33480. Prop: Jack M.D. Owen. TN: (305) 588-5129. Est: 1965. Shop. Medium stock used. Spec: Marine, Biographies. Cata: Occasionally.

PARKERS BOOKS, 1465 Main Street, Sarasota, FL 33577.

EVANELL K. POWELL, 420 West Platt, Tampa, FL 33606. TN: (305) 833-3920 and 844-8640. Est: 1962. Shop, open normal business hours October through June, other times by appointment. Medium stock used; a few new books and moderately priced jewelry.

RARE BOOKS MAPS AND PRINTS, 138 Markland Place, Saint Augustine, FL 32084. Prop: A. Mueller. TN: (904) 829-9782. Shop in Lightner Museum Mall, Saint Augustine. Spec: graphic arts; maps.

CARROLL MINHER ROBINSON, P.O. Box 501, Palm Beach, FL 33480. (251 Park Avenue.) TN: 833-2028. Est: 1966. Shop open 11.00 to 18.00 hours. Spec: fine literature, leather bindings, biography.

SAN MARCO BOOK STORE, 1971 San Marco Boulevard, Jacksonville, FL 32207. Prop: John Blauer. TN: (904) 396-7597. Est: 1960. Shop. Medium stock used, out-of-print and rare. Spec: history; Florida.

THE SCRIBBLING BOOKMONGER, 1613 Silverwood, North Fort Myers, FL 33903. Shop, appointment advisable. Small stock used.

SOUTHEAST BOOK AUCTION SERVICE, P.O. Box 184, 254 W. Central Avenue, Winter Haven, FL 33880. TN: (813) 294-1772. Auction Service.

TAPPIN BOOK MINE, 705 Atlantic Blvd., Atlantic Beach, FL 32233.

TRIANGLE BOOKS, P.O. Box 1923, Eustis, FL 32726. (820 South Bay Street.) Prop: Wendell Davis. TN: (904) 357-3101. Est: 1963. Shop. Medium stock used, also new. Spec: Florida, old comic books, remainders.

D.E. WHELAN-SAMADHI, Box 729, Newberry, FL 32669. Spec: metaphysical literature.

14. GEORGIA (GA.)

ATLANTA	AVONDALE ESTATES
AUGUSTA	FOLKSTON

131

MARIETTA	SHARPSBURG
POWERSVILLE	STONE MOUNTAIN
ROME	THOMASVILLE
SAVANNAH	

HARVEY DAN ABRAMS, P.O. Box 13763, ATLANTA, GA 30324. TN: (404) 982 0460. Est: 1966. Appointment necessary. M: A.B.A.A.

K. TILDEN ADAMSON, 1833 WOODROW STREET, AUGUSTA, GA 30904. Spec: obstetrics and gynaecology.

THEODORE G. AHRENDT, 535 MOUNT VISTA ROAD, STONE MOUNTAIN, GA 30087.

W. GRAHAM ARADER III, 1317 BERWICK AVENUE, ATLANTA, GA 30306. TN: (404) 872 5039.

BEST BOOKS, P.O. Box 701, FOLKSTON, GA 31537. Prop: Eugene F. Kramer. TN: (912) 496-2193. Spec: Americana, biography, Military, World Wars I and II, 19th century prints. A.B.A.A.

BOOK SEARCH SERVICE, 36 KENSINGTON ROAD, AVONDALE ESTATES, GA 30002. Prop: Edmond D. Keith. TN: 294-5398. Est: 1953. Private premises, appointment necessary. Very small stock used. Spec: hymnology and books on church music. Cata: on foregoing, 8 a year.

HERB BRIDGES, SHARPSBURG, GA 30277. TN: (404) 253-4934. Est: 1965. Private premises, appointment necessary. Very small stock used, some new. Spec: American and foreign editions of *Gone with the Wind*.

JULIAN BURNETT, P.O. Box 229, ATLANTA, GA 30301. Prop: John Burnett Morris. TN: (404) 252-5812. Est: 1980. Private premises; appointment necessary. Small stock used. Spec: nautical, maritime. Cata.

GEORGE E. CARNAHAN, GREENLEAF LANE, THOMASVILLE, GA 31792. TN: (912) 228-4812. Est: 1981. Private premises; appointment necessary. Very small stock used, also new books. Spec: fox hunting books only.

COOSA VALLEY BOOK SHOP, 15 EAST THIRD AVENUE, ROME, GA 30161. Prop: Mrs. John Grigsby. TN: (404) 234-3253. Est: 1963. Shop. Large stock used, some new. Spec: local history, genealogy, American Indian, Georgia and other Southeastern States. Cata: on foregoing and general, 3-4 a year. A.B.A.

C. DICKENS, 3393 PEACH TREE ROAD NORTH-EAST, ATLANTA, GA.

DOWNS BOOKS, 774 MARY ANN DRIVE, N.E. MARIETTA, GA 30067 Prop: Jack Downs. Shop. Spec: books by or about Joel Chandler Harris; children's. M: Georgia Antiquarian Booksellers' Association.

V. & J. DUNCAN, 137 BULL STREET, SAVANNAH, GA 31401. Prop: Ginger Duncan. Spec: maps and prints.

WILLIAM HARTLEY RARE BOOKS, 3273 TETON DRIVE N.W., ATLANTA, GA 30339.

O.G. LANSFORD, POWERSVILLE, GA 31074. TN: 956-3484. Est: 1924. Mail order only. Large stock used, also new books, Edison springwind phonographs and records. Spec: Edgar Rice Burroughs, Vardis Fisher, Ben Ames Williams.

JACQUELINE LEVINE, 107 E. OGLETHORPE AVENUE, SAVANNAH, GA 31401. Prop: Jacqueline & Stanley Levine. TN: (912) 233-8519. Est: 1938. Private premises, appointment necessary. Medium stock. Spec: Americana, nautical, limited editions, fine bindings, fore-edge paintings. Cata: 2 annually. M: A.B.A.A.

MIDNIGHT BOOK COMPANY, 3929 EBENEZER ROAD, MARIETTA, GA 30066. Prop: H. Dricks. TN: (404) 926-1102. Private premises; appointment necessary. Large stock used. Spec: fantasy, science fiction; first editions.

ROBERT MURPHY, 3113 BUNKER HILL ROAD, MARIETTA, GA 30062. TN: (404) 973-1523. Private premises; appointment necessary. Small stock used. Spec: Civil War and regional Americana.

OLD NEW YORK BOOKSHOP, 1069 JUNIPER STREET NORTH EAST, ATLANTA, GA 30309. Prop: Cliff Graubart. TN: (404) 881-1285. Est: 1970. Very large stock, general. Spec: signed limited editions, first editions.

PEACHTREE BOOKS INC., P.O. Box 54501, ATLANTA, GA 30308. (68 Peachtree Street North West, 2nd floor.) TN: (404) 523-5494. Est: 1940. Shop. Very large stock used; also new books in special fields. Spec: Southern Americana, Georgiana, Civil War; modern first editions. Cata: Georgiana, annually to libraries only.

PRINTED PAGE, 211 WEST JONES STREET, SAVANNAH, GA 31401. Prop: Rita Trotz. Private premises; by appointment or by mail-order only.

SOUTHERN HIGHLANDS BOOKS, 47 WEST PACES FERRY ROAD, ATLANTA, GA 30305. Prop: Frank & Starr Adamson. Shop. General stock sec. and antiq. books. Spec: bestsellers; self-help books; regional cookbooks; children's; war books, esp. Civil War and World War II.

SOUTHERN SEARCH SERVICE, P.O. Box 54404, ATLANTA, GA 30308. Est: 1970. Private premises, storeroom; business by mail only. Medium stock used. Spec: Southern Americana, Civil War. Cata: on foregoing, 1 a year.

STONE MOUNTAIN RELICS INC., 968 MAIN STREET, STONE MOUNTAIN, GA 30083. TN: (404) 469-1425. Store. Spec: Civil War.

YESTERYEAR BOOK SHOP INC., 3201 MAPLE DRIVE NORTH-EAST, ATLANTA, GA 30305. Prop: Frank O. Walsh III & Polly G. Fraser. TN: (404) 237-0163. Shop. Medium stock used. Spec: Americana (Georgia and Southern States); modern first editions; books about books; Civil War history; maps and prints. M: A.B.A.A.

15. HAWAII (HI.)

HILO	KAILUA
HONOLULU	WAILUKU

BOOKFINDERS OF HAWAII, 150 HAILI STREET, HILO, HI 96720. TN: (808) 961-5055. Shop.

SHELBY ANNE FLOYD, 4094 ROUND TOP DRIVE, HONOLULU, HI 96814.

MARY HARTMAN'S BOOKSTORE, 1164, FORT STREET MALL, HONOLULU,. HI 96813. Prop: Mary Lou Hartman. TN: (808) 533-1551. Est: 1978. Shop. Large stock used. Spec: Architecture & related engineering. New books in architecture only.

PACIFIC BOOK HOUSE, KILOHANA SQUARE, 1016-G KAPAHULU AVENUE, HONOLULU, HI 96816. Shop. Large stock used. Spec: Hawaii, Pacific history. Cata: on foregoing and general, irregularly. A.B.A.A.

PRINTS PACIFIC, R.R.I., BOX 276, WAILUKU, MAUI, HI 96793. TN: (808) 244-8171.

SANDWICH ISLAND BOOKS, 125 MERCHANT STREET, HONOLULU, HI 96813. Prop: B. Lee Reeve. Shop. Stock sec. and antiq. books. Spec: Hawaii and South Pacific.

TUSITALA, 116 HEKILI STREET, KAILUA, HI 96734. TN: (808) 262-6343. Shop.

16. IDAHO (ID.)

BOISE   NAMPA

BOISE BOOK MART, 5600 HILL ROAD, BOISE, ID 83703.

THE BOOK SHOP, 908 MAIN STREET, BOISE, ID 83702. Prop: Harry Schuppel & Jean Wilson. TN: (208) 342-2659. Est: 1890. Shop. Small stock used; also new books. Spec: Western Americana.

THE YESTERYEAR SHOPPE, 1211 FIRST STREET SOUTH, NAMPA, ID 83651.

17. ILLINOIS (IL.)

ANTIOCH	ELMHURST
AURORA	EVANSTON
BARRINGTON	GALENA
BERWYN	GALESBURG
BLOOMINGTON	GLENVIEW
BROOKFIELD	HIGHLAND PARK
CHAMPAIGN	LA GRANGE
CHICAGO	LAKE BLUFF
CLARENDON HILLS	LAKE FOREST
DECATUR	LIBERTYVILLE
DEERFIELD	LINCOLN
DOWNERS GROVE	LOMBARD

MACOMB	SCHAUMBURG
MATTOON	SKOKIE
MOLINE	SOUTH HOLLAND
MOUNT PROSPECT	SPRINGFIELD
MOUNT MORRIS	SYCAMORE
NORMAL	TINLEY PARK
OAK PARK	URBANA
OSWEGO	VERNON HILLS
PARIS	VILLA PARK
ROCKFORD	WHEELING
ROLLING MEADOWS	WINTHROP HARBOUR
SAINT CHARLES	

AARIANA'S USED BOOK STORE, 1001 S. WRIGHT STREET, CHAMPAIGN, IL 61820.

ABOUT BOOKS, 3303 35TH AVENUE, P.O. BOX 8409, MOLINE, IL 61265. Prop: Michael Winne. TN: (309) 797-1584. Visits by appointment only; otherwise business by mail order. Large stock. Spec: bibliography; book-collecting; bookbinding; book-selling, paper-making.

ABRAHAM LINCOLN BOOK SHOP, 18E CHESTNUT STREET, CHICAGO, IL 60611. Prop: Daniel Weinberg. TN: (312) 944-3085. Est: 1933. Shop. Medium stock used. Spec: Lincolniana, U.S. Civil War. U.S. Presidency. New books in these fields of specilisation. M: A.B.A.A.

RICHARD ADAMIAK, 1545 EAST 60TH STREET, CHICAGO, IL 60637.

R.H. ADAMS, P.O. BOX 11131, CHICAGO, IL 60611. TN: (312) 327-6542. Spec: Americana; natural history.

JANE ADAMS BOOKSHOP, 208 NORTH NEIL, CHAMPAIGN, CHICAGO, IL 60603. Prop: Nancy Finke & Flora Faraci. Est: 1976. Shop. Small stock used. Spec: Women's Literature, Children's books, Illustrated books. M: A.B.A.

NORMA ADLER, 59 EASTWOOD DRIVE, DEERFIELD, IL 60015. TN: (312) 945-8575.

THE AMERICAN BOTANIST, 3751 Grand Boulevard, Brookfield, IL 60513. Prop: D. Keith Crotz. TN: (312) 485-7805. By appointment only. Spec: horticulture, botany.

W. GRAHAM ARADER III, 110 East Delaware Place, Suite 1504, Chicago, IL 60611. TN: (312) 337 6033.

ARTICLES OF WAR LIMITED, 8806 Bronx Avenue, Skokie, IL 60077-1823. TN: (312) 674-7445. Prop: R. Ruman & M. Cobb. Est: 1964. Shop. Large stock new and used. Spec: military history and related fields. Cata: frequent.

ASPIDISTRA BOOKSHOP, 2630 North Clark St., Chicago, IL 60614.

AVATAR BOOKS, 423 15th Street, Moline, IL 61265. TN: (309) 764-7271.

BANK LANE BOOKS, P.O. Box 782, North Bank Lane, Lake Forest, IL 60045. Prop: Jan Hudson. TN: (312) 234-2912. Est: 1978. Shop. Large stock sec. and antiq. books. Spec: mass media: movies, radio, television. Cata: occasionally. Corresp: Français, Deutsch. B: First Midwest Bank, Lake Forest, IL 60045.

P BARATH BOOKS, P.O. Box 30027, Chicago, IL 60630. Prop: Patricia A. Barath. TN: (312) 777-3573. Est: 1965. Private premises: appointment necessary. Medium stock used. Spec: music: American history; Chicago; hunting and fishing, Cata: bi-monthly.

RICHARD S. BARNES & CO., 821 Foster Street, Evanston, IL 60201. TN: (312) 869-2272. Shop. Large stock used. Spec: history and literature.

BARRINGTON OLD BOOK SHOP, 310 West Northwest Highway, Barrington, IL 60010. Spec: sporting (dogs and horses).

BEASLEY BOOKS, 1533 West Oakdale (2nd Floor) Chicago, IL 60657. Prop: Paul & Elizabeth Garon. TN: (312) 472-4528. Est: 1979. Private premises; appointment necessary. Small stock out-of-print. Spec: modern first editions; science fiction, detective fiction; proletarian literature. Cata: 6 per year. M: A.B.A.A.

THE BIBLIOPHILE, 2146 YALE BOULEVARD, SPRINGFIELD, IL 62703.
Prop: David M. Hunter. TN: (217) 525-0081. Est: 1984. Private
premises, postal business only. Very small stock used; also new books.
Spec: Christianity, history, anthropology. Cata: several times a year.

BLUE DAHLIA BOOKSHOP, 124 BEAUFORT STREET, NORMAL, IL
61761. TN: (309) 452-6014.

BOOKMAN'S ALLEY, 1712 REAR, SHERMAN AVENUE, EVANSTON, IL
60201. TN: (312) 869-6999.

BOOKNOOK PARNASSUS, 2000 MAPLE, EVANSTON, IL 60201. TN:
(312) 475-3445. Store. Spec: Judaica, Jungian psychology.

BOOKSTALL OF ROCKFORD, 606 GREGORY, ROCKFORD, IL 61108.
TN: (815) 963-1671.

THE BOOK STORE, 316 WESTMORELAND DRIVE, VERNON HILLS, IL
60061. Prop: Richard M. KinKaid. TN: (312) 362-2011. Est: 1956.
Private premises, appointment necessary. Medium stock. Spec: Arctic,
Canada, Horses, American Indians, Irish. B: Premier Bank of Vernon
Hills. Account 100774901. Bank of Ireland, Letterkenny, Co. Donegal.
28483788.

JAMES M.W. BORG, INC., 8 S. MICHIGAN, SUITE 401, CHICAGO, IL
60603. TN: (312) 236-5911. TA: Bibliopole, Chicago. Est: 1977. Shop
closed on Saturdays. Small stock used. Spec: British and American
literature. Cata: 4-6 times per year. B: Michigan Avenue National
Bank. Acc.No: 053 703 9.

M. BRANDE BOOKS, 810 EAST FRANKLIN, MACOMB, IL 61455.

THOMAS BRISCH, 304 SOUTH MAIN STREET, GALENA, IL 61036. TN
(815) 777-0814. Medium stock sec. and antiq. Spec: American
Mid-West and West.

BERTRAM W. BROWN, 4927 SOUTH SEELEY AVENUE, CHICAGO, IL
60609. TN: (312) 778-1799. Est: 1936. Private premises; appointment
necessary. Medium stock used; also remainders. Spec: Illinois. Cata:
Americana occasionally.

J.R. BURDETT & R.E. STOKER, P.O. Box 77, LOMBARD, IL 60148. (21W470 Burdett Road.) TN: (312) 629-0223 and 469-3647. Est: 1962. Storeroom; appointment necessary. Medium stock used.

BURKWOOD BOOKS, Box 172, URBANA, IL 61801. TN: (217) 344-1419. Shop. Western Americana.

THOMAS W. BURROWS, P.O. Box 400, DOWNERS GROVE, IL 60515. TN: (312) 960-1028. Private premises; business by mail only. Medium stock used. Spec: history, literature, classical antiquity, religion. Cata: Occasionally.

RICHARD CADY — RARE BOOKS, 1927 NORTH HUDSON AVENUE, CHICAGO, IL 60614. TN: (312) 944-0856. Est: 1980. Private premises, appointment necessary. Small stock. Spec: Rare books and autographs, first editions, fine bindings, the English Nineties, fine printing, press books; bibliography. B: Mid-town Bank and Trust, Chicago.

CANDLELIGHT BOOKSHOP, 112 CHICAGO ROAD, (RT.34) OSWEGO, IL 60543. TN: (312) 554-3199. Private premises; appointment necessary.

CANTERBURY BOOKSHOP, 63 EAST ADAMS STREET (ROOM 300), CHICAGO, IL 60603. Prop: J.F. von Berg. TN: (312) 939-2923. Est: 1962. Shop. Large stock used; also publishers. Spec: literary biography and criticism, the arts, out of print fiction, books on books, Chicago and Illinois history. A.B.A.A.

JOHN E. CHANDLER, 3454 NORTH SOUTHPORT, CHICAGO, IL 60657. TN: (312) 929-8298.

GERALD J. CIELEC, 2248 NORTH KEDVALE AVENUE, CHICAGO, IL 60639. TN: (312) 235-2326. Private premises; postal business only. Small stock used. Spec: Americana.

CHESTNUT COURT BOOKSHOP, INC., 411 NORTH WOLF ROAD, WHEELING, IL 60090.

COGITATOR BOOKS, P.O. Box 405, LIBERTYVILLE, IL 60048. Prop: Donald V. & Jackie Vento. Est: 1964. Medium stock used. Spec: literary, Americana, History, Biography. A.B.A.A.

OWEN DAVIES, 200 WEST HARRISON STREET, OAK PARK, IL 60304. Prop: Thomas R. Bullard. TN: (312) 848-1186. Est: 1929. Shop. Small stock used, also new books. Spec: railroad and maritime history. Cata: 6 a year.

DOWD'S BOOK SHOPPE, 16 NORTH FIRST AVENUE, SAINT CHARLES, IL 60174. TN: (312) 584-1930. Est: 1974. Private premises, appointment necessary. Small stock used. Spec: Chicago & Illinois, Indians, West, also colour plate and Literary biography. Cata: Once a year. New books also. B: State Bank of St. Charles. M: Fox Valley Booksellers Assn.

JANE DUNNE, 1209 NORTH ASTOR STREET, CHICAGO, IL 60610. TN: (312) 664-0231. Printed works on food and wine. Cata: Issued.

EDENROCK BOOKS, 42720 NORTH HUNT CLUB ROAD, ANTIOCH, IL 60002. Prop: John Swan. TN: (312) 395-7069.

FIRST IMPRESSIONS, 26 WEST 580 BUTTERFIELD ROAD, WHEATON, IL 60187. TN: (312) 668-9418.

MICHAEL R. FLEISCHHACKER, 1642 NORTH FAIRFIELD AVENUE, CHICAGO, IL 60647. TN: ARmitage 6-4512. Mail order only. Spec: dictionaries.

D.J. FLYNN BOOKS, 421 EAST WESTLEIGH ROAD, LAKE FOREST, IL 60045. TN: (312) 234-1146. (Formerly at Bank Lane Books.)

FOLLETT COLLEGE BOOK CO., 1000 WEST WASHINGTON BOULEVARD, CHICAGO, IL 60607. TN: (312) M06-5859. Cables: Wilfol, Chicago. Telex: 25 3225. Warehouse and offices open normal business hours. Stock of six million volumes new and used. Spec: college textbooks. N.A.C.S.

FUR, FIN, FEATHER BOOKS, P.O. BOX 326, SOUTH HOLLAND, IL 60473.

HERBERT FURSE, 1461 BAFFIN ROAD, GLENVIEW, IL 60025. TN: (312) 724-4594.

GALLERY BOOKSHOP, 404 NORTH CLARK STREET, CHICAGO, IL 60610.

THE GAME BAG, 973 NORTH PRINCETON, VERNON HILLS, IL 60061. TN: (312) 362-6562. Spec: hunting, fishing, etc.

CAROL HACKER BOOKS, 5 SHAGBARK ROAD, ROLLING MEADOWS, IL 60008. TN: (312) 387-3896.

HAMILL & BARKER, 400 NORTH MICHIGAN AVENUE, CHICAGO, IL 60611. TN: (312) 644-5933. Spec: first editions, autographs, early illustrated books, incunabula. Closed July and August. A.B.A.A.

HANLEY'S BOOK SHOP, 1750 WEST JARVIS AVENUE, CHICAGO, IL 60660.

HISTORICAL NEWSPAPERS AND JOURNALS, 9850 KEDVALE-SKOKIE, IL 60076. Prop: Steve & Linda Alsberg. TN: (312) 676-9850. Est: 1976. Private premises; appointment necessary. Medium stock newspapers and magazines. Spec: historical papers and documents; maps, atlases and engravings.

KING V. HOSTICK, 901 SOUTH COLLEGE STREET, SPRINGFIELD, IL 62704. TN: (217) 544-8283. Est: 1940. Appointment necessary. Stock of rare books and manuscripts. Cata: occasionally.

JACKS USED BOOKS, 718 EAST NORTHWEST HIGHWAY, MOUNT PROSPECT, IL 60056. Prop: Jack Huggard. TN: (312) 398-7767. Est: 1975. Shop. Large stock used. Spec: First editions, modern and history, and mysteries.

JEWISH BOOKMART, 127 NORTH DEARBORN STREET, CHICAGO, IL 60602.

THOMAS J. JOYCE AND COMPANY, 431 SOUTH DEARBORN, CHICAGO, IL 60605. Prop: Thomas J. Joyce. TN: (312) 922-0980. Est: 1974. Office, business hours (please telephone to confirm) and by appointment. Small stock sec. and antiq. Spec: books about books; Americana; literary first editions; law; printing. Cata: 4 a year. B: Standard Chartered. M: A.B.A.A., I.L.A.B., Midwest Bookhunters.

DOROTHY V. KECK, 1360 WEST RIVERVIEW, DECATUR, IL 62522. TN: (217) 428-5100. Est: 1968. Mail order only. Medium stock used.

E.F. KEENAN, 506 NORTH AVENUE, LAKE BLUFF, IL 60044. TN: (312) 234-5054.

KENNEDY'S BOOKS, 1307 ROSALIE STREET, EVANSTON, IL 60201. Prop: Ashley Kennedy. Manager: Joan Kennedy Wilson. TN: (312) 475-2481. Est: 1962. Private premises, appointment necessary. Large stock used. A.B.A.A.

JOYCE KLEIN, NORTH BOULEVARD ANTIQUES CENTRE, 818 NORTH BOULEVARD, OAK PARK, IL 60304. TN: (312) 383-3033.

EDGAR KREBS, 5849 N. TALMAN AVENUE, CHICAGO, IL 60659. TN: (312) 275-4611. Est: 1945. Private premises, appointment necessary. Large stock used. Spec: humanities.

KROCH'S & BRENTANO'S, 29 SOUTH WABASH AVENUE, CHICAGO, IL 60603. Prop: Carl A. Kroch. TN: (312) 332-7500. Est: 1907. Shop. Medium stock used, also new. A.B.A.A.

N.L. LAIRD, 1240 WEST JARVIS, CHICAGO, IL 60626. TN: (312) 761-4380.

A. LARSEN, 400 SPRING STREET, GALENA, IL 61036. Medium stock sec. and antiq.

J. STEPHEN LAWRENCE, 1301 S. WABASH, CHICAGO, IL 60605.

LEEKLEY BOOK SEARCH, 711 SHERIDAN ROAD, WINTHROP HARBOR, IL 60096. Prop: Brian Leekley. TN: (312) 872-2311. Est: 1961. Shop, closed on Mondays. Large stock used. Spec: Out of print scholarly books in literature, history, social sciences, the humanities, etc. Search service. Occasional sales lists. B: Bank of Waukegan, Illinois. M: A.B.A.A.

LEFT BANK BOOKSTALL, 104 SOUTH OAK PARK AVENUE, OAK PARK, IL 60302. Prop: Carol Zientek & Carole Goodwin. TN: (312) 383-4700. Est: 1978. Shop. Medium stock used, also speciality and small press new books.

RICHARD LOBIN RARE BOOKS, 21 KRISTIN DRIVE, SUITE 412, SCHAUMBURG, IL 60195. TN: (312) 310 9453.

THE LONDON BOOKSHOP, 79 WEST MONROE STREET (SUITE 1122), CHICAGO, IL 60603. Prop: Glen Norman Wiche. TN: (312) 782-2261. Est: 1974. Shop. Small stock. Spec: British history and literature; prints. Cata: occasionally.

J. McGOVERN, 1831 SOUTH HARVEY, BERWYN, IL 60402. TN: (312) 484-8499. Est: 1963. Private premises, appointment necessary. Small stock used. Spec: fantasy, science fiction. Cata: on foregoing, occasionally.

MAGIC INC., 5082 NORTH LINCOLN AVENUE, CHICAGO, IL 60625. Prop: Jay Marshall & David C. Meyer. TN: (312) 334-2855. Spec: conjuring, playing cards, Street entertainers, marionettes, Punch and Judy. A.B.A.A.

CLAIRE MAGEE, 16840 ELM LANE DRIVE, TINLEY PARK, IL 60477. TN: (312) 532-2098. Est: 1965. Private premises; appointment necessary. Very small stock used; also a few new.

ANTHONY MAITA, 813 GREENWOOD ROAD, GLENVIEW, IL 60025. Spec: Military books.

MARSHALL FIELD AND COMPANY, 111 NORTH STATE STREET, CHICAGO, IL 60690. TN: (312) 781-4281. Rare Book Dept. Est: 1930. Department store. Medium stock used, also new. Spec: 18th and 19th century English and American literature, fine bindings, manuscripts, letters, early maps and prints. A.B.A.A.

JOHN WM. MARTIN—BOOKSELLER, 231 SOUTH LA GRANGE ROAD, LA GRANGE, IL 60525. TN: (312) 352-8115. Est: 1973. Private premises, appointment necessary. Small stock used. Spec: British & American Literature 18th-20th Century. Cata: 5 per year. B: Continental. Acc.No: 66-27528.

MUNSON BOOKS, 3436 WILLOW DRIVE, MATTOON, IL 61938.

KENNETH NEBENZAHL, INC., 333 NORTH MICHIGAN AVENUE, CHICAGO, IL 60601. TN: (312) 641-2711. Cables: Nebenbooks Chicago. Est: 1957. Shop. Spec: rare Americana, voyages, atlases, maps, manuscripts, American historical prints. Cata: on foregoing, several a year. A.B.A.A. I.L.A.B.

JACK L. NELSON, 1693 ROBERTSON AVENUE, GALESBURG, IL 61401.

RALF GEOFFREY NEWMAN INC., 175 EAST DELAWARE PLACE, CHICAGO, IL 60611.

NORTHWEST BOOK AUCTION, 3 BLODGETT, CLARENDON HILLS, IL 60514.

JOSEPH O'GARA, 1311 EAST 57th STREET, CHICAGO, IL 60637. TN: (312) 363-0993. Est: 1937. Shop and storeroom. Stock of 150,000 volumes used and antiq. Spec: history; literature; fine arts. A.B.A.A. A.B.A. (Int.)

J.E. PEARSON, P.O. BOX 446, CHICAGO, IL 60690. (5255 South California, Chicago, IL 60632.) TN: (312) 776-9566. Est: 1970. Private premises; appointment necessary. Stock primarily out-of-print; also new books. Spec: aviation; military; railroad; buses and trolley-coaches (especially articulated buses). Cata: on foregoing, occasionally.

POWELL'S BOOKSHOP, 1501 E. 57TH STREET, CHICAGO, IL 60637.

POWELL'S BOOK WAREHOUSE, 8TH FLOOR, 1020 S. WABASH AVENUE, CHICAGO, IL 60605.

PRAIRIE ARCHIVES BOOKSELLERS, P.O. BOX 2264, 641 WEST MONROE, SPRINGFIELD, IL 62704. TN: (217) 522-9742.

PRAIRIE AVENUE BOOKSHOP, 711 SOUTH DEARBORN STREET, CHICAGO, IL 60605.

A. AND A. PROSSER, BOOKSELLERS, 3118 NORTH KEATING AVENUE, CHICAGO, IL 60641. TN: (312) 685-7680. Est: 1936. Private premises and storeroom, appointment necessary. Large stock used. Spec: Pre-Vatican II Catholic authors: Chesterton, Belloc, Newman etc. Cata: At irregular intervals. B: Community Savings and Loan Association, Chicago.

THE PUTMAN BOOKSHOP, 305, SOUTH MCLEAN STREET, BLOOMINGTON, IL 61801. Prop: Ruth Putman. TN: (309) 827-6574. Est: 1934. Private premises, appointment necessary. Large stock used. Spec: Lincolniana, Illinois History, Americana, Literature, O.P. titles. Cata: 1 or 2 annually. B: National Bank of Bloomington, Acct. No: 170-460.

GEORGE RITZLIN BOOKS AND MAPS, P.O. BOX A3398, CHICAGO, IL 60690. Prop: George Ritzlin. TN: (312) 528-6228. Est: 1977. Stock can only be seen by appointment. Medium stock. Spec: antiquarian maps, atlases, books about maps, voyages and travel. Cata: Occasionally. Some new map reference books also kept. B: Dai-Ichi Kangyo Bank, Chicago Branch. M: A.B.A.A.

RICHARD OWEN ROBERTS, BOOKSELLERS, 5N740 DUNHAM ROAD, SAINT CHARLES, IL 60174. TN: (312) 584-8069. Est: 1962. Shop and storeroom. Very large stock used; also new books. Spec: religion and theology. Cata: on foregoing, 4 a year.

ROGER'S PARK USED BOOKSTORE, 1422 WEST MORSE AVENUE, CHICAGO, IL 60660.

PAUL ROHE & SONS, 2002 CENTRAL ST., EVANSTON, IL 60202.

JOHN RYBSKI, 2319 West 47th Place, Chicago, IL 60609. TN: (312) 847-5082. Est: 1968. Private premises, appointment necessary. Large stock used. Spec: Latin America, American history, social sciences. Cata: on foregoing, 2-3 a year.

C.E. SANDSTROM, 310 Emily, Mount Morris, IL 61054.

SELECTED WORKS, 3619 North Broadway, Chicago, IL 60613. Prop: Keith Peterson. TN: (312) 975-0002. Shop, open afternoons Tuesday, Wednesday and Thursday and all day Friday to Monday.

HARRY L. STERN, Suite 206, 1 North Wacken Drive, Chicago, IL 60606. TN: (312) 372-0388.

STONEHILL'S BOOKS, 611 South Wright Street, Champaign, IL 61820. Prop: Allan L. Steinberg. TN: (217) 359-2607. Est: 1975. Shop. Medium stock used. Spec: Americana; anthropology. Cata: occasionally.

STORYBOOK ANTIQUES AND BOOKS, 1325 East State Street, Sycamore, IL 60178. TN: (815) 895-5910. Shop.

JOHN E. SWAN, 42720 North Hunt Club Road, Antioch, IL 60002. TN: (312) 395-7069.

T. A. SWINFORD, Box 93, Paris, IL 61944. TN: (217) 465-5182. Shop. Spec: Western Americana.

SULLIVAN SPORTING BOOKS, 3748 North Damen Avenue, Chicago, IL 60618. Prop: John Sullivan. TN: (312) GR 2-2638. Est: 1957. Private premises, open normal business hours. Very small stock used. Spec: baseball, football. Cata: on foregoing and hockey, 2 a year.

HELENA SZEPE, 1525 East 53rd Street (Suite 902), Chicago, IL. TN: (312) 493-4470. Private premises, appointment necessary.

PHYLLIS THOLIN, 824 Ridge Terrace, Evanston, IL 60201. TN: (312) 475-1174. Private premises, appointment necessary.

TITLES, INC., 1931 Sheridan Road, Highland Park, IL 60035. Prop: Florence Shay. TN: (312) 432-3690. Est: 1972. Shop. Medium stock. Spec: All categories of rare, fine and first editions. Cata: Annually. B: First National Bank of Highland Park, Ill. M: A.B.A.A.

VAN NORMAN BOOK COMPANY, 422-424 BANK OF GALESBURG BUILDING, GALESBURG, IL 61401. Prop: C.E. Van Norman, Sr. Est: 1928. Office, appointment necessary. Large stock used. Spec: Americana. Cat: Americana, American literature, 2-5 a year.

VINTAGE VOLUMES, 1451 HULL DRIVE, WHEATON, IL 60187. TN: (312) 690-8749.

MARY WEHLER, 244 SOUTH ELMWOOD DRIVE, AURORA, IL 60506. TN: (312) 896-0169.

BERN WHEEL, BOOKS, 834 WENONAH AVENUE, OAK PARK, IL 60304. Est: 1972. Private premises; postal business only. Spec: New and Used Esperanto Books and Magazines.

YELLOWSTONE BOOKS, P.O. BOX 69, VILLA PARK, IL 60181. TN: (312) 627-9175.

YE OLDE BOOK WORM, 161 NORTH YORK ROAD, ELMHURST, IL 60126. Prop: Dale & Ann Brownewell. TN: (312) 279-0123. Shop, closed Sunday and Monday. General stock sec. and antiq. books, also new.

YESTERYEAR, 420 LINCOLN AVENUE, LINCOLN, IL 62656.

18. INDIANA (IN.)

ANDERSON	LA PORTE
BLOOMINGTON	MUNCLE
CHESTERTON	SOUTH BEND
DECATUR	TERRE HAUTE
DYER	VALPARAISO
ELKHART	WEST LAFAYETTE
FORT WAYNE	ZIONSVILLE
INDIANAPOLIS	

THE ABSTRACT, 5538 NORTH PENNSYLVANIA STREET, INDIANAPOLIS, IN 46220.

ALMAGIE BOOKS, 3271 SPRING BRANCH ROAD, BLOOMINGTON, IN 47401. TN: (812) 334-0465.

AMERICANA BOOKS, P.O. Box 243, DECATUR, IN 46733. (144 South Second Street.) Prop: David G. MacLean. Est: 1956. Small stock used. Spec: Americana. Cata: 6 to 10 a year. (During the winter months address is: P.O. Box 481, Pinellas Park, FL 33565.)

BACK TRACTS, INC., P.O. Box 30008, INDIANAPOLIS, IN 46220. Prop: Joan H. Morris. TN: (317) 257-3686. Est: 1975. Shop, closed on Mondays. Medium stock used. Spec: Indiana history and literature, Cookbooks, Women. Cata: Occasionally. B: Indiana National Bank. Acc. No: 10-024-506.

BARNETTE'S, 22727 ADAMS ROAD, SOUTH BEND, IN 46628. TN: (219) 272-9880. Appointment necessary. Spec: the Colonies, American Revolution, War of 1812, the old Northwest Territory.

BOOKS BELOW, 1625 NORTH 8th STREET, TERRE HAUTE, IN 47804. Prop: Elizabeth H. Bevington. TN: (812) 234-8989. Private premises, appointment necessary. Medium stock used.

BOOKSTACK, 112 WEST LEXINGTON AVENUE, ELKHART, IN 46514.

BROAD RIPPLE BOOKSHOP, 6407 FERGUSON STREET, INDIANAPOLIS, IN 46220.

CAVEAT EMPTOR, 208 SOUTH DUNN, BLOOMINGTON, IN 47401. Props: James A. Rock, Janis Starcs, Don Wilds. TN: (812) 332-9995. Est: 1971. Shop. Very large stock used; also new books and collectibles, phonograph albums and stationery. Spec: science fiction, fantasy, comics; Indiana authors; 19th and 20th century British and American authors. Cata: 2 to 4 a year. A.B.A.

CORNER CUPBOARD COOKBOOKS, P.O.Box 171, ZIONSVILLE, IN 46077. Prop: Helen L. Jump TN: (317) 255-6153. Est: 1976. Shop, but appointment advisable. Small stock used; also special interest new books. Spec: regional cookbooks.

COUNTRY BOOKSHELF, P.O. Box 372, RR1, CHESTERTON, IN 46304.

FOREST PARK BOOK SHOP, 1412 DELAWARE, FORT WAYNE, IN 46805. Prop: L.M. Morris. TN: (219) 424-1058. Est: 1970. Shop, closed on Mondays. Large stock used. Spec: Americana, Indiana, Illustrated, Mystery and Detective. B: Summit Bank, Fort Wayne.

A HOOSIER SCHOOLMASTER'S BOOKS, 1228 MICHIGAN AVENUE, LA PORTE, IN 46350. Prop: G. Linnemann. Est: 1960. Mail order only. Medium stock used, some new. Spec: books about Indiana or by Hoosiers, American Presidents, American literature, Indians. Cata: on foregoing and general, occasionally.

WILLIAM S. JOHNSON, 829 EAST DR. WOODRUFF PLACE, INDIANAPOLIS, IN 46201. TN: (812) 639-1256. Est: 1964. Private premises, appointment necessary. Small stock used. Spec: literary criticism, humanities, Russian literature, Orientalia, fantasy.

MIDNIGHT BOOKMAN, 237 SCHILLING, WEST LAFAYETTE, IN 47906.

ODDS AND EADS, 1127 PROSPECT, INDIANAPOLIS, IN 46203. Prop: Hereford & Winona Eads. TN: (317) 635-2592. Stockroom open normal business hours. Very large stock used, also a few new books.

KATHLEEN RAIS BOOKS, 612 NORTH DUNN, BLOOMINGTON, IN 47401. TN: (812) 336-7687. Est: 1978. Private premises; appointment necessary. Very small stock used, also occasionally new books. Spec: fine and rare books on the dog, field, sporting; A.P. Terhune.

G. JAY RAUSCH, BOX 2346, BLOOMINGTON, IN 47402. TN: (812) 333-1178. Est: 1981. Private premises, appointment necessary. Large stock sec. and antiq. Spec: searches for libraries. Cata: 4 a year. B: First National Bank of Bloomington, P.O.B. 608, Bloomington; and Lloyds Bank, 48-50 Minories, London EC3N 1JE.

ROLLIN KING, LONG AGO BOOKS, 800 UMBARGER, MUNCLE, IN 47304.

WILLIAM SUTFIN—BOOKS, P.O. BOX 16144, INDIANAPOLIS, IN 46216. Medium stock used. Spec: children's; western Americana; social sciences.

THE USED BOOK PLACE, 2027 HART ST., P.O. BOX 206, DYER, IN 46311.

DON WALKER, 3302 EAST 38th STREET, ANDERSON, IN 46013.

WALLACE M. WOJTKOWSKI, 257 LOCUST ST., VALPARAISO, IN 46383.

19.   IOWA (IA.)

19.   IOWA (IA.)

AKRON	MAQUOKETA
CEDAR RAPIDS	MARION
DAVENPORT	OTTUMWA
DES MOINES	WINTHROP
IOWA CITY	

ABLE BEAM BOOKS, P.O. Box 3771, Davenport, IA 52808. Prop: George Pekios, 2515 Iowa Street, Davenport. TN: (316) 323-7262. Private premises; appointment necessary. Small stock used. Spec: Greek culture, Classical, Hellenistic, Byzantine, Modern.

ANDROMEDA BOOK SHOP, 111 East Platt, Maquoketa, IA 52060. Prop: David Lawrence Rosheim. TN: (319) 652-5694. Est: 1976. Shop. Very large stock used; also a few selected new books. Spec: history; science fiction.

KARL ARMENS, 621 Walnut Street, Iowa City, IA 52240.

BROKEN KETTLE BOOKS, R.R.1, Akron, IA 51001. Prop: Eldon J. Bryant. TN: (712) 568-2114. Est: 1965. Private premises, appointment necessary. Medium stock used. Spec: trade catalogues and manufacturer's literature for farm machinery, airplane, motorcycle. Cata: Occasional lists. B: First National Bank, LeMars, Iowa.

EL-ZAR BOOK BAR, P.O. Box 1904, Cedar Rapids, IA 52406. Prop: Jannette A. & John H. Nehl. TN: (319) 396-3444. Private premises; appointment necessary. Small stock used; also new books. Spec: horses, driving, coaching, riding. Cata: 4 a year.

R. RUSSELL ERNEST, 22455 N. Court Street, Ottumwa, IA 52501.

WILLIAM A. GRAF, 717 Clark Street, Iowa City, IA 52240. Prop: William & Mary Graf. TN: (319) 337-7748. Est: 1969. Storeroom, appointment necessary. Medium stock used, some new. Spec: General Custer, U.S. Army, Iowa, books about books. Cata: general, monthly.

THE HAUNTED BOOKSHOP, 227 South Johnson, Iowa City, IA 52240. TN: (319) 337-2996. Shop. Closed Sundays.

150

MIKE MADDIGAN, BOX 824, CEDAR RAPIDS, IA 52406. TN: (319) 363-4821. Private premises; appointment necessary. Very small stock used. Spec: Torch Press.

PAULINE MILLEN, BOOKS, 3325 CRESCENT DRIVE, DES MOINES, IA 50312. TN: (515) 255-1588. Est: 1965. Private premises; appointment necessary. Medium stock used. Spec: Americana, Iowa, Mid-west, West; private press; maps and prints. Cata: on foregoing, 1 a year.

MURPHY-BROOKFIELD BOOKS, 219 NORTH GILBERT, IOWA CITY, IA 52240. TN: (319) 338-3077. Shop, closed Mondays.

PIERCE BOOK COMPANY, WINTHROP, IA 50682. Prop: Mr. & Mrs. Fred J. Pierce. TN: (319) 935-3361. Est: 1944. Shop. Small stock used, also new books. Spec: Natural History. Cata: twice a year.

PRAIRIE LIGHTS BOOKS, 15 SOUTH DUBUQUE STREET, IOWA, IA 52240. TN: (319) 337-2681.

SELECTED WORKS, 610 SOUTH DUBUQUE, IOWA CITY, IA 52240. TN: (319) 337-9700.

O.G. WAFFLE BOOK CO., MARION, IA 52302.

20. KANSAS (KS.)

GOFF	SHAWNEE MISSION
LAWRENCE	TOPEKA
PRAIRIE VILLAGE	WICHITA

ADVENTURE, 1010 MASSACHUSETTS STREET, LAWRENCE, KS 66044.

AL'S OLD AND NEW BOOK STORE, 1710 WEST DOUGLAS, WICHITA, KS 67203.

GREAT PLAINS BOOK COMPANY, GOFF, KS 66428. TN: (913) 939-4575.

GREEN DRAGON BOOKSTORE, 2730 BOULEVARD PLAZA, P.O. BOX 17338, WICHITA, KS 67217. Prop: Charles & Larue Basom. TN: (316) 681-0746. Est: 1973. Shop. Large stock used. Spec: U.S. history, aviation, biography, fine and rare. Boulevard State Bank.

20. KANSAS (KS.)

J. HOOD, BOOKSELLERS, 1401, MASSACHUSETTS, LAWRENCE, KS 66044. TN: (913) 841-4644. Est. 1973. Shop. Large stock used, out-of-print, scholarly. Spec: history; music; religion; psychology; philosophy; literary criticism.

S. JACOBS, RURAL ROUTE 6, P.O. BOX 264, TOPEKA, KS 66608. (3240 North West 25th Street.) TN: (913) 233-7049. Est: 1970. Shop and storeroom: appointment preferable. Medium stock used. Spec: first editions, literary periodicals. Cata: first editions literature, rare books, 6 a year.

T.N. LUTHER, P.O. BOX 6083, SHAWNEE MISSION, KS 66206. TN: (913) 381-9619. Private premises, appointment necessary. Est: 1962. Medium stock used, a few new. Spec: Western Americana, American Indians. Cata: on foregoing, 4-6 a year.

THE NEMAHA BOOKSELLERS, GOFF, KS 66428. Prop: S. Jacobs & Daniela Lang. TN: (913) 939-2192. Est: 1976. Private premises, appointment necessary. Medium stock used. Spec: Kansas, Western Americana and General. Cata: 4 annually on Kansas and W. Americana; other subjects occasionally.

R & B BOOKS, GOFF, KS 66428. Prop: H. Catlin Beal. TN: (913) 939-2130. Est: 1977. Private premises, appointment necessary. Very small stock used. Spec: Music, Americana, Scholarly non-fiction. Cata: Occasionally.

WHISTLER'S BOOKS, 5316 WEST 95TH ST., PRAIRIE VILLAGE, KS 66207.

21. **KENTUCKY (KY.)**

COVINGTON   LEXINGTON
HOPKINSVILLE   LOUISVILLE

CYNTHIA K. FOWLER BOOKS, 4101 STONE VIEW DRIVE (APT. 4), LOUISVILLE, KY 40207. TN: (502) 896-2079.

W.C. GATES, BOOKS, 1279 BARDSTOWN ROAD, LOUISVILLE, KENTUCKY 40204. TN: (502) 451-8386. Est: 1937. Shop—not open to the public. Spec: Kentuckiana, Americana, First Editions. Cata: Lists issued on request for specific author, title or subject. B: Citizens Fidelity Bank & Trust Co. M: A.B.A.A.

GLOVER'S BOOKS, 862 SOUTH BROADWAY, LEXINGTON, KY 40586. Prop: John T. Glover. TN: (606) 253-0614. Est: 1976. Shop. Very large stock sec. and antiq. Spec: Americana, Kentucky; horse racing. Cata: 2 a year.

LEGACY BOOK STORE, 1916 BARDSTOWN ROAD, LOUISVILLE, KY 40705. Prop: Jeff Dean. Spec: Kentucky and Kentucky-related material; modern first editions; U.S. Civil War.

G.T. McWHORTER—RARE BOOKS, 1425 SAINT JAMES COURT, LOUISVILLE, KY 40208.

OLD LOUISVILLE BOOKS, 426 WEST OAK ST., LOUISVILLE, KY 40203.

PENNYROYAL BOOKS, 2538 COX MILL ROAD, HOPKINSVILLE, KY 42240. Prop: D.D. Cayce III. TN: (502) 885-9609. Est: 1958. Private premises; appointment necessary. Very small stock used. Spec: Kentucky history and related subjects.

PHILATELIC BIBLIOPOLE, P.O. Box 36006, LOUISVILLE, KY 40233. Prop: Leonard H. Hartmann. TN: (502) 451-0317. Est: 1965. Private premises; appointment necessary. Large stock used; also new books. Spec: authoritative philatelic literature only.

DON SMITH, 3930 RANKIN STREET, LOUISVILLE, KY 40214.

T & S BOOKS, 1545 SCOTT BOULEVARD, COVINGTON, KY 41014. Prop: Dan Nagle. TN: 261-6435. Shop. Large stock.

22. LOUISIANA (LA.)

BATON ROUGE	SHREVEPORT
GRETNA	SLIDELL
NEW ORLEANS	

ARK-LA-TEX BOOK COMPANY, P.O. Box 564, SHREVEPORT, LA 71162. (525 Marshall Street.) Prop: L.S. Hooper. TN: 221-6820. Est: 1951. Storeroom, appointment necessary. Small stock used, also coins, stamps, letters, maps, ephemera. Spec: Louisiana, South, Confederate.

BAYOU BOOKS, 1005 MONROE STREET, GRETNA, LA 70053. Prop: Milburn Calhoun. TN: (504) 368-1171. Est: 1961. Shop. Large stock used, also new. Spec: Louisiana and Lower Mississippi Valley. A.B.A.

BECKHAM'S BOOK SHOP, 228 DECATUR STREET, NEW ORLEANS, LA 70130. TN: (504) 522-9875. Shop. Large stock used. Spec: local history (Louisiana and New Orleans).

CITY BOOK AND COIN STORE, 521 CROCKETT ST., SHREVEPORT, LA 71101.

CLAITOR'S LAW BOOKS AND PUBLISHING DIVISION INC., P.O. BOX 3333, BATON ROUGE, LA 70821. (3165 South Acadian Street I-10.). Prop: Robert G. Claitor. Est: 1920. TN: DI 3-9506. Shop. Stock of about 100,000 used law books, 20,000 other used books, also new. Spec: Law. Cata: law, 1 a year, charged $1.00 A.B.A. A.B.A.A.

TAYLOR CLARK'S, INC., 2623 GOVERNMENT STREET, BATON ROUGE, LA 70806. Prop: Taylor Clark, Jr. TN: (504) 383-4929. Est: 1935. Shop. Small stock used, some new. Spec: color-plate books. Cata: general books, prints and paintings, 1 a year. A.B.A.A.

A COLLECTOR'S BOOKSHOP, 3119 MAGAZINE ST., NEW ORLEANS, LA 70115. TN: (504) 899-7016. M: A.B.A.A.

CORONET BOOK SHOP, 1622 FRONT STREET, SLIDELL, LA 70458. Prop: Cecil Davis. TN: (504) 643-6740. Est: 1942. Shop. Medium stock used; also new books. Spec: cat books, Americana, occult. A.B.A.

De VILLE BOOKS AND PRINTS, 32 CORONDELET STREET, NEW ORLEANS, LA 70130. TN: (504) 522-2363.

HARRIS FINE PRINTS, 3726 GOVERNMENT ST., BATON ROUGE, LA 70806. TN: (504) 387-1344.

LIBRAIRIE BOOKSHOP, 823 CHARTRES STREET, NEW ORLEANS, LA 70116. Prop: Carey Beckham. TN: (504) 525-4837. Est: 1967. Shop. Large stock used; also a few specialized new. Spec: local history (New Orleans and Louisiana). A.B.A.

OLD BOOKS, 811 ROYAL STREET, NEW ORLEANS, LA 70116. Shop.

J. RAYMOND SAMUEL LIMITED, 2727 Prytania Street, New Orleans, LA 70130. TN: (504) 891-9061. Shop. Large stock sec. and antiq. Spec: New Orleans, Mississippi River, Deep South.

SOUTHERN BOOK MART, 742 Royal Street, New Orleans 16, LA. Prop: Mrs. Edyth Renaud. TN: RAymond 6835. Est: 1937. Shop. Medium stock used. Spec: Americana, color-plates, maps, fine bindings.

TALIESSINS'S BOOKS, 3054 Perkins Road, Baton Rouge, LA 70808. Prop: Lindon Stall; J.G. & C.B. Gilbert. TN: (504) 343-1266. Est: 1978. Shop. Medium stock used, also new books. Spec: Anglo-Catholic, Literature, Louisiana. B: Louisiana National Bank.

23. MAINE (ME.)

BELGRADE	LEWISTON
BREWER	MADISON
BRUNSWICK	MANCHESTER
BUCKFIELD	MOUNT VERNON
CAMDEN	NEW GLOUCESTER
CAPE ELIZABETH	NORTH BERWICK
CASTINE	PENOBSCOT
DENMARK	PORTLAND
EDGECOMB	SOUTH CHINA
ELIOT	SOUTHWEST HARBOR
ELLSWORTH	SPRINGVALE
EUSTIS	SPRUCE HEAD
FREEPORT	STOCKTON SPRINGS
GARDINER	WELLS
HALLOWELL	WESTBROOK
KENNEBUNK	YARMOUTH

ACADIA BOOK SERVICE, Box 244, Castine, ME 04421. Prop: John & Gloria Artz. TN: (207) 326-8672. Open June—September 9.00 a.m. to 5 p.m. Spec: Marine, Children's books and General non-fiction.

AMERICAN ANTIQUE PAPER AND PRINTS, 2 Hemlock Hill Road, Cape Elizabeth, ME 04107. Prop: Milo Matrazzo. TN: (207) 799-7182 or 774-7861. Mail or appointment only. Spec: Old & rare American Sporting Prints, Books, Advertising, Broadsides, Posters, Periodicals & Art Objects.

BEDFORD'S USED BOOKS, 54 HIGH STREET, ELLSWORTH, ME 04605. Prop: Bedford Riggs. TN: (207) 667-7308. Est: 1978. Shop. Very large stock used books including 15,000 paperbacks.

LILLIAN BERLIAWSKY, 23 BAY VIEW STREET, CAMDEN, ME 04843. TN: (207) 236-3903. Spec: Americana, European history, biography, music, the arts. A.B.A.A.

THE BOOKBARN, 286 MAIN STREET, SPRINGVALE, ME 04083. Prop: Allen Scott. TN: (207) 324-8255. Shop. September to May appointment necessary. June, July, August 9 a.m. to 10.00 p.m. Spec: Books for collectors, First Editions, Nature, History, Art, Children, Literature, Medicine, Technical, Cookery, Psychology, Travel, Americana, Religion, Occult and General O.P.

BOOK CELLAR, 36 MAIN STREET, FREEPORT, ME 04032. Prop: Dean Chamberlin. TN: (207) 865-3157. Mail order and search service.

BOOKS AND AUTOGRAPHS, 287 GOODWIN ROAD, ELIOT, ME 03903. TN: (207) 439-4739. Spec: theatre, film, opera.

BOOKS FROM MAINE, 15 SUMMER ST., KENNEBUNK, ME 04043.

THE BOOK NOOK, 54 HIGH STREET, ELLSWORTH, ME 04605.

BUNKHOUSE BOOKS, RT 126, 5 LEWISTON ROAD, GARDINER, ME 04345. Prop: Isaac Davis, Jr. TN: (207) 582-2808. Open May—October 1.00 p.m. to 5.00 p.m. but wise to make appointment. October—May appointment necessary. Spec: Maine town histories, Fishing. Free search service.

CARLSON-TURNER BOOKS, 241 CONGRESS STREET, PORTLAND, ME 04101. Prop: Norma C. Carlson & David John Turner. TN: (207) 773-4200. Open Tuesdays to Saturdays 10.00 a.m. to 5.00 p.m. and by appointment. Medium stock used. Spec: Rare books, Literature and Scholarly books. Mail order speciality: Fencing and Duelling.

DONALD C. CHANDLER—BOOKS, RT. 231, NEW GLOUCESTER, ME 04260. TN: (207) 926-4653. Appointments necessary. Spec: Maine categories, Americana.

CHARLES' BOOKS, South China, ME 04358. Prop: Mabel Charles. TN: (207) 445-2245. Shop, but advisable to telephone for appointment. Large stock used.

CIDERPRESS BOOKSTORE, Rt. 41, Mount Vernon, ME 04352. Prop: Virginia Chute. TN: (207) 293-3570. Appointment necessary.

CROSS HILL BOOKS, P.O. Box 798, 9 Noble Street, Brunswick, ME 04011. Prop: William W. Hill. TN: (207) 729-8531. Est: 1976. Private premises, appointment necessary. Medium stock used. Spec: Nautical, Sailing ships, Rare books and First Editions. Cata: Occasionally.

DOUGHTY'S FALLS OLD BOOK SHOP, P.O. Box 93, Rt. 9 West, North Berwick, ME 03906. Prop: Bill & Eleanor Riviere. TN: (207) 676-4490. Shop. Open from April to December. Spec: Maine titles, Hunting and Fishing.

DOWNEAST BOOK SERVICE, Pierce's Pond Road, Penobscot, ME 04476. Prop: Thomas Stotler. TN: (207) 326-4771. Est: 1975. Shop and storeroom; appointment necessary. Medium stock used. Spec: Americana, early juvenile, first editions. Cata: occasionally.

ROBERT E. DYSINGER, 5 Stanwood Street, Brunswick, ME 04011. TN: (207) 725-5873. Spec: early science; natural history; Americana.

EAST COAST BOOKS, P.O. Box 849, Rt. 109, Wells, ME 04090. Prop: Kaye & Merv Slotnick. TN: (207) 646-3584. Shop. Open April to November. Spec: Rare & Out-of-print books. Paintings, Prints and Drawings, 17th to 20th Centuries. Autographs and Manuscripts in all fields.

EDGECOMB BOOK BARN, Cross Point Road, No. Edgecomb, ME 04556. Prop: Frank McQuaid. TN: (207) 882-7278. Open May—October 11.00 a.m. to 6.00 p.m. Year round by appointment. Spec: Illustrated books, Children's, Americana, Maine, Marine.

ESTES BOOK SERVICE, 13 Haley St., Lewiston, ME 04240.

BARBARA FALK, West Castine Road, P.O. Box 356, Castine, ME 04421. Private premises, appointment necessary. Spec: Maine.

FLYNN BOOKS, 466 Ocean Avenue, Portland, ME 04103. TN: (207) 772-2685.

LARRY & PEG GERAGHTY—BOOKS, 1 POPE ROAD, WESTBROOK, ME 04092. TN: (207) 892-6518. Open every day from 9.00 a.m. to 6 p.m., open evening by appointment. Very large stock used. Spec: Maine related items, General Americana, Periodicals.

C.E. GUARINO—OLD PRINTS & MAPS, BOX 49, BERRY ROAD, RT. 117, DENMARK, ME 04022. TN: (207) 452-2123. Appointment necessary. Spec: Early Americana maps and prints, historical documents. Choice lithographs from Kurz to Currier and oddities from America's printed past. Cata: Frequently.

DOUGLAS N. HARDING RARE BOOKS, P.O. BOX 184, RTE 1, WEDHANNET FARM, WELLS, ME 04090. TN: (207) 646-8785. Est: 1962. Shop, open daily from 1st April to Christmas. Very large general stock used; also prints and new art books. Corresp: Français. B: Maine National Bank, Portland, Maine. M: A.B.A.A.

INTERNATIONAL HOUSE BOOKS, P.O. BOX 343, BREWER, ME 04412. Prop: John E. Cayford, M.S.D. TN: (AC207) 945-6995. Cables: Interserv. Est: 1926. Shop; appointment preferable. Medium stock used. Spec: history; maritime; travel. Quarterly lists.

DEBORAH ISAACSON, 11 ASH STREET, BOX 932, LEWISTON, ME 04240. TN: (207) 784-3937. or (207) 782-7153-home. Shop. Medium stock used. Spec: art.

PATRICIA LEDLIE—BOOKSELLER, BOX 46, BUCKFIELD, ME 04220. TN: (207) 336-2969. Spec: Natural history.

LOBSTER LANE BOOK STORE, RT. 73, SPRUCE HEAD, ME 04859. Prop: Vivian York. TN: (207) 594-7520. Shop. Open June—September 12.30 to 5.00 p.m. daily, October—November, 9.00 a.m. to 5.00 p.m. Saturdays & Sundays. General stock of out-of-print and used books.

MacDONALD'S MILITARY MEMORABILIA & MAINE MEMENTOES, COBURN GORE, EUSTIS, ME 04936. Prop: Thomas L. MacDonald. TN: (207) 297-2751. Appointment necessary. Spec: Civil War books, paper and photos. All periods covered from Colonial to World War 2. Cata: Every six weeks.

AIMEE B. MacEWEN, Victorian House, Stockton Springs, ME 04981. Est: 1960. Shop. Very large stock used. Spec: Americana, Maine. Cata: subject or author lists on request. A.B.A.A.

F.M. O'BRIEN, 34 and 36 Highstreet, Portland, ME 04101. TN: (207) 774-0931. Est: 1934. Shop. Very large stock used. Spec: Americana, State of Maine, literature, early education. Cata: occasionally. A.B.A.A. I.L.A.B.

OLD BOOKS, 136 Maine Street, Brunswick, ME 04011. Prop: Clare Creighton Howell. TN: (207) 725-4524. Est: 1977. Shop, closed Thursdays (mid-June to mid-September) and Sundays. Medium stock. Spec: Literature & Books by and about women.

THE OWL AND THE TURTLE INC., 8 Bay View, Camden, ME 04843.

CHARLES L. ROBINSON, Box 299, The Pond Road, Manchester, ME 04351. TN: (207) 622-1885. Appointment necessary. Spec: Rare and fine books in many fields.

ROWES' OF BOOKS, Knowles Road, Belgrade, ME 04917. Prop: F. Roberts & Charlene C. Rowe. TN: (207) 495-2243. Appointment necessary. Spec: O.P. books on all subjects, Fiction and Non-fiction.

CAROL SIMPSON, ANTIQUARIAN BOOKBINDER, Rfd 2, Hiltons Lane, North Berwick, ME 03906. TN: (207) 646-7151. Private premises, appointment necessary. Restoration of old and rare books; fine period bindings.

SNOWBOUND BOOKS, R F D Box 510, Madison, ME 04950. Prop: Nancy Wright & Marla Bottesch. TN: (207) 696-5081. Est: 1977. Private premises, mail orders only. Medium stock. B: Federal Trust Co. Waterville, Maine 140-610-8.

SOUTHWEST HARBOR ANTIQUES GALLERY, P.O. Box 732, Southwest Harbor, ME 04679. Prop: Lee Freedman. TN: (207) 244-3162. Est: 1960. Shop and storeroom. Medium general stock. Spec: first editions, fine editions; illustrated; children's; natural history; rare, scarce, documents, paper memorabilia. Also antiques and paintings.

SUMNER & STILLMAN, P.O. Box 225, YARMOUTH, ME 04096. Prop: Richard S. Loomis, Jr. TN: (207) 846-6070. Est: 1980. Private premises, appointment necessary. Very small stock sec. and antiq. Spec: first editions English literature 1825-1950. Cata: 6 a year. B: Maine National Bank, Yarmouth, ME. M: A.B.A.A.

LEON TEBBETTS BOOK SHOP, 164 WATER ST., HALLOWELL, ME 04347. TN: (207) 623-4670. Open Monday—Saturday 10.00 a.m. to 5.00 p.m. Very large stock used.

24. MARYLAND (MD.)

BALDWIN	KENSINGTON
BALTIMORE	LA PLATA
BETHESDA	LAUREL
BRINKLOW	POOLESVILLE
CENTREVILLE	RIVERDALE
COLLEGE PARK	ROCKVILLE
COLUMBIA	SALISBURY
EASTON	SEVERNA OAK
ELKTON	SILVER SPRING
FREDERICK	SYKESVILLE
GAITHERSBURG	TOWSON
GREENBELT	WESTMINSTER
HAGGERSTOWN	

ARC BOOKS, P.O. Box 16282, ROLAND PARK STATION, BALTIMORE, MD 21210. Prop: Arthur Cheslock. TN: (301) 653-0218. Est: 1981. Private premises; postal business only. Very small stock used. Spec: computer science; antiquarian science.

ARISTA BOOK SERVICE, 2222 PARK AVENUE, BALTIMORE, MD 21217.

B.R. ARTCRAFT COMPANY, 6701 CHERRY HILL ROAD, BALDWIN, MD 21013. Prop: Bernhard Rogge. TN: (301) 592-2847. Est: 1934. Mail order only. Medium stock used, also new. Spec: architecture, fine art, crafts. Cata: on foregoing and hobbies, collecting, 1 a year. A.B.A.A.

ATTIC BOOKS, 357 MAIN STREET, LAUREL, MD 20707. Prop: Richard Cook. TN: (301) 725-3725. Est: 1970. Shop. Very large stock used.

BARTLEBY'S BOOKSHOP, BETHESDA SQUARE MALL, 7710 WOODMONT AVENUE, BETHESDA MD 20814. TN: (301) 654-4373. Shop.

E. BERGER, 126 NORTH COURT STREET, FREDERICK, MD 21701.

STEVEN C. BERNARD [FIRST EDITIONS], 138 NEW MARK ESPLANADE, ROCKVILLE, MD 20850.

THE BOOK CELLAR, 8227 WOODMONT AVENUE, BETHESDA, MD 20014. Prop: Mildred P. Bell. TN: (301) 652-4522. Est: 1976. Shop, open 7 days a week. Very large stock. Some Library of Congress Copyright duplicates. B: Suburban Trust Co. Chevy Chase, Maryland. No: 23-2276-8.

BOOKS PLUS INC., 661 CREEK ROAD, SEVERNA OAK, MD 21146.

BORGEN'S BOOKS, 1901 WEST ROGERS AVE., BALTIMORE, MD 21209.

BOWSERS FOR BROWSERS, ROUTE 12, BOX 96, FREDERICK, MD 21701. TN: (301) 473-5473. Est: 1974. Private premises, appointment necessary. Very small stock used. Spec: Out of print dog books.

MARILYN BRAITERMAN, 20 WHITFIELD ROAD, BALTIMORE, MD 21210. TN: (301) 235-4848. Est: 1976. Private premises, appointment necessary. Small stock used. Spec: Fine printing, 18th to 20th century, first editions, Architecture and Landscape. Cata. B: Equitable Bank; Acc. No: 601-0756-9. M: A.B.A.A.

VIRGINIA CARMICHAEL, 425 N. POTOMAC ST., HAGGERSTOWN, MD 21740.

CARROCEL BOOKSHOP, P.O. BOX 2294, ROCKVILLE, MD 20852. TN: (301) 881-0817.

MARY CHAPMAN, P.O. BOX 304, COLLEGE PARK, MD 20740. Spec: Embroidery and Lace.

THE CHIRURGICAL BOOKSHOP, 1211 CATHEDRAL STREET, BALTIMORE, MD 21201. TN: (301) 539-0872 (ext. 255). Spec: medical. Cata.

CHRISTIAN CLASSICS, P.O. BOX 30, WESTMINSTER, MD 21157. Prop: John J. McHale. TN: (301) 848-3065. Est: 1966. Storeroom. Large stock used, also new. Spec: Catholic books. Cata: Catholic theology, 4 a year. Also publishers of Catholic books.

CORSICA BOOKSHOP, 1 COMMERCE, CENTREVILLE, MD 21617.

DE RE MEDICINA, P.O. BOX 23105, BALTIMORE, MD 21203-5105. Spec: medicine.

JOHN A. DESCH, 11701 JUDSON ROAD, SILVER SPRINGS, MD 20902.

E. DON BULLIAN, 7-D RIDGE ROAD, GREENBELT, MD 20770. TN: (301) 345-7430. Est: 1930. Storeroom, open normal business hours. Very large stock of backnumber magazines. Spec: medical, scientific and technical periodicals.

JEFF DYKES, P.O. BOX 38, COLLEGE PARK, MD 20740. TN: (301) 864-0666. Spec: Western Americana. A.B.A.A.

LIONEL EPSTEIN, 9909 OLD SPRING ROAD, KENSINGTON, MD 20895. TN: (301) 949 8622. Est: 1965. Private premises; postal business only. Small stock used. Spec: law; economics.

FOLKWAYS, SCHOLARLY BOOKS, 5309 TUSCARAWAS ROAD, BETHESDA, MD 20816. Prop: Bradford H. Gray. TN. (301) 320-5672. Est: 1978. Private premises, appointment necessary. Very small stock used. Spec: History of Social and Behavioral Sciences, Medicine. Cata. One a year.

FRANCIS LIMITED, 205 E. JOPPA ROAD, TOWSON, MD 21204. TN: (301) 321-7178. Spec: Bibles in exotic languages.

DORIS FROHNSDORFF, P.O. BOX 2306, GAITHERSBURG, MD 20879. TN: (301) 869-1256. Est: 1967. Private premises; appointment necessary. Medium stock used. Spec: rare children's books, illustrated and miniature books, fine bindings. Cata: children's books, 4 a year. A.B.A.A. I.L.A.B.

JOHN GACH BOOKS, 5620 WATERLOO ROAD, COLUMBIA, MD 21045. Prop: John Gach. TN: (301) 465-9023. Est: 1973. Private premises, appointment necessary. Large stock sec. and antiq. also some new books. Spec: psychology, psychiatry, psychoanalysis, philosophy. Cata: 4 a year. B: Maryland National, Account No. 871 3497. M: A.B.A.A.

GOLDMAN & GOLDMAN, INC., 5225 POOKS HILL ROAD, 1822 N. BETHESDA, MD 20814.

J.W. HARMAND & SONS, 3789 MELODY LANE, HAGGERSTOWN, MD 21740.

HARRIS AUCTION GALLERIES, 873-875 NORTH HOWARD STREET, BALTIMORE, MD 21201. Prop: Mr. Barr Harris. TN: (301) 728-7040. Est: 1912. Shop. Auction sales of books, paper Americana, autographs, graphics, photographs & ephemera. Catalogs by subscription.

KARDY'S BOOK STORE, 105A WEST MAIN STREET, SALISBURY, MD 21801. Prop: Ellen Kardy. TN: (301) 749-0491. Est: 1977. Shop, closed on Wednesdays. Large stock used. Spec: Local history, humour. Cata: Approximately 3 monthly. B: Maryland National. Acc. No. 527.13.066.0.20.

KELMSCOTT BOOKSHOP, 32 W. 25TH ST., BALTIMORE, MD 21218. TN: (301) 539-5020.

KEY BOOKS, 2 WEST MONTGOMERY STREET, BALTIMORE, MD 21230. Prop: R.D. & Mrs C.L. Cooper. TN: (301) 539-5020. Private premises, appointment necessary. Spec: history of science and technology, bibliography; mystery fiction.

EDWARD A. LEHWALS—BOOKS, 3509 NORTH CALVERT ST., BALTIMORE, MD 21218. TN: (301) 366-6249. Est: 1976. Private premises, mail order only. Appointments can be made. Very small stock. Spec: P.G. Wodehouse firsts & ephemera; Automobile. Cata: Infrequently. New books stocked under trade name of 'Bookman Dan.' B: Maryland National Bank (Bookman Dan). Acc. No: 361 694 3.

LOST GENERATION BOOKSHOP, 1719 CORWIN DRIVE, SILVER SPRING, MD 20910.

THE 19TH CENTURY SHOP, 1100 HOLLINS STREET, BALTIMORE, MD 21233. Prop: Stephan Loewentheil. TN: (301) 539-2553. Spec: 19th century autographs and literature; Charles Darwin, Napoleon; first editions; rare science; Americana; travel and exploration. Cata: 2 a year.

OLD HICKORY BOOKSHOP, 20225 NEW HAMPSHIRE AVENUE, BRINKLOW, MD 20862. Prop: Ralph & Johanna Grimes. TN: (301) 924-2225. Private premises, appointment necessary. Large stock used. Spec: medical books—old, rare and out-of-print. A.B.A.A.

OLD PRINTED WORD INC., 3808 HOWARD AVE., KENSINGTON, MD 20795.

OLD SOLDIER BOOKS & MILITARIA, P.O. BOX 291, POOLESVILLE, MD 20839.

POE BOOKSHOP IN FELL'S POINT, 1706 FLEET STREET, BALTIMORE, MD 21231.

JEAN-MAURICE POITRAS & SONS, 107 EDGERTON ROAD, TOWSON, MD 21204. Prop: Helen M. Poitras. TN: (301) 821-6284. Est: 1981. Private premises, appointment necessary. Very large stock sec. and antiq. medical books and journals. Cata: 2 a year. Corresp: Français, Italiano.

QUILL & BRUSH, 7649 OLD GEORGETOWN ROAD, BETHESDA, MD 20014. Prop: Allen & Patricia Ahearn. TN: (301) 951-0919. Shop. Large stock used. Spec: 19th and 20th century first editions: fine books.

JOHN C. RATHER, P.O. BOX 273, KENSINGTON, MD 20895. TN: (301) 942-0515. Est: 1976. Private premises, mail order only. Spec: Chess, Photography, art, magic. Cata: 2 or 3 per year.

RIVERDALE BOOKSHOP, 6104 RHODE ISLAND AVENUE, RIVERDALE, MD 20737. Prop: Mary E. Sorrell. Est: 1956. Shop. Medium stock used.

CECIL ARCHER RUSH, 1410 NORTHGATE ROAD, BALTIMORE, MD 21218. TN: (301) 323-7767. Cables: Rushbooks Baltimore. Appointment necessary. Est: 1940. Large stock new and used. Spec: Erotic art and illustrated books, scholarly curiosa, fine press, Tibet. Cata: Yearly. M: A.B.A.A. I.L.A.B., American Appraisers Assoc. *Also at* 2605 NORTH CHARLES STREET, BALTIMORE, MD, TN: (301) 467-2622.

SECOND STORY BOOKS, 7730 OLD GEORGETOWN ROAD, BETHESDA, MD 20814. Prop: Tim Kugel. TN: (301) 656-0170. *Also shop at* 3322 GREENMOUNT AVENUE, BALTIMORE, MD 21218; TN: (301) 467-4344.

LAWRENCE SEEBORG—BOOKS, 8423 GREENBELT ROAD, GREENBELT, MD 20770. TN: (301) 552-2111. Est: 1975. Private premises, appointment necessary. Very small stock used. Spec: Children's illustrated books and original art, polar exploration, books about disasters. B: Bank of Virginia. Acc: 1018787.

SHERLOCK BOOK DETECTIVE, 2624 SAINT PAUL STREET, BALTIMORE, MD. Prop: William Forshaw. Spec: fiction.

JEROME SHOCKET, 6144 OAKLAND MILLS ROAD, SYKESVILLE, MD 21784. TN: (301) 795-5879. Private premises, postal business only. Very small stock sec. and antiq. books on boxing; also magazines, programmes, ephemera.

ROBERT SMITH, 6012 SOUTHPORT DRIVE, BETHESDA, MD 20014.

STONE HOUSE BOOKS, 71 STONE HOUSE LANE, ELKTON, MD 21921. Prop: Robert M. Eisenberg. TN: (301) 398-6835. Private premises; appointment necessary. Small stock used. Spec: natural history; detective fiction; local history.

STUDIO NORTH, 8 ALLEGHENY AVENUE, BALTIMORE, MD 21204. Prop: Shirley L. Balser. TN: (301) 825-2022. Est: 1961. Shop. Very large stock used. Spec: Americana, Art and Illustrated, Literature. Cata: general, occasional. 17th to 20th century paintings and prints bought, sold and appraised.

UNICORN BOOKSHOP, 24 NORTH WASHINGTON STREET, EASTON, MD 21601. Prop: Dawson TN: (301) 822-0148. Est: 1975. Shop. Medium stock. Spec: Maryland; history; civil war; art.

SAMUEL WARD, LA PLATA, MD 20646. Est: 1938. Warehouses; appointment necessary. Very large stock used. Spec: U.S. Government publications; early printing. Cata: occasionally.

25. MASSACHUSETTS (MA.)

ACTON	ASHLEY FALLS
AMHERST	ASSONET
ANDOVER	AUBURN
ARLINGTON	AUBURNDALE
ASHFIELD	BEDFORD

25. MASSACHUSETTS (MA.)

BELMONT
BERNARDSTON
BEVERLEY
BLANDFORD
BOSTON
BRAINTREE
BRIDGEWATER
BROOKLINE
CAMBRIDGE
CANTON
CARVER
CHELMSFORD
CHESTNUT HILL
CONCORD
DRACUT
EAST LONGMEADOW
EAST ORLEANS
EAST OSIS
EVERETT
FAIRHAVEN
FRAMINGHAM
GARDNER
GEORGETOWN
GLOUCESTER
GREAT BARRINGTON
HADLEY
HARWICK
HULL
HUNTINGTON
ISLINGTON
JAMAICA
LANESBOROUGH
LEXINGTON PLAIN
LUNENBORG
MARBLEHEAD
MARLBORO'
MARSHFIELD HILLS
MARTHA'S VINEYARD
MASHPEE
MELROSE
MIDDLEBORO
MONTAGUE

NANTUCKET
NEEDHAM
NEW BEDFORD
NEWBURYPORT
NEW SALEM
NEWTON
NORTHAMPTON
NORTHFIELD
OAK BLUFFS
ONSET
ORANGE
ORLEANS
PALMER
PEABODY
PETERSHAM
PITTSFIELD
SALEM
SHARON
SHEFFIELD
SOMERVILLE
SOUTHBRIDGE
SOUTH EGREMONT
SOUTH HAMILTON
SOUTH LEE
SOUTH YARMOUTH
SPENCER
SPRINGFIELD
STOCKBRIDGE
STOUGHTON
TEMPLETON
UXBRIDGE
WABAN
WALTHAM
WATERTOWN
WAYLAND
WELLESLEY HILLS
WESTBOROUGH
WEST BROOKFIELD
WESTFIELD
WESTPORT
WESTON
WHITMAN

166

ABACUS BOOK CO., 43 BARNES ROAD, STOUGHTON, MA 02072.

ABARJONA BOOKSHOP, P.O. BOX 263, WINCHESTER, MA 01890.

ABRAXAS, 84 MAIN STREET, GLOUCESTER, MA 01930. TN: (617) 283-8802. Shop, open Tues. to Sat., 12-4. General stock sec. and antiq. books. Spec: mythology and occult.

MARION F. ADLER, BOX 744, STOCKBRIDGE, MA 01262. TN: (413) 298-3394. Est: 1976. Private House, appointment necessary. Small stock. Spec: Children's books—old, rare and out-of-print. Cata: Occasionally.

LORRAINE ALLISON, BOOKSELLER, 235 WASHINGTON STREET, MARBLEHEAD, MA 01945.

KENNETH ANDERSEN, P.O. BOX H, AUBURN, MA 01501. TN: (617) 832-3524. Private premises: postal business only. Spec: hunting, fishing, mountaineering, golf. Cata: occasionally. M: A.B.A.A.

ANDOVER ANTIQUARIAN BOOKS, 68 PARK STREET, ANDOVER, MA 01810. Prop: V. David Rodger. TN: (617) 475-1645. Shop, open Thursdays, Fridays and Saturdays. (Closed August). Spec: first editions, illustrated, New England M: A.B.A.A.

ANTIQUARIAN BOOKWORM, 54 HARVARD STREET, BROOKLINE, MA 02146.

THE ANTIQUARIAN SCIENTIST, P.O. BOX 367, DRACUT, MA 01826. Prop: Raymond V. Giordano. TN: (617) 957-5267. Est: 1976. Private premises; appointment necessary. Very small stock used. Spec: antiquarian science and medicine; also scientific instruments.

EVA AROND, 52 TURNING MILL ROAD, LEXINGTON, MA 02173. TN: (617) 862-6379. Est: 1980. Private premises, appointment necessary. Medium stock. Spec: Juveniles; modern first editions; illustrated. Cata: occasionally. Corresp: Deutsch.

167

ARS LIBRI LIMITED, 286 SUMMER STREET, BOSTON, MA 02210. Prop: Elmar W. Seibel. TN: (617) 357-5212. Est: 1976. Shop. Large stock used. Spec: fine arts; architecture; illustrated books; photography. M: A.B.A.A., Verband Deutscher Antiquare.

ARTISTIC ENDEAVORS, INC. 24 EMERSON PLACE, BOSTON, MA 02114. Prop: Barbara Ratner Gantshar. TN: (617) 227-1967. Est: 1975. Private premises, appointment necessary. Small stock used. Spec: Fine arts, the lively arts; paintings, prints, photographs, autographs. Cata: 2-3 times yearly. M: Mass. & Rhode Island Antiquarian Books, A.B.A.A.

ASIAN BOOKS INC., 12 ARROW ST., CAMBRIDGE, MA 02138. Cata: occasionally and newsletters.

ASTRONOMY BOOKS, P.O. BOX 217, HUCKLE HILL ROAD, BERNARDSTON, MA 01337. Prop: Paul W. Luther. TN: (413) 648-9500. Est: 1976. Private premises, appointment necessary. Very small stock used. Spec: physical sciences, history of science, astronomy. Cata: Approx. 4 per year.

ATLANTIC BOOK SERVICE, POB 218, CHARLESTOWN STATION, BOSTON, MA 02129. Prop: Paul Dembicki. Est: 1946. Mail order. Medium stock used, also new books and direct mailing services. Spec: marine and nautical. Cata: general.

PHIL BARBER, P.O. BOX 8694, BOSTON, MA. TN: (617) 492-4653. Spec: Antiquarian Newspapers.

THE BARROW BOOKSTORE, 79 MAIN STREET, CONCORD, MA 01742. Prop: Mrs. William Dawes. TN: (617) 369-6084. Est: 1971. Shop. Small stock used. Spec: Concord history and local authors: Bronson and Louisa May Alcott, Emerson, Thoreau, Hawthorne. Active search service for out-of-print books.

THE BEACON HILL BOOK & MUSIC SHOPPE, 17 MYRTLE STREET, BOSTON, MA 02114. TN: (617) 523-5807. Prop: Edward F. Durbeck, III. Est: 1970. Shop. Medium stock used. Spec: music, show business. Also rare phonograph records. Cata: occasionally.

PAUL E. BELISLE, 74 SPRUCE STREET, WATERTOWN, MA 02172. TN:
WA 3-9079. Est: 1955. Mail order only. Medium stock used. Spec:
American historical books, pamphlets and manuscripts,
Mesoamericana. Cata: on foregoing, occasionally. M.S.A.

BLAND'S BOOK BIN, 37 GLENDALE ROAD, SHARON, MA 02067. Prop:
Francis E. Memoe. TN: (617) 784 8303. Private premises: by appointment or by mail only. Medium stock sec. and antiq. books. Book search
service.

BLUE RIDER BOOKS, 1640 MASSACHUSETTS AVE, (REAR), CAMBRIDGE,
MA 02138. Prop: Robin Bledsoe. TN: (617) 576-3634 or 354-4894.
Est: 1973. Shop, open Tues-Sat 10-5, or by appointment. Medium
stock used. Spec: horses, equestrian sports and pastimes; scholarly; art
reference; oriental art, archaeology; architecture; women artists. Cata:
4 to 6 a year.

THE BOOK AND TACKLE SHOP, 29 OLD COLONY ROAD, CHESTNUT
HILL, MA 02167. Prop: Bernard Ludwig Gordon. TN: (617) 965-0459.
Private premises, appointment necessary. Winter only. Spec: science
and medicine; sporting; natural history; travel and exploration;
Americana; fish and fishing. M: A.B.A.A. (Summer shop in Rhode
Island).

THE BOOK BEAR, WEST MAIN STREET, BOX 663, WEST BROOKFIELD,
MA 01585. Prop: Albert Nevitski. TN: (617) 867-8705. Est: 1972.
Shop, closed Mondays and Tuesdays, open other days, including
Sundays. Very large stock used. Spec: psychology; anthropology; social
sciences. M: Massachusetts and Rhode Island Antiquarian Booksellers
Association.

BOOK COLLECTOR, 375 ELLIOT STREET, NEWTON UPPER FALLS, MA
02164.

THE BOOK DEN EAST, P.O. BOX 721, NEW YORK AVENUE, OAK
BLUFFS, MARTHA'S VINEYARD, MA 02557. Prop: Cynthia & Ivo
Meisner. TN: (617) 693-3946. Est: 1977. Converted barn open every
day June to September; Appointment advised Fall, Winter and Spring.
Large stock. Cata: Occasional lists.

BOOK FRIENDS, 75 MAIN STREET, PEABODY, MA 01960. TN: (617) 532-2100. Shop, open Tues. to Sat., 11-4. Large general stock sec. and antiq. books. Spec: modern first editions, Civil War, mystery and detective.

BOOK MARKS, 1 EAST PLEASANT STREET, (CARRIAGE SHOPS), AMHERST, MA 01002. Prop: Fred & Barbara Marks. TN: (413) 549-6136. Shop. open Mon. to Sat., 10-5. Spec: photography; music; art; literature and criticism; illustrated.

BOOK STORE, 67 MAIN STREET, GLOUCESTER, MA 01930.

BOOK STORE, 76 CHESTNUT ST., BOSTON, MA 02108.

THE BOOK STORE OF WEST BRIDGEWATER, 222 NORTH MAIN STREET, WEST BRIDGEWATER, MA 02379. Prop: David E. Johnson. TN: (1-617) 588-4774. Est: 1972. Shop, closed Mondays and Tuesdays. Open, Wed, Thurs, Sat & Sun 12.00 to 18.00 hrs. Fridays open until 21.00 hrs. Very large stock used, some new books published by Arkham House publishers. Cata: 1 a year.

BOOKS, Box 404, RTE 23 & TYREL ROAD, SOUTH EGREMONT, MA 01258. Prop: Bruce & Sue Gventer. TN: (413) 528 2327 or (413) 528 9499 (home). Shop, closed Monday and Tuesday.

BOOKS WITH A PAST, 113 COMMONWEALTH AVENUE, WEST CONCORD, MA 01742. Prop: Susan Tucker & Anne Wanzer. TN: (617) 371-0180. Est: 1981. Shop. Medium stock used. Spec: Concord authors and history; transcendentalism.

BOOKS FOR EMBROIDERY, 96 ROUNDWOOD ROAD, NEWTON, MA 02164. Prop: Betty Feinstein. TN: (617) 969-0942. Est: 1979. Private premises; appointment necessary. Medium stock used, also new books. Spec: embroidery, needlework, lace, fashion, quilting, tapestry, design, color. Cata: 3 a year. B: US Trust Co., Box 373, Boston, Mass., and Midland Bank, Church Street, London. M: A.B.A.

THOMAS G. BOSS, 80 MONMOUTH STREET, BROOKLINE, MA 02146. TN: (617) 277-1527. Private premises, appointment necessary. Spec: Press books, first editions, bindings; bibliography.

BOSTON BOOK ANNEX, 906 BEACON STREET, BOSTON, MA 02215. Prop: Helen Kelly & Francine L. Ness. TN: (617) 266-1090. Est: 1980. Shop, open seven days a week. Very large stock used. Spec: modern literary first editions.

OSEE H. BRADY BOOKS, 12 ELM STREET, ASSONET, MA 02702. TN: 644-5073. Est: 1975. Storeroom, appointment necessary. Large stock used. Spec: Diversified general stock. B: Bristol County Savings, Acc. No: 14663; Fall River 5 Cent Savings: Acc. No: 80-000169; 74-000384. Cheque Acc. No. Bristol County Savings—2340130-3.

BRATTLE BOOK SHOP, 9 WEST STREET, BOSTON, MA 02111. Prop: George Gloss. TN: (617) 542-0210. Est: 1825. Shop. Stock of over 350,000 volumes used and antiq. A.B.A.A.

FRANCIS JOHN BRECK, Jr., 52 MOUNTAINVIEW STREET, SPRINGFIELD, MA 01108. TN: (413) 733-3523. Est: 1982. Private premises; open Mon. to Sat. by appointment only. Small stock. Spec: occult; foreign languages, esp. French and Spanish. Cata: irregularly. Corresp: Français, Español.

E.C. BREEDING, 99 WASHINGTON STREET, NANTUCKET, MA 02554.

BROMER BOOKSELLERS, 607 BOYLSTON STREET, BOSTON, MA 02116. Prop: David J. & Anne C. Bromer. TN: (617) 247-2818. Est: 1965. Open Monday to Friday 9.30 to 17.30 hrs. Most Saturdays 10.00 to 16.00 hrs. Medium-stock. Spec: Early printed books, fine bindings, literary first editions, private press, illustrated, miniature books, juveniles. Cata: 3 a year. M: A.B.A.A.

MAURY A. BROMSEN ASSOCIATES, INC., 770 BOYLSTON STREET, BOSTON, MA 02199. TN: (617) 266-7060. Cables: Bromsenbooks Boston. Est: 1954. Private premises, appointment necessary. Very large stock used. Spec: rare Americana, Latin Americana, autographs, manuscripts, bibliography, rare periodicals, reference books. Cata: occasional lists. M.S.A., A.B.A.A.

BROOKLINE VILLAGE BOOKSHOP, 23 HARVARD STREET, BROOKLINE, MA 02146. Prop: James Lawton. TN: (617) 734-3519. Est: 1980. Shop. Large stock used and antiq. Spec: nautical and local history. M: A.B.A.A.

F. THURLOW BROWN, 7 SCHOOL STREET, GEORGETOWN, MA 01830. Prop: Patsy J. Brown. TN: (617) 352-6259. Est: 1946. Shop, open November to June but appointment advised. Medium stock used. Spec: historical material on Essex County, New England history and authors, books on antiques. Cata: lists, 8-12 a year. *Also at:* CORNER NEWMAN AND HIGH ROADS, NEWBURY, MA; shop, open June through October.

BUCEPHALUS, 465 PUTNAM AVENUE, CAMBRIDGE, MA 02139.

BULL MOOSE REPUBLICAN BOOKSHOP, 6 N. MAIN STREET, ORANGE, MA 01364.

HAROLD M. BURSTEIN, 36 RIVERSIDE DRIVE, WALTHAM, MA 02154. Prop: Eunice K. Burstein TN: (617) 893-7974. Est: 1953. Shop and storeroom. Very large stock used; also large stock pamphlets, old and rare prints, graphics and maps. Spec: American history and literature. Cata: history, literature, juvenilia, occasionally. A.B.A.A. I.L.A.B.

J.S. CANNER & COMPANY, 49-65 LANSDOWNE STREET, BOSTON, MA 02215. TN: (617) 437-1923. Cables: Cannbooks Boston. Telex: 940649. Storeroom, appointment necessary. Spec: periodicals, serial publications, and reference works.

CAPE COD BOOK CENTER, ROUTE 28, MASHPEE, MA 02649. Prop: Carole Warth Aronson.

ROGER F. CASAVANT, 88 Dudley Road, Wayland, MA 01778. TN: (617) 653-4104. Est: 1971. Private premises, appointment necessary. Medium stock used. Spec: Americana, English & American Lit. Collectibles in mostly 19th Century in all fields. B: Bay Bank, Middlesex.

MILDRED C. CHAMBERLIN, CAPE COD BOOKS, P.O. Box 794, East Orleans, MA 02643. TN: (617) 255-4921. Est: 1970. Private premises: mail order only. Very small stock. Spec: Cape Cod, Nantucket, Martha's Vineyard books and maps; Cape Cod authors (Joseph C. Lincoln, Gladys Taber, Sara Bassett, Phoebe A. Taylor). Cata: one a year.

CHILD'S GALLERY, 169 Newbury Street, Boston, MA 02116. Prop: D. Roger Howlett. TN: (617) 266-1108. Spec: fine prints, Americana, 19th and 20th century drawings, American illustrators. M: A.B.A.A.

CHOREOGRAPHICA, 82 Charles Street, Boston, MA 02114. Prop: Jack Sherman & Ernie Morrell. TN: (617) 227-4780. Shop, open 7 days a week. General stock sec. and antiq. books.

CHRISTOPHERS, 347 Park Avenue, Worcester, MA. Prop: Christopher Paul. TN: (791) 050-8617. Est: 1932. Shop. Very large stock used, also new. Spec: Americana and railroadiana—papers, books, documents, advertising, newspapers, magazines, periodicals. Cata: general, occasionally. Also antiques, gold, silver and stamps.

COMBAT SPORTS SERVICE, P.O. Box 33, Worcester, MA 01613. Prop: Osmo U. Tuiskula. Est: 1960. Mail order only. Very small stock used, also new. Spec: self-defense books. Cata: aikido, boxing, wrestling, judo, karate, etc., 1 a year.

COMMON READER BOOKSHOP, P.O. Box 32, Old Main Street, New Salem, MA 01355.

COOKE BOOKS, 436 Webster St., Needham, MA 02194.

THE CHARLES DALY COLLECTION, 66 Chilton St., Cambridge, MA 02138.

NATHANIEL DAME & COMPANY, INC., 133 Walden Street, Cambridge, MA 02140. TN: (617) 876-6846. Est: 1937. A.B.A.A.

WILLIAM A. DELUCA, P.O. Box 313, UXBRIDGE, MA 01569.

JOSEPH A. DERMONT, 155 ONSET AVENUE, P.O. BOX 654, ONSET, MA 02558. TN: (617) 295-4760. By appointment only. Spec: autographs, modern first editions, poetry, little magazines, English literature. M: A.B.A.A.

REBECCA B. DESMARAIS, 1 NIXON ROAD, P.O. BOX 2286, FRAMINGHAM, MA 01701.

WEBB DORDICK, 15 ASH AVENUE, SOMERVILLE, MA 02145. TN: (617) 776-1365. Private premises, postal business only. Spec: medicine and life sciences. Cata: occasionally.

DOWER HOUSE, BOX 387, MARLBORO, MA 01366.

DUNHAM'S BOOK STORE, 50 GREAT ROAD, BEDFORD, MA 01730. Prop: Carroll H. Dunham. TN: (617) 275-9140. Est: 1960. Shop. Large stock used, general.

DWYER'S BOOKSTORE, P.O. BOX 426, 44 MAIN ST., NORTHAMPTON, MA 01060.

ELMCRESS BOOKS, 161 BAY ROAD, SOUTH HAMILTON, MA 01982. Prop: A.C., Jr & Britta K. Cressy. TN: (617) 468-3261. Est: 1978. Shop, closed Mondays. Small stock used. Spec: ships and sea; books on books; book arts.

DOROTHY ELSBERG, BOX 178, WEST STOCKBRIDGE, MA 01266. TN: (413) 232-8560. Est: 1974. Private premises, appointment necessary. Very small stock used. Spec: Music. Cata: 2 or 3 per year. M: Massachusetts and Rhode Island Antiquarian Booksellers Inc.

ENGLISH BOOKSHOP, 85 MOUNT PLEASANT AVENUE, GLOUCESTER, MA 01930.

FONDA BOOKS, P.O. Box 1826, NANTUCKET, MA 02554. Prop: Douglass C. Fonda. TN: (617) 228-8501. Est: 1961. Private premises, appointment necessary. Small stock used, a few new. Spec: whaling, ships and the sea (manuscripts, books, prints, printings, charts and ephemera). A.B.A.A.

FOX HILL BOOKS, 436 Main Street, Palmer, MA 01069. Prop: Dick & Joan Taylor. TN: (413) 283-7681. Est: 1979. Shop, open 6 days a week. Medium stock used.

MICHAEL GINSBERG, P.O. Box 402, 60 Lincoln Road, Sharon, MA 02067. TN: (617) 784-8181/6929. Spec: Western Americana, American history, Canadiana, voyages and travel, US Govt. pubs. M: A.B.A.A.

KARL E. GOEDECKE, 382A Great Road, Apartment 102, Acton, MA 01720. TN: (617) 263-7998. Est: 1932. Private premises, by appointment only. Very small stock. Spec: American, English literature. A.B.A.

GOODSPEED'S BOOK SHOP, INC., 7 Beacon Street, Boston, MA 02108. Prop: George T. Goodspeed. TN: (617) 523-5970. Shop. Est: 1898. Large stock used. Spec: Americana, autographs, genealogy, first editions, prints. A.B.A.A. A.B.A. (Int.) *Also at*: 2 Milk Street, Boston, MA 02108.

GREENO, HADDEN & COMPANY, LTD., 168 Brattle Street, Cambridge, MA 02138. Prop: Richard R. Hadden. Est: 1959. Storeroom, appointment necessary. Small stock used, also new. Spec: theology, Cata: theology, 1-2 a year.

GROLIER BOOKSHOP, 6 Plympton Street, Cambridge, MA 02138. Prop: Louisa Solano. TN: (617) 547-4648. Est: 1927. Shop. Very small stock used, also new books and appraisals. Spec: poetry, modern first editions, women's literature. Cata: first editions and new poetry, annually. A.B.A.

W.D. HALL, 99 Maple Street, East Longmeadow, MA 01028. Prop: Douglas and Marjorie Hall. TN: (413) 525-3064. Est: 1963. Private premises, appointment necessary. Medium stock used. Spec: Americana. Cata: general, monthly lists.

BARBARA B. HARRIS, BOOKS, 212 Main Street, Northfield, MA 01360.

HARVARD BOOK STORES INC., 12 PLYMPTON STREET, CAMBRIDGE, MA. (Shop at 1256 Massachusetts Avenue, Cambridge, MA 02138.) Prop: Frank S. Kramer. TN: (617) 661-1515. Est: 1932. Shop. Large stock of new hardcovers and paperbacks. Also used textbooks, paperbacks and mags. A.B.A. N.A.C.S.

HILARY HOUSE, 29 CLARK STREET, SPENCER, MA 01562. Prop: Gerard J. Gagne. TN: (617) 885-3759. Est: 1955. Private premises, appointment necessary. Very large stock used. Spec: Americana, reference works. A.B.A.

HISTORY HOUSE, P.O. BOX 146, ASHLEY FALLS, MA 01222. Prop: Howard Crockett. TN: (413) 229-6605. Est: 1970. Shop; appointment preferable. Very small stock used; also memorabilia. Spec: rare books, maritime Americana, prints. Cata: Americana, once a year.

HOMAN'S PRINT SHOP, INC., 28 COURT SQUARE, BOSTON, MA 02108. TN: (617) LAfayette 3-8187. A.B.A.A.

LINDA HONAN ART BOOKS, 49 CHURCH STREET, WESTBOROUGH, MA 01581. TN: (617) 366-0860. Est: 1976. Private premises; appointment necessary. Medium stock used; also new books. Spec: art reference, art history; art of all periods and regions.

HORSE IN THE ATTIC BOOKSHOP, 50-52 BOYLSTON STREET, BROOKLINE, MA 02146. Prop: Margaret Lockwood. TN: (617) 566-6070. Est: 1975. Shop. Large stock used, also remainders and some new. Spec: art; children's; literature. M. Massachusetts and Rhode Island Booksellers Association.

HOWLAND AND COMPANY, 100 ROCKWOOD STREET, JAMAICA PLAIN, MA 02130. Prop: Llewellun Howland. TN: (617) 522-5281. Est: 1978. Private premises: appointment necessary. Small stock used. Spec: yachting; 20th century first editions.

HUDSON BOOK SHOP, P.O. BOX A2091, NEW BEDFORD, MA 02741. Prop: M.R. Hudson. Est: 1953. Appointment necessary. Large stock used. Spec: first editions.

HUNTINGTON BOOKS, 25 HUNTINGTON AVE, (SUITE 422), BOSTON, MA 02116. Prop: James O'Neil. TN: (617) 236 1925. Spec: Photography, first editions. M: A.B.A.A.

INCREDIBLE BARN, MAIN STREET, ORLEANS, MA 02653. Prop: Wendell Smith. TN: (617) 255-1259. Est: 1965. Shop. Medium stock used. Spec: Cape Cod, literature. Cata: general, occasionally. Also antiques.

IRENE'S BOOKSHOP, 49 WEST BROADWAY, GARDNER, MA 01440. TN: (617) 632-5574. Est: 1966. Shop. Stock of 30,000 used, and rare.

ISLINGTON BOOK COMPANY, P.O. Box 127, ISLINGTON, MA 02090. (217 Washington Street). Prop: Dr. Abraham Portman. TN: 326-2912. Est: 1948. Private premises, appointment necessary. Large stock used. Spec: Americana, American fiction, biography. Lists on request.

JOHNSON'S, 1379 MAIN STREET, SPRINGFIELD, MA 01103. Prop: Charles, Peter, and Paul Johnson. TN: (413) 732-6222. Est: 1893. Shop. Very large stock used; also reprint and remainders; also new books and stationery, office supplies, cards, hobby, art and craft materials. A.B.A. Massachusetts and Rhode Island Antiquarian Booksellers Association.

PRISCILLA JUVELIS INC., 150 HUNTINGTON AVENUE, BOSTON, MA 02115. TN: (617) 424-1895. Est: 1980. Private premises, appointment necessary. Small stock used. Spec: rare books and fine printing; manuscripts. Cata: frequent.

MARK A. KALUSTIAN, 259 PLEASANT STREET, ARLINGTON, MA 02174. TN: (617) 648-3437. Private premises, appointment necessary. Spec: Armenia, Turkey, Asia Minor, Near East.

RALPH KRISTIANSEN — BOOKSELLER, P.O. Box 524, KENMORE STATION, BOSTON, MA 02215. TN: (617) 424-1527. Spec: Science fiction, fiction, detective fiction. M: A.B.A.A.

LEIF LAUDAMUS RARE BOOKS, 62 ORCHARD STREET, AMHERST, MA 01002. TN: (413) 253-5188. By appointment only. Spec: fine, rare and unusual books in many fields.

CHARLES E. LAURIAT COMPANY, INC., 30 FRANKLIN STREET, BOSTON, MA 02110. TN: (617) 482-2850. Est: 1872. Shop. Medium stock used, also new. Spec: standard sets, fine bindings, sea books. Also stationery, gifts, greeting cards. A.B.A.A. A.B.A.

EDWARD J. LEFKOWICZ, INC., P.O. BOX 630, FAIRHAVEN, MA 02719. (43 Fort Street.) TN: (617) 997-6839. Private premises; appointment necessary. Very small stock of rare and antiquarian books. Spec: the sea and its islands, nautical science (maritime subjects only), whaling. Cata: several every year.

LITERARY HERITAGE, 1613 CENTRAL STREET, STOUGHTON, MA 02072. Prop: Western Hemisphere, Inc. TN: (617) 344-8200. Est: 1967. Shop. Medium stock used, also new. Spec: first editions of American and English literature, modern and 19th century. Cata: on foregoing, 4 a year. A.B.A.A. I.L.A.B.

PETER V. LOCKE—BOOKS, 310 FRANKLIN ST., BOSTON, MA 02110.

KEN LOPEZ—BOOKSELLER, 51 HUNTINGTON ROAD, HADLEY, MA 01035. TN: (413) 584-4827. Est: 1980. Premises open daily; visits by appointment only. Small stock used and antiq. Spec: modern first editions; American Indian fiction and poetry, literature related to Viet-Nam War; detective fiction, Ken Kesey, Robert Stone, Peter Matthiessen, Leslie Silko. Cata: 6 per year.

SAMUEL L. LOWE, JR., ANTIQUES INC., 80 CHARLES STREET, BOSTON, MA 02114. TN: (617) 742-0845. Est: 1964. Shop. Very small stock used, also marine art and antiques. Spec: marine books and original material. Americana Dealers.

PHILIP LOZINSKI, SCHOLARLY BOOKS, 1504 DRIFT ROAD, BOX C97, WESTPORT, MA 02790. TN: (617) 636-2044. Est: 1960. Private premises; appointment necessary. Medium stock used. Spec: Slavica, Russica, Eastern Europe (all languages). Cata: Slavica, (bibliography, history, literature, linguistics, serials).

J. & J. LUBRANO, P.O. BOX 127, SOUTH LEE, MA 01260. Prop: John P. Lubrano. TN: (413) 243-2218. Est: 1977. Private premises, appointment necessary. Small stock used. Spec: performing arts (music, dance, theatre). Cata: 2 per year. B: Berkshire Bank and Trust. Acc. No: 94053873. M: A.B.A.A. Mass. & Rhode Island Antiquarian Bookdealers Assoc., Music Library Assoc., Manuscript Society, Sonneck Society.

ROBERT F. LUCAS, P.O. Box 63, Main Street, Blandford, MA 01008. TN: (413) 848-2061. Est: 1977. Private premises, appointment necessary. Small stock used. Spec: Rare Americana, Whaling, Hawaii, H.D. Thoreau, transcendentalists. Mass. & Rhode Island Antiquarian Booksellers Assoc., A.B.A.A., Manuscript Society, Ephemera Society.

LYMAN BOOKS, P.O. Box 83, East Osis, MA 01029. Prop: Sam & Reg Freedman. TN: (413) 269-6311. Est: 1981. Private premises, appointment necessary. Small Stock sec. and antiq. Spec: theatre. Cata: 2 a year. B: multi-Bank National, Springfield, Mass.

JOHN F. McGRANN, 16 Sandra Drive, Chelmsford, MA 01824. TN: 256-6218. Est: 1961. Private premises, appointment necessary. Very small stock used, also new books, arms and weapons. Spec: arms and armour, especially oriental.

M. & S. RARE BOOKS, INC., P.O. Box 311, Weston, MA 02193. (45 Colpitts Road.) Prop: Daniel G. Siegel. TN: (617) 891-5650. Est: 1969. Shop, appointment advised. Medium stock used. Spec: 19th century American thought and literature, history, medicine, science. Cata: on foregoing and history, author collections, 2 a year.

JEAN S. McKENNA, P.O. Box 397, 15 Oak Street, Beverly Farms, MA 01915. TN: (617) 927 3067.

JEFFREY D. MANCEVICE INC. P.O. Box 413, West Side Station, Worcester, MA 01602. TN: (617) 755-7421. Spec: Renaissance, Reformation, classics, history, early theology, early science, bibliography.

PETER L. MASI, 17 Central Street, Montague, MA 01351. TN: (413) 367-2628. Est: 1979. Shop; appointment advisable. Medium stock used. Spec: agriculture; trade catalogs; early children's; science; technology.

MATTSON BOOKS, 739 Chase Road, Lunenburg, MA 01462. (Route 13.)

H. L. MENDELSOHN, 1640 Massachusetts Avenue, Cambridge, MA 02138. TN: (617) 576-3634. Est: 1981. Private premises; appointment necessary. Very small stock used. Spec: architectural history; art reference.

179

ROBERT L. MERRIAM, NEWHALL ROAD, CONWAY, MA 01341. TN: (413) 369-4052. TA: Merriam, Newhall, Conway, MA 01341. Est: 1965. Shop; open Sundays 1 to 5 p.m. or by appointment. Medium stock used including some new. Spec: Bibliography, Books on books, Americana, Decorative arts. Cata: 2 monthly. M: Western Massachusetts Booksellers Assoc., Mass. & Rhode Island Booksellers Assoc., Dealers Assoc.

MILITARY HISTORY BOOKSHOP, 104 CHARLES STREET, P.O. BOX 296, BOSTON, MA 02114. TN: (617) 742-9153 (after 12 noon). Spec: military, naval, aeronautics; China and the Far East. Cata: regularly.

GEORGE ROBERT MINKOFF, INC., R.F.D. 3, BOX 147, ROWE ROAD, GREAT BARRINGTON, MA 01230. TN: (413) 528-4575. Cables: Minkoffbooks Great Barrington. Est: 1966. Private premises, appointment necessary. Medium stock used. Spec: modern first editions, English and American literature, Americana, manuscripts. Fine Press Books, original drawings for book illustrations. Cata: 9 a year. A.B.A.A. I.L.A.B.

EDWARD MORRILL & SON, INC., 27 COUNTRY CLUB ROAD, NEWTON CENTER, MA 02159. President: Samuel R. Morrill. TN: (617) 527-7448. Spec: Americana, prints and autographs, science, sports, nature, travel. Cata: Americana, 10 a year. A.B.A.A.

HOWARD S. MOTT INC., P.O. BOX 309, SOUTH MAIN STREET, SHEFFIELD, MA 01257. Prop: Donald N., Howard S. & Phyllis N. Mott. TN: (413) 229-2019. Est: 1936. Private premises, appointment necessary. Large stock used. Spec: first and rare editions, 16th to 20th century, Americana and Caribbean. Cata: on foregoing, occasionally. Also manuscripts, autographs, paintings, drawings and prints. A.B.A.A., A.B.A. (Int.), I.L.A.B

SEAN O. MOYE, 115 COMMONWEALTH AVENUE, WEST CONCORD, MA 01742.

MUCH ADO, 1 PLEASANT STREET, MARBLEHEAD, MA 01945. TN: (617) 639-0400. Shop, open Tues. to Sun 10-5. General stock sec. and antiq. books.

ROBERT MURPHY, 14 DERBY SQUARE, SALEM, MA 01970. TN: (617) 745-6406. Est: 1970. Shop, closed on Tuesdays. Large stock used. B: Noumkerg Trust Co. Acc. No: 0113-0179: 02 0829 9. M: Mass. & Rhode Island Booksellers Assoc.

ROBINSON MURRAY III, 150 LYNDE STREET, MELROSE, MA 02176. TN: (617) 665-3094. Private premises, appointment necessary.

MURRAY BOOKS, 473-477 MAIN STREET, WILBRAHAM, MA 01095. Prop: Samuel & Paul M. Murray. TN: (413) 596-3801. Est: 1950. Private premises, appointment necessary. Very large stock used. Spec: color plate books, juvenilia, bibliography, Americana. M: A.B.A.A.

D. R. NELSON AND COMPANY, P.O. BOX B954, NEW BEDFORD, MA 02741. Prop: David R. Nelson. TN: (617) 996-6234. Est: 1970. Private premises; appointment necessary. Small stock used.

S. S. NEMEROFF, P.O. BOX 606, WILLIAMSTOWN, MA 01267. TN: (413) 458-9212. Shop at 35 Spring Street (2nd Floor) Williamstown. Medium stock, sec and antiq. Spec: Art History, Iconography, Mythology.

NEWBURYPORT RARE BOOKS, 32 OAKLAND ST., NEWBURYPORT, MA 01950. TN: (617) 462 7398.

DAVID L. O'NEAL, 131 NEWBURY STREET, BOSTON, MA 02215. TN: (617) 266-5790. Est 1970. Large stock used rare and antiquarian; also undertakes appraisals. Spec: rare books from 15th century to modern first editions. Cata. on foregoing, 4 a year. M: A.B.A.A., I.L.A.B.

ISAAC J. OELGART, 30 MILK STREET, NEWBURYPORT, MA 01950. A.B.A.A.

OLD BOOK SHOP, SPRING STREET, WILLIAMSTOWN, MA.

OLD BOOK STORE, 32 MASONIC STREET, NORTHAMPTON, MA 01060. Prop: Carl Walz. TN: (413) 586-0576. Est: 1958. Shop. Large stock used.

OLD COLONY BOOK SHOP, P.O. BOX 12, CARVER, MA 02330. Prop: Thomas C. Barham. TN: Union 6-3647. Shop. Large stock used, a few new. Spec: scholarly. Cata: scholarly, occasionally.

181

THE ORGAN LITERATURE FOUNDATION, 45 NORFOLK ROAD, BRAINTREE, MA 02184. Prop: Henry Karl Baker. TN: (617) 848-1388. Est: 1950. Private premises, appointment necessary. Very small stock used, very large stock new books, recordings and filmstrips. Spec: organ building, history, tuning. Cata: on foregoing, every year. M: American Guild of Organists; Organ Club, London and Boston; Organ Historical Society.

THE OPEN CREEL, 25 BRETON ST., PALMER, MA 01069. Prop: Dick & Joan Taylor. TN: (413) 283-3960. Est: 1976. Private premises, appointment necessary. Very small stock used. Spec: Fishing. Cata: 4 per year.

PANGLOSS BOOKSHOP, 65 MOUNT AUBURN STREET, CAMBRIDGE, MA 02138. Prop: Herbert R. Hillman, Jr. TN: (617) 354-4003. Est: 1950. Shop. Stock of over 50,000 volumes used. Spec: scholarly books in the humanities and social sciences. Cata: general, 2 a year. A.B.A.A. I.L.A.B.

ELLIE PANOS, 402 BEDFORD STREET, WHITMAN, MA 02382. Est: 1955. Shop; appointment preferable. Very large stock used. Spec: cookery; early fiction; Americana; biography. Cata: 2 a year.

PARNASSUS BOOK SERVICE, BOX 33, ROUTE 6A, YARMOUTH PORT, MA 02675. TN: (617) 362-6420. Est: 1950. Shop. Very large stock used; also new books. Spec: Latin America; Maritime history; antiques. Cata: Latin America bi-monthly; Russian annually. A.B.A.A.

RANDALL PASS, 159 JASON STREET, ARLINGTON, MA 02174.

ROBERT AND BARBARA PAULSON, ALLEN COIT ROAD, HUNTINGTON, MA 01050. TN: (413) 667 3208. Shop, open 7 days a week. Spec: Rockwell Kent, children's books; Victorian ephemera; detective fiction; industry and labor. M: A.B.A.A.

PAYSON HALL BOOKSHOP, 80 TRAPELO ROAD, BELMONT MA 02178. Prop: T. E. Murphy. TN: (617) 484 2020.

PEPPER & STERN — RARE BOOKS, P.O. BOX 160, SHARON, MA 02067. Prop: Peter L. Stern. TN: (617) 784-7618. Spec: Detective fiction, first editions, autographed material. M: A.B.A.A.

PERCEPTION PLUS, P.O. Box 283, ARLINGTON, MA 02174. Prop: Shirley Utudjian. TN: (617) 643-9022. Private premises, appointment necessary. Small stock used. Spec: Music and the Arts, selected general stock.

JOHN E. PETERS, 19 TANAGER STREET, ARLINGTON, MA 02174. Spec: mountaineering, sea and ships.

THE PRINTER'S DEVIL, 25 HUNTINGTON AVENUE, (SUITE 209), BOSTON, MA 02116. Prop: Barry A. Weidenkeller. TN: (617) 646-6762. Spec: History of medicine, collections. M: A.B.A.A.

QUABOAG BOOKSHOP, 47 HIGH STREET, THORNDIKE, MA 01079. Prop: Edward A. Reynolds. TN: (413) 283-8456. House premises, open normal business hours or by appointment. Medium stock used, a few new books, also antiques and collectors' items.

LORD RANDALL BOOK with PRINT SHOP, 22 MAIN ST., MARSHFIELD, MA 02050. Prop: Gail Wills. TN: 837-1400. Est: 1972. Shop, closed on mornings. Appointment advised. Medium stock. M: Mass. & R.I. Booksellers Assoc.

RASIMAS BOOK BARN, 239 MAIN, SPENCER, MA 01562.

DIANA J. RENDELL, INC., 177 COLLINS ROAD, WABAN, MA 02168. TN: (617) 969-1774. By appointment only. Spec: Autograph letters, manuscripts. M: A.B.A.A.

THE RENDELLS INC., 154 WELLS AVENUE, NEWTON, MA 02159. Prop: Kenneth W. Rendell. TN: (617) 969-7766. TA: Autographs, Newton. Est: 1961. Offices; appointment preferable, but not essential. Largest stock of autographs and manuscripts in the world. Spec: Autograph letters, Manuscripts and Documents from ancient & medieval times to the present, early printings, fine bindings, voyages and travels, Western Americana, classical western antiquities. Cata: on autographs and manuscripts in all fields and languages, 10 a year. A.B.A. A.B.A.A. S.L.A.M.

FRANK E. REYNOLDS, P.O. Box 805, NEWBURYPORT, MA 01950. (13 Essex Street.) TN: (617) 462-3258. Est: 1952. Private premises; appointment necessary. Very small stock. Spec: Civil War, Americana, West. Cata: 5 a year.

PAUL C. RICHARDS, HIGH ACRES, TEMPLETON, MA 01468. TN: (800) 637-774. By appointment only. Spec: autographs and manuscripts; signed limited editions, inscribed and associated first editions. A.B.A.A.

STEPHEN C. ROSE FIRST EDITIONS, P.O. Box 249, STOCKBRIDGE, MA 01272.

ROBERT H. RUBIN, BOOKS, P.O. Box 558, STOUGHTON, MA 02072. TN: (617) 344-0740. TA: Rubooks, Stoughton. Est: 1978. Private premises, appointment necessary. Small stock used. Spec: Antiquarian books in political economy, social thought, Americana, law, economics and business, philosophy. Cata: twice yearly. M: A.B.A.A.

JOHN R. SANDERSON, ANTIQUARIAN BOOKSELLER, Box 285, WEST MAIN STREET, STOCKBRIDGE, MA 01262. TN: (413) 274-6093. Est: 1976. Private House, appointment necessary. Small stock. Spec: Literary First Editions, Important books in most fields. B: Lee Savings, Lloyds-Birmingham.

PETER R. SARRA, ISHTAR BOOKS, 318 SHERMAN STREET, CANTON, MA 02021. Spec: Arabian House Books.

SAVOY BOOKS, P.O. Box 271, BAILEY ROAD, LANESBOROUGH, MA 01237. Prop: Robert H. Fraker. TN: (413) 499-9968 Spec: Agriculture, gardening and horticulture; Americana. M: A.B.A.A.

SAXIFRAGE BOOKS, 13 CENTRAL STREET, SALEM, MA 01970. TN: (617) 745-7170. Shop: Closed Mondays. Spec: Childrens; art; national history; first editions Bookbinding and repair work done.

SUZANNE SCHLOSSBERG, 529 WARD STREET, NEWTON CENTER, MA 02159. TN: (617) 964-0213. Spec: Children's books; illustrated. M: A.B.A.A.

SCIENTIA BOOKS, P.O. Box 433, ARLINGTON, MA 02174, (432A MASSACHUSETTS AVENUE). Prop: Malcolm Jay Kettler. TN: (617) 643-5725 or 641-3254. Private premises; appointment necessary. Small stock. Spec: medicine; science; history of medicine and science; evolution. Cata.

TIM SCONCE BOOKSHOP, FULLER STREET, RFD2, MIDDLEBORO, MA 02346.

SCOTTISH BOOKS, 110 HIGH STREET, NEWBURYPORT, MA 01950. Prop: Grace Munsell.

SECOND FIDDLE BOOKSHOP, 62 ELM STREET, SOUTHBRIDGE, MA 01550. Prop. Roland Boutwell. TN: (617) 765-0370. Shop: appointment preferred. Large stock used.

SECOND FLOOR BOOKS, 47 NORTH STREET, PITTSFIELD, MA 01201. Prop: Eric Wilska. TN: (413) 442-6876. Est: 1974. Shop. Medium stock used. Spec: Berkshire County (Massachusetts) History,and books by Hal Borland.

SECOND LIFE BOOKS, P.O. BOX 242, QUARRY ROAD, LANESBOROUGH, MA 01237. Prop: Russell & Martha Freedman. TN: (413) 447-8010. Est: 1972. Private premises, open every day except Monday in the summer; by appointment in the winter. Large stock used. Spec: first editions, inscribed books; horticulture, agriculture; feminism. Cata: 4 to 6 a year. M: A.B.A.A.

THEODORE SMALL, P.O. BOX 457, SOUTH YARMOUTH, MA 02664.

S. CLARE SMITH, P.O. BOX 562, NEEDHAM, MA 02192. TN: (617) 449-1814. Spec: Children's Books. Cata.

STARR BOOK SHOP INC., 37 KINGSTON STREET, BOSTON, MA 02111. Prop: Milton Starr. TN: (617) 547-6864. Est: 1931. Shop. Very large stock used. Spec: literature, American and English. Cata: occasionally. A.B.A.A.

STATEN HOOK BOOKS, 705 MAIN STREET, HARWICK, MA 02642.

PETER L. STERN, P.O. BOX 160, SHARON, MA 02067. TN: (617) 784-7618. Est: 1973. Private premises, appointment necessary. Small stock used. Spec: Detective fiction, Sherlockiana. Cata: 3-4 per year. A.B.A.A., Massachusetts and Rhode Island Antiquarian Booksellers.

I. STORMGART, P.O. BOX 1232, BOSTON, MA 02205. TN: (617) 268-3942. Private premises, appointment necessary. Spec: Erotica, sexology. Cata.

ANNE SWINDELLS, DOWER HOUSE, BOX 354, PETERSHAM, MA 01366. TN: (617) 724-3283. Private premises; appointment necessary. Spec: Children's; mysteries; gardening.

TEMPLE BAR BOOKSHOP, 9 JOHN F. KENNEDY STREET, CAMBRIDGE, MA 02138. Prop: James & Eugene O'Neill. TN: (617) 876-6025. Spec: photography, fine press books, American and English literature, modern first editions. A.B.A.A.

TEN POUND ISLAND BOOK CO. 108 MAIN ST., GLOUCESTER, MA 01930. Prop: G. Gibson. TN: (617) 283-7312 and 281-3864. Est: 1976. Shop. Medium stock used. B: Gloucester National. 0018 3466.

ISAIAH THOMAS BOOKS & PRINTS, 980 MAIN STREET, WORCESTER, MA 01603. Prop: James A. Visbeck. TN: (617) 754-0750. Est: 1970. Shop. Large stock used and antiq., also print gallery. Spec: First editions. M: A.B.A.A.

THE THOREAU LYCEUM, 156 BELKNAP STREET, CONCORD, MA. TN: (617) 369-5912.

TIME AND AGAIN BOOKS, P.O. BOX 13, BEDFORD, MA 01730. Prop: Kathy Phillips. Spec: first edition mysteries and thrillers.

MAGDA TISZA, RARE BOOKS, 130 WOODCHESTER DRIVE, CHESTNUT HILL, MA 02167. TN: (617) 527-5312. Spec: Foreign: German books; illustrated; Judaica; scholarly books. M: A.B.A.A.

TROTTING HILL PARK, P.O. BOX 1324, SPRINGFIELD, MA 01101.

UNIVERSITY BOOK RESERVE, P.O. BOX 905, ALLERTON STATION, HULL, MA 02045. (75 Main Street and 815 Nantasket Avenue.) Prop: Paul Bassinor. TN: 925-0570 and 925-0005. Est: 1941. Storeroom, appointment necessary. Very large stock used. Spec: literature, religion, history, social sciences. A.B.A.A.

VALLEY BOOKS, 5 EAST PLEASANT STREET, AMHERST, MA 01002.

VANVORAH'S, P.O. BOX 671, EVERETT, MA 02149. Postal business only.

HENRY J. VICKEY, 9 BROOK STREET, STOUGHTON, MA 02072. TN: (617) FIeldbrook 4-3649. A.B.A.A.

WAITING FOR GODOT BOOKS, 137 MAGAZINE STREET, CAMBRIDGE, MA 02139. TN: (617) 661-1824. Private premises, appointment necessary. Spec: first editions; modern art.

BARBARA WALL, 66 CHILTON STREET, CAMBRIDGE, MA 02138.

WESTERN HEMISPHERE, INC., 144 WEST STREET, STOUGHTON, MA 02072. Prop: Eugene L. Schwaab & Eugene L. Schwaab Jr. TN: (617) 344-8200. Cables: Sharonbooks Stoughton. Est: 1967. Shop. Large stock used, some new. Spec: Americana, Publications of U.S. Government, Political and social science, back-files of periodicals, economics. Cata: and lists irregularly. A.B.A.A. I.L.A.B.

E. WHARTON & CO., 3 HIGHLAND TERRACE, WINCHESTER, MA 01890. Prop: Sarah Baldwin. TN: (617) 729 8408. Est: 1981. Private premises; appointment necessary. Literary first editions; also new signed copies. Some illustrated and children's titles. Spec: 19th and 20th century literature (British and American, especially women writers). M: Mass & Rhode Island Antiquarian Booksellers; A.B.A.A.; Manuscript Society.

ROBIN WILKERSON, BOOKS, 24 GROVELAND STREET, AUBURNDALE, MA 02166. TN: (617) 969-2678. By appointment only. Spec: Horticulture, landscape design, gardening, decorated trade bindings. M: A.B.A.A.

WILLIAMS BOOK STORE, 52 PROVINCE STREET, BOSTON, MA. Prop: H.E. Williams. TN: (617) CApitol 7-7520. Shop. Very large stock used and rare, also new books and publishing.

A.A. WILLS & SONS, INC., P.O. BOX 148, MARSHFIELD HILLS, MA 02051. (161 Prospect Street.) TN: (617) 834-8572. Est: 1958. Private premises, appointment necessary. Medium stock used, also prints. Spec: medical books, old, rare and out of print.

WILLIAM WYER RARE BOOKS, P.O. BOX 111, WILLIAMSTOWN, MA 01267. TN: (413) 458-3369. Est: 1981. Private premises; appointment necessary. Very small stock used. Spec: rare early printed books, early Americana, natural history, early science and medicine.

DAN YACK BOOKS, 888 MASSACHUSETTS AVENUE, CAMBRIDGE, MA 02139.

YESTERDAY'S BOOKS, BAPTIST CORNER ROAD, ASHFIELD, MA 01330. TN: (413) 628-3249.

25. MASSACHUSETTS (MA.)

25. MASSACHUSETTS (MA.)

YESTERDAY'S PAPER, POST OFFICE SQUARE, WESTFIELD, MA 01085. Prop: Robert T. Brown, Elizabeth Meredith & Robert F. Lucas. TN: (413) 568-1052. Shop in small shipping mall. Small stock used and rare. Spec: Americana: (books, postcards, posters, magazines, trade catalogues and other ephemera).

WILLIAM YOUNG & COMPANY, P.O. Box 282, WELLESLEY HILLS, MA 02181. Private premises; appointment necessary. A.B.A.A.

BOHDAN ZAREMBA, 3 LIVERMORE PLACE, CAMBRIDGE, MA 02141. TN: (617) 491-3246.

26. MICHIGAN (MI.)

ALBION	HIGHLANDS PARK
ALGONAC	JACKSON
ANN ARBOR	KALAMAZOO
AUBURN HEIGHTS	LANSING
BATTLE CREEK	LAWTON
BIRMINGHAM	NILES
BLOOMFIELD HILLS	ROCHESTER
DEARBORN	SAUGATUCK
DETROIT	SOUTHFIELD
EAST LANSING	SUTTONS BAY
EATON RAPIDS	THREE OAKS
FLINT	TRAVERSE CITY
GRAND RAPIDS	WEST BLOOMFIELD
GRASS LAKE	WEST ROCKFORD
HARSENS ISLAND	

D.C. ALLEN, P.O. Box 3, THREE OAKS, MI 49128. (503 North Elm Street.) TN: (616) 756-9218. Est: 1960. Shop and storeroom. Very large stock used. Spec: all Americana. Cata: on foregoing, 8 a year. A.B.A.A.

ALLEN'S BOOKSHOP, 26 NORTH DIVISION AVENUE, GRAND RAPIDS, MI 49502.

ARNOLD'S OF MICHIGAN, 511 SOUTH UNION STREET, TRAVERSE CITY, MI 49684. Prop: Elizabeth Griffin. TN: (616) 946-9212. Est: 1931. Shop. Large stock used. Spec: fine out-of-print books. A.B.A.A. I.L.A.B.

ATHENA BOOK SHOP, 471 WEST SOUTH STREET, KALAMAZOO, MI 49006. Prop: Dale & Berenice Johnson. TN: (616) 342-4508. Est: 1944. Shop. Very small stock used. Mostly new.

JAMES M. BABCOCK, P.O. BOX 160, HARSENS ISLAND, MI 48028. TN: (313) 748-9779. Est: 1968. Private premises, appointment necessary. Spec: American history, literature (rare printings) fine books; Michigania.

BAKER BOOK HOUSE, 2768 EAST PARIS, GRAND RAPIDS, MI 49506. TN: 957 3110. Est: 1939. Shop. Very large stock used, also new. Spec: theology. Christian Booksellers Association.

BAKER STREET BOOKS, 130E SQUARE LAKE ROAD, BLOOMFIELD HILLS, MI 48013.

BENZ BOOKHOUSE, 14230 OHIO STREET, DETROIT, MI 48238. TN: WE 3-3564. Private premises, appointment necessary. Very small stock used. Spec: hard-to-find items.

BICENTENNIAL BOOKSHOP, 820 SOUTH WESTNEDGE, KALAMAZOO, MI 49008. Prop: Vaughn Baber. TN: (616) 345-5987. Est: 1975. Shop, open Monday to Saturday, 10 to 5.30. Very large stock used. Spec: Americana.

BIG BOOK STORE, 3915 WOODWARD, DETROIT, MI 48201. Prop: John K. King. TN: (313) TE 1-8511. Est: 1923. Shop. Very large stock used. Spec: back-issue magazines.

RICHARD T. BOHAN, 4401 AUDUBON, DETROIT, MI 48224.

BOHLING BOOK COMPANY, P.O. BOX 215, LAWTON, MI 49065. Prop: Curt Bohling TN: (616) 624-6002. Spec: Regional Americana, Civil War, travel guides, pamphlets, old Northwest.

BOOKPEOPLE INC., 6399 ORCHARD LAKE ROAD, WEST BLOOMFIELD, MI 48023.

BORDERS BOOK SHOP, 316 SOUTH STAKE STREET, ANN ARBOR, MI 48108. Prop: Tom & Louis Borders. TN: (313) 668-7654. Est: 1970. Shop. Medium stock used, also remainders. Spec: literature, art, Americana. Cata: general, 4 a year.

BRUCE'S BOOKS, 444 WEST MARGARET, DETROIT, MI 48203.

BYGONE BOOK HOUSE, 12922 MICHIGAN AVENUE, DEARBORN, MI 48126. Prop: John K. King. TN: (313) 581-1588. Est: 1980. Shop. Large stock used. Spec: art, antiques; military; trains, cars; children's illustrated.

'CALL ME ISHMAEL' BOOKS, Box 595, SAUGATUCK, MI 49453. Prop: P. Vinge. TN: (616) 857-2661. Est: 1977. Private premises, not possible to visit. Spec: Michigan and Great Lakes. Cata: 8 times a year. General list and Michigan list. B: First Michigan Bank & Trust, Douglas, Acc. No: 094-394-7-1682.

CASPERSON BOOKS, 1303 BUCHANAN ROAD, NILES, MI 49120. TN: (616) 683-2888.

THE CELLAR BOOK SHOP, 18090 WYOMING, DETROIT, MI 48221. Prop: Morton J. & Petra F. Netzorg. TN: (313) 861-1776. Cables: Cellarbook Detroit. Est: 1946. Shop. Medium stock used, also new. Spec: Southeast Asia (with emphasis on Philippines), Pacific Islands. Cata: on foregoing, regularly, on subscription only. A.B.A.A. I.L.A.B.

CEYX, P.O. Box 73, Dearborn, MI 48121. Prop: David & Carole Orkoskey. TN: (313) 571-8871. Est: 1976. Private premises, not possible to visit. Small stock used. Spec: Aeronautica. Cata: 1 a year. Some new books. B: National Bank of Detroit.

B.C. CLAES BOOKSHOP, 1670 Leverette, Detroit, MI 48216.

CLASSIC BOOKSHOP, 1515 Broadway, Detroit, MI 48226.

ALBERT C. CLEGG, 312 West Broad Street, Eaton Rapids, MI 48827. TN: (517) 663-8428.

CURIOUS BOOK SHOP, 307 East Grand River, East Lansing, MI 48823. TN: (517) 332-0112. Shop. Very large sec. & antiq. stock.

THE DAWN TREADER BOOKSHOP, 525 East Liberty, Ann Arbor, MI 48104. Prop: William Gillmore. TN: (313) 995-1008. Est: 1978. Shop. Very large stock used. Spec: poetry; mysteries, science fiction; voyages; folklore.

DON'S BOOK STORE, 663 Bridge North West, Grand Rapids, MI 49504. Prop: Donald D. Teets. TN: (616) 454-7300. Est: 1951. Shop. Large stock used; also a few new books, and publishing (Blackletter press). Spec: Michigan history; Civil War; first editions.

ELLISON BOOKSHOP, 101 East Washtenaw Street, Lansing, MI 48933. TN: (517) IVanhoe 5-0451. Cables: Ellsonbook Lansing. Est: 1930. Shop. Very large stock used, also new. Spec: Americana. A.B.A. A.B.A.A.

THE FINE BOOKS CO., 781 East Snell Road, Rochester, MI 48064.

GALERIE DE BOICOURT, 250 Martin Street, Birmingham, MI 48011.

GRUB STREET-A BOOKERY, 17194 East Warren, Detroit, MI 48224. Prop: Mary C. Taylor. TN: (313) 882-7143. Est: 1975. Shop, closed Mondays. Large stock used. Spec: antiquarian; bindings, press books; literature.

GUNNERMAN BOOKS, P.O. Box 4292, Auburn Heights, MI 48057. TN: (313) 879-2779. Spec: Hunting, fishing; bird dogs; big game; shooting.

HARTFIELD BOOKS, 117 DIXBORO ROAD, ANN ARBOR, MI 48105. Prop: Ruth Iglehart. TN: (313) 662-6035. Est: 1968. Private premises, mail order or by appointment. Large stock used. Spec: English & American literature 18th and 19th Century. Cata: Quarterly. B: National Bank & Trust Co. Acct. No: 9050016. M: M.A.B.A. Ann Arbor Antiquarian Bookman's Assoc., Oxford Bibliographic Society.

HIGHWOOD BOOK SHOP, 711 SHADY LANE ROAD, SUTTONS BAY, MI. Prop: Lewis L. Razek. TN: (616) 271-3898. 1977. Shop. Large stock. Spec: hunting, fishing, guns, hunting dogs, archery. Also 40,000 back-numbers of sporting magazines. Cata: 2 a year.

JOHN K. KING, P.O. Box 363-A, 901 W. LAFAYETTE BLVD., DETROIT, MI 48232. Prop: John K. King and Thomas R. Schlientz. TN: (313) 961-0622. Est: 1965. Shop. Very large stock. Spec: Americana, literature. Cata: on foregoing, monthly.

KREGEL'S BOOKSTORE, 525 EASTERN AVENUE SOUTHEAST, P.O. BOX 2607, GRAND RAPIDS, MI 49501. TN: (616) 459-9444. Est: 1910. Store. Very large stock used, also new books and Church and Sunday School Supplies. Spec: religion and theology. Christian Booksellers Association.

LEAVES OF GRASS, 2433 WHITMORE LAKE ROAD, ANN ARBOR, MI 48103. Prop: Tom Nicely. TN: (313) 995-2300. Est: 1973. Private premises, appointment necessary. Medium stock used. Spec: Literature, Americana, Books on books, Early imprints. Cata: twice a year (free on request). B: Ann Arbor Trust, Acc. No: 02123-6. M: Ann Arbor Booksellers' Assoc.

JOSEPH L. LEPCZYK, P.O. Box 751, EAST LANSING, MI 48823.

LITTLE READ BOOKS, 12501 WOODWARD AVENUE, HIGHLANDS PARK, MI 48203.

MUCH LOVED BOOKS, P.O. Box 2005, SOUTHFIELD, MI 48037. Prop: Paul M. Branzburg. TN: (313) 355-2040. Est: 1978. Private premises, appointment necessary. Stock of about 10,000 rare and scarce, used. Some new books—bibliography and selected titles of use to collectors. Spec: First editions, Americana, bibliography, Michigan, New York and New Jersey local history, Books about books, Private Press books, illustrated and signed books, Mark Twain.

JULIA SWEET NEWMAN, P.O. Box 99, Battle Creek, MI 49016. TN: (616) WOodward 5-3637. Mail order only. Spec: American historical materials. A.B.A.A. M.S.A.

PAIDEIA BOOKS, 313 South State Street, Ann Arbor, MI 48104. Prop: Tom Prims. TN: (313) 995-5200. Est: 1974. Very small stock used. Spec: Classical studies, Medieval studies. Cata: Used and O.P. about twice a year, new books every 2-3 months.

PEREGRINE BOOKS, P.O. Box 17, East Lansing, MI 48823.

PISCES & CAPRICORN BOOKS, 514 Lindon Avenue, Albion, MI 49224. Prop: Joseph V. Wilcox. TN: (517) 629-3267 or (616) 258-2972. Est: 1975. Private premises, appointment necessary. Very small stock used. Spec: Angling & other sporting books, Notable British trials series. Cata: Annually (in March) occasional lists. B: Alden State Bank, Alden, Michigan.

RAY RUSSELL, 111 East Fourth Street, Rochester, MI 48063.

M. SAVAGE BOOKS, 200 West Mason Street, Jackson, MI 49203. Prop: Mollie Savage. TN: (517) 782-5260. Est: 1975. Shop. Small stock used; also fine art restoration, paintings, prints, china and porcelain.

SCIENCE BOOKSHELF, 525 Fourth Street, Ann Arbor, MI 48103.

DOROTHY SLOAN'S BOOKSHELF, 1651 N. Grand Traverse, Flint, MI 48503. TN: (313) 239-5160. Est: 1976. Private premises, appointment necessary. Small stock used. B: Genesee Bank, Acc. No: 10427-3.

SQUIRE'S LANE BOOKSHOP, 30 Bridge Street, West Rockford, MI 49341.

GEORGE STAHL, 5720 Calhoun Road, Albion, MI 49224.

STALKER & BOOS INC., 280 North Woodward Avenue, Birmingham, MI 48011.

STATE STREET BOOKSHOP, 316 South State, Ann Arbor, MI 48108.

DALE WEBER BOOKS, 5740 LIVERNOIS, ROCHESTER, MI 48063.

WEST SIDE BOOK SHOP, 113 WEST LIBERTY, ANN ARBOR, MI 48108. Prop: Jay Platt. TN: (313) 995-1891. Store. Large stock sec. and antiq. Spec: Arctic and Antarctic, Great Lakes and Michigan. M: A.B.A.A.

THE WINE & FOOD LIBRARY, 1207 W. MADISON, ANN ARBOR, MI 48103. Prop: Jan Longone. TN: (313) 663-4894. Est: 1974. Private premises, appointment necessary. Medium stock used. Spec: Wine, food, cookery, gastronomy, herbs, gardening. Cata: Yearly and lists. M: Ann Arbor Antiquarian Bookdealers Assoc.

WOODEN SPOON BOOKS, 200 NORTH FOURTH AVENUE, ANN ARBOR, MI 48108. Prop: Darleen K. Marshall. TN: (1-313) 769-4775. Est: 1968. Shop. Very large stock used. General fiction and non-fiction.

PETER A. WOODRUFF, P.O. BOX 311, GRASS LAKE, MI 49240. Spec: counter culture, beat generation.

27. MINNESOTA (MN.)

ANOKA	MONTICELLO
DULUTH	SAINT PAUL
HUTCHINSON	VIRGINIA
MANKATO	WAYZATA
MINNEAPOLIS	WINONA

MATTHEW G. ALFS. 3355 QUEEN AVENUE NORTH, MINNEAPOLIS. MN 55412. Est: 1979. Private premises; appointment necessary. Very small stock used; also occasional new books. Spec: 'Watchtower' publications (old and scarce); obscure translations of the Bible and New Testament into English.

A.B.C. ANTIQUES & BOOKS, C/O JAMESONS, TERRITORIAL ROAD, MONTICELLO, MN 55362. Prop: Robert & Marion Jameson. TN: 295-2950. Est: 1950. Shop. Medium stock used, also some new books and antiques. Spec: Americana, travel, biography, books on antiques and collecting. Minnesota prints.

ARCH BOOKS, 5916 DREW AVENUE SOUTH, MINNEAPOLIS, MN 55410. TN: (612) 927-0298. Very large stock sec. and antiq. Spec: children's; illustrated.

ATC BOOKS, 321 East Superior Street, Duluth, MN 55802. Prop: Big League Game Company. TN: (218) 722-1275. Est: 1955. Shop, Medium stock used; also new books, and games, and sport novelties. Spec: military; team sports. Cata: on foregoing, 6 a year. A.B.A.

J.A. BAUMHOFER, P.O. Box 65493, Saint Paul, MN 55165. Spec: Zane Gray, Gene Stratton-Porter; Civil War.

BOOKSEARCH, 105 West Third Street, Winona, MN 55987.

CAISSA BOOKS, 121 South East 5th Street, Minneapolis, MN 55414. TN: (612) 379-7841. Private premises; appointment necessary. Spec: Chess

CRIST BOOK SHOP, 473 Saint Peter Street, Saint Paul, MN 55102. Prop: Harry Fredkove. TN: (612) 222-3155. Est: 1900. Shop. Large stock used; also some new books, and news business.

JAMES & KRISTEN CUMMINGS, 303 Book House, 14 S.E. 14th Avenue, Minneapolis, MN 55414. Private premises, appointment necessary. Large stock. Spec: printed diaries and journals; folklore, mythology; social histories. Cata: on foregoing, 1 a year.

DALE SEPPA, 103 Sixth Avenue North, Virginia, MN 55792. Manageress: Carmen Arroyo. TN: (218) 749-8108. Est: 1980. Shop, appointment preferable,. Medium stock sec. and antiq.; also new books, Spec: Latin America. Cata: 3 or 4 a year. Corresp: Français, Italiano, Español. B: Queen City Federal Bank, 501 Chestnut Street, Virginia MN 55792.

DINKYTOWN ANTIQUARIAN BOOKSTORE, 1316 South East, 4th Street, Minneapolis, MN 55414. Prop: Lawrence Dingman. TN: (612) 378-1286. Spec: modern first editions, poetry, history, crafts and trades. M: A.B.A.A.

ENIGMA BOOKSTORE, 307 Oak Street, S.E. Minneapolis, MN 55414.

HAROLD'S BOOKSHOP, 186 West 7th Street, Saint Paul, MN 55102. Prop: Harold H. Lensing. TN: (612) 222-4524. Est: 1949. Shop. Very large stock used; also some new books. Spec: Minnesota history.

HAWKEYE BOOK & MAGAZINE COMPANY, P.O. Box 529, HUTCHINSON, MN 55350. Prop: Geo. Pierson. TN: (612) 897-8195. Est: 1957. House premises, open normal business hours. Small stock used, also new. New book jobbers to school libraries.

JAMES AND MARY LAURIE, 251 SOUTH SNELLING AVENUE, SAINT PAUL, MN 55105. TN: (612) 699-1114. Shop. Large stock sec and antiq. Spec: Bibliography; press books, limited editions. Cata. M: A.B.A.A.

LIEN'S BOOK SHOP, 413 SOUTH 4th STREET, MINNEAPOLIS, MN 55415. Prop: Leland Lien TN: (612) 332-7081. Spec: Western Americana, Civil War, Confederacy, history. M: A.B.A.A.

NORTHERN LIGHTS BOOKSHOP, 77 EAST STREET, WINONA, MN 55982. Prop: Jim Donahue.

J. & J. O'DONOGHUE BOOKS, 1926 2ND AVENUE SOUTH, ANOKA, MN 55303. Prop: Jean O'Donoghue. TN: (612) 427-4320. Est: 1970. Shop. Large stock used. Spec: science fiction, mystery; Children's series.

ONCE READ, 629 SOUTH FRONT STREET, MANKATO, MN 56001.

OUDAL BOOK SHOP, 315 SOUTH 9th STREET, MINNEAPOLIS, MN 55402. Prop: Justin T. Oudal. TN: (612) 332-7037. Est: 1901. Shop. Very large stock used. Spec: Americana, occult, religious, rare.

PERINE BOOK COMPANY, 315 14th AVENUE SOUTH EAST, MINNEAPOLIS, MN 55414. TN: (612) 338-5618. Est: 1914. Shop. Large stock used, also new. Spec: college texts, juveniles, paperbacks. A.B.A. N.A.C.S.

MARY H. PRIMEAU, 246 EAST STANLEY AVENUE, SAINT PAUL, MN 55118. Est: ca. 1930. Private premises. Large stock used: general out-of-print.

ROSS & HAINES OLD BOOKS COMPANY, 639 EAST LAKE STREET, WAYZATA, MN 55391.

ERLING ROVICK, 7104 WOODDALE AVENUE SOUTH, MINNEAPOLIS, MN 55435. TN: (612) 927-7518. Private premises; appointment necessary. Very small stock used; also new books. Spec: fishing.

RULON-MILLER BOOKS, 212 NORTH SECOND STREET, MINNEAPOLIS, MN 55401. Prop: Robert Rulon-Miller, Jr. TN: (612) 339-5779. Est: 1980. Private premises, appointment advised. Medium stock, primarily antiquarian. Spec: Dictionaries and grammar; women's history; American; voyages and travel. M: A.B.A.A.; Manuscript Society; Grolier Club; I.L.A.B.

S and S BOOKS, 80 N. WILDER, SAINT PAUL, MN 55104. Prop: Jack & Pat Sticha. TN: (612) 645-5962. Est: 1971. Private premises, mail order only. Medium stock used. Spec: Search service. Science Fiction, Fantasy, Horror, Mystery, Religion. Cata: Upon request. A few new books available. B: Minnesota Federal, St. Paul, MN 55105 (Acct.No. 058821-0).

GENE TERRES BOOKS, 4051 BLAISDELL AVENUE, MINNEAPOLIS, MN 55409.

MARY TWYCE, 601 EAST 5th STREET, WINONA, MN 55987. Prop: John, Mary & David Pendleton. TN: (509) 454-4412. Stock of 10,000 used. Spec: Americana, children's books.

28. MISSISSIPPI (MS.)

CARLISLE	JACKSON
GULFPORT	KOSCIUSKO

CHOCTAW BOOKS, 406 MANSHIP STREET, JACKSON, MS 39202. Prop: Fred Smith. Shop. Spec: Mississippi history, Mississippi writers; mystery books

JAMES A. DILLON, STAR ROUTE, BOX 23, CARLISLE, MS 39049.

MAGIC LANTERN BOOKS, ROUTE 1, BOX 84-T, KOSCIUSKO, MS 39090.

NOUVEAU RARE BOOKS, 5005 MEADOW OAKS PARK DRIVE, P.O. BOX 12471, JACKSON, MS 39211. TN: (601) 956-9950. Private premises, appointment necessary. Spec: 20th century first editions. Cata.

SUE THOMPSON BOOKS, 476 EVANS AVENUE, GULFPORT, MS 39501.

29. MISSOURI (MO.)

COLUMBIA	SAINT LOUIS
GREENWOOD	SPRINGFIELD
KANSAS CITY	WESTON

ABC THEOLOGICAL INDEX, MINISTERS BOOK SERVICE, P.O. BOX 2786, COMMERCIAL STATION, SPRINGFIELD, MO 65803. Prop: Gerard J. Flokstra, Jr. TN: (417) 833-2019. Est: 1962. Private premises, appointment necessary. Very large stock used. Spec: American theology, church history, ecclesiastical biographies.

ADAMS BOOKS & HOBBIES, 214 NORTH 8th STREET, COLUMBIA, MO 65201. Prop: I.C. Adams, Jr. TN: (314) 449-6416. Est: 1946. Shop. Medium stock used, large stock pocket-books, a few new books.

AMITIN'S BOOK SHOP, 811 WASHINGTON AVENUE, SAINT LOUIS, MO 63101. Prop: Samuel & Janet Amitin. TN: GA 1-2908. Shop. Spec: Saint Louis, Missouri.

MRS. G.B. CAMPBELL, 2413 LAWN, KANSAS CITY, MO 64127.

BOOKENDERS, 517 MAIN, P.O. BOX 279, WESTON, MO 64098. TN: (816) 386-5800. Shop, closed Mondays.

THE BOOKSELLER, 3841 MAIN STREET, KANSAS CITY, MO 64111. TN: (816) 756-3717. Shop.

THE BOOKSELLER, 27 NORTH NINTH STREET, COLUMBIA, MO 65201. TN: (314) 874-4100. Large stock sec. and antiq.

WILLIAM J. CASSIDY, 109 EAST 65th STREET, KANSAS CITY, MO 64113. TN: (816) 361-4271. Est: 1950. Storeroom, appointment necessary. Very large stock used. Spec: economics, dance and related disciplines. Cata: economics, 2 a year. A.B.A.A. I.L.A.B.

C. CHITTENDEN, 524 CYPRESS, KANSAS CITY, MO 64124.

CLIFFSIDE BOOKS, P.O. BOX 7235, KANSAS CITY, MO 64113. Prop: P.A. Anderson. TN: (816) 444-8056. Est: 1970. Warehouse, appointment necessary. Medium stock used. Spec: science, medicine, social sciences, transportation.

COLUMBIA BOOKS, P.O. Box 27, 111 Strollway, Columbia, MO 65205.

R. DUNAWAY, 6138 Delmar Boulevard, Saint Louis, MO 63112. TN: (314) 725-1581. Est: 1960. Shop. Medium stock used, also new. Spec: literary criticism and biography, first editions bibliography, Americana. Cata: on foregoing, monthly.

ELIZABETH F. DUNLAP, 6063 Westminster Place, Saint Louis, MO 63112. TN: (314) 863-5068. Est: 1951. Private premises, appointment necessary. Small stock used, also maps. Spec: Americana. Cata: Americana, maps.

ANTHONY GARNETT, P.O. Box 4918, Saint Louis, MO 63108. (5399 Lindell Boulevard, Saint Louis, MO 63112.) TN: (314) 367-8080. Est: 1967. Private premises; appointment necessary. Large stock. Spec: English and American literature in first editions; private presses; the fine arts illustrated books. Cata: on foregoing, occasionally.

GLENN BOOKS, INC., 1227 Baltimore Avenue, Kansas City, MO 64105. Prop: Ardis L. Glenn. TN: (816) 842-9777. Est: 1933. Shop. Medium stock rare and fine and a few new. Spec: Literature, Western Americana, Graphic arts, Private presses, Fine bindings. Cata: Occasional, free. A.B.A.A. I.L.A.B. A.B.A.

FRANCIS T. GUELKER, 4052 Flora Place, Saint Louis, MO 63110. TN: (314) 772-6342. Est: 1978. Private premises, appointment necessary. Medium stock sec. and antiq. Spec: books about books; 18th century English literature. B: Mercantile Trust Company 8th and Locust Streets, Saint Louis, MO 63116.

HENDERSON AND PARK, Fifth & Main Streets, Greenwood, MO 64034. TN: (816) 537-6388. Spec: Hunting, fishing, natural history.

HOOKED ON BOOKS, 2756 South Campbell, Springfield, MO 65807. Collector's room. American first editions; illustrated, art, etc.

EUGENE M. HUGHES, ANTIQUARIAN BOOKSELLER, 4109 Wilmington Saint Louis, MO 63116. (Shop at 927 Demun, Saint Louis, MO 63105.) TN: Home. (314) 353-1009 & (314) 727-9777. Shop. Est: 1974. Shop and private premises. Normal business hours for shop but appointments can also be made. Small stock used. Spec: English and American Literature & History, and Art.

THOMAS LAW BOOK COMPANY, 1909 WASHINGTON AVENUE, SAINT LOUIS, MO 63103. TN: (314) 621-2236. Shop. Very large stock used law books, also new.

MISSOURI BOOKSTORE, 909 LOWRY, COLUMBIA, MO 65201.

RED BRIDGE BOOKS, 2523 RED BRIDGE TERRACE, KANSAS CITY, MO 64131. Prop: Frank W. & Joan E. Hood. TN: (816) 942-0106. Est: 1976. Private premises, appointment necessary with weekend shop. Large stock out-of-print. Spec: Literature, History, Humanities.

HARRY B. ROBINSON, 915 TEXAS AVENUE, COLUMBIA, MO 65202. TN: (314) 449-1611. Private premises: appointment necessary.

ROUSH'S LOAN & SECONDHAND STORE, 318 EAST COMMERCIAL STREET, SPRINGFIELD, MO. Prop: Stanley Roush. TN: UN 6-4635. Est: 1942. Very small stock used.

SMOKY HILL BOOKSELLERS, P.O. BOX 2, KANSAS CITY, MO 64141. (4531 Kenwood Avenue, Kansas City, MO 64110). Prop: Kenneth D. & Elaine Sender. TN: (816) 531-2524. Est: 1950. Shop; appointment preferable. Large stock used. Spec: Western Americana (Kansas, Missouri, County histories, cattle history etc.). Cata: on foregoing, occasionally.

DAVID R. SPIVEY, 1708 WEST 45TH STREET, KANSAS CITY, MO 64111. Manager: Mike Borserine. TN: (816) 531-6088. Store: Spec: Americana.

30. MONTANA (MT.)

ALBERTON	HELENA
BIGFORK	KALISPELL
BILLINGS	LEWISTOWN
BOZEMAN	MISSOULA
HAMILTON	PLAINS

BARJON'S BOOKS & GRAPHICS, 2718 THIRD AVENUE NORTH, BILLINGS, MT 59101. Prop: Barbara Shenkel. TN: (406) 252-4398. Est: 1977. Shop. Small stock used; mostly new books. Spec: Montana history; Native American History. Complete search service for books on all subjects.

BLACKTAIL MOUNTAIN BOOKS, P.O. Box 1699, KALISPELL, MT 59901.

BOOKS FROM YESTERDAY, P.O. Box 6, 507 NORTH LAST CHANCE GULCH, HELENA, MT 59601. Prop: Dorothy & Walter A. Coslet. TN: (406) 442-7950. Est: 1985. Shop. Small stock sec. and antiq. Spec: British Christianity, Scripture versions in English, Jean Guyon. B: First Bank of Helena, Last Chance Gulch at 6th Avenue, Helena, MT 59601.

GALLERY OF THE OLD WEST, Box 556, EAST LAKE SHORE, BIGFORK, MT 59911. TN: (406) 982-3221. Visit welcome by appointment. Spec: Old West. Cata.

GOLDEN HILLS ANTIQUARIAN BOOKS, P.O. Box 5598, HELENA, MT 59604. TN: (406) 443-0678. Appointment only. Search service.

JANE GRAHAM TREASURED BOOKS, 316 WEST LAMME, BOZEMAN, MT 59715. TN: (406) 587-5001. Est: 1974. Private premises, appointment is suggested. Small stock used. Spec: Montana & Yellowstone Park. Cata: Approx 6 times per year. B: First National Bank, Bozeman.

HATCH'S, 9 GATEWAY, WEST MALL, KALISPELL, MT 59901.

DAVID A. LAWYER, PLAINS, MT 59859. TN: (406) 826-3229. Est: 1930. Storeroom; appointment necessary. Stock of several thousand used books on botany and horticulture (including French and German language). Cata: occasional lists.

THOMAS MINCKLER, 111 NORTH 30TH (SUITE 221), BILLINGS, MT 59101. TN: (406) 245-2969. Est: 1977. Shop. Small stock antiquarian. Spec: Western Americana.

MONTANA VALLEY BOOK STORE, MAIN STREET, ALBERTON, MT 59820. Prop: Kenneth & Alicia Wales. TN: (406) 722-4950. Est: 1978. Shop, open 7 days a week except from December-May. Very large stock.

OASIS, 1104 WEST MAIN ST., LEWISTOWN, MT 59457. TN: (406) 538 5200. Mail order only. Spec: Medicine and Science.

GERALD B. PETTINGER, 326 ADIRONDAC AVENUE, HAMILTON, MT 59840.

SIDNEY'S USED BOOKS, 518 SOUTH 4TH STREET WEST, MISSOULA, MT 59801. Prop: Carol Stem. TN: (406) 543-5343. Est: 1976. Shop. Small stock used. Spec: Western Americana, Liberal Arts.

31. NEBRASKA (NE.)

LINCOLN   SIOUX CITY
OMAHA

THE BOOK BARN, Box 304H, RR.1, SOUTH SIOUX CITY, NE 68776. Prop: Miss Darleen Volkert. TN: (402) 494-2936. Est: 1977. Shop, mail order only. Large stock used and out-of-print. Spec: Rare, Wide variety subjects, Books of 1600's to early 1900s. No catalogues but wants lists invited. B: Dakota County State Bank. Acc. No: 38/310/4/0244.

D.N. DUPLEY, 9118 PAULINE STREET, OMAHA, NE 68124. TN: (402) 393-2906. Est: 1964. Private premises; appointment necessary. Small stock. Spec: Nebraska and Iowa.

LONG'S BOOK STORE, P.O. BOX 81704, 905 'O' STREET, LINCOLN, NE 68501. TN: (402) 474-4697. Est: 1914. Shop.

32. NEVADA (NV.)

LAS VEGAS   VIRGINIA CITY
RENO

BOOK STOP III, 3732 EAST FLAMINGO ROAD, LAS VEGAS, NV 89121.

THE BOOKEND, P.O. BOX 2967, LAS VEGAS, NV 89104. (806 East Sahara Avenue.) Prop: Paul D. Porter. TN: (702) 735-9490. Est: 1965. Shop. Small stock used, a few new. Spec: first editions, Nevada history, fine bindings. Also prints and general book supplies.

CAMELBACK BOOKS, 1344 SOUTH WELLS, RENO, NV 89502.

DONATO'S FINE BOOKS, 2202 WEST CHARLESTON BOULEVARD (SUITE 9), LAS VEGAS, NV 89102. TN: (702) 384-5838. Shop, open Mon. to Sat, 10-6. Spec: out of print and rare books; fantasy and science fiction.

GAMBLER'S BOOK CLUB/GBC PRESS INC., P.O. Box 4115, Las Vegas, NV 89147. (630 S. 11th St.) President, John Luckman. TN: (702) 382-7555. Est: 1964. Shop. Small stock used, also new. Spec: gambling—casino games, horseracing, poker, etc. Cata: on foregoing, 1 a year. A.B.A.

GRAHAME HARDY, P.O. Box 449, Virginia City, NV 89440. Spec: transportation, Western Americana.

33. NEW HAMPSHIRE (NH.)

ANDOVER	LEBANON
ANTRIM	MANCHESTER
BRADFORD	MARLBOROUGH
CONCORD	MARLOW
CONTOOCOOK	MEREDITH
CONWAY	MILFORD
DERRY	NASHUA
EPPING	NEW LONDON
EXETER	NEWINGTON
FARMINGTON	NEWPORT
FRANCESTOWN	NORTH WEARE VILLAGE
FRANKLIN	NORTHWOOD
GILFORD	OSSIPEE
GILMANTON	PORTSMOUTH
GOFFSTOWN	ROCHESTER
GREENFIELD	RUMNEY
GUILD	SALISBURY
HANOVER	SOUTH TAMWORTH
HAVERHILL	SPOFFORD
HENNIKER	STRATHAM
HILSBORO	TEMPLE
HOLLIS	WARNER
HOPKINTON	WESTMORELAND
LACONIA	

ABBIE'S SEARCH SERVICE, P.O. Box 36, Temple, NH 03084.

ADAMS BROWN COMPANY, P.O. Box 399, Exeter, NH 03833. (Linden Street.) Prop: Herschel B. Burt. TN: (603) 772-4067. Est: 1954. Shop. Medium stock used, also new. Spec: horology. Cata: horology, 2 a year. Fellow, National Association Watch and Clock Collectors.

AEROPRINT, SOUTH SHORE ROAD, SPOFFORD, NH 03462. Prop: Robert Westervelt. TN: (603) 363 4713. Est. 1971. Storeroom, catalogue and mail order only. Small stock used. Spec: aviation. Cata: 6 monthly. Some new books also.

THE ANTIQUARIAN BOOK STORE, 1070 LAFAYETTE ROAD, U.S.RTE 1. PORTSMOUTH, NH 03801. TN: (603) 436-7250. Est: 1973. Shop. Stock of over 70,000 used. Spec: erotica; paper ephemera; periodicals and serials (over 250,000 in stock).

APPLE TREE BOOK SHOP, 24 WARREN STREET, CONCORD, NH 03301.

DON AND CLAIRE ARNOLD, MAPLE STREET, CONTOOCOOK, NH 03229. TN: (603) 746-3624. Shop. Appointment advisable.

BERT BABCOCK, P.O. BOX 1140, 9 EAST DERRY ROAD, DERRY, NH 03038. TN: (603) 432-9142 Appointment preferable. Small stock sec. and antiq. Spec: first editions, limited and press books, poetry, literary manuscripts and letters. M: A.B.A.A.

BARN LOFT BOOKSHOP, 96 WOODLAND AVENUE, LACONIA, NH 03246. Prop: Lee Burt. TN: (603) 524-4839. Appointment preferable. Medium stock sec. and antiq.

BOOK FARM, BOX 515, CONCORD ROAD, HENNIKER, NH 03242. Prop: Walter K. Robinson. TN: (603) 428-3429. Est: 1955. Barn premises, open normal business hours. Large stock used. Spec: Americana, New England, literature, history. Cata: on foregoing and general, 6 a year.

THE BOOK GUILD OF PORTSMOUTH, 85 DANIEL STREET (SECOND FLOOR), PORTSMOUTH, NH 03801. TN: (603) 436-1758. Shop. Medium stock of sec. and antiq. Spec: maritime; New England; children's.

THE BOOKCASE, P.O. BOX 33, FOREST ROAD, GREENFIELD, NH. Prop: Mrs William Walsh. TN: (603) 547-3354. Shop. Very large stock sec. and antiq.

THE BOOKERY, 62 NORTH MAIN STREET, FARMINGTON, NH 03835. Prop: Robert Colpitt. TN: (603) 755-4471. Store, open Friday and Saturday or by appointment. Large stock of sec. or antiq. books, also magazines and paper items.

BOOKSHELF SHOP, 3 PLEASANT STREET, CONCORD, NH 03301. Prop: Polly Powers. TN: (603) 224-8496. Shop, open winter seven days, summer closed Saturdays. Small stock sec. and antiq. Spec: cookbooks, children's.

THE BROWSERY, MAIN STREET, CONTOOCOOK, NH 03229.

BURPEE HILL BOOKS, BURPEE HILL ROAD, NEW LONDON, NH 03257. Prop: Alf. E. Jacobson. TN: (603) 526-6654. Appointment preferable. Spec: Central America; Early printed books; art and collecting.

CALLAHAN AND COMPANY, BOX 42, TEMPLE, NH 03084. Spec: sporting and hunting. Cata.

CARRY BACK BOOKS, P.O. BOX 68, DARTMOUTH HIGHWAY, HAVERHILL, NH 03765. Prop: Donald & Ruth St. John. TN: (603) 989-5943. Est: 1970. Private premises: appointment preferred. Medium stock used. Spec: Vermont, White Mountains, Americana, British and American literature. Cata: general, 2 a year. A.B.A.A.

CELTIC CROSS BOOKS, RR1, BOX 160, WESTMORELAND NH 03467. Prop: Henry Hurley. TN: (603) 399-4342. Medium stock used. Spec: 20th century Roman Catholic and Anglican. Cata.

CHEAPE'S THRILLERS, 14 NORTH PARK STREET, 2-5, HANOVER, NH 03755. Prop: C.W. Cheape. TN: (603) 643-4165. Est: 1978. Private premises, appointment necessary. Very small stock. Spec: Mystery-detective fiction. Cata: 2-3 times per year. M: New Hampshire Antiquarian Booksellers Assoc.

THE CILLEYVILLE BOOKSTORE, BOX 127, ANDOVER, NH 03216. Prop: Eleslie & Sands B. Robart. TN: (603) 735-5667. Store, very large stock sec. and antiq. Spec: Ireland; juvenile.

CLELAND'S BOOKS, 63 MARKET STREET, PORTSMOUTH, NH 03801. Prop: Dave & Jane Cleland. TN: (603) 431-2369. Shop: open May to August, Monday to Saturday; September to January Tuesday to Saturday; February to April Saturdays only. Large stock sec. and antiq. Spec: Civil War, American Revolution.

EVELYN CLEMENT, 45 CENTRAL STREET, FRANKLIN, NH 03235. TN: (603) 934-5496. Appointment advisable.

COLD RIVER BOOKSTORE, BOX 58, RTE. 25 EAST, SOUTH TAMWORTH, NH 03883. Prop: Pat Kyprides. TN: (603) 323-8609. Appointment desirable: Small stock sec. and antiq. Philosophy; Homeopathy; New Hampshire & Maine.

COLONIAL PLAZA ANTIQUES, RRI, BOX 472, BAKER'S CROSSING, LEBANON, NH 03766. Prop: Karl & Kathleen Neary. TN: (603) 448-5880. Shop, open seven days a week. Medium stock sec. and antiq. books, also antiques. Spec: Childrens; Cookbooks.

COLOPHON BOOK SHOP, P.O. BOX E, EPPING, NH 03042. Prop: Robert Liska. TN: (603) 679-8006. Est: 1971. Private premises, appointment necessary. Spec: 19th and 20th century literary first editions, literary bibliography, press books, association and inscribed books, bibliography. Cata: 6 a year. M: A.B.A.A., I.L.A.B.

CONTENTS AND MALCONTENTS, 80 LEBANON STREET, HANOVER, NH 03755. Prop: Wayne Van Voorhees. TN: (603) 643-4382. Appointment advisable.

FRED COSTELLO BOOKS, GILMANTON IRON WORKS, NH 03837.

COTTON HILL BOOKS, RFD 6, BOX 298, LACONIA, NH 03246. Prop: Elizabeth K. Emery. TN: (603) 524-4967. Private premises, appointment necessary. Spec: art; gardens.

CRICKET HILL BOOKS, BOX 66, 33 DEPOT ROAD, STRATHAM, NH 03885. Prop: Edith M. Spurr. TN: (603) 772-5166. House premises: appointment necessary. Medium stock used, some new.

CAROL DELLE, 78 MERROW STREET, MANCHESTER, NH 03104. TN: (603) 627-4477. Private premises, appointment necessary.

EBEN'S BOOK BARN, P.O. Box 52, MILFORD, NH 03055. Prop: Martha & Joseph Donne. TN: (603)) 673-6115. Private premises, appointment necessary. Small stock sec. and antiq.

EMERY'S BOOKS, RTE 2, DUSTON ROAD, CONTOOCOOK, NH 03229. Prop: Ron Emery. TN: (603) 746-5787 Est: 1975. Private premises, appointment necessary. Small stock used. Spec: Books before 1800, Americana, Travel, Maps. Cata: Issued occasionally. B: New Hampshire Savings Bank, Concord, NH. Acc.No: 23110304. M: New Hampshire Antiquarian Booksellers Assoc.

FAIRHAVEN FARM BOOKS, RTE 9, HOPKINTON ROAD, CONCORD, NH 03301. Prop: Bruce R. Luneau. TN: (603) 225-4743. Private premises, appointment necessary. Very small stock sec. and antiq. Spec: botany, horticulture.

EDWARD C. FALES, RTE 4, SALISBURY, NH 03268. TN: (603) 648-2484. Est: 1952. Shop, appointment preferred. Large stock used. Spec: Americana, manuscripts, gardening, cookery. Cata: on foregoing, 2 a year. A.B.A.A. I.L.A.B. M.S.

FARMHOUSE BOOKSHOP, 123 NORTHSHORE ROAD, DERRY, NH 03038. Prop: Kathryn Howard Snyder. TN: 898-9280. Est: 1962. House premises, appointment necessary. Small stock used.

LOUISE FRAZIER, RFD 6, BOX 417, LACONIA, NH 03246. TN: (603) 524-2427. Appointment advisable. Very large stock sec. and antiq. *Also at* MORRILL STREET, GILFORD, NH 03246.

GIBSON MAGIC, 55 LAKE STREET, NASHUA, NH 03060. Prop: Wendell & Gran Gibson. TN: (603) 882-9287 and 880-4218. Shop, open afternoons on Thursdays and Fridays, all day Saturday. Very small stock sec. and antiq. books: also booklets, magazines and manuscripts. Magic only.

J. & J. HANRAHAN, OLD DOVER ROAD, NEWINGTON, NH 03801. Prop: Jack Hanrahan. TN: (603) 436-6234. Est: 1960. Shop. Medium stock used. Spec: Old and rare books in all fields, U.S.A. and England. Cata: Occasionally. B: Ind. Head Bank, N.A. Market Square, Portsmouth. Acc.No: 0761 07209. M: A.B.A.A., I.L.A.B., New Hampshire Antique Dealers' Assoc., Bibliog. Society of America, Milton Society.

PAUL HENDERSON—BOOKS, 50 BERKELEY STREET, NASHUA, NH 03060. TN: (605) 883-8918. Est: 1970. Private premises. Small stock used. Spec: Local histories and genealogies. Cata: 1 per year. B: Nashua Trust Co. 194 Main St., Nashua, NH 03060. M: New Hampshire Antiquarian Booksellers Assoc.

JOHN F. HENDSEY, THE RED BARN, RTE 125, EPPING, NH 03042. TN: (603) 679-2428. Est: 1960. Private premises; appointment necessary. Small stock used. M: A.B.A.A. Spec: American bindings; cookery; hunting, fishing, angling; Civil War and Confederacy.

HILLSIDE BOOKS, RTE 103, BOX 246, WARNER, NH 03278. Prop: Tom & Christopher Stotler. TN: (603) 456-3338. Appointment desirable. Medium stock sec. and antiq. Spec: science; Americana.

HODSDON FARM BOOKS, OSSIPEE, NH 03864. Prop: Jerry Powers. TN: (603) 539-2252. Shop.

HOMESTEAD BOOKSHOP, RTE. 101, P.O. BOX 90, MARLBOROUGH, NH 03455. Prop: Harry, Robert & Connie Kenney. TN: (603) 876-4213. Shop. Large stock sec. and antiq. Spec: Children's.

HURLEY BOOKS, RRI, BOX 160, WESTMORELAND, NH 03467. (WALPOLE ROAD.) Prop: Henry Hurley. TN: (603) 399-4342. Est: 1966. Shop. Large stock used. Spec: early farming; 18th and 19th century theology, particularly the Protestant religion; miniature books. M: A.B.A.A. Cata: general.

JUNIPER HILL BOOKS, P.O. BOX 119, NEWPORT, NH 03773. Prop: Mrs Anne D. Purnell. TN: (603) 863-3919. Private premises, appointment necessary. Juvenile; travel; first editions.

KALON BOOKS, P.O. BOX 16, RT. 114, BRADFORD, NH 03221. Prop: Rod Jones. TN: (603) 938-2380. Est: 1977. Private premises—open all year round on Saturdays and Sundays 1-5 p.m.; daily during July and August. Medium stock used. Spec: Literary Biography, Science Fiction, History, Biography. Cata: 8-10 lists per year. M: New Hampshire Antiquarian Booksellers Association.

BARBARA KREIENSIECK, HALF PRICE BOOK SHOP, 170 PORTLAND STREET, ROCHESTER, NH 03867.

RON KURZ, P.O. Box 164, Antrim, NH 03440. TN: (603) 588-2916. Private premises, appointment necessary.

LA TIENDA EL QUETZAL, P.O. Box 298, Conway, NH 03813. Prop: James C. Andrews. TN: (603) 447-5518. Est. 1978. Private premises; appointment necessary. Very small stock sec. and antiq. Spec: Central America, mainly Guatemala. Cata: occasionally. Corresp: Español. B: Indian Head Bank, Keene, NH.

LANDSCAPE BOOKS, P.O. Box 483, Exeter, NH 03833. Prop: Jane W. Robie. TN: (603) 964-9333. Est: 1972. Private premises, appointment necessary. Very small stock sec. and antiq. Spec: Landscape architecture, garden history. Cata: 1 a year.

PAUL AND ROSEMARIE MAJOROS, Sunapee Road, Rtes. 11 and 103, P.O. Box 36, Guild, NH 03754. TN: (603) 863-3165. Appointment desirable.

MARTEL ET FILS, 104 Bridge Street, Manchester, NH 03105.

ELIZABETH OLCOTT BOOKS, Quincy Road, Rumney, NH 03266. TN: (603) 786-9898. Appointment desirable; very large stock sec. and antiq. Spec: cookbooks; biographies; detective fiction.

THE OLD ALMANACK SHOP, 5 South State Street, Concord, NH 03301. Prop: Craig B. Holmes. TN: (603) 225-5411. Basement Store. Medium stock sec. and antiq., also prints, maps and ephemera. Spec: 18th to 20th century.

OLD NUMBER SIX BOOK DEPOT, Box 525, 26 Depot Hill Road, Henniker, NH 03242. Prop: Ian and Helen Morrison. TN: (603) 428-3334. Est: 1977. Premises open every afternoon; appointment advised in winter. Stock of 75,000 used. Spec: History; Natural, Social and Behavioural Sciences; Medicine; Economics and business; law.

WILLIAM E. REILLY & PEGGY SYSYN, 1 Goodell Road, Antrim, NH 03440. TN: (603) 588-2466. Private Premises, appointment necessary. Small stock sec. and antiq. Spec: Americana; travel.

RISING SUN BOOKS, 228 Ray Street, Manchester, NH 03104.

MARY ROBERTSON, BOOKS, P.O. Box 296, MEREDITH, NH 03253. (U.S. Route 3.) TN: (603) 279-8750. Est: 1950. Shop. Small stock used; also new books. Spec: crafts, antiques; Americana; Nature. A.B.A.

ROBERTSON'S BOOKSHOP, 85 DANIEL STREET, PORTSMOUTH, NH. TN: (603) 436-1758.

SACRED AND PROFANE, RTE 13, NEW BOSTON ROAD, P.O. Box 321, GOFFSTOWN, NH 03045. Prop: H. Donley Wray. TN: (603) 645-6282. Store, open Monday evenings, Saturday and Sunday afternoons. Small stock sec. and antiq.

THE 1784 SHOP, RTE. 4, Box 550, NORTHWOOD, NH 03261. Prop: Richard G. Puffer. TN: (603) 942-8583. Appointment desirable. Large stock sec. and antiq. Spec: New England; Sporting.

THE SHADOW SHOP, Box 942, HILLSBORO, NH 03244. Prop: Lois & Barbara Meredith. TN: (603) 464-5413. Appointment preferable in summer, essential in winter. Large stock sec. and antiq. books, also ephemera.

STINSON HOUSE BOOKS, QUINCY ROAD, RUMNEY, NH 03266. Prop: George & Ann Kent. TN: (603) 786-3412. Est: 1963. Large stock used. Spec: New Hampshire, mountaineering, White Mountains. Cata: Americana, 1 a year. Also antiques. A.B.A.A.

STILES BARN, 108 DEPOT ROAD, HOLLIS, NH 03049. Prop: Arthur & Josephine Stiles. TN: (603) 465-2543. Appointment desirable. Small stock sec. and antiq. Spec: colorplate books.

SYKES & FLANDERS, P.O. Box 86, ROUTE 77, NORTH WEARE VILLAGE, NH 03281. Prop: Richard L. Sykes & Mary Flanders Sykes. TN: (603) 529-7432. Est: 1975. Shop. Medium stock used. Spec: Natural history, Travel and exploration, Illustrated books, Detective fiction, First editions and Americana. Cata: 4-6 times per year. M: A.B.A.A., I.L.A.B., New Hampshire Antiquarian Booksellers Association.

TAINTER'S CHICK BOOK SHOP, P.O. Box 36, TEMPLE, NH 03084. Prop: Lewis & Olga Tainter. TN: (603) 878-1758. Est: 1949. Mail order only. Very large stock used.

JAMES C. TILLINGHAST, P.O. Box 556, Marlow, NH 03456. TN: 446-3460. Est: 1961. Shop. Small stock used 2,000 to 5,000 volumes, also new books. Spec: ammunition, arms, firearms, gun catalogs. Cata: on foregoing, about 1 a year.

THE TYPOGRAPHEUM BOOKSHOP, The Stone Cottage, Bennington Road, Francestown, NH 03043. Prop: R.T. Risk. Est: 1976. Private premises. Very small stock used. Spec: Modern British/European literature, First editions, Press Books, Rare books. Cata: Hand-printed 4 times a year.

VISUALLY SPEAKING, Rte. 11A, Rfd 7, Box 405, Gilford, NH 03246. Prop: Charles & Barbara French. TN: (603) 524-6795. Appointment advisable. Small stock sec. and antiq.

JENNY WATSON, 121 Water Street, P.O. Box 915, Exeter, NH 03833. TN: (603) 772-4010. Shop, open Tuesday to Saturday. Small stock sec. and antiq. Spec: Asia.

WOMEN'S WORD BOOKS, RR4 Box 322, Straw Road, Hopkinton, NH 03229. Large stock sec. and antiq. Spec: books by or about women.

34. NEW JERSEY (NJ.)

ALLENTOWN	FREEHOLD
ASBURY PARK	GLEN RIDGE
ATLANTIC CITY	HADDONFIELD
BERGENFIELD	HAZLET
BERKELEY HEIGHTS	HILLSDALE
BLOOMFIELD	HOBOKEN
BRICK TOWN	HOPEWELL
BRIELLE	HOWELL
CLOSTER	KENDALE PARK
CRANBURY	KENVIL
DOVER	LEONIA
EGG HARBOUR	LINCROFT
ENGLEWOOD	LINDEN
FAIRFIELD	LIVINGSTON
FANWOOD	LONG VALLEY
FORT LEE	LYNDHURST
FRANKLIN LAKES	MADISON

MATAWAN	POTTERSVILLE
MAYWOOD	PRINCETON
METUCHEN	RANCOCAS
MIDDLETOWN	RED BANK
MIDDLEVILLE	ROOSEVELT
MILLVILLE	RUMSON
MONTCLAIR	SADDLE RIVER
MONTVALE	SOMERVILLE
MORRISTOWN	SUMMIT
NEWARK	TENAFLY
NEW BRUNSWICK	TOM'S RIVER
NORTH BRUNSWICK	TRENTON
NORWOOD	UNION
OLDWICK	VERONA
PARK RIDGE	WALDWICK
PARLIN	WAYNE
PASSAIC	WEST END
PENNINGTON	WESTFIELD
PITTSTOWN	WEST NEW YORK
PLAINFIELD	WESTWOOD
PLEASANTVILLE	

ADAMS BROWN COMPANY, P.O. Box 357, Cranbury, NJ 08512. Medium stock used. Spec: horology.

AMERICANA BOOKS, 46 Sycamore Road, Manahawkin, NJ 08050. Prop: Bob Dawson. TN: (201) 842-8890. Est: 1961. Storeroom, appointment necessary. Small stock used. Spec: Western Americana and literature. Cata: on foregoing, 6 a year.

ANDY AND JEAN ANDRUSKO, 211 Princeton Road, Parlin, NJ 08859. TN: (201) 727-1618.

ANTIC HAY BOOKS, P.O. Box 2185, Asbury Park, NJ 07712. Prop: D. Darryl Stine. TN: (201) 774-4590. Est: 1977. Private premises, appointment necessary. Large stock used. Spec: American literary first editions autographs, all periods. Cata: monthly.

ARNOLD'S USED BOOK, 357 Cold Soil Road, Princeton, NJ 08540 TN: (609) 921-3495.

THE BAGGAGE CAR, 128 LAKE DRIVE EAST, WAYNE, NJ 07470. Prop: Susan & Thomas Bjorkman. TN: (201) 694-6749. Private premises, appointment necessary. Spec: Railroads.

LEONARD BALISH, 124A, ENGLE STREET, ENGLEWOOD, NJ 07621. TN: (201) 871-3454. Private premises, by appointment only. Spec: Color plate books, ephemera, photography, typography, trade catalogues. M: A.B.A.A.

BAUMAN RARE BOOKS, 14 SOUTH LA CLEDE PLACE, ATLANTIC CITY, NJ 08401. Prop: David and Natalie Bauman. TN: (609) 344-0763. Est: 1973. Private premises; appointment necessary. Rare books. Spec: fine books in all fields — law, travel, exploration; science; natural history; Americana; signed and association copies; literature. M: A.B.A.A., International Society of Appraisers.

BEL CANTO BOOKS, P.O. BOX 55, METUCHEN, NJ 08840. Prop: Robert Hearn. Est: 1956. Private premises, appointment necessary. Medium stock used. Spec: Music and Musicians. Cata: At times but not regularly. B: First Fidelity, Metuchen, NJ (Metuchen) 209-119546-4.

BEVERLY BOOKS INC., 36 EAST PRICE STREET, LINDEN, NJ 07036. President: M. Sedacca. TN: (201) 486-6500. Est: 1972. Storeroom and offices, open normal business hours. Spec: scientific and technical.

BLACK HORSE BOOKS, Box 13, MIDDLEVILLE, NJ 07855. Prop: John & Mary Hall, TN: (201) 383-5430. Est: 1981. Private premises; appointment necessary. Large stock used. Spec: English and American fiction and literary criticism.

BOOK GARDEN, 27 SOUTH MAIN STREET, ALLENTOWN, NJ 08501. Prop: Joyce & George Engle. TN: (609) 259-3792. Shop, open weekdays and Sunday mornings.

BOOK PEDDLERS, 23 WEST DELAWARE AVENUE, PENNINGTON, NJ 08534. No stock of used; search service only and new books.

BOOK SHOP, 83 SOUTH STREET, MORRISTOWN, NJ 07960.

THE BOOK SHOP, 430 HILLSDALE AVENUE, HILLSDALE, NJ 07642. Prop: Martha Fornatale. TN: (201) 391-9101. Shop, closed Mondays. Spec: Mysteries.

213

THE BOOK STORE AT DEPOT SQUARE, 8 DEPOT SQUARE, ENGLEWOOD, NJ 07631. Prop: Rita Alexander. TN: (201) 568-6563. Est: 1977. Shop. Large stock used. Spec: Cookbooks, Women. B: United Jersey Bank. Acc.No: 103054669.

BOOKS AND COLLECTIBLES, 2 CRABTREE ROAD, MATAWAN, NJ 07747.

BOOKS-ON-FILE, P.O. Box 195, UNION CITY, NJ 07087. TN: (201) 869-8786. Prop: Mary Snyder. Spec: cinema, autographs and manuscripts; genealogy. A.B.A.A.

BOOKWOOD BOOKS, P.O. Box 263, WESTWOOD, NJ 07675. Prop: P.R. Goodman. TN: (201) 664-3946. Est: 1974. Private house, appointment necessary. Small stock. Spec: Soccer (English football), 19th-20th century fiction. B: UJB, Oradell, N.J. M: A.B. Northern New Jersey.

HARVEY W. BREWER, BOX 322, CLOSTER, NJ 07624. (270 Herbert Avenue.) Prop: Alice F. Brewer. TN: (201) 768-4414. Est: 1959. Private premises; appointment necessary. Small stock used. Spec: Textiles, color plate books, photography.

CALDERWOODS BOOKS, BOX F, LONG VALLEY, NJ 07853. Prop: Don Frazier & Jo Koch. TN: (201) 876-3001. Private premises, appointment necessary.

CANTERBURY BOOKS, R.D.I, BOX 392, PITTSTOWN, NJ 08867. TN: (201) 735-9614.

THE CHATHAM BOOKSELLER, 8 GREEN VILLAGE ROAD, MADISON, NJ 07940. Prop: Frank Deodene. TN: (201) 822-1361. Shop, general stock.

COLONIAL TOWNE BOOKS, P.O. BOX 23, MIDDLETOWN, NJ 07748. Prop: Olen P. Glenn. TN: (201) 671-0704. Est: 1965. Private premises; business by mail only. Medium stock used. Spec: health and longevity; Christian Religion.

CONCORD BOOKSHOP, 216 MAIN AVENUE, PASSAIC, NJ 07055.

JAMES CUMMINS BOOKSELLER INC., P.O. Box 232, POTTERSVILLE, NJ 07979. TN: (201) 439-3803. Private premises; appointment necessary. Very large stock used; also fine press books new. Spec: sporting, fine press; illustrated; travel and exploration. M: A.B.A.A. *Also at* MADISON AVENUE, NEW YORK, q.v.

CRANBURY BOOK WORM, 54 NORTH MAIN STREET, CRANBURY, NJ 08512. Prop: Ralph Schremp. TN: (609) 655-1063. Shop, open seven days.

GERRY DE LA REE, 7 CEDARWOOD LANE, SADDLE RIVER, NJ 07458. TN: (201) 327-6621. Est: 1950. Private premises, appointment necessary. Medium stock used, some new. Spec: science fiction, fantasy, weird books and magazines. Cata: on foregoing, monthly.

DESKINS AND GREENE, P.O. Box 1092, ATLANTIC CITY, NJ 08404-1092. TN: (609) 646-6920. Spec: erotica, curiosa, lesbiana.

RICHARD P. De VICTOR, 3 DOVE PLACE, KENDALL PARK, NJ 08824. TN: (201) 279 0296

EGG HARBOR BOOKS AND RECORDS, 612 WHITE HORSE PIKE, EGG HARBOR, NJ 08215. Prop: Norman Arrington and William Spangler. TN: (609) 965-1708. Est: 1977. Shop. Very large stock used.

ESCARGOT BOOKS, 503 RT. 71, BOX 332, BRIELLE, NJ 08730. Prop: Richard Weiner. TN: (201) 528-5955. Est: 1979. Shop. Large general stock used.

JOSEPH J. FELCONE INC., P.O. BOX 366, PRINCETON, NJ 08540. TN: (609) 924 0539. Est: 1971. Private premises, appointment necessary. Large stock. Spec: New Jerseyana, early Americana; sporting; fine and rare chiefly before 1860. Cata: about 6 a year.

T. FESSLER, NEW STREET, NEWARK, NJ 07102.

RONALD GARILLI, 248 CLINTON TERRACE, LYNDHURST, NJ 07071.

GILL BOOKS, 409 MOUNTAIN AVENUE, FRANKLIN LAKES, NJ 07417.

TOM GLOVER, 320-B ATLANTIC AVENUE, TRENTON, NJ 08629.

JAMES TAIT GOODRICH, 214 EVERETT PLACE, ENGLEWOOD, NJ 07631. TN: (201) 567-0199. Est: 1980. Private premises; appointment necessary. Small stock used; also new books. Spec: history of medicine and science.

GREENLEE BOOKS, PACKARD'S FARM MARKET, HIGHWAY 206S, SOMERVILLE, NJ 08876. TN: (201) 725 1045. Store, open Wednesdays, Fridays and Saturdays.

HAMMER BOOK COMPANY, 308 HILLSIDE AVENUE, LIVINGSTON, NJ 07039. TN: (201) 992-5387. Spec: Bibles, Hebraica, Greek and Latin Classics.

HEINOLDT BOOKS, 1325 WEST CENTRAL AVENUE, EGG HARBOR, NJ 08215. Prop: T.H. Heinoldt. TN: (609) 965-2284. Est: 1959. Private premises, open normal business hours. Medium stock used. Spec: the American Scene. Cata: on foregoing, twice a year. A.B.A.A.

HELIOCHROME BOOKS, 75 WEBSTER DRIVE, BERKELEY HEIGHTS, NJ 07922. Prop: David Klappholz & Lisa Kraus. TN: (201) 464-0805. Est: 1984. Private premises, postal business only. Very small stock of books on photography only. Cata: 3 a year. Corresp: Français, Español, Hebrew. B: City Federal Bank, Berkeley Heights, NJ 07922.

ERNEST S. HICKOK, 382 SPRINGFIELD AVENUE, SUMMIT, NJ 07901. Prop: Sally H. Bockus. TN: (201) 277-1427. By appointment only. Spec: Americana, ornithology, sporting prints, angling, hunting. M: A.B.A.A.

H.T. HICKS — OLD COOKBOOKS, BOX 462, HADDONFIELD, NJ 08033. Prop: Harmon & Jean Hicks. TN: (609) 854-2844. Private premises, appointment necessary. Small stock sec. and antiq. Spec: cookery and related, pre 1918. Cata: 2 a year. B: First Peoples Bank of New Jersey.

HOBBIT RARE BOOKS, 305 WEST SOUTH AVENUE, WESTFIELD, NJ 07090. Prop: Arby Rolband. TN: (201) 654-4115. Spec: General stock, documents and prints, restoration.

HORLINE BOOKS, 174 DAVEY STREET, BLOOMFIELD, NJ 07003. Prop: R.W. Horline. TN: (201) 748-0006. Est: 1975. Private premises, mail order only. Very small stock used. Spec: Americana. Cata: Occasionally.

WALTER J. JOHNSON INC., 355 CHESTNUT STREET, NORWOOD, NJ 07648. TN: (201) 767-1303. Telex 135-393. Cables: Bookjohns Norwood Newjersey. Very large stock used, also new books. Spec: science and technology, medicine, scientific and social science periodicals, book collections and publications of Learned Societies. Cata: regularly. (Branch offices in London, England and Frankfurt am Main, Germany.) A.B.A.A.

JOSE'S USED BOOKS, 206 MAIN STREET, TOM'S RIVER, NJ.

JUNIUS BOOK DISTRIBUTORS, 6606 JACKSON STREET, WEST NEW YORK, NJ 07093. Prop: Michael Cordasco. TN: (201) 868-7725. Open Monday, Thursday, Fridays, 10.00 a.m. to 9.00 p.m., Tuesdays, Wednesdays and Saturdays 10.00 a.m. to 6.00 p.m. Sundays by appointment. Spec: paperbacks, general history.

KEITH LIBRARY, MONMOUTH ANTIQUES SHOPPES, 217 WEST FRONT STREET, RED BANK, NJ 07701. Prop: Quentin & Sylvia Keith. TN: (201) 842-7377. Est: 1950. Shop. Medium stock of old and fine. Spec: maps and prints; New Jersey; English literature; fine bindings, limited editions; English classics.

HUGH T. KERR, 707 ROSEDALE ROAD, PRINCETON, NJ 08540.

VIRGINIA KLEPPER, 41 LOCUST AVENUE, FANWOOD, NJ 07013.

STEPHEN KOSCHAL, 159 WOODLAND AVENUE, VERONA, NJ 07044. TN: (201) 239-7299. Private premises: appointment necessary. Spec: signed and association copies; autographs.

THE KEITH LIBRARY

Antiquarian Books, Maps & Prints

217 West Front Street, Red Bank, N.J. 07701 U.S.A.

THE LITERARY SHOP, 736 WASHINGTON STREET, HOBOKEN, NJ 07030. Prop: Paul Duardo. TN: (201) 420-7917. Shop, open seven days afternoons.

LITTLE MERMAID BOOKS, 411 PARK STREET, UPPER MONTCAIR, NJ 07043. Prop: Frederick, Nora & Harry Wertz. TN: (201) 744-9157. Private premises, appointment necessary. Spec: 19th century; biographies.

CHARLES LLOYD RARE BOOKS, 6 LORI LANE, HOWELL, NJ 07731. TN: (201) 363-3634.

LEO LOEWENTHAL, P.O. BOX 938, FOUR NORTH ELK AVENUE, DOVER, NEW JERSEY. TN: (201) 328-7196. Est: 1973. Stockroom, mail order only. Medium stock. Spec: Dance, architecture, art, poetry, cookbooks, photography. Cata: two a year. Corresp: Deutsch, Français, Yiddish.

WHITNEY McDERMUT, BOOKSELLER, 49 SPRING VALLEY ROAD, MONTVALE, NJ 07645. Prop: Whitney McDermut. TN: (201) 391 5905. Est: 1934. Mail order only. Spec: New Jerseyana; books about books, bookplates; art books. M: A.B.A.A.

MARLEY & SCROOGE, P.O. BOX 358, MAIN STREET, OLDWICK, NJ 08858. Prop: William Michalski. TN: (201) 439-2271 & (201) 735-7485. Shop, closed Mondays. Spec: early printed books.

FRANK MICHELLI BOOKS, P.O. BOX 3037, TOMS RIVER, NJ 08756. Prop: Frank Michelli & Paul Grippo. TN: (201) 623-4289. Est: 1952. Shop. Large stock used; also a few new books.

MIDTOWN MAGAZINES, INC., P.O. BOX 917, MAYWOOD, NJ 07607. TN: (212) 993-6579. Est: 1932. Mail order only. Stock of over 2 million periodicals. Spec: back issues of periodicals.

ARTHUR MOLIN, P.O. BOX 42, BERGENFIELD, NJ 07621. TN: (201) 385-7116. Private Premises; appointment necessary. Medium stock used. Spec: Americana; old juvenile.

MONTCLAIR BOOK CENTER, 221 GLEN RIDGE AVENUE, MONTCLAIR, NJ 07042.

MICHAEL NAKONEZNY, JAMESTOWN VILLAGE BUILDING 16 (APT. 11) TOM'S RIVER, NJ 08753.

HAROLD NESTLER, 13 PENNINGTON AVENUE, WALDWICK, NJ 07463. TN: (201) 444-7413. Est: 1952. Private premises, appointment necessary. Small stock used. Spec: Americana; ephemera; industry and labor; manuscripts; technology. Cata: general, about 10 a year. M: A.B.A.A.

NOYES ART BOOKS, MILL ROAD AT GRAND AVENUE, PARK RIDGE, NJ 07656.

JOHN O'CONNOR, 54 NORMAN PLACE, TENAFLY, NJ 07670.

OLD BOOK SHOP, 75 SPRING STREET, MORRISTOWN, NJ 07960. Prop: Virginia Faulkner & Chris Wolff. TN: (201) 538-1210. Est: 1945. Shop. Large stock used. General out-of-print and scholarly.

OLD YORK BOOKS, Box 1850 (122 FRENCH STREET), NEW BRUNSWICK, NJ 08901. Prop: Cecile Hopkins. TN: (201) 249-0430. Est: 1965. Shop. Medium stock used.

RENA & MERWIN L. ORNER, 39 NO. BROWNING AVENUE, TENAFLY, NJ 07670. TN: (201) 568-5796. Appointment necessary. Spec: Kennedy assassination and related items. Left-wing literature.

P.M. BOOKSHOP, 321 PARK AVENUE, PLAINFIELD, NJ 07060. Prop: Sidney Pinn. TN: (201) 754-3900.

PAPER AND INK BOOKSHOP, 44 BEECH AVENUE, BERKELEY HEIGHTS, NJ 07922. Prop: R. Chris Wolff. TN: (201) 464-2391. Est: 1968. Private premises, appointment necessary. Very small stock used, a few new. Spec: New Jersey history and literature. Cata: occasionally.

PASSAIC BOOK CENTER, 594 MAIN AVENUE, PASSAIC, NJ 07055.

PAST HISTORY, 136 PARKVIEW TERRACE, LINCROFT, NJ 07738. Prop: B. & M. Massey. TN: (201) 842-4545. Est: 1962. Private premises; business by mail only. Large stock used. Spec: Americana and New Jersey. Cata: on foregoing, 4 a year.

R. AND A. PETRILLA, ROOSEVELT, NJ 08555-0306. TN: (609) 448-5510. Private premises, appointment necessary.

PHILOSOPHER'S STONE, 557 ROUTE 46, KENVIL, NJ 07847. Prop: James B. Collins. TN: (201) 584-1369. Shop. Monday through Friday afternoons, Saturday and Sunday all day. Spec: Esoteric, Mystical.

PRINCETON ANTIQUES BOOKSHOP, 2915-17 ATLANTIC AVENUE, ATLANTIC CITY, NJ 08401. Prop: Robert E. Ruffolo. TN: (609) 344-1943. Est: for three generations, incorporated 1974. Three shops and warehouse. Very large stock. Also antiques.

RARE BOOK COMPANY, P.O. BOX 957, FREEHOLD, NJ 07728. (292 Route 9, Howell Township.) Prop: Gerard Lupo. TN: (201) 780-1393. Est: 1920. Storeroom; appointment necessary. Large stock used; also new books. Spec: Christian Science Literature. Cata: every two years.

RED BANK BOOK STORE, 6 LINDEN PLACE, RED BANK, NJ. Prop: Margaret & John Connelly. TN: (201) 747-1412. Est: 1922. Shop. Very large stock used, also new books and greetings cards. A.B.A.

WALTER L. RENZ, 18 ALLEN STREET, RUMSON, NJ 07760.

ROLAND ROBERGE, 491 ROSEDALE ROAD, PRINCETON, NJ 08540. TN: (609) 924 6329. Cata: Books on Visual Arts.

JOSEPH RUBINFINE, RFD 1, PLEASANTVILLE, NJ 08232. TN: (609) 641-3290. Spec: autographs; manuscripts; historical Americana. M: A.B.A.A.

LA SCALA AUTOGRAPHS, P.O. BOX 268, HOPEWELL, NJ 08525. Prop: James Camner. TN: (609) 466 3071. Private premises, appointment necessary. Spec: opera, music, theatre.

MYRON B. SCHNELLER, 15 PETUNIA DRIVE 1K, NORTH BRUNSWICK, NJ 08902.

JACQUES V. SICHEL, 1024 SAYRE ROAD, UNION, NJ 07083.

PATTERSON SMITH, 23 PROSPECT TERRACE, MONTCLAIR, NJ 07042. TN: (201) 744-3291. Est: 1957. Private premises; appointment necessary. Very large stock used. Spec: criminology, social history, business & technological history. A.B.A.A.

RICHARD W. SPELLMAN, 610 MONTICELLO DRIVE, BRICKTOWN, NJ. TN: (201) 863-2758. Private premises; appointment necessary. Stock of over 50,000 newspapers, also framed newspapers for wall decor. Spec: historical newspapers of 1600s to 1800s. Cata: 10 to 12 a year.

SPORTING BOOK SERVICE, BOX 177, RANCOCAS, NJ 08073. (38 East Main Street). Prop: A. Aldridge Williams. TN: (609) 267-5506. Est: 1940. Private premises; appointment necessary. Medium stock used; also new books. Spec: hunting and fishing, guns, dogs, natural history. Cata: on foregoing, 2 a year.

TIME AGAIN BOOKS, P.O. BOX 385, STRAUBE CENTER, BUILDING K REAR, WEST FRANKLIN AVENUE, PENNINGTON, NJ 08534. Prop: Charles & Faith McCracken. TN: (609) 737-0361 and (201) 363-2401. Shop, open Wednesdays, Saturdays and Sundays.

TRANSATLANTIC BOOKS, P.O. BOX 44, MATAWAN, NJ 07747. Prop: William H. Groveman. TN: (201) 566-8689. Mail order only. Very small stock used, also new. Spec: British books.

TROTTING BOOK SHOP, SHALEBROOK DRIVE, MORRISTOWN, NJ 07960. TN: (201) 766-6111.

JOHN C. VAN DOREN, P.O. BOX 221, HOPEWELL, NJ 08525. TN: (609) 466-2196. Spec: Movie magazines.

VATHEK BOOKS, 250 SLOCUM WAY, FORT LEE, NJ 07024. Prop: Daniel Rich. TN: (201) 585-1760. Est: 1984. Telephone or mail business only. Large general stock sec. and antiq. books. Spec: scholastic titles; monographs; 3rd century A.D. Imperial Rome and Persia.

VERITAS BOOKS, 68 CHESTNUT STREET, MONTCLAIR, NJ 07042. Prop: Alfonse Battista. TN: (201) 746-7250. Private premises, appointment only. Spec: theology, philosophy.

STEPHEN VIEDERMAN, 108 HIGH STREET, LEONIA, NJ 07605. TN: (201) 947-5292. Private premises, appointment necessary. Spec: Travel, voyages, Africa, Asia, Italy.

WANGNER'S BOOKSHOP, 9 MIDLAND AVENUE, MONTCLAIR, NJ 07042. Prop: Victor & Lorraine Wangner. TN: (201) 744-4211. Mon.-Fri. 11 a.m. to 4.00 p.m., Sat. 11 a.m. to 5.00 p.m., Sundays by appointment. Spec: Theatre and art books, general stock.

WEST END CULTURAL CENTER, 101 BRIGHTON AVENUE, WEST END, NJ 07740. TN: (201) 870-6005. Store, open Wednesday through Sunday.

WHITE'S GALLERIES, 607 LAKE AVENUE, ASBURY PARK, NJ 07712. TN: (201) 774-9300 and 531-4535. Spec: New Jersey, Americana, biography, fiction.

WILSEY RARE BOOKS, 80 WATCHUNG AVENUE, UPPER MONTCLAIR, NJ 07043. Prop: Edward Ripley-Duggan & Carol Maltby. TN: (201) 744-8366. Office premises; appointment necessary. Spec: The Arts of the Book (binding, paper-making, calligraphy); fine printing; major illustrated, etc. Cata: 4 a year. M: A.B.A.A.

WIND CHIMES BOOK EXCHANGE, 210 NORTH HIGH STREET, MILLVILLE, NJ 08332. Dave & Diann Ewan. TN: (609) 327-3714. Shop, large stock paperbacks.

WITHERSPOON ART & BOOK STORE, 12 NASSAU STREET, PRINCETON, NJ 08540. TN: (603) 924-3582. Est: 1925. A.B.A.A.

ERICH A. WITZEL, 15 HIGHLAND AVENUE, GLEN RIDGE, NJ 07028.

ELISABETH WOODBURN, BOOKNOLL FARM, HOPEWELL, NJ 08525. Prop: Elisabeth Woodburn Robertson. TN: (609) 466-0522. Est: 1946. Private premises; appointment necessary. Medium stock used; also a few new. Spec: horticulture, early farming, early botany. Cata: 2 or 3 a year. A.B.A.A.

YESTERDAY'S BOOKS & RECORDS, 559 BLOOMFIELD AVENUE, MONTCLAIR, NJ 07042. Prop: John & Mary Areson. TN: (201) 783-6262. Shop, open afternoons, closed Mondays.

35. NEW MEXICO (NM.)

ALBUQUERQUE	SANTA FE
GALLUP	TAOS
LAS VEGAS	

ABACUS BOOKS, P.O. BOX 5555, SANTA FE, NM 87502-5555.

ADOBE BOOKSELLERS, 2416 Pennsylvania Street, N.E., Albuquerque, NM 87110.

ANCIENT CITY PRESS, P.O. Box 5401, Santa Fe, NM 87502.

THE BOOK STOP, 110 Hermosa Drive S.E., Albuquerque, NM 87106. Prop: Jerry Lane. TN: (505) 268-8898. Est: 1974. Shop. Very large stock sec.

BOOKS BY MAIL, 1833 Central Avenue, N.W., Albuquerque, NM 87104. Prop: Katharine Ransom. TN: (505) 247-3043. Est: 1959. Shop. Very small stock used; also new books. Spec: Southwest history, archaeology; out of print search service.

CHAMISA BOOKS, 3611 Simms Avenue, SE., Albuquerque, NM 87108.

TOM DAVIES BOOKSHOP, 414 Central Avenue Southeast, Albuquerque, NM 87102. Prop: Eric Holmes Patterson. TN: (505) 247-2072. Est: 1963. Shop. Medium stock used; also a few new books. Spec: archaeology; anthropology; American Indians. Cata: general, 6 a year.

EL PAISANO BOOKS, 1000 Park Avenue South West, Albuquerque, NM 87102. Prop: Katherine Stamm. TN: (505) 242-9121. Est: 1965. Shop. Medium stock used, also new. Spec: Americana, New Mexico and Southwest. A.B.A.

EMERSON–LANE BOOKSELLERS, 111 Amherst Drive S.E., Albuquerque, NM 87106. Prop: R. & D. Emerson & Jerry Lane. TN: (505) 265-7113. Est: 1985. Shop. Small stock antiq. Spec: fine books. M: A.B.A.A., I.L.A.B.

LA GALERIA DE LOS ARTESANOS, P.O. Box 1657, Las Vegas, NM 87701.

LANE'S REPOSITORY, 10412 Chapala Place, Albuquerque, NM 87111. Prop: Florence Larry Lane.

MARGOLIS AND MOSS, 129 West San Francisco Street, P.O. Box 2042, Sante Fe, NM 87501. Prop: David M. Margolis. TN: (505) 982-1028. Spec: Western Americana, illustrated books, photography, prints, printed ephemera. M: A.B.A.A.

PARKER BOOKS OF THE WEST, 300 LOMITA, SANTA FE, NM 87501. Prop: Riley G. Parker. TN: (505) 988-1076. Spec: South-western Americana, American Indians. M: A.B.A.A.

NICHOLAS POTTER, 203 EAST PALACE AVENUE, SANTA FE, NM 87501. TN: (505) 983-5434. Spec: Southwestern U.S.A. history; modern first editions, photographic. A.B.A.A.

QUIVIRA BOOKSHOP & PHOTOGRAPH GALLERY, P.O. BOX 4147, ALBUQUERQUE, NM 87106. (111 Cornell Drive South East.) Prop: Ann E. Dietz. TN: (505) 266-1788. Est: 1964. Shop. Small stock used, also new. Spec: history of photography, and photography as a fine art. A.B.A.

JACK D. RITTENHOUSE, P.O. BOX 4422, 600 SOLANO DRIVE S.E., ALBUQUERQUE, NM 87106. TN: (505) 255 2479. Spec: Western Americana only.

FRANK L. RUSSELL, P.O. BOX 389, SANTA FE, NM 87501. (132 East De Vargas.) TN: (505) 982-8829. Est: 1956. Storeroom, open normal business hours. Medium stock used. Cata: general.

THE SOUTHWESTERNER BOOKS, P.O. BOX 2409, GALLUP, NM 87301.

TAOS BOOK SHOP INC., P.O. BOX 827, TAOS, NM 87571. (216 East Kit Carson.) TN: (505) 758-3733. Est: 1947. Shop. Small stock used; also new books. Spec: D.H. Lawrence; Southwest Americana, Cata: 2 a year.

TEN DIRECTIONS BOOKS, P.O. BOX 330, TAOS, NM 87571. Prop: Allan Clevenger. TN: (505) 758-1897. Est: 1985. Used books. Spec: southwestern Americana, New Mexico, Taos; D. H. Lawrence, Freida, Mabel Dodge Luhan, Lady Brett; Eastern religions; mysticism.

TERRITORIAL EDITIONS, INC., P.O. BOX 8394, SANTA FE, NM 87504-8394. TN: (505) 983-8346. Spec: Southwestern Americana.

JANE ZWISOHN BOOKS, 524 SOLANO DRIVE N.E., ALBUQUERQUE, NM 87108. TN: (505) 255-4080. Private premises; appointment necessary. Very small stock used and rare. Spec: Western and Latin Americana; travel especially travel books of literary interest. Cata: 2 or 3 a year.

36.   NEW YORK (NY.) (MANHATTAN AND BRONX)

ABRAHAMS MAGAZINE SERVICE INC., 56 EAST 13TH ST, NEW YORK, NY 10003. Prop: G. Hornstein. TN: (212) 777-4700. Telex: 710-581-2302 (amspress nyk). Est: 1889. Store, open normal business hours, closed Saturdays. Very large stock used. Spec: humanities and social sciences.

ACADEMY BOOK STORE, 10 WEST 18 STREET, NEW YORK, NY 10011. Prop: Alan Weiner. TN: (212) 242-4848. Est: 1973. Shop, open 7 days a week. Very large stock. Spec: Psychology, Philosophy, literature, Art, History, Performing Arts, First Editions. B: Manufacturers Hanover Trust Co. Acc.No.: 39-0-35526.

ABBOT BOOKS AND PRINTS, 100-26L BENCHLEY PLACE, BRONX, NY 10475. Prop: Mr. Ira Unschuld. TN: (212) 671 9800. Private premises, appointment necessary. Spec: Wall Street, Financial History. Cata: occasional.

ACANTHUS BOOKS, 52 WEST 87TH STREET, NEW YORK, NY 10024. Prop: Barry Cenower. TN: (212) 787-1753. Est: 1982. Private premises, appointment necessary. Very small stock sec. and antiq. Spec: decorative arts, architecture, prints. Cata: 4 a year. Corresp: Français, Deutsch. B: Chemical Bank, 53 West 86th Street, New York.

ALPHABETALIA BOOK COMPANY, 60 EAST 96th STREET, NEW YORK, NY 10028.

AMPERSAND BOOKS, P.O. BOX 674, COPPER STATION, NEW YORK, NY 10276. Prop: G. Bixby. TN: (212) 674-6795. Est: 1968. Private premises, appointment necessary. Small stock used, some new. Spec: modern first editions. Cata: on foregoing, about 4 a year.

APPELFELD GALLERY, 1372 YORK AVENUE, NEW YORK, NY 10021. Prop: Louis Appelfeld. TN: (212) 988-7835. Est: 1940. Large stock old and rare. Spec: fine bindings, rare books, color plate, sets, Americana. Cata: on foregoing, 2 a year. A.B.A.A.

W. GRAHAM ARADER III, 23 EAST 74TH STREET, NEW YORK, NY 10021. TN: (212) 628-3668.

YORK

ANTIQUARIAN BOOKSELLERS

As one of the earliest centres of printing in Britain outside London, it is appropriate that York today is the centre of the antiquarian book-trade in the North of England.

YORK OFFERS THE BOOK COLLECTOR

* **Fifteen Antiquarian Booksellers,** with over 300,000 books for sale. Most of the shops are within a short walk of each other, and there is a specialist dealer on most subjects.

* **Easy Access** – York is under two hours from London and two hours from Edinburgh by high-speed train; with close proximity to both the main motorway network, and air terminal.

* **Antiquarian Book Fairs.** Two of the largest fairs outside London are held in York each May and September.

* **Catalogues** produced by members will be sent free on request.

York offers the beauty of a walled medieval city, dominated by the splendour of one of the finest churches in Europe – York Minster. The visitor is well provided for – should you wish for detailed information regarding hotels, places of interest & c, please write and your request will be forwarded direct to York City Tourist Authority.

A leaflet containing full details of all the antiquarian booksellers in the city is available from:

The Hon. Secretary,
York Antiquarian Booksellers,
25 Fossgate, York. YO1 2TA.

Telephone (0904) 27467

ARCADE BOOKS, 575 Madison Avenue, New York, NY 10022. Prop: Michael T. Sillerman.

ARGOSY BOOK STORE, 116 East 59th Street, New York, NY 10022. Prop: Louis Cohen. TN: (212) 753-4455. Est: 1927. Store. Very large stock used. Spec: early medical, early maps, first editions, Americana. Cata: general, 10 a year. A.B.A.A.

RICHARD B. ARKWAY INC., 538 Madison Avenue, New York, NY 10022. TN: (212) 751-8135. Cables: Mapmaker, New York. Est: 1975. Shop, but appointment desirable. Spec: early maps, atlases, travels; early science; 16th and 17th century illustrated. M: A.B.A.A.

THE ASIAN AMERICAN MATERIALS CENTER, 165 West 66th Street, New York, NY 10023. Prop: Y. Kishi. TN: (212) 787-7954. Est: 1971. Business by mail only. Very small stock used; also new books. Spec: Asians in the Americas, (North, Central, South). Cata: on foregoing, occasionally.

ASIAN RARE BOOKS INC., 234 Fifth Avenue, (Third Floor), New York, NY 10001. Prop: Stephen Feldman. TN: (718) 259-3732. Cables: Asianrare, New York. Est: 1975. Private premises; appointment necessary. Medium stock used and rare. Spec: Asia and Middle East.

DAVID AXELROD, 235 West 76th Street, New York, NY 10023.

RICK BARANDES, 61 Fourth Avenue, New York, NY 10003. TN: (212) 505 7065. Spec: decorative, applied and fine arts.

BARNES & NOBLE, INC., 105 Fifth Avenue, New York, NY 10003. TN: ALgonquin 5-8100. Cables: Barnobinc. Shop. Very large stock used, also new. Spec: textbooks and scholarly. Cata: Americana, anthropology, drama, Greece and Rome, Hibernica, literature, modern history, middle ages, orient philosophy, religion, sets and journals. One annually on each subject. A.B.A.A. A.B.A. (Int.). N.A.C.S.

C. VIRGINIA BARNES, 2 Fifth Avenue – 16M, New York, NY 10011. Private premises. Est: 1954. Very small stock used. Spec: art of memory, mnemonics.

J.N. BARTFIELD BOOKS, INC., 45 WEST 57th STREET, NEW YORK, NY 10019. Prop: George Bartfield. TN: (212) 753-1830. Est: 1937. Shop. Very large stock used. Spec: rare, color plate, atlases, Canadiana, Americana, fine bindings, scholarly sets and sporting books. Also art gallery, 19th century American and European paintings. Cata: irregular. A.B.A.A.

BENNETT BOOK STUDIO CORP., 920 BROADWAY, NEW YORK, NY 10010.

BLACK SUN BOOKS, 220 EAST 60TH STREET, NEW YORK, NY 10072. Prop: Harvey Tucker. TN: (212) 688-6622. Est: 1970. By appointment. Small stock; also old and modern master drawings. Spec: 18th-20th century first editions, rare and fine press editions. Cata: 4 or 5 a year. A.B.A.A.

THE BOOK CHEST, 300 EAST 75TH STREET, NEW YORK, NY 10021. Prop: Estelle Chessid. TN: (212) 772 3498. Est: 1972. Private premises, appointment necessary. Spec: historical humor, satire, caricature; natural history; travel. Cata: 2/3 a year. M: A.B.A.A., I.L.A.B.

BOOKFINDERS GENERAL, INC., 145 EAST 27th STREET, NEW YORK, NY 10016. TN: (212) 689-0772. Not possible to see stock. Spec: History, Literature, Sciences, Cinema.

BOOKLORD'S, P.O. BOX 177, PETER STUYVESANT STATION, NEW YORK, NY 10009. Prop: Bern Meyer. TN: (212) 677-4547. Est: 1970. Mail order only. Medium stock. Spec: radio, television, cinema, mass media, journalism. Cata: on foregoing, 1 a year.

BOOKRANGER, 105 CHARLES STREET, NEW YORK, NY 10014.

BOOKS OF WONDER, 464 HUDSON STREET, NEW YORK, NY 10014. Prop: Peter Glassman. TN: (212) 989-3270. Est: 1980. Shop. Small stock used; also new books. Spec: children's illustrated, Oz and Baumiana, juvenile fantasy, folklore and mythology.

WILLIAM BOYER, P.O. BOX 70, PLANETARIUM STATION, NEW YORK, NY 10024.

ABE B. BRAYER, 417 GRAND STREET, NEW YORK, NY 10002. TN: (212) LF 3-4872. Est: 1956. Private premises, appointment necessary. Small stock used. Spec: Literature of the Scouting Movement. Cata: Scouting, Americana, miscellaneous, occasionally.

BRENTANO'S, 586 FIFTH AVENUE, NEW YORK, NY 10036. TN: (212) PL7-8600. Est: 1885. Shop. Medium stock of rare books. Spec: Binding, First editions, Illustrated books and Sports. Cata: 2 per year. M: A.B.A.A.

MARTIN BRESLAUER, INC., P.O. BOX 607, NEW YORK, NY, 10028. Prop: B.H. Breslauer. TN: (212) 794-2995. Spec: Autographs, fine bindings, illustrated books, incunabula, manuscripts. M: A.B.A.A.

BROUDE BROTHERS LIMITED, 170 VARICK STREET, NEW YORK, NY 10013. Prop: Dr Ronald Broude. TN: (212) 242-7001. Private premises; by appointment only. Spec: music and musicology, theatre, art; early books. A.B.A.A.

ROBERT K. BROWN BOOKS, 120 EAST 86th STREET, NEW YORK, NY 10028. TN: (212) 427-4014. Est: 1970. Apartment premises; appointment necessary. Very small stock of used and antiq. books; also rare posters. Spec: early modern art, architecture, design. Cata: 2 or 3 a year. A.B.A.A. I.L.A.B.

JUTTA BUCK, 4 EAST, 95TH STREET, NEW YORK, NY 10128. TN: (212) 289-4577. By appointment only. Spec: Botany; natural history; children's books; old prints. M: A.B.A.A.

JAMES F. CARR, 227 EAST 81ST STREET, NEW YORK, NY 10028. TN: (212) 535-8110. Est: 1959. Shop and private premises. Large stock used, also new. Spec: Western Americana, historical Americana, fine and decorative arts. Cata: on foregoing, 6 a year. Also publishing and art gallery.

WM. J. CARR, BASE EXCHANGE OFFICE, APO, NEW YORK, NY 09023. Est: 1959. Small stock used. Spec: Baha'i World Faith. Cata: on foregoing.

H. CELNICK, 2144 MULINER AVENUE, BRONX, NY 10462. Est: 1941. Storeroom, appointment necessary. Medium stock used. Spec: medical, health, Judaica in English, occult, phrenology, theology, religion and natural history, natural healing.

CHARTWELL BOOKSELLERS, PARK AVENUE PLAZA, 55 EAST 52ND STREET, NEW YORK, NY 10055. Prop: Barry Singer. TN: (212) 308-0643. Est: 1983. Shop. Very small stock sec. and antiq. Spec: Winston Churchill first editions and ephemera; angling. Corresp. Français. B: Chemical Bank, 633 Third Ave, New York, NY 10017.

CHIP'S BOOKSHOP, BOX 123, PLANETARIUM STATION, NEW YORK, NY 10024. Prop: Seymour Greenberg. Est: 1957. Shop. Medium stock used. Spec: literature and literary criticism, Conrad, modern first editions. Cata: on foregoing, quarterly.

CLARK BOARDMAN CO. LTD., 435 HUDSON STREET, NEW YORK, NY 10014. TN: 929-7500. Est: 1916. Shop. Very large stock. Spec: legal. Cata: legal, 1 a year.

COHASCO, INC., 321 BROADWAY, NEW YORK, NY 10007. TN: (212) 962-0399. Cables: Cohascoa New York. Office, appointment necessary. Small stock used, also new. Spec: American history. Cata: American history and general, occasionally. MS.

J.M. COHEN, P.O. BOX 542, BRONX, NY 10463. TN: (212) 548-7160. Private premises, appointment necessary. Spec: Decorative and Applied Arts.

LAWRENCE H. CONKLIN, 2 WEST 26th STREET, NEW YORK, NY 10036.

CRISS CROSS BOOKS, BOX 829, CANAL STREET STATION, NEW YORK, NY 10013.

JAMES CUMMINS BOOKSELLER INC., 859 Lexington Avenue, New York, NY 10021. Prop: Carol R. Cummins. TN: (212) 249 6901/6902. Shop, closed Saturdays. Very large stock used; also fine press books new. Spec: sporting; fine press; illustrated; travel and exploration; fine and rare. M: A.B.A.A. *Also at* Pottersville, NJ. q.v.

KIT CURRIE BOOKS, 101 West 12th Street, New York, NY 10011.

MITCHELL CUTLER BOOKS, 61 West 37th Street, New York, NY 10018. TN: (212) 921-9234. Est. 1977. Private premises: appointment necessary. Small stock, art books and exhibition catalogues. Spec: 19th and 20th century American and European art, and twentieth century decorative arts.

HOWARD C. DAITZ—PHOTOGRAPHICA, P.O. Box 530, Old Chelsea Station, New York, NY 10113-0530. (446 West 20th Street, New York, NY 10011). TN: (212) 929-8987. Est: 1972. Private premises; appointment necessary. Very small stock used: also original photographic images from the daguerreotype to contemporary prints, and optical toys. Spec: 19th century books illustrated with original photographs and early photomechanical examples; 20th century books showing work of contemporary photographers; diverse book and/or photograph collections e.g. Negro; Medical; Bourke-White; Hine; Stieglitz; Weston.

B. DALTON, 666 Fifth Avenue, New York, NY 10021.

BEVAN DAVIES BOOKS, 680 Broadway, New York, NY 10012. TN: (212) 925-9132. Spec: Photography, 20th century art. M: A.B.A.A.

JORDAN DAVIES BOOKS, 356 Bowery, New York, NY 10012. TN: (212) 477-3891. Spec: modern fiction and poetry, first editions. M: A.B.A.A.

PETER DECKER, 45 West 57th Street, New York, NY 10019. TN: (212) PLaza 5-8945. Est: 1899. Office, appointment necessary. Small stock used. Spec: American history, travel and voyages. A.B.A.A.

DE SIMON COMPANY, 793 Lexington Avenue, New York, NY 10021. TN: (212) 319-0577 Spec: Italian books 1650-1800, English and American books about Italy printed before 1850.

DOLPHIN BOOK SHOP, P.O. Box 20370, NEW YORK, NY 10025. Prop: Linda K. Montemaggi. TN: (212) 866-8454. Est: 1976. Private premises, postal business only. Medium stock used. Spec: Book Arts. Scholarly out-of-print. Cata: On foregoing, 2 per year. Some new books stocked. B: Manufacturers Hanover Trust. M: A.B.A.

DONAN BOOKS INC., 235 EAST 53rd STREET, NEW YORK, NY 10022. Prop: D. Dryfoos. TN: (212) 421-6210. Est: 1969. Shop. Small stock used only. A.B.A.

PAUL J. DRABECK, 2886 ROOSEVELT AVENUE, BRONX, NY 10465. Est: 1957. Business by post only. Small stock. Spec: Big game hunting, shooting, firearms, ordnance. Cata: on foregoing, several a year.

WILLIAM DREMETTEL, 21 E 22ND ST, (SUITE 1DE), NEW YORK, NY 10010. Fine books; prints. Cata.

MARGARET Du PRIEST – BOOKSELLER, 35 WEST, 16TH STREET, NEW YORK, NY 10011. Spec: Art, books about books, press books, fine printing, scholarly. M: A.B.A.A.

PHILIP C. DUSCHNES, INC., 201 EAST, 66TH STREET, NEW YORK, NY 10011. TN: (212) 861-7832. Cables: Goodbooks. Est: 1930. Store, open normal business hours. Spec: Illuminated manuscripts, rare Bibles, press books, first editions, autographs. Cata: on foregoing, 7 or 8 a year. A.B.A.A. A.B.A.(Int.) I.L.A.B. M.S.A.

HANNS EBENSTEN & COMPANY, P.O. Box 127, GRAND CENTRAL STATION, NEW YORK, NY 10017. TN: (212) 683-7328. Est: 1968. Baedeker and similar travel guides only. Mail order only.

EL CASCAJERO, THE OLD SPANISH BOOK MINE, 506 WEST BROADWAY, NEW YORK, NY 10012. Prop: A. Gran. TN: 254-0905. Est: 1956. Private premises, appointment desirable. Medium stock used. Spec: Hispanica. Cata: on scholarly subjects, irregularly.

PHILIPP FELDHEIM, INC., 96 EAST BROADWAY, NEW YORK, NY 10002. TN: WA 5-3180. Est: 1941. Store. Very large stock used, also new. Spec: Judaica and Hebraica. Cata: once yearly.

EX LIBRIS, 160A EAST 70TH STREET, NEW YORK, NY 10021. Prop: Arthur A. Cohen. TN: (212) 249-2618. Spec: Art, art reference, illustrated books, photography. M: A.B.A.A.

FANTASY ARCHIVES, 71 EIGHTH AVENUE, NEW YORK, NY 10014. Prop: Eric Kramer. TN: (212) 929 5391. Est: 1978. Private premises, appointment necessary. Very large stock sec. and antiq. Spec: fantasy, science fiction. Cata; occasionally. B: Lloyds Bank, 48 Minories, London, and N.Y. City Manufacturers, NY.

PETER THOMAS FISHER, 41 UNION SQUARE WEST, NEW YORK, NY 10008.

JOHN F. FLEMING, INC., 322 EAST 57th STREET, NEW YORK, NY 10022. TN: 755-3242. Spec: rare, manuscripts, fine, A.B.A.A.

LEONARD FOX, LTD., 790 MADISON AVENUE, NEW YORK, NY 10021. TN: (212) 888-5480. Spec: Art Nouveau and Art Deco illustrated books, fashion, watercolours, paintings. M: A.B.A.A.

JANET MacADAM GATTO, 235 WEST 76TH STREET, NEW YORK, NY 10023.

STANLEY GILMAN, P.O. BOX 131, COOPER STATION, NEW YORK, NY 10003. Spec: American history.

LUCIEN GOLDSCHMIDT, 1117 MADISON AVENUE, NEW YORK, NY 10028. Prop: Marguerite S. Goldschmidt. TN: (212) 879-0070. Cables: Printsmith. Est: 1953. Shop. Medium stock. Spec: European continental, French books, rare, illustrated books, prints, drawings. Cata: on foregoing, several a year. A.B.A.A.

ALFRED GOODMAN, P.O. BOX 724, GRAND CENTRAL STATION, NEW YORK 10017. TN: (212) 544-1026. Est: 1890. Private House, appointment necessary. Medium stock. Spec: Manuscripts, Diaries, Journals, Old letters. M: Manuscript Society.

GOTHAM BOOK MART, 41 WEST 47th STREET, NEW YORK, NY 10036. Prop: Andreas Brown. TN: (212) 719-4448. Est: 1920. Shop. Large stock. Spec: modern literature, little magazines, cinema, modern first editions, manuscripts. Cata: small press literature, cinema, theatre, and lists of individual writers, 3 or 4 a year. A.B.A. A.B.A.A.

GRAMERCY BOOK SHOP, 22 EAST 17th STREET, NEW YORK, NY 10003. TN: (212) ALgonquin 5-5568. Prop: L. Wilbur. Est: 1940. Office, appointment necessary. Medium stock used. Spec: rare, English books before 1701 and American literature. Cata: on foregoing, 4 a year.

L.S. GRANBY, 1168 LEXINGTON AVENUE, NEW YORK, NY 10028. TN: (212) 249-2651. Spec: rare, graphics, photography.

GREENWICH BOOKS LTD., 127 GREENWICH AVENUE, NEW YORK, NY 10014. Prop: R. Richards & B. Bailey. TN: (212) 242-3095. Est: 1976. Shop. Small stock used. Spec: New and used Art Books, Limited editions and contemporary first editions, Autographs, some leather bound. Cata: 2 or 3 times per year. B: Manufacturer's Hanover Trust.

K. GREGORY, 222 EAST 71st STREET, NEW YORK, NY 10021. TN: (212) 288-2119. Est: 1931. By appointment only. Spec: illustrated books, botanical, prints, color plate books, miniature books. Cata: on foregoing, annually. A.B.A.A.

GRYPHON BOOKSHOP, 216 WEST 89TH STREET, NEW YORK, NY 10024. TN: (212) 362-0706. Est: 1974. Shop, open seven days a week. Medium stock used. Spec: children's; illustrated, modern first editions; music.

ALBERT GUTKIN, 1133 BROADWAY, NEW YORK, NY 10010. TN: (212) CH 3-3600. Est: 1942. Storeroom; any time in business hours by appointment. Medium stock used and antiq. Spec: natural history and view books.

B. HACKER, 7 PARK AVENUE, NEW YORK, NY 10016. Spec: Literary manuscripts and first editions.

HACKER ART BOOKS, 54 WEST 57th STREET, NEW YORK, NY 10019. TN: PLaza 7-1450. Shop. Est: 1946. Stock of over 100,000 volumes new; also rare. Spec: art, costume. Cata: fine and applied arts occasionally.

RENATE HALPERN GALLERIES INC., 325 EAST 79TH STREET, 10E, NEW YORK, NY 10021. Prop: Renate Halpern & Arthur B. Halpern. TN (212) 988-9316. Est: 1974. Private premises; appointment necessary. Very small stock used; also new books. Spec: oriental rugs, tapestries, textiles and early travel to weaving area.

CHARLES HAMILTON GALLERIES, 200 WEST 57TH STREET, NEW YORK, NY 10019.

LATHROP C. HARPER INC., 300 MADISON AVENUE, NEW YORK, NY 10017. Prop: Felix B. de Marez Oyens. TN: (212) 490-3412. Cables: Lactage. Est: 1881. Office Building, appointment preferred. Spec: incunabula; historical bindings; illustrated books. A.B.A.A. I.L.A.B. A.B.A.

HARRIS SEARCH AND RESEARCH, 1145 EAST 37th STREET, NEW YORK, NY 10016.

W.S. HEINMAN, 225 WEST 57TH STREET, (SUITE 404), NEW YORK, NY 10019. TN: (212) 757-7628. Spec: Africa, dictionaries, foreign languages, Europe. A.B.A.A.

J.-N. HERLIN, 108 WEST 28th STREET, NEW YORK, NY 10001. TN: (212) 741-1880. Est: 1972. Private premises, open 10.30-19.00 Monday thru Saturday. Medium stock. Spec: art from 1850; film, radio, television, mass communications; French literature. Cata: on foregoing, irregularly.

JONATHAN A. HILL, BOOKSELLER, INC., 470 WEST END AVENUE, NEW YORK, NY 10024. TN: (212) 496-7856. By appointment only. Spec: Science, medicine, bibliography, voyages, travels and exploration, press books, fine printing, printing and printing history. M: A.B.A.A.

GLENN HOROWITZ BOOKSELLER INC., 141 EAST 44TH STREET, NEW YORK, NY 10017. Prop: Aaron & Glenn Horowitz. TN: (212) 557-1381. Est: 1979. Storeroom, open normal business hours, closed Saturdays. Small stock used. Spec: modern first editions, (galleys, proofs, manuscripts, letters).

HOUSE OF BOOKS LIMITED, 667 MADISON AVENUE, NEW YORK, NY 10021. Prop: Mrs. Louis Henry Cohn. TN: (212) 755-5998. Office. Spec: modern first editions, autographs, manuscripts. Cata: occasionally. A.B.A.A. I.L.A.B. A.B.A.

NMAN'S BOOK SHOP, 50 EAST 50th STREET, NEW YORK, NY 10022. Prop: Nathan Ladden. TN: (212) 755-2867. Est: 1926. Shop. Small stock used and antique. Spec: first editions; rare books; fine bindings. A.B.A.A. A.B.A. (Int.).

INTERNATIONAL UNIVERSITY BOOKSELLERS, INC., I.U.B. BUILDING, 30 IRVING PLACE, NEW YORK, NY 10003. Prop: Max J. Holmes. TN: (212) 254-4100. Spec: Periodicals in all fields, reference materials and book collections. M: A.B.A.A.

HARMER JOHNSON BOOKS LIMITED, 38 EAST 64TH STREET, NEW YORK, NY 10021. Prop: Harmer Johnson and Peter Sharrer. TN: (212) 752-1189. Shop. Medium stock used; also new books. Spec: tribal and ancient art and anthropology.

ELLIOT KLEIN, LTD., 19 WEST 44th STREET, NEW YORK, NY 10036. TN: (212) 840-6885. Est: 1975. Shop, closed Saturdays and Sundays except by appointment. Small stock used. Spec: Folklore, Mythology and related fields. Cata: 5 per year. New books also stocked.

JESSE'S BOOKS, 110 GREENWICH AVENUE, NEW YORK, NY 10014. Prop: Jesse Joseph. TN: (212) 691-6070. Est: 1979. Shop open normal business hours. Small stock used, also new. Spec: Paperbacks, philosophy.

KIM KAUFMAN, 1370 LEXINGTON AVENUE, SUITE 1E, NEW YORK CITY NY 10128. TN: (212) 369-3384. Spec: Children's, illustrated books, autograph material, fiction, drawings. M: A.B.A.A.

JUDITH AND PETER KLEMPERER, 400 SECOND AVENUE, NEW YORK, NY 10010.

H.P. KRAUS, 16 EAST 46th STREET, NEW YORK, NY 10017. TN: (212) 687-4808. Cables: Krausbooks, Newyork. Spec: rare, mediaeval manuscripts, incunabula, early science and medicine, early general Americana. A.B.A.A.

LEE AND LEE BOOKSELLERS, 424 BOOME STREET, NEW YORK, NY 10013. Prop: Virginia Lee Green. TN: (212) 226-8135. Est: 1970 Private premises; appointment necessary. Small stock used. Spec: fine arts, architecture, classical archaeology. Cata: on foregoing, 3 or 4 a year.

LANDMARK BOOK COMPANY, 119 WEST 57TH STREET, NEW YORK NY 10019. Prop: Norman Baustein. TN: (212) 765-5252. Est: 1975 Showroom, open normal business hours. Wholesalers of remainders o scholarly reprints for the antiquarian trade; stock of 5,000 titles.

JANET LEHR, INC., P.O. Box 617, GRACIE STATION, NEW YORK, NY 10028. TN: (212) 288-6234/1802. Est: 1971. Private premises, appointment necessary. Small stock used. Spec: Photographically illustrated books, Photographic reference books, Photographs, architecture, autographed material. Cata: Annually. B: Manufacturers Hanover. M: A.B.A., International Photography Art Assoc., A.B.A.A.

WILLIAM B. LIEBMANN, 5700 ARLINGTON AVENUE, RIVERDALE, NY 10471. Prop: James E. Liebmann. TN: (212) 548-6014. By appointment only. Spec: First editions, manuscripts, press books, fine printing. M: A.B.A.A.

BARBARA LEIBOWITS, GRAPHICS LTD., 80 CENTRAL PARK WEST, NEW YORK, NY 10023. TN: (212) 799-0570. By appointment only. Spec: Illustrated books, press books, fine printing, fine bindings, drawings. M: A.B.A.A.

MADELINE M. LESNEVICH, 1160 FIFTH AVENUE, NEW YORK, NY 10029.

LIBER LIBRORUM, 551 HUDSON STREET, NEW YORK, NY 10014.

JAMES LOWE AUTOGRAPHS LTD., 30 EAST 60TH STREET, (SUITE 907), NEW YORK, NY 10022. Prop: James Lowe. TN: (212) 759-0775. Est: 1970. Shop, open Mon.-Fri. 11 a.m. to 6 p.m., Saturdays: 1 p.m. to 5 p.m. Spec: Historic and Literary Autographs, Letters, Documents, Manuscripts, Signed First Editions, Photographica. Cata: Quarterly. M: A.B.A.A. I.L.A.B.

MANNYE'S BOOKSTORE, 114 4th AVENUE, NEW YORK, NY 10003.

MARTIN'S BOOK SHOP, 162 WEST 4th STREET, NEW YORK, NY 10003. Shop open normal business hours. Small stock used.

J.M. MARTIN, 2039 CRUGER AVENUE, BRONX, NY 10462. TN: (212) 931-9784 and TY2-3743. Est: 1966. Private premises; appointment necessary. Medium stock used; also some new. Spec: correspondence courses all subjects; management, business books, vocational books, marketing. Cata: on foregoing, 2 a year. A.B.A.

M.M. EINHORN MAXWELL, AT THE SIGN OF THE DANCING BEAR, 80 EAST 11TH STREET, NEW YORK, NY 10003. Prop: Marilyn M. Einhorn. TN: (212) 228-6767 and 477-5066. Est: 1977. Office: visitors by appointment only. Medium stock used, out of print and rare. Spec: food and drink, dance, puppetry and theatre. Cata: 4 per year. M: A.B.A.A.

BENJAMIN MAYO BOOKS, P.O. BOX 694, COOPER STATION, NEW YORK, NY 10003.

MEMORY SHOP, P.O. BOX 365, COOPER STATION, NEW YORK, NY 10003. (100 Fourth Avenue). Prop: Mark Ricci. TN: (212) GR 3-2404. Very large stock of photographs and magazines, movies, theatre and general items from 1900 to date. Cata: movies, 1 a year.

ISAAC MENDOZA BOOK COMPANY, 15 ANN STREET, NEW YORK, NY 10038. Prop: Walter L. Caron. TN: (212) 227-8777. Est: 1894. Shop. Large stock used, also new books. Spec: science fiction, modern first editions, detective fiction. M: A.B.A.A.

THE MILITARY BOOKMAN LTD., 29 EAST 93RD STREET, NEW YORK, NY 10128. Prop: Harris & Margaretta Colt. TN: (212) 348-1280. Est: 1976. Shop, closed on Mondays. Large stock used. Military, Naval and Aviation History only. Cata: three a year by subscription. B: Republic National Bank. No. 280002319.

ARTHUR H. MINTERS, INC., 39 WEST 14TH STREET (ROOM 401), NEW YORK, NY 10011. TN: (212) 989-0593. Est: 1957. Storeroom, appointment necessary. Medium stock used. Spec: art, architecture, archaeology, illustrated, literature. Cata: on foregoing, 4 a year. A.B.A.A. I.L.A.B.

MOVABLE TYPE BOOKSHOP, 1377 LEXINGTON AVENUE, NEW YORK, NY 10028. Props: H. Weitz & S. Neill. TN: (212) 831-2213. Est: 1909. Shop. Large stock of used; also a few new. Spec: illustrated, sporting, press books, first editions. Cata: on foregoing.

MURDER INK, 271 WEST 87TH STREET, NEW YORK, NY 10024. Prop: Carol Brener. Manager Jane Dentinger. TN: (212) 362-8905. Est: 1972. Shop, open afternoons. Small stock sec. and antiq. Also new books. Spec: Mystery and crime fiction including reference books: Newsletters twice a year. Corresp: Français, Deutsch and Español. B: Citybank, 86th Street and Broadway, New York, NY 10024.

N.A.S. BOOKS, 1181 AMSTERDAM AVENUE, NEW YORK, NY 10027. TN: (212) 666-3060 Very large stock used; also records. Spec: poetry, drama, performing arts, humanities, fiction.

NEW YORK BOUND BOOKSHOP, 43 WEST 54TH STREET, NEW YORK, NY 10019. Prop: Barbara L. Cohen. TN: (212) 245-8503. Est: 1974. Shop, closed on Wednesdays. Small stock used. Spec: New York City, Americana. Cata: 3-4 times per year. Some new books kept relating to New York. B: European-American Bank. Acc. No: 028 03968 3 0253.

NORTH AMERICAN MAPS AND AUTOGRAPHS, 97 FORT WASHINGTON AVENUE, NEW YORK, NY 10032. Prop: E. Forbes Smiley III & Lisa A. Benson. TN: (212) 568-0639. Spec: Maps, topograph, travel. Cata.

NUDEL BOOKS, 135 SPRING STREET, NEW YORK, NY 10012. Prop: Harry Nudel. TN: (212) 966-5624. Est: 1979. Private Premises, appointment necessary. Large stock used. Spec: First Editions, Photography, Black Literature, Art. Cata: Twice a year. B: East River. No: 03-262661-6. Post cheque a/c No: 2260-7036-003001 0995-0218. M: Soho Merchants Ass.

OCEANIC PRIMITIVE ARTS, 88 EAST 10th STREET, NEW YORK, NY 10003. Prop: Lynda Cunningham. TN: (212) 982-8060. Est: 1967. Shop open normal business hours. Gallery by appointment only. Very small stock used, also new. Spec: Primitive art, anthropology of Africa, Oceania, Americas and Indonesia. Cata: Yearly.

OLANA GALLERY, 2390 PALISADE AVENUE, BRONX, NY 10463. Prop: Bernard Rosenberg. TN: (212) 796-9822. Est: 1971. Private premises, appointment necessary. Small stock, also new books. Spec: American art, Japanese prints, photography. Cata: on foregoing.

OLD BLOCK BOOKS, 240 WEST 10th STREET, NEW YORK, NY 10014. Prop: Davied Preiss. TN: (212) 255-0416. Est: 1978. Shop open normal business hours. Small stock used, also new. Spec: Illustrated books. Cata: Yearly.

OLD GLORY TRADING POST, P.O. BOX 1327, GRACIE STATION, NEW YORK, NY 10028. Prop: Gloria K. Davidson. Est: 1971. Private premises, stock not able to be seen. Small stock used. B: Citibank, Acc.No: 22892986 28.

THE OLD PRINT SHOP, INC., 150 LEXINGTON AVENUE, NEW YORK, NY 10016. Prop: Kenneth M. Newman TN: (212) 683-3950. Spec: Americana in old prints, drawings and maps. A.B.A.A.

PAGEANT BOOK AND PRINT SHOP, 109 EAST 9th STREET, NEW YORK, NY 10003. Prop: Sidney B. & Shirley Solomon. TN: (212) 674-5296. Est: 1945. Shop. Stock of 100,000 books and over a million old prints. Spec: old prints and maps, art, American fiction, literature, Americana. Cata: on foregoing. A.B.A.A.

PARAGON BOOK GALLERY LIMITED, 2130 BROADWAY, NEW YORK, NY 10023. TN: (212) 532-4920. Cables: Paragalery. Est: 1938. Shop. Very large stock used; also new books. Spec: Orient, Africa, Near and Middle East.

PHOENIX BOOK SHOP, 22 JONES STREET, NEW YORK, NY 10014. Prop: R.A. Wilson. TN: (212) OR5-2795. Est: 1938. Shop. New books. Spec: modern first editions; 20th century poetry and little magazines. Cata: first editions, 4 a year.

PIMPERNEL BOOKS, 41 UNION SQUARE WEST, NEW YORK, NY 10003.

POMANDER BOOKSHOP, 252 WEST 95th STREET, NEW YORK, NY 10025. Prop: William Hamilton & Carlos Goez. TN: (212) 866-1777. Est: 1975. Shop. Medium stock used. Spec: 19th and 20th Century literature, Art, Philosophy and Religion. B: Chemical Bank No: 074 014021.

PUTNAM BOOK STORE, 85 GREENWICH STREET, NEW YORK, NY 10006. Prop: Ian Chattan. TN: (212) 425-8422. Est: 1950. Books about New York City only, bought and sold. M: Book League of New York City.

RADIO CITY BOOK STORE, 324 WEST 47th STREET, NEW YORK, NY 10036. Prop: Seymour Gaynor. TN: (212) 245-5754. Est: 1934. Shop: appointment preferable. Large stock used; also new books. Spec: books for hotels, culinary and food industry. Cata: on hotel management, professional cooking, food books, once a year.

BRUCE J. RAMER, 401 EAST 80TH STREET, NEW YORK, NY 10021. TN: (212) 772-6211. TA: Experiment-NY. Est 1981. Private premises, appointment necessary. Small stock sec. and antiq. Spec: Old and rare science, medicine, natural history, technology, mathematics. Cata: 1 or 2 a year. Corresp: Français, Deutsch.

RICHARD C. RAMER, 225 EAST 70th STREET, NEW YORK, NY 10021. TN: (212) 737-0222/0223. Cables: Livroraro. Est: 1969. Apartment, appointment necessary. Medium stock old and rare and some new (mostly Portuguese). Spec: Latin America, Spain, Portugal, and Portuguese-speaking Asia and Africa; nautical books, voyages and travel. Cata: occasionally. A.B.A.A. I.L.A.B.

REFERENCE BOOK CENTER, INC., 175 FIFTH AVENUE, NEW YORK, NY 10010. Prop: Saul Shine. TN: (212) 677-2160. Est: 1961. Shop. Small Stock used; also new books. Spec: general reference books, and encyclopedias. Cata: 2 a year.

RETRIEVER BOOKS, P.O. Box 119, NEW YORK, NY 10024. Prop: Marvin Stern. TN: (212) TR 3-0757. Est: 1965. Private premises, appointment necessary. Medium stock used. Spec: economics, social history, literary criticism.

RIVENDELL BOOKSHOP, 109 SAINT MARK'S PLACE, NEW YORK, NY 10009. Prop: Eileen Gordon. TN: (212) 533-2501. Est: 1977. Shop open normal business hours. Medium stock used, also new. Spec: Celtic myth, Lore and legend, Arthurian and Norse legend, fantasy, faerie, search service.

JOLLY ROGER, 190 COLUMBUS AVENUE, NEW YORK, NY 10025.

PAULETTE ROSE, FINE AND RARE BOOKS, 360 EAST 72ND STREET, NEW YORK, NY 10021. TN: (212) 861-5607. By appointment only. Spec: Women; French literature and France. M: A.B.A.A.

MARY S. ROSENBERG INC., 17 WEST 60TH STREET, NEW YORK, NY 10023. TN: (212) 362-4873. Cables: Findall, New York. Est: 1940. Upstairs shop and storeroom, open normal business hours. Very large stock of used and antiq. and also new books, records and educational games. Spec: German and French Books in any subject, Judaica, Middle Ages. A.B.A.A. I.L.A.B.

LEONA ROSTENBERG—RARE BOOKS, P.O. Box 188, GRACIE STATION, NEW YORK, NY 10028. Prop: Leona Rostenberg & Madeleine B. Stern. TN: (212) 831-6628. Est: 1944. Private premises, appointment necessary. Small stock used. Spec: Renaissance, Reformation, 17th century, France, political science. Cata: on foregoing, 4 a year. A.B.A.A. I.L.A.B. A.B.A.

ARTHUR ROTHMAN FINE ARTS, 1123 BROADWAY, NEW YORK, NY 10010. TN: (212) 255-0760. Est: 1947. Storeroom, open normal business hours. Small stock used. Spec: fine arts and illustrated books with originals. Also fine arts prints, reproductions and originals.

ROWLAND'S, 50 EAST 96th STREET, NEW YORK, NY 10028. Prop: Ted Rowland. TN: (212) 369-6581. Est: 1960. Private premises; appointment necessary. Very small stock used.

RUSSICA BOOK AND ART SHOP INC., 799 BROADWAY, NEW YORK, NY 10003. Prop: Mrs. R. Zheleznyak. TN: 473-7480. Est: 1976. Shop, appointment necessary. Very large stock used. Spec: Russian and Slavic books. Cata: Once a year. New books also kept.

WILLIAM H. SCHAB, 11 EAST 57TH STREET, NEW YORK, NY 10022. Prop: Frederick G. Schab. TN: (212) 758-0327. Spec: woodcut books, manuscripts, drawings, Americana. A.B.A.A.

HOWARD SCHICKLER, 48 EAST 13TH STREET, NEW YORK, NY 10003. TN: (212) 674-1953. Est: 1975. Private premises; appointment necessary. Very small stock used. Spec: photography. M: Association of International Photography Art Dealers.

WOLFGANG SCHIEFER BOOKS, 220 EAST 22ND STREET, (SUITE GLM), NEW YORK, NY 10010. TN: (212) 475-3139. Private premises; appointment necessary. Small stock used. Spec: Braziliana. *Also in* CONNECTICUT, Q.V.

JUSTIN G. SCHILLER LIMITED, P.O. BOX 1667, F.D.R. STATION, NEW YORK, NY 10150. (1 East 61st Street, New York, NY 10021.) Pres: Justin G. Schiller; Treasurer: Raymond M. Wapner. TN: (212) 832-8231. Cables: Kinderbook. Est: 1970. Shop; Medium stock used also appraisals. Spec: Children's historical literature; 18th and 19th century graphics; Decorative arts (Art Deco and Nouveau). Cata: 4 a year. A.B.A.A. I.L.A.B. A.B.A.

E.K. SCHREIBER, 135 EAST 63TH STREET, NEW YORK, NY 10021. Prop: Fred Schreiber. TN: (212) 772-3150. Est: 1971. Private premises, appointment necessary. Small stock. Spec: classical antiquity; Renaissance humanism; rare and early editions of the Greek and Latin classics, emblem books, incunabula. Cata: on foregoing, 2-3 a year.

OSCAR SCHREYER BOOKS, 230 EAST 79th STREET, NEW YORK, NY 10021. Prop: Dr. Oscar Schreyer. TN: (212) 628-6227. Est: 1961. Private premises, appointment necessary. Small stock used. Spec: Medicine before 1800; Economy before 1850; Pacifism; Morocco. B: Chase Manhattan Bank.

SCIENTIFIC LIBRARY SERVICE, 29 EAST 10TH STREET, NEW YORK, NY 10003. Prop: Samuel Orlinick. Est: 1946. Shop. Stock of 20,000 used and some new books. Spec: music; history of science. Cata: 2 a year. A.B.A.A.

NATHAN SIMONS, 1816 SEMINOLE AVENUE, NEW YORK, NY 10461. TN: 863-4328. Est: 1911. Mail order only. Small stock used. Spec: atheism, freethought.

ROSEJEANNE SLIFER, 30 PARK AVENUE, NEW YORK, NY 10016. TN: (212) 685-2040. By appointment only. Spec: autographs and manuscripts; historical documents, old maps, atlases. A.B.A.A.

SOKAL RESEARCH SERVICE, 2953 BAINBRIDGE AVENUE, BRONX, NY 10458.

SOTHEBY'S, BOOK DEPT., 1334 YORK AVENUE, NEW YORK, NY 10021. TN: (212) 606-7000. Auctioneers of fine books and autograph letters. M: A.B.A.A.

MILTON SPAHN, 1370 SAINT NICHOLAS AVENUE, NEW YORK, NY 10033. TN: (212) 568-9593. Est: 1946. Private premises, appointment necessary. Small stock used. Spec: first editions, bibliography, fantasy. Cata: general.

PETER SPERLING, OLD CHELSEA STATION, P.O. BOX 300, NEW YORK, NY 10113-300. Prop: Lucy Kalk & Peter Sperling. TN: (212) 242-5167. Est: 1977. Private premises; postal business only. Very large stock used. Spec: P.G. Wodehouse, Jack London, Rufus M. Jones.

CHARLES STEIR, 630 WEST 246th STREET, BRONX, NY 10471.

CHRISTOPHER P. STEPHENS, 347 E. 52nd ST. & 10, N.Y. 10022. TN: (212) 759-2152. Est. 1966. Private premises, appointment necessary. Large stock used (about 20,000 volumes), also own reprints. Spec: fiction (modern, science, detective, translations), poetry, scholarly congresses and symposia. Cata: on foregoing 3 per year.

STEVENS & CO., BOOKS, INCORPORATED, 200 PARK AVENUE SOUTH, NEW YORK, NY 10003. Pres: M. Leleiko. TN: (212) 477-2930. Est: 1951. Storeroom; appointment necessary. Very large stock used; also new books. Spec: mathematics, chemistry, physics, history of science, technology. Cata: once a year.

RICHARD STODDARD, PERFORMING ARTS BOOKS, 90 EAST 10th STREET, NEW YORK, NY 10003. TN: (212) 982-9440. Est: 1975. Shop, closed on Mondays and Tuesdays. Medium stock used. Spec: Theatre, Film, Dance, Popular Entertainments. Cata: 5 times a year.

STRAND BOOKSTORE, 828 BROADWAY, NEW YORK, NY 10003. Prop: Fred Bass. TN: (212) 473-1452. Est: 1930. Shop, open Monday to Saturday 9.30 to 18.30 hrs; main floor only open till 21.30 Mon. to Fri, Sunday 11.00 to 17.00 hrs. Stock of 2,000,000 books on all subjects, used, antiquarian, rare, remainders, reviewers' copies.

STUBBS BOOKS AND PRINTS, INC., 28 EAST 18TH STREET, NEW YORK, NY 10003. TN: (212) 982-8368. Est: 1981. Gallery/Shop. Medium stock used and rare. Spec: architecture, classical archaeology, Egyptology; decorative arts; landscape architecture.

SWANN GALLERIES, INC., 104 EAST 25TH STREET, NEW YORK, NY 10010. Prop: George S. Lowry. TN: (212) 254-4710. Auctioneers and appraisers. M: A.B.A.A.

THEATREBOOKS, INC., 1576 BROADWAY, ROOM 312, NEW YORK CITY, NY 10036. Prop: Robert & Jane Emerson. TN: (212) 757-2834. Est: 1979. Shop. Medium stock used. Spec: Theatre. Cata: 4 times per year. B: Chase Manhattan Bank, 1211 Ave. of the Americas, NYC 10036. Acc. No: 226-1-041756. M: A.B.A.

TOTTERIDGE BOOK SHOP, 667 MADISON AVENUE (SUITE 305), NEW YORK, NY 10021. Prop: Oliver Twigg. TN: (212) 421-1040. Spec: sporting books, fine bindings, English and American first editions. A.B.A.A.

TREBIZOND RARE BOOKS, 667 MADISON AVENUE, NEW YORK, NY 10021. Prop: Williston R. Benedict. TN: (212) 371-1980. Spec: English, American and Continental literature and travel A.D. 1600 to 1900. Catalogues issued regularly.

PETER TUMARKIN, FINE BOOKS INC., 310 EAST 70TH STREET, NEW YORK, NY 10021. TN: (212) 348-8187. Spec: German books; rare and first editions. M: A.B.A.A.

DAVID TUNICK INC., 12 EAST 81TH STREET, NEW YORK, NY 10028. TN: (212) 570-0090. Private premises; appointment necessary. Spec: illustrated books; also old and modern engravings, sets of fine prints, etc. A.B.A.A.

URSUS BOOKS LIMITED, 39 EAST 78TH STREET (CORNER MADISON AVENUE), NEW YORK, NY 10021. Prop: T. Peter Kraus. TN: (212) 772-8787. Est: 1972. Shop. Large stock out-of-print. Spec: Arts, architecture, fine printing, illustrated books, decorative prints. Cata: on foregoing, 5 or 6 a year. A.B.A.A.

VANITY FAIR, 108 FOURTH AVENUE, NEW YORK, NY 10003. Prop: Herbert Oxer. TN: 475-4352. Est: 1950. Shop. Very large stock used. Spec: theater, literature, fiction, American history. Cata: general, 3-4 a year. Also prints.

VICTORIA BOOK SHOP, 303 FIFTH AVENUE (SUITE 8DG), NEW YORK, NY 10016. Prop: Milton Reissman. TN: (212) 683-7849. Est: 1965. Private premises, appointment preferred. Medium stock used. Spec: Children's books and illustrated books 16th to 20th centuries; miniature books, most 19th century and earlier; Original Art of the Illustrator. Cata: 3 times per year. B: Merchant Bank of N.Y. Acc.No: 5007260. M.: A.B.A.A. I.L.A.B.

CHARLES WALBERG, 72 BARUCH DRIVE, NEW YORK, NY 10002.

ANDREW WASHTON, 411 EAST 83RD STREET, NEW YORK, NY 10028. TN: (212) 751-7027, or (212) 861-0513. Est: 1979. Private premises: appointment necessary. Small stock used. Spec: art reference and art history, standard monographs, exhibition catalogues. Lists and catalogues issued.

PETER MALLON WALSH, 123 EAST 90th STREET, NEW YORK, NY 10028.

W.A. WAVROVICS, 224 FIRST AVENUE, NEW YORK, NY 10009. Est: 1939. Shop, open 1-30 p.m. to 6 p.m. Very large stock used. Spec: Americana, technical, collectors' items.

MICHAEL R. WEINTRAUB, INC., 306 WEST 100TH STREET, NEW YORK, NY 10025. TN: (212) 678-0174. Spec: Modern illustrated books from France, Germany, Austria, Eastern Europe; stage design; architecture. M: A.B.A.A.

SAMUEL WEISER INC., 132 EAST 24TH STREET, NEW YORK, NY 10010. Prop: Donald Weiser. Est: 1926. Shop. Large stock used; also new books. Spec: Esoteric; oriental; metaphysical. M: A.B.A.A.

E. WEYHE, INC., 794 LEXINGTON AVENUE, NEW YORK, NY 10021. Prop: Gertrude Weyhe Dennis. TN: (212) 836-5466. Spec: Art, architecture. M: A.B.A.A.

PHILIP WILLIAMS, NON SEQUITUR, 329 COLUMBUS AVENUE, NEW YORK, NY 10023.

FRED WILSON, 80 EAST 11TH STREET, SUITE 334, NY 10003. TN: (212) 533-6381. Est: 1972. Shop. Small stock. Spec: Antiquarian chess literature. Cata: on foregoing, 4 per year.

THE WITKIN GALLERY, 41 East 57th Street, New York, NY 10022.

WITTENBORN ART BOOKS INC., 1018 Madison Avenue, New York, NY 10021. President: Gabriel Austin. TN: (212) 288-1558. Est: 1937. Shop. Medium stock used; also new books. Spec: Visual arts and architecture. Cata: monthly.

WURLITZER-BRUCK, 60 Riverside Drive, New York, NY 10024. Prop: Marianne Wurlitzer. TN: (212) 787-6431. By appointment only. Spec: Music, prints of musical subjects, musical autographs and ephemera. M: A.B.A.A.

XIMENES: RARE BOOKS, INC., 19 East 69th Street, New York, NY 10021. Prop: Stephen Weissman. TN: (212) 744-0226. Est: 1963. Shop. Medium stock rare. Spec: Rare books, Economics, English and American Literature; Medicine and science, Americana, Voyages and travel.

Dr MORRIS N. YOUNG, 170 Broadway, New York, NY 10038. TN: BE 3-2344. Private premises, appointment necessary. Very small stock used. Library of memory systems, mnemonics and hocus pocus.

ALFRED F. ZAMBELLI, 156 5th Avenue, New York, NY 10010. TN: (212) 734-2141. Est: 1941. Storeroom; business by mail only. Large stock used. Spec: mediaeval, Renaissance, Reformation, early modern history, philosophy, religion, culture; bibliography; palaeography. Cata: on foregoing, 4 a year. A.B.A.A.

ZITA BOOKS, 760 West End Avenue, New York, NY 10025. Prop: G. Laderman. TN: (203) 222-1993. Est: 1959. Storeroom, appointment necessary. Medium stock used. Spec: caricature and comic illustration, languages (Japanese and Chinese), Judaica and Hebraica. Cata: on foregoing, 2 a year and lists.

IRVING ZUCKER ART BOOKS, INC., 303 Fifth Avenue (Suite 1503), New York, NY 10016. Prop: Irving Zucker. TN: (212) 679-6332. Est: 1939. Shop, closed on Saturdays. Medium stock used. Spec: Art, Colour plate, Illustrated Books. Cata: Occasionally. B: Manufacturers Hanover. M: A.B.A.A., M.A.C.

37. NEW YORK (NY.) (LONG ISLAND AND STATEN ISLAND)

AMITYVILLE   AURORA

BAYSIDE
BOICEVILLE
BRONXVILLE
BROOKLYN
CEDARHURST
COLD SPRING HARBOR
DEANSBORO
DIX HILLS
ELMHURST
FARMINGDALE
FLUSHING
FOREST HILLS
FREEPORT
GARDEN CITY
GLEN COVE
GLEN HEAD
GLENDALE
GREAT NECK
GREAT RIVER
GREENPORT
HAUPPAUGE
HICKSVILLE
HILTON
HOPEWELL JUNCTION
HUNTINGTON
JACKSON HEIGHTS
JAMAICA
JERICHO
KATONAH
KEW GARDENS

KINGS PARK
LIDO BEACH
LINDENHURST
LONG ISLAND CITY
MILLER PLACE
MONTICELLO
NEW HYDE PARK
NORTH BELLMORE
NORTHPORT
OCEANSIDE
OLD BETHPAGE
PATCHOGUE
PIERMONT
PLANDOME
PLAINVIEW
PORT JEFFERSON
PORT WASHINGTON
REGO PARK
RICHMOND HILL
ROCKVILLE CENTRE
ROCKY POINT
ROSLYN
SAINT JAMES
SEARINGTOWN
SOUTHAMPTON
STATEN ISLAND
STONY BROOK
WADING RIVER
WEST HEMPSTEAD

ALBEE BOOKS, 2163 77TH STREET, BROOKLYN, NY 11214. Prop: Alfred M. Slotnick. TN: (212) CL 6-7872. Est: 1955. Private premises, appointment necessary. Small stock used, also new. Spec: violin family. Cata: violin family, irregularly.

JOYCE ACKERMAN, 441 MAXWELL STREET, WEST HEMPSTEAD, NY 11552.

ANTHEIL BOOKSELLERS, 2177 ISABELLE COURT, NORTH BELLMORE, NY 11710. Prop: Nate & Sheila Rind. TN: (516) TA 6-2094. Est: 1958. Storeroom, appointment necessary. Large stock used, also new. Spec: naval, maritime, aviation. Cata: naval and military; 4 a year.

JAMES E. ARNAY, 110-56, 71ST AVENUE, FOREST HILLS, NY 11375. Prop: J.E. Arnay. Est: 1955. Spec: precious stones and related items.

RUTH ARNOLD, 345 NORTH OCEAN AVENUE, PATCHOGUE, NY 11772.

AUSTIN BOOK SHOP, 82-60A AUSTIN STREET, P.O. BOX 36, KEW GARDENS, NY 11415. Prop: Bernard Titowsky. TN: (212) HI1-1199. Est: 1954. Business by post only. Large stock. Spec: American history; literature; immigration, woman, the law, Cata: on foregoing, 6 a year. Retail outlet shop at 82-64 Austin St., Kew Gardens, NY 11415.

B. AND J. BOOKS, 91-16 63RD DRIVE, REGO PARK, NY 11374. Prop: Barry Skolnick. TN: (212) 896-1272. Shop. Medium stock used. Spec: war and military. Cata: 2 a year.

B C BOOKS, 6-10 POND VIEW, EAST PATCHOGUE, NY 11772.

BARTEL DENTAL BOOK CO. INC., 112 CROWN STREET, BROOKLYN, NY 11225. Prop: Mrs. Thelma Loeb. TN: (212) 772-8170. Est: 1970. Storeroom, appointment necessary. Medium stock. Spec: dentistry. Cata: dental books and backfiles of periodicals, irregularly.

BATTERY PARK BOOK COMPANY, P.O. BOX 710, FOREST HILLS, NY 11375. TN: (718) 261-1216. Private premises, appointment necessary. Spec: bibliography; performing arts; bindings and typography.

ELEANOR BECKHARD, RED SPRING LANE, GLEN COVE, NY 11542.

EMIL J. BERGMANN, 66-69 FRESH POND ROAD, BROOKLYN, NY 11227. TN: (212) VA 1-2713. Est: 1947. Business by post only. Very small stock. Spec: Americana printed before 1860. Cata: Americana, irregularly.

GEORGE A. BERNSTEIN, BOOKDEALER, 67 REMSEN STREET, BROOKLYN, NY 11201. TN: (212) 875-7582. Est: 1972. Private premises, appointment necessary. Small stock used. Spec: Anthropology, Archaeology, Exploration, Judaica, Islamica etc. Cata: Irregularly.

BERRY HILL BOOK SHOP, R.D. BOX 118, DEANSBORO, NY 13328. TN: (315) 821-6188.

BIBLION, INC., P.O. Box 9, Forest Hills, NY 11375. Prop: Ludwig Gottschalk. TN: (718) 263-3910. Est: 1948. Appointment necessary. Medium stock. Spec: history of science and medicine, scientific periodicals. Cata: occasionally.

BIEBER ART BOOKS, 778 East 9th Street, Brooklyn, NY 11230. Prop: Sheldon Bieber. TN: (212) 859-0677. Est: 1965. Private premises, appointment necessary. Medium stock new. Spec: fine arts. Cata: 4 a year.

BILL THE BOOKY, P.O. Box 6228, 30-91 Crescent Street, Long Island City, NY 11102. Prop: Bill Epstein. TN: (718) 728-4791. Est: 1982. Private premises; appointment necessary. Medium stock. Spec: autographs; historical newspapers; photography; journalism; cartoon books; American sports. Cata: 4 a year. B: Atlantic Bank, New York City. M: United Autograph Collectors Club, Manuscript Society.

BINKIN'S BOOK CENTER, 54 Willoughby Street, Brooklyn, NY 11201. Prop: Irving Binkin. TN: (212) ULster 5-7813. Est: 1935. Entire building of five floors open 11 a.m. to 7 p.m. Very large stock used.

BLEECKER BOOK SERVICE, 231 Berkeley Place, Brooklyn, NY 11217. Prop: William S. Hauser. TN: ST 3-1651. Est: 1953. Private premises, appointment necessary. Large stock. Spec: Literature in English language. Cata: 3 a year.

MRS. GERTRUDE K. BOGART, 29 Frankel Avenue, Freeport, NY 11520.

BONMARK BOOKS, 182 Old Country Road, Hicksville, NY 11801. Spec: Art, cookbooks, history.

THE BOOK END, 521 Jewett Avenue, Staten Island, NY 10302.

BOOK JOURNEYS, 15 Bowen Place, Stony Brook, NY 11790.

BOOK MARX, 28 Lincoln Avenue, Roslyn Heights, NY 11577. Prop: Evan Marx. TN: (516) 621-0095. Shop. Medium stock used. Spec: modern firsts; A.C. Doyle; E.R. Burroughs, Jack London, Jack Kerouac. M: Long Island Antiquarian Bookdealers Association.

THE BOOK SCOUT, 455 MAIN STREET, GREENPORT, NY 11944.

BOOKSWAPPERS, 1 SORGI COURT, PLAINVIEW, NY 11803. Prop: Bengta Woo. TN: (516) 692-4426. Est: 1980. Private premises; appointment necessary. Very large stock of used. Spec: collectible paperbacks; romances; mysteries; science fiction. M: Long Island Antiquarian Bookdealers Association.

BORO BOOKSTORE, 146 LAWRENCE STREET, BROOKLYN, NY 11201.

CHARLES BRAGIN, 1525 WEST 12th STREET, BROOKLYN, NY 11204. TN: BEnsonhurst 6-1816. Storeroom, appointment necessary. Spec: juveniles.

CHARLES CANFIELD BROWN, 43 HICKS STREET, BROOKLYN, NY 11201. TN: (212) 580-1684. Est: 1967. Private premises: appointment necessary. Stock of 10,000 volumes. Spec: Americana; Archaeology; travel and exploration; maritime history; Bibliography and arts of the book; books about women.

CHARLIE BROWN'S BOOK GALLERIE, 34 MIDDAGH STREET, BROOKLYN HEIGHTS, NY 11201. TN: (212) 624-1373. Est: 1968. Store. Stock of 60,000 volumes. Spec: Ancient cultures; Mythology, symbolism, folklore; Occult, psychic phenomena; mysticism.

A. BUSCHKE, 200 HART BOULEVARD, STATEN ISLAND, NEW YORK, NY 10301. TN: (212) 254 2555. Est: 1939. Large stock used. Spec: chess and checkers/draughts. Russian scholarly periodicals. Cata: occasionally. B: Manufacturers Hanover Trust Company 600 01574.

CARAVAN-MARITIME BOOKS, 87-06 168th PLACE, JAMAICA, NY 11432. Prop: Mrs. Anne Klein. Est: 1947. Private premises. Mail order only. Very large stock rare and out-of-print; some new. Spec: books and pamphlets only. Naval history, piracy, seamanship, ship bldg., ship modelling, Voyages, whaling & yachting. A.B.A.A. I.L.A.B. A.B.A.

JO ANN AND RICHARD CASTEN ANTIQUE MAPS, RR2, LITTLE BAY ROAD, WADING RIVER, NY 11792. Prop: Jo Ann Casten. TN: (516) 929-6280. Cables: Casmaps. Est: 1975. Private House, appointment necessary. Small stock. Spec: Antique maps, atlases, books on travel and exploration. Cata: Occasionally. B: Bank of Suffolk, County Shirley, N.Y. M: A.B.A.A.

CITY WIDE BOOK AND PREMIUM CO., 735 WYTHE AVENUE, BROOKLYN, NY 11211. Prop: Robert Chalfin. TN: (212) UL2-3650. Est: 1934. Storeroom; appointment necessary. Very large stock used. Wholesalers, used books, geographic magazines, comics and paperbacks.

A COLLECTORS LIBRARY, 520 NORTH GREECE ROAD, HILTON, NY 14468. Prop: Carmen Pitman. TN: (1-716) 392-7720. Est: 1975. Shop, appointment necessary. Small stock used. Spec: Signed books, Sporting, Taylor Caldwell and general stock. B: Chemical Bank of Hilton. Acc.No: 510-532349.

A COLLECTOR'S LIST, 68 NORTH VILLAGE, ROCKVILLE CENTRE, NY 11570. Prop: Herman Abromson. TN: (576) 536-3757.

CORE COLLECTION BOOKS, 11 MIDDLE NECK ROAD, GREAT NECK, NY 11021.

JOHN CRISCIONE, 10 CHURCHILL DRIVE, NEW HYDE PARK, NY 11040.

DALIES DEVINE BOOKS, RD2, BOX 121-C, KATONAH, NY 10536. TN: (914) 962-7750.

THE DANCE MART, BOX 48, HOMECREST STATION, BROOKLYN, NY 11229. Prop: Tennessee Wild. TN: (718) 627-0477. Private premises, appointment necessary. Medium stock. Spec: dance. Cata: dance, two a year.

DOUBLE DEALINGS, 149 CLINTON STREET, BROOOKLYN, NY 11201. Prop: Vilma Diamond & Carol Greenberg. TN: (718) 643-1075. Spec: Mystery and Detective Fiction.

RAYMOND DOW, 2922 164th STREET, FLUSHING, NY 11358. Est: 1938. Business by post only. Large stock used, some new. Spec: anything by Sigmund Spaeth and Gustavus Myers, pirates, spies, riots, conspiracies, metrication.

EDITIONS, BOICEVILLE, NY 12412. Prop: Norman Levine. TN: (914) 657-7000. Est: 1948. Mail order only. Very large stock used. Spec: Literature, Fiction, History. Cata: Every 3 weeks.

ELGEN BOOKS, 336 DeMott Avenue, Rockville Centre, NY 11570. Prop: Esther Geller. TN: (516) 536-6276. Private premises: appointment necessary. Spec: mathematics, medicine; sciences; technology. Cata: occasionally.

ELYSIAN FIELDS BOOKSELLERS, 80-50 Baxter Avenue, Suite 339, Elmhurst, NY 11373. Prop: Ed. Drucker. TN: (718) 424-2789. Est: 1971. Mail order only. Medium stock. Spec: homosexuality, homosexuals, gay literature. Cata: on foregoing, occasionally.

EPCO PUBLISHING COMPANY, 62-19 Cooper Avenue, Glendale, NY 11385. Prop: Peter Hlinka & Edward P. Siess. TN: (212) 497-1100. Est: 1970. Shop. Very small stock. Spec: military, Western, antiques. Cata: 2 a year. Also publishers.

GEORGE A. ERB, P.O. Box 464, Locust Valley, Long Island, NY 11560.

EUROPE UNIE BOOKS, 60 Reynolds Street, Staten Island, NY 10305. Prop: R. Michael Speer. TN: (212) 273-0475. Est: 1974. Private premises, appointment necessary. Large stock used. Spec: German books of all types. Cata: 2 or 3 times per year.

HENRY FELDSTEIN, P.O. Box 398, Forest Hills, NY 11375. TN: (718) 544-3002. Spec: Photography before 1973.

JACK H. FABER (ANTIQUARIAN BOOKS), Box 24, Millwood, NY 10546. Prop: Jack H. & Jane Faber. Est: 1981. Mail order only. Very small stock sec. and antiq. Spec: military, naval and aviation history. Cata: 4 a year.

FOREIGN & INTERNATIONAL BOOK COMPANY, INC., P.O. Box 126, Flushing, NY 11364. President: Robert N. Schreiner. TN: (212) 352-1245. Est: 1933. Private premises, appointment necessary. Very small stock used.

J. FRANKLIN, 3111 Brighton 1st Place, Brooklyn, NY 11235.

FREE LANCE BOOKS, Suite 1060, 163 Joralemon Street, Brooklyn, NY 11201. TN: (718) 522-5455. Private premises, postal business only. Spec: Radicalism, Revolution, Utopian movements.

CHARLES E. GARDINER, 39-20 220th STREET, BAYSIDE, NY 11361. TN: (212) 229-3260. Est: 1965. Private premises; appointment necessary. Very small stock used. Spec: railroad and nautical steam. Monthly lists.

G.F.S. BOOKS, P.O. BOX 12, GREAT RIVER, NY 11739. Prop: Gertrude F. Schweibish. TN: (516) 581-7076. Est: 1977. Private House; appointment necessary. Small stock.

ROSE H. GIBEL, 367 ATLANTIC AVENUE, BROOKLYN, NY 11217. TN: (212) ULster 2-2594. Est: 1963. Shop. Large stock used, also new. Spec: first editions, out of print fiction and non-fiction. Also antiques.

THE GOOD TIMES, 150 EAST MAIN STREET, PORT JEFFERSON, NY 11777.

GOLDEN AGE, 81 BUTTON DRIVE, DIX HILLS, NY 11746.

JEAN GONZALEZ RARE BOOKS, 21 Hobson Avenue, St. James, NY 11780.

ANNE GORDON, BOOKS, 175 Adams Street, 11C, Brooklyn, NY 11201.

PAULETTE GREENE, BOOKS, 140 Princeton Road, Rockville Centre, NY 11570. TN: (516) R06-8602. Est: 1967. Private premises; appointment necessary. Medium stock used. Spec: 19th and 20th century American and English literature; first editions; mystery, detective and Sherlock Holmes fiction.

HAITIAN BOOK CENTRE, P.O. Box 324, Flushing, NY 11369-0324. Spec: all books on Haiti.

MORRIS HELLER, Box 529, Monticello, NY 12701. TN: (914) 583-5879. Est: 1964. Private premises, not possible to see stock. Small stock used. Spec: Natural history, Hunting and Fishing. Cata: Twice a year. B: Marine Midland. Acc.No: 086713640.

HERE'S A BOOK STORE, INC., P.O. Box 117, Quentin Road, Brooklyn, NY 11229. Prop: S. Bailes Levy. TN: (718) 645-6675. Est: 1976. Shop. Very large stock sec. and antiq. Spec: Judaism and occult. Corresp: Français, Deutsch, Hebrew. M: A.B.A.

HERPETOLOGICAL SERVICE, 117 East St. Barbara Road, Lindenhurst, NY 11757.

BENZION HIBEL, 375 First Street, Brooklyn, NY 11215. Spec: 19th and 20th century graphic arts and books; Judaica, Hebraica.

HILLTOP HOUSE, 1 The Loch, Roslyn, Long Island, NY 11576. Prop: Tobie Heller. TN: (516) MAnhasset 1-0257. A.B.A.A.

DANIEL HIRSCH—BOOKS, P.O. Box 315, Hopewell Junction, NY 12533. TN: (914) 462-7404. Est: 1972. Private premises, appointment necessary. Very small stock used. Spec: Children's and Illustrated books, Reference books. Cata: 6 per year. M: A.B.A.A. I.L.A.B.

JAMAICA BOOK CENTER, 146-16 Jamaica Avenue, Jamaica, NY 11435. Prop: Harry Pollack. TN: (718) 658-2500. Stock of 500,000 books in all fields, mostly used.

V. JANTA, 88-28 43RD AVE, ELMHURST, NY 11373. TN: (718) 898-6917. Private premises by appointment only. Spec: Eastern Europe, Slavica, Baltic and Balkan countries, Russia in all languages. Cata. M: A.B.A.A.

KATONAH BOOK SCOUT, 75 MEADOW LANE, KATONAH, NY 10536.

ROBERT KEENE BOOKSHOP & GALLERY, P.O. BOX 303, SOUTHAMPTON, NY 11968. (21 South Main). TN: (516) 283-1612. Est: 1950. Shop. Very large stock used and rare books. Spec: whaling, New York history, Kenneth Roberts.

DAVID M. KING — ROLLS-ROYCE ARCHIVES, 5 BROUWER LANE, ROCKVILLE CENTRE, NY 11570. TN: (516) 766-1561. Est: 1980. Private premises, postal business only. Small stock sec. and antiq. Spec. Rolls-Royce and Bentley literature: also other automotive books. Cata: occasionally. B: Chemical Bank, Rockville Centre NY, 11570.

FRANCES KLENETT, 13 CRANBERRY STREET, BROOKLYN, NY 11201. TN: (718) 852-2424. Est: 1950. Private premises, appointment necessary. Large stock used. Spec: New York.

RUTH KRAVETTE, 9 LEWIS AVENUE, JERICHO, NY 11753.

A. AND S. KUSTIN, 127 REID AVENUE, PORT WASHINGTON, NY 11050.

LIBER MUSICALS, 40 HOLLY LANE, ROSLYN HEIGHTS, NY 11577. Prop: Sheldon L. Tarakan. TN: (516) 621-2445. Private premises, appointment necessary. Medium stock sec. and antiq. Spec: music, dance, theatre, drama. Cata.

HERBERT A. LUFT, P.O. BOX 91, OAKLAND GARDENS, BAYSIDE, NY 11364. (69-11, 229th Street.) TN: (212) 428-2770. Est: 1950. Private premises, appointment necessary. Mainly new, some used, astronomy and related sciences.

KAREN AND JOHN McKENNA, 341 ELWOOD ROAD, EAST NORTHPORT, NY 11731.

MAIN STREET BOOKSELLERS, BOX 103, VANDERVEER STATION, BROOKLYN, NY 11210. Prop: Arnold Cohen. TN: (212) 381-8084. Est: 1968. Shop. Large stock used. Spec: first editions and out-of-print: biography, drama, fiction, literature, poetry, short stories. Cata: 4 per year.

MALITSKY ART BOOKS, P.O. Box 15, BAYSIDE, NY 11361. (39-44 222nd Street.) TN: Bayside 4-5121. Est: 1953. Private premises, appointment necessary. Spec: art. Cata: 5 or 6 a year.

MAPLETON HOUSE BOOKS INC., 413 LIBERTY AVENUE (ENTRANCE ON VERMONT STREET), BROOKLYN, NY 11225. TN: (718) 345-6176/6177. Office and warehouse. Small stock used books, mainly backfiles of periodicals on all subjects, technical, medical, scientific.

MERCURIUS BOOKS AND PERIODICALS, 36 UNQUA PLACE, AMITYVILLE, NY 11701. Prop: Alexej Ugrinsky. TN: (516) 598-2187. Storeroom; appointment necessary. Large stock used books; also new books, old phonograph records for the collector, music and spoken word. Spec: Russian history, language and literature in all languages.

MERLIN, 28 ORTON DRIVE, EAST NORTHPORT, NY 11731.

E.H. MILLER, 2105 EAST 21st STREET, BROOKLYN, NY 11229.

S. MILLMAN BOOKSELLER, P.O. Box 23, NEW LOTS STATION, BROOKLYN, NY 11208. TN: (212) 649-0111. Est: 1958. Storeroom; appointment necessary. Very large stock used; also new books. Spec: economics. Cata: annually.

G. MONTLACK, 12 HARROW LANE, OLD BETHPAGE, NY 13322.

ED MORAN, P.O. Box 1231, ROCKY POINT, NY 11778. Prop: Ed Moran. Est: 1954. Private premises, postal business only. Very small stock. Spec: Transportation and natural history. Includes back numbers of natural history journals and new issues.

JAMES C. MOREL, 83-33 AUSTIN STREET, KEW GARDENS, NY 11415. TN: (212) 849-7226. Est: 1974. Private premises; appointment necessary. Very small stock used. Spec: Modern American and English literature. Cata: on modern literature, occasionally.

NATIONWIDE BOOK SERVICE, 150 MANHATTAN AVENUE SP, BROOKLYN, NY 11206. Prop: Isidore Suarez. TN: 782-4328. Est: 1976. Storeroom. Very large stock used. Cata: 6 per year. Some new books, remainders. B: Chemical Bank. Acc.No: 071 021108.

NORTH SHORE BOOKS LTD., 8 GREEN STREET, HUNTINGTON, NY 11743. Prop: Ruth Nottman. TN: (516) 271-5558. Est: 1975. Shop, open 7 days a week. Large stock used. Spec: Modern First Editions, interesting and scholarly books on all subjects. Cata: 3 per year. M: L.I.B.A.

NOSEGAY BOOKS, 46 GLENWAY, COLD SPRING HARBOR, NY 11724.

OCEANSIDE BOOKS UNLIMITED, 2856 SAINT JOHN'S ROAD, OCEANSIDE, NY 11572. TN: (516) 764-3378. Spec: Mystery and detective first editions; bibliography. Cata: regularly.

EMIL OFFENBACHER, P.O. BOX 96, KEW GARDENS, NY 11415. (84-50 Austin Street.) TN: (212) 849-5834. Private apartment, appointment necessary. Medium stock. Spec: 15th and 16th century imprints, early science and medicine. Cata: science and medicine, annually. A.B.A.A.

PAUL OLINKIEWICZ/SAL LOMBARDO, P.O. BOX 381, MILLER PLACE, NY 11764.

THE OPERA BOX, P.O. BOX 46, HOMECREST STATION, BROOKLYN, NY 11229. Prop: Mrs. Tennessee Wild. TN: (718) 627-0477. Private premises, appointment necessary. Medium stock used, also new books, prints, autographs, scores. Spec: opera.

ORSAY BOOKS, 86-32 ELIOT AVENUE, REGO PARK, NY 11374. Prop: Theodore Orsay. TN: (212) OL 1-6177. Est: 1940. Private premises, appointment necessary.

OUT-OF-PRINT BOOK CENTER, P.O. BOX 6122, LONG ISLAND CITY, NY 11106. Prop: G.D. Chinn. TN: (212) 937-2965. Est: 1949. Storeroom; appointment necessary. Very large stock used. Spec: scholarly subjects; collectors items.

PASTIMES PAPER COLLECTIBLES, 369 OAK AVENUE, CEDARHURST, NY 11516.

PATCHOGUE BOOK SHOP, 116 WEST MAIN STREET, PATCHOGUE, NY 11772. Prop: Benjamin Schifferson. TN: (516) 475-3520. Est: 1954. Shop. Very large stock used. Spec: Long Island, New York history.

PIER BOOKS, INC., P.O. BOX 5, PIERMONT, NEW YORK, NY 10968. Prop: David C. Roach. TN: (914) 353-0232. Business by mail order or by appointment only. Spec: Rare, Used and Out of Print Books on Maritime Subjects: shipbuilding, naval architecture, ship modeling.

POGONIA PRESS, 8 SIDNEY PLACE, BROOKLYN, NY 11201.

W.J. QUINN, 128 EAST ZORANNE DRIVE, FARMINGDALE, LONG ISLAND, NY 11735. TN: (516) 249-7283. Est: 1962. Business by post only. Very small stock. Spec: Islam, Mediaeval theology, philosophy, Catholica.

BLOSSOM RESNIK, 58 MIDLAND ROAD, ROSLYN HEIGHTS, NY 11577.

H. FRANK RESSMEYER, OLDEN BOOKS, P.O. BOX 396, GARDEN CITY, NY 11530.

H. AND R. SALERNO, 1 GIVEN COURT, HAUPPAUGE, NY 11788.

SANDYS, 16 CRESCENT DRIVE, SEARINGTOWN, NY 11507.

C.J. SCHEINER BOOKS, 275 LINDEN BOULEVARD, BROOKLYN, NY 11226. TN: (718) 469-1089. Est: 1976. Private premises; appointment necessary. Medium stock used; also new books. Spec: erotica, curiosa, sexology. Cata: charged $2 or £1.

M. SHAMANSKY, G.P.O. BOX 1482, 10 PLAZA STREET, BROOKLYN, NY 11238.

NICHOLAS T. SMITH BOOKSELLER/PUBLISHER, P.O. BOX 66, 51 PONDFIELD ROAD, BRONXVILLE, NY 10708. TN: (914) 337-2794. Est: 1977. Shop; closed on Mondays. Very small stock. Spec: Press books, Marbling, Papermaking, Bookbinding, Beverages, Bibliography. Cata: will be issued. B: Bank of New York, Bronxville 92-214044.

SOUTH SHORE BOOK RESERVE, BOX 768, SOUTHAMPTON, NY 11968. Prop: Philip E. Tulchin. TN: (212) 861-2080. Private premises, appointment necessary. Large stock sec. and antiq. Spec: Art and Architecture.

SPECTOR THE COLLECTOR, 34-10 94th STREET, 1-B, JACKSON HEIGHTS, NY 11372.

SHELLY SPINDEL, 1 Blackheath Road, Lido Beach, NY 11561.

SPIRATONE, INC., 135-06 Northern Boulevard, Flushing, NY 11354. Pres: S.F. Spira. TN: (212) 8886-2000. Est: 1942. Very small stock. Spec: photography and photographic supplies.

THE STANLEYS, 280 Schenck Avenue, Great Neck, NY 11021.

STEPHEN'S BOOK SERVICE, P.O. Box 321, Kings Park, NY 11754. Prop: Stephen J. Takacs. TN: (516) AN 5-6563. Est: 1946. Private premises, appointment necessary. Medium stock used, also new. Spec: science fiction, fantasy, mystery, detective. Cata: on foregoing, monthly.

PAUL A. STROOCK, 35 Middle Lane, Jericho, Long Island, NY 11753. TN: (516) GE 3-9018. Est: 1932. Appointment necessary. New books, also small stock of rare books. Spec: arts, reference, bibliography.

TALBOTHAYS BOOKS, P.O. Box 118, Aurora, NY 13026. TN: (315) 364-7550.

LEE AND MIKE TEMARES, 50 Heights Road, Plandome, NY 11030. Prop: Lee B. Temares. TN: (516) MA7-7822. Est: 1965. Private premises; appointment necessary. Very large stock used. Spec: children's illustrated and series books; heritage; art. M: Long Island Book Dealers' Association.

THEORIA, P.O. Box 369, Forest Hills, NY 11375. Spec: Philosophy, Religion.

THOMOLSEN BOOKS, P.O. Box 180, Bayside, NY 11361. Prop: Joan O. Golder. TN: 718-3942. Est: 1977. Private premises; appointment necessary. Small stock. Spec: mystery, detective crime. Cata: Spring and Fall. M: Long Island Antiquarian Bookdealers Association.

BEATRICE C. WEINSTOCK, 14 Brook Bridge Road, Great Neck, NY 10021. TN: (516) 482-0904. Est: 1965. Private premises, appointment necessary. Small stock used, some new. Spec: applied arts. Cata: applied and fine art. A.B.A.

EDWARD L. WEISS, 2282 Ocean Avenue, Brooklyn, NY 11229.

WELLREAD BOOKS, 2 Folly Field Court, Cold Spring Harbor, NY 11724.

HARRY WINZENRIED, BOOKS, 91 Vermont Avenue, Oceanside, NY 11572. TN: (516) 766-6140. Est: 1973. Private premises, appointment necessary. Medium stock used. Spec: Modern American First editions, Americana. Cata: Occasionally. M: Long Island Antiquarian Book Dealers Assn.

BENGTA WOO, 1 Sorgi Court, Plainview, NY 11803. TN: (516) 692-4426. Est: 1972. Private premises; appointment necessary. Medium stock used. Spec: mystery, detective and romance fiction. Cata: monthly. M: Long Island Antiquarian Booksellers Association.

XERXES RARE BOOKS AND DOCUMENTS, P.O. Box 428, 818 Glen Cove Avenue, Glen Head, NY 11545. Prop: Carol & Dennis Travis. TN: (516) 671-6235. Est: 1980. Private premises; appointment necessary. Large stock. Spec: rare; Orientalia, travel; Judaica, theology; Italian literature and language; Americana. Also back-numbers of journals. Cata: 6 a year. Corresp: Français, Español, Russki yazyk. B: 1st National of Glen Head.

JOYCE W. ZUK, 172 4th Avenue, Huntington Station, Long Island, NY 11746.

38. NEW YORK STATE (NY.)

ALBANY	HARTSDALE
AMENIA	HEMPSTEAD
AMHERST	HILLSDALE
AMSTERDAM	HILTON
ANCRAM	HOPEWELL JUNCTION
ANCRAMDALE	HUDSON FALLS
BANGALL	HUNTER
BEARSVILLE	ILION
BINGHAMPTON	ITHACA
BREWSTER	JAMESTOWN
BRONXVILLE	JOHNSTOWN
BUFFALO	KINGSTON
CALEDONIA	LA FAYETTE
CANAAN	LAKE PLACID
CATSKILL	LARCHMONT
CAZENOVIA	LIMA
CLARYVILLE	LITTLE FALLS
CLINTON CORNERS	LIVINGSTONE
COBLESKILL	MAMARONECK
COLD SPRING	MANHASSET
COOPERSTOWN	MEDINA
CORNING	MIDDLETOWN
CROTON-ON-HUDSON	MILLWOOD
DELANSON	MILTON
DOBBS FERRY	MOUNT KISCO
EAST CHESTER	MOUNT VERNON
EAST CHATHAM	NEPONSIT
EDMESTON	NEVERSINK
ELIZABETHTOWN	NEW HARTFORD
ELMA	NEW PALZ
ELMSFORD	NEW ROCHELLE
FORESTBURGH	NIAGARA FALLS
FORT PLAIN	ONEONTA
GENEVA	ORCHARD PARK
GETZVILLE	OSSINING
GLENS FALLS	OWEGO
GREENWICH	PECONIC

PEEKSKILL

PLATTSBURGH

PLEASANTVILLE

POUGHKEEPSIE

RHINEBECK

ROCHESTER

ROTTERDAM JUNCTION

RYE

SARANAC LAKE

SARATOGA SPRINGS

SCARSDALE

SCHENECTADY

SCOTIA

SENECA FALLS

SLOATSBURG

SPRING VALLEY

STONE RIDGE

SWAN LAKE

SYRACUSE

TALLMAN

TARRYTOWN

TROY

TUCKAHOE VALLEY

UTICA

VALHALLA

VALLEY COTTAGE

VALLEY STREAM

VOORHEESVILLE

WAPPINGERS FALLS

WARRENSBURG

WARWICK

WATKINS GLEN

WESTBURY

WHITE PLAINS

WILLIAMSON

WOODSTOCK

WYNANTSKILL

YONKERS

ABC—ANTIQUES, ART & AMERICANA BOOK CLUBS, OLD IRELANDVILLE, WATKINS GLEN, NY 14891. TN: (607) 535-4004. Est: 1946. Business by post only. Large stock used, also new books. Spec: art, architecture, antiques, arts and crafts, Americana, landscape gardening. Cata: 4 a year.

ADIRONDACK YESTERYEARS INC., P.O. BOX 209, SARANAC LAKE, NY 12983. Prop: Maitland C. & Sylvia de Sormo. TN: (518) 891-3206. Est: 1967. Shop; appointment necessary. Large stock used; also new books on Adirondacks. Spec: Adirondacks; S.R. Stoddard pictures; paintings and maps. Cata: 1 or 2 a year.

ADRIAN'S, 175 WHITE SPRINGS ROAD, GENEVA, NY 14456. Prop: Adrian Hicks. TN: 305-6667. Est: 1952. Private premises; appointment necessary. Small stock used. Spec: Americana; scholarly; paper. Cata: 4 or 5 times a year.

a'GATHERIN' HISTORICAL PAPERS, P.O. BOX 175, WYNANTSKILL, NY 12198. Prop: Robert Dalton Harris. TN: (518) 674-2979. Est: 1972. Private premises; appointment necessary. Very small stock used. Spec: American Ephemera (esp. letters), postal history, telegraph history, 19th century drug trade. Cata: ephemera, manuscript and printed, 1 a year.

MRS AGNES ALBERTS, 67 SHOREVIEW DRIVE, YONKERS, NY 10710. Spec: Theatre; Western Hemisphere history: Illustrated.

ALBION BOOK SHOP, 378 BROADWAY, ALBANY, NY. Prop: Z. Cohn. Shop.

ALEPH-BET BOOKS, 670 WATERS EDGE, VALLEY COTTAGE, NY 10989. Prop: Helen Younger. TN: (914) 268-7410. Est: 1977. Private premises; appointment necessary. Small stock used. Spec: children's and illustrated books. Cata. $2.

ALICAT GALLERY, 64 LUDLOW STREET, YONKERS, NY 10705. Prop: Florenz Baron. TN: (914) 963-9774. Est: 1937. Private premises; appointment necessary. Very large stock used; also paintings and prints.

ALL PHOTOGRAPHY BOOKS, P.O. BOX 429, YONKERS, NY 10702. Prop: Arnold Sadow. TN: (914) 423-6473. Est: 1973. Private House, appointment necessary. Small stock. Spec: Photography. Cata: 2-3 per year.

AMERICANA BOOKS AND GALLERY, 36 OAK AVENUE, TUCKAHOE, NY 10707.

ANCRAMDALE BOOK BARN, WOOD'S DRIVE, ANCRAMDALE, NY 12503. TN: (518) 329-0913. Est: 1950. Storeroom, open normal business hours. Medium stock used.

ANTIPODEAN BOOKS, MAPS AND PRINTS, P.O. BOX 189, COLD SPRING, NY 10516. (66 Main Street). Prop: David & Cathy Lilburne. TN: (914) 265-3785 and (914) 265-4058. Est: 1977. Shop closed Mondays. Small stock sec. and antiq. Spec: Australia, Antarctica, Southeast Asia, Hudson River, Maps and prints. Cata: 3 a year. M: A.B.A.A., P.B.F.A. (England).

CHARLES APFELBAUM BOOKS, 39 FLOWER ROAD, VALLEY STREAM, NY 11581. TN: (212) 783-4466.

PAUL P. APPEL, 216 WASHINGTON STREET, MOUNT VERNON, NY 10553. TN: (914) 667-7365. Shop. Spec: Modern first editions, art, out-of-print, literary criticism, little magazines. A.B.A.A.

ARCTURUS BOOK SERVICE, 263 North Ballston Avenue, Scotia, NY 12302. TN: (518) 372-2373. Spec: paranormal, UFOs, folklore.

ARGONAUT BOOK SEARCH, P.O. Box 18, Claryville, NY 12725.

FREDERICK ARONE, 377 Ashforde, Dobbs Ferry, NY 10522. TN: (914) OW3-1832.

AS YOU LIKE IT BOOKSHOP, 2185 Bullis Road, Elma, NY 14059.

BONNIE AUCHMOODY, P.O. Box 123, Delanson, NY 12053. TN: (518) 895-2125. Private premises; appointment necessary.

AVONLEA BOOKS, Box 74, Main Station, White Plains, NY 10602. Prop: Leone E. Bushkin. TN: (914) 946-5923. Est: 1979. Private premises; postal and phone business only. Search service.

BAOBAB BOOKS, 14 Voorheesville Avenue, Voorheesville, NY 12186.

BARBER'S BOOK STORE, 28 Prospect Avenue, Ilion, NY 13357.

WALTER R. BENJAMIN AUTOGRAPHS INC., P.O. Box 255, Hunter, NY 12442. (Scribner Hollow Road.) Pres: Mary A. Benjamin. TN: (518) 263-4133. Est: 1887. Private office building; appointment necessary. Autograph letters and manuscripts: historical, literary, musical, presidential. Cata: 6 to 8 a year. A.B.A.A. I.L.A.B.

CARL SANDLER BERKOWITZ, 7 Crane Road, Middletown, NY 10940. TN: (914) 692-5324. Est: 1975. Private premises; appointment necessary. Small stock used. Spec: old world archaeology, ancient art, civilisations, history, languages, religions, Mediaeval and Renaissance Europe.

F.A. BERNETT, 2001 Palmer Avenue, Larchmont, NY 10538. TN: (914) 834-3026. Est: 1944. Spec: fine art, architecture, archaeology, bibliography. A.B.A.A.

BIBLIOMANIA, 129 Jay Street, Schenectady, NY 12305. Prop: Bill Healy. TN: (518) 393-8069. Est: 1981. Shop. Medium stock used; also some new books. Spec: modern fiction; mystery; art and photography.

B.K. BOOKS, P.O. BOX 1681, MAIN STATION, WHITE PLAINS, NY 10602. Prop: Kenneth & Barbara Leish. TN: (914) 9977184. Est: 1982: Private premises, postal business only. Medium stock sec. and antiq. Spec: Literature: history, performing arts.

THE BOOKERY, DEWITT MALL, ITHACA, NY 14850. Prop: Jack Goldman. TN: (607) 273-5055. Est: 1975. Shop. Medium stock used. New books in French and German. B: 1st Bank/Ithaca. Acc.No: 267-71147-6.

BOOK EXCHANGE, 90 WEST MARKET STREET, CORNING, NY 14830. Prop: Elizabeth Iraggi. TN: 936-8536. Est: 1977. Shop. Medium stock. Spec: Glass working. Cata: 1 per year.

THE BOOK FINDER, 471 EXCHANGE STREET, GENEVA, NY 14456. Prop: Mrs. Jeanne S. Busch. TN: (315) 789-9388. Est: 1978. Shop. Medium stock. B: National Bank of Geneva (NY) Acc.No: 277 21687 7.

THE BOOK GALLERY, 15 OVERLOOK ROAD, BOX 26, GEDNEY STATION, WHITE PLAINS, NY 10605. Prop: Mrs. Ruth Berman. TN: (914) 949-5406. Est: 1960. Appointment necessary. Spec: fine and applied arts. Cata: on foregoing, 3-4 a year. A.B.A.A.

BOOK LOOK, 51 MAPLE AVENUE, WARWICK, NY 10990.

BOOKS REMEMBERED, P.O. BOX 1157, SCHENECTADY, NY 12301. Prop: Jill Titus. TN: (518) 346-0269. Private premises, appointment necessary.

R.F. BRANI, 83 FRONT STREET, OWEGO, NY 13827. Est: 1960. Mail order only. Large stock used. Cata: 1 a year.

ANNE P. BRENNAN, 1318 THORNDALE AVENUE, NIAGARA FALLS, NY 14305.

THE BROWN BAG BOOKSTORE, 127A MAIN STREET, P.O. BOX 276, DOBBS FERRY, NY 10522. Prop: Ruth Rosenblatt. TN: (914) 693-2322.

BRYN MAWR BOOK SHOP, 135 EAST AVENUE, ROCHESTER, NY 14604. Prop: Bryn Mawr College Club of Rochester, Inc. TN: (716) 454-2910. Est: 1975. Shop, closed on Fridays. Small stock used. B: Lincoln First Bank of Rochester. Acc.No: 022300173 238 626 6.

BRYN MAWR BOOK SHOP, 1 Spring Street, Albany, NY 12210. Prop: Bryn Mawr College Alumnae Club. TN: 465-8126. Est: 1968. Shop, open Tuesdays-Saturdays, 10.30 a.m. - 4 p.m. and by appointment. Very large stock used, some new, also prints and records. Search service.

BUFFALO BOOK STORE, 3131 Sheridan Drive, Amherst, NY 14226.

ROBERT BUMP, 281 Main Street, Fort Plain, NY 13339. TN: (518) 993-3534. Small stock used; also new books. Spec: shooting, hunting, fishing.

CALHOUN'S BOOKS, RD4, Box 39, Geneva, NY 14456. TN: (315) 789 8599.

CARNEY BOOKS, 44 Elm Street, Oneonta, NY 13820. Prop: John J. and Margaret Carney. TN: (607) 432-5360. Est: 1978. Private premises; appointment necessary. Large stock used.

IRENE CARR, 456 Madison Avenue, Albany, NY 12208. TN: (518) 462-2729. Est: 1970. Private premises, appointment necessary. Very small stock sec. and antiq. Spec: American History and fiction; art; children's.

THE CAT BOOK CENTER, P.O. Box 112, Wykagyl Station, New Rochelle, NY 10804. Prop: G. Zeehandelaar. TN: (914) 235-2698. Est: 1965. Private premises, appointment necessary. Small stock used, also new books. Spec: Cats. Cata: cats, one a year.

CHANG TANG BOOKS, 35 Di Rubbo Drive, Peekskill, NY 10566. Prop: Don Roy. TN: (914) 739-8167. Est: 1979. Private premises; visits any time by appointment. Small stock used; also imported new books. Spec: early history and domestication of dogs, dogs of Tibet and related Asiatic breeds.

BEV. CHANEY JUNIOR, 73 Croton Avenue, Ossining, NY. TN: (914) 941-1002. Private premises, by appointment only.

JENS J. CHRISTOFFERSEN, 221 South Barry Avenue, Mamaroneck, NY 10543. TN: (914) 698-3495. Spec: illustrated and press books; bibliography; Eastern Americana (esp. New York State).

ROY W. CLARE, 47 WOODSHIRE SOUTH, GETZVILLE, NY 14068. TN: (716) 688-8723. Est: 1969. Private premises; appointment necessary. Medium stock antiq. Spec: incunabula, early printed books, occult and magic, STC and Wing books, woodcut books. Cata: on foregoing, one a year, A.B.A.A. I.L.A.B.

ANTHONY P. COLLINS BOOKSELLER, P.O. BOX 566, BANGALL, NY 12506. TN: (914) 868-7188. Est: 1970. Private premises; appointment necessary. Small stock used.

COLONIAL 'OUT-OF-PRINT' BOOK SERVICE, INC., P.O. BOX 451, PLEASANTVILLE, NEW YORK, NY 10570. Prop: A.N. Scheinbaum. Est: 1934. Storeroom, private premises: postal business only. Small stock used.

THE CORNER-STONE BOOKSHOP, 110 MARGARET STREET, PLATTSBURGH, NY 12901. Prop: Terence L. Duniho. TN: (518) 561-0520. Est: 1973. Shop. Medium stock used. Spec: C.S. Lewis, Tolkein, George MacDonald, Charles Williams. Cata: Occasionally. B: State Bank of Albany. M: A.B.A.

COUNTRY BOOKS, R.D.1., DELANSON, NY 12053. TN: (518) 895-2054. Spec: children's and general non-fiction.

COUNTRYSIDE BOOKS AND ANTIQUES, 3698 MOHAWK STREET, NEW HARTFORD, NY 13413.

NATHANIEL COWEN, 16 SCHOONMAKER LANE, WOODSTOCK, NY 12498. TN: (914) 679-6475. Est: 1932 in Chicago. Private premises, by mail only. Small stock. Spec: English and American history and literature. M: A.B.A.A., Emeritus.

L.W. CURREY ANTIQUARIAN BOOKSELLER INC., CHURCH STREET, ELIZABETHTOWN, NY 12932. Prop: L.W. & Alida Currey. TN: (518) 873-6477. Est: 1968. Shop, appointment necessary. Medium stock used. Spec: 19th century Americana, American literary first editions, science fiction and fantasy. Cata: on foregoing, 4-5 a year. A.B.A.A.

MRS. K.R. DORN BOOK SERVICE, 8 WALNUT AVENUE, JOHNSTOWN, NY 12095. Prop: Mrs. K.R. Dorn. TN: (1-518) 762-9466. Est: 1960. Premises open daily, from 9 a.m. to 9 p.m. Medium stock used; also new books. Spec: Americana, New York State; natural history.

LEO DUFFY, 79 Madison Street, Geneva, NY 14456.

EDUCO SERVICES INTERNATIONAL LTD., 75 No. Kensico Avenue, Valhalla, NY 10595. Prop: Charles Cecere. TN: (914) 997-7044 General stock antiq. books. M: A.B.A.A.

EX LIBRIS/MAZEL, P.O. Box 285, Larchmont, NY 10538. Prop: Ella Mazel. TN: (914) 633-7173. Est: 1975. Private premises; appointment necessary. Very small stock used. Spec: Psychoanalysis, Psychiatry, Psychology, Hypnotism, Phrenology. Cata: Annually. B: Chemical Bank, Acc. No: 007-050151. M: A.B.A.A.

DON FAY, 4329 Avon-Caledonia Road (Rte.5), Caledonia, NY 14423. TN: (716) 226-2288. Stock of 50,000 volumes used.

C.G. FISHER, 62 East Main Street, Cobleskill, NY 12043. TN: (518) 234-3374. Est: 1961. Private premises, appointment advisable. Very small stock. Spec: New York State local history. Americana.

FORDHAM BOOK COMPANY, P.O. Box 6, New Rochelle, NY 10801. Prop: Mrs. Helen Hirsch. TN: (914) 632-7771. Spec: philosophy, history, literature. A.B.A.A.

FOX AND SUTHERLAND INC, 15 South Moger Avenue, Mount Kisco, NY 10549.

HOWARD FRISCH, P.O. Box 75, Livingston, NY 12541. (Old Post Road). Prop: Howard Frisch and Fred Harris. TN: (518) 851-7493. Est: 1954. Shop, appointment necessary. Small stock sec. and antiq. Spec: Art and illustrated books, costume and fashion. Cata: 2 a year. B: Norstar Bank of Upstate New York, Hudson, NY 12534. M: A.B.A.A.

GENESEE BOOK SHOP, 2420 Monroe Avenue, Rochester, NY 14618.

RACHEL GOODKIND, 151 FENIMORE ROAD, MAMARONECK, NY 10543. Prop: Rachel G. Goodkind. TN: (914) 698-7854. Est: 1925. Private premises, appointment necessary. Small stock used. Spec: Violins, Violas, Cellos and their Bows. Also own books on Antonio Stradivari and Index and Sup. to the Musical Quarterly. M: The Violin Society of America, Inc.

GRANT'S BOOK SHOP, 255 GENESEE STREET, UTICA, NY 13501.

GREEN THOUGHT BOOKSELLERS, 283 LEE AVENUE, YONKERS, NY 10705.

RICK GRUNDER, 669 WEST KING ROAD, ITHACA, NEW YORK, NY 14850. TN: (607) 272-3448. Est: 1981. Private premises, appointment necessary. Very small stock rare. Spec: early printing; European and American history; Mormons before 1850. M: A.B.A.A., I.L.A.B.

HAMMER MOUNTAIN BOOK HALLS, 841 UNION STREET, SCHENECTADY, NY 12308. Prop: Wayne Somers. TN: (518) 393 5266. Est: 1971. Shop, open afternoons and saturdays. Medium stock used. Spec: Out-of-print scholarly books; Economics, European history and literature. Cata: 1 or 2 a year. M: A.B.A.A.

LION HARVEY'S FALLS BOOKSHOP, P.O. BOX 331, WAPPINGERS FALLS, NY 12590. TN: (914) 297-2119. Est: 1968. Shop. Medium stock used. Spec: books about music (biography, history, technique etc.,). Cata: very occasionally.

MARCIA HASKELLS, 122 SOUTH THIRD AVENUE, MOUNT VERNON, NY 10550. TN: (914) MO 7-2238. Mail order only. Large stock used.

CHARLES E. HASTINGS, 11 HORICON AVENUE, WARRENSBURG, NY 12885. TN: (518) 623-2940. Est: 1972. Mail order only. Small stock. Spec: Americana; literary first editions; occult.

CLAUDE HELD, P.O. BOX 140, BUFFALO, NY 14225. TN: (716) 634-4842. Est: 1940. Private premises; appointment necessary. Medium stock used; also some new books. Spec: fantasy, science fiction, mysteries (Edgar Rice Burroughs, G.A. Henty), first editions; old comics, books and magazines. Cata: on foregoing, several a year.

HOMER W. HENDEE, 6763 EAST QUAKER ROAD, ORCHARD PARK, NY 14127.

HEMLOCK BOOKS, 170 Beach 145th Street, Neponsit, NY 11694. Prop: Norman & Sheila Shaftel. TN: (212) 474-1372. Est: 1977. Private premises; appointment necessary. Small stock, old and rare medicine only.

PETER HENNESSEY, P.O. Box 393, Peconic, NY 11958. TN: (516) 734-5650. Private premises, postal business only. Medium stock sec. and antiq. Cata. 1 a year.

THE HENNESSEYS, Fourth and Woodlawn, Saratoga Springs, NY 12866. Prop: J.P. & Helen B. Hennessey. TN: (518) 584-4921. Est: 1962. Shop; appointment preferred. Medium stock used and rare. Spec: Americana, sporting books, history, art. A.B.A.A.

MARK D. HEWES, 1 Beryl Avenue, Seneca Falls, NY 13148.

HIGH RIDGE BOOKS INC., P.O. Box 286, Rye, NY 10580. Prop: Frederick U. Baron. TN: (914) 967-3332. Private premises; appointment necessary. Large stock sec. and antiq. Spec: Americana, railroads, color plate books, maps and atlases, New York City. M: A.B.A.A.

DANIEL HIRSCH, P.O. Box 315, R.D. 3, Route 52, Hopewell Junction, NY 12533. Prop: Ruth Hirsch. TN: (914) 462-7404. Spec: Children's, 16th-20th century illustrated, 17th-19th century literature, original art and illustration. M: A.B.A.A.

SAMUEL HIRSCH, 22 Arden Drive, Hartsdale, NY 10530.

OLGA HOEFLIGER'S BOOK CORNER, 438 Vermont Street, Buffalo, NY 14213.

HOFFMAN LANE BOOKS (NICKLAS & PARKER), 31 Second Street, Troy, NY 12180. (518) 273-4826. Large stock used. Spec: old and rare.

PATRICIA A. HOLLAND, 8 Tiemson Road, Scotia, NY 12302.

GRAHAM HOLROYD, 19 Borrowdale Drive, Rochester, NY 14626. TN: (716) 225-4879. Large stock sec. and antiq. books. Spec: science fiction, fantasy, horror, mystery. Cata: on foregoing.

38. NEW YORK STATE (NY.)

JAMES C. HOWGATE, STAR ROUTE, ROTTERDAM JUNCTION, NY 12150. Prop: Mrs. Dorothea R. Howgate. Shop. Large stock used. Cata: occasionally.

JOHN C. HUCKANS, BOOKS, P.O. BOX 270, CAZENOVIA, NY 13035 (16 Farnham Street). Prop: John Curtis Huckans. TN: (315) OL 5-9654; Office: OL 5-8499. Private Office, appointment necessary. Small stock. Spec: Rare books in all fields, 18th and 19th century Travel and Exploration, 18th century pamphlets; Utopian communities, abolitionist movement. Cata: Occasionally.

JOHNSON AND O'DONNELL RARE BOOKS, 1015 STATE TOWER BOULEVARD, SYRACUSE, NY 13202. Prop: Bruce Johnson. TN: (315) 476-5312. Spec: 19th and 20th century American and English literature, literary documents and autographs, signed and association copies. M: A.B.A.A.

JAMES KLENOTIZ, 14 SCHUBERT STREET, BINGHAMTON, NY 13905.

KRAUS REPRINT AND PERIODICALS, ROUTE 100, MILLWOOD, NY 10546. TN: (914) 762-2200. Spec: Scholarly periodicals, bibliographies, reference works. M: A.B.A.A.

EDWARD L. KREINHEDER, 197 MAIN STREET, WARRENSBURG, NY 12885. TN: (518) 623-2149. Shop, open 09.00 to 17.00. Medium stock used.

NORMAN LEVINE'S BOOK SHOP, ROUTE 28, KINGSTON, NEW YORK, NY 12401. Prop: Joan & Norman Levine. TN: (914) 338-5555. Store, open seven days a week. Very large stock sec. and antiq.

GEORGE LEWIS GOLFIANA, P.O. BOX 291, MAMARONECK, NY 10543. Prop: George Lewis. TN: (914) 698-4579. Est: 1982. Private premises, appointment necessary. Very small stock sec. and antiq. Spec: Golf. Cata: 2 a year. B: Bank of New York, Post Road, Mamaroneck, NY 10543.

LIBERTY ROCK BOOK SHOPPE, 4A, MUNICIPAL PLAZA, SLOATSBURG, NY 10974.

LIBRARIUM, RD 190, BLACK BRIDGE ROAD, EAST CHATHAM, NY 12060. Prop: Richard B. Socky; Manager: Sharon S. Lips. TN: (518) 392-5209. Est: 1979. Shop open Fridays, Saturdays, Sundays, Mondays, or by appointment. Large stock used.

LINCOLN HILL BOOKS, 20 HARRIS AVENUE, ALBANY, NY 12208.

LITTWIN & FEIDEN, BOOKS, 135 EAST BOSTON POST ROAD, MAMORONECK, NY 10543. Props: Suzanne Littwin & Elaine S. Feiden. TN: (914) 698-6504. Est: 1975. Shop; stock can be seen Wednesday and Friday and by appointment. Small stock. Spec: Art, illustrated and literature. Cata: twice a year. B: Barclay's Bank. Acc.No: 189 908 2. M: A.B.A.A.

WILLIAM LOEWY, P.O. BOX 186, TALLMAN, NY 10982. Spec: Early Judaica and Hebraica in all languages; manuscripts and prints.

LUBRECHT AND CRAMER, RFD 11 BOX 244, FORESTBURGH, NY 12777. Prop: Harry D. Lubrecht. TN: (914) 794-8539. Spec: Botany, geology, natural history, science. M: A.B.A.A.

LYRICAL BALLAD BOOKSHOP, 7 PHILADELPHIA STREET, SARATOGA SPRINGS, NY 12866. Prop: John & Carolyn De Marco. TN: (518) 584-8779. Est: 1971. Shop. Medium stock used. Spec: general antiquarian and fine illustrated, children's, folklore. A.B.A.A.

McDONALD'S BOOK ENDS, 125 WATER STREET, CATSKILL, NY 12414. Prop: Mrs. Frank J. McDonald. TN: (518) 943-3520. Est: 1959. Store, open after 10 a.m. Monday through Saturday, by appointment on Sundays. Very large stock used. Cata: occasionally.

RALPH AND GERTRUDE McKENSIE, 237 ASBURY AVENUE, WESTBURY, NY 11590.

MAHONEY AND WEEKLY, BOOKSELLERS, 513 VIRGINIA STREET, BUFFALO, NY 14202. Prop: Jon Weekly. TN: (716) 856-6024. Est: 1972. Shop, open normal business hours on Wednesday, Thursday, Friday and Saturday. Medium stock used; also prints and framing. Spec: Niagara Falls, literature, Private press, illustrated.

ELLEN A. MANDIVELLE, 586 MERCHANTS ROAD, ROCHESTER, NY 14609.

MAXWELL SCIENTIFIC INTERNATIONAL, FAIRVIEW PARK, ELMSFORD, NY 10523. TN: (914) 592-7700. Pres: Dr. Edward Gray. Spec: periodicals (scholarly), collections, social sciences, history (esp. French), history of economics, Shakespereana. M: A.B.A.A.

MAXWELL'S TREASURES—BOOKS, ROUTE 15A AT 5 AND 20, LIMA, NEW YORK (shop). 8053 Canadice Road, Springwater, NY 14560 (mailing address). Prop: George & Ruth Kennedy. TN: (716) 669-2568 after 7 pm. Shop, open weekends and holidays, or by appointment. Stock secondhand and out of print books, ephemera, prints and maps.

KARL MILLER BOOKS, RD2, BOX 20, JOHNSTOWN, NY 12095. TN: (518) 762 3551. Private premises; postal business only. Spec: maritime.

WILLIS MONIE BOOKS, RD1, BOX 336, COOPERSTOWN, NY 13326. TN: (607) 547-8363. Est: 1979. Private premises; appointment necessary. Regular hours in summer. Medium stock used. Spec: Americana, New York State, literature; theology; World Fairs. M: A.B.A.A. *Also at:* 52 PIONEER STREET, COOPERSTOWN, NY 13326.

MORE'S OLD RARE BOOKS, 169 ALLEN STREET, BUFFALO, NY 14201. Prop: Moris Sultanik. TN: 886-5800. Est: 1950. Shop. Large stock used. Spec: 16th and 17th century. Also small antiques.

NEW YORK BOUND BOOK SHOP, R.F.D.1, ANCRAM, NY 12502. Prop: Barbara L. Cohen. TN: (518) 851-7896. Est: 1974. Shop; appointment necessary, summer and spring weekends. Small stock used. Spec: Americana, New York City and State.

OLANA GALLERY, 2 CARILLON ROAD, BREWSTER, NY 10509.

OLD AND RARE LOVE AFFAIR, 215 SPRING STREET, JAMESTOWN, NY. Prop: Marjorie Coons. TN: (716) 488-1020.

OLD BOOK ROOM, 111 GRAND STREET, CROTON ON HUDSON, NY 10620. Prop: Jane Northshield. TN: (914) 271-6802. Shop. Medium stock sec. and antiq. Spec: New York & Westchester County.

OLD EDITIONS BOOKSHOP, 3124 MAIN STREET, BUFFALO, NY 14214. Prop: Ronald Cozzi. TN: (716) 836 7354. Shop. Large stock used. Spec: General, Used, Antiquarian. Cata: Periodically.

ONCE UPON A TIME BOOKSEARCH, 146 FRONT STREET, HEMPSTEAD, NY 11550. Prop: James Dore & Harvey Stanson. TN: (516) 486-9427. Est: 1980. Shop open 11.00 to 18.00 hrs. Stocks of 15,000 used volumes. Spec: art and photography.

OWL PEN BOOKS, RTE.2, BOX 202, GREENWICH, NY 12834. Prop: Hank Howard & Eddie Brown. TN: (518) 692-7039. Est: 1960. Storeroom (Barns). Open May-October, closed on Mondays and Tuesdays. Very large stock. B: 1st National Bank of Glen Falls, N.Y. Acc.No: 840 462 4.

PALENQUE BOOKS, R.R.1, BOX 12, MILTON, NY 12547. Prop: Edith J. Stickle. Est: 1958. Private premises; business by mail only. Medium stock used. Spec: Franklin D. Roosevelt and period (1932-1945).

PARNASSUS BOOK SHOP, 26 MONTGOMERY STREET, RHINEBECK, NY 12572.

N. & N. PAVLOV, 37 OAKDALE DRIVE, DOBBS FERRY, NY 10522. Props: Nicolai & Nina Pavlov. TN: (914) 693-1776. Est: 1970. Shop and private house. Stock can be seen at weekend or by appointment. Small stock. Spec: Rare books, N.Y. Metro Area, early printed books, Prints, Maps. B: Bank of New York, Hastings-on-Hudson, NY 08 825009. M: A.B.A.A.

VELTON PEABODY, 4548 MAIN STREET, BUFFALO, NY 14226.

ALBERT J. PHIEBIG, INC., P.O. BOX 352, WHITE PLAINS, NY 10602. (5 Rutherford Avenue). TN: (914) 948-0138. Book search service only. Spec: foreign books and periodicals, world-wide search service, building collections, international congresses, irregular serials. Represents foreign publishers in America and prepares their catalogues. A.B.A.A.

CARMEN PITMAN, 520 NORTH GREECE ROAD, HILTON, NY 14468.

JAMES PUGLIESE, 39 NORTH CHESTNUT STREET, NEW PALTZ, NY 12561.

QUESTION MARK BOOK SHOP, MADISON AVENUE AT LARK, ALBANY, NY. Prop: Michael Lenihan. Shop. Medium stock used.

DOROTHY QUINN, 2698 MOHAWK STREET, NEW HARTFORD, NY 13413.

INGEBORG QUITZAU, ANTIQUARIAN BOOKS, P.O. BOX 5160, EDMESTON, NY 13335. TN: (607) 965-8605. Est: 1971. Private house, appointment necessary. Small stock. Spec: Children's, Books about books, General Antiquarian, Miniature books.

KEVIN T. RANSOM, P.O. BOX 176, AMHERST, NY 14226. TN: (716) 839-1510. Private premises, appointment necessary. Spec: First editions. Cata.

RARE BOOKS AT WEBSTER'S LANDING, P.O. BOX 2154, SYRACUSE, NY 13220.

STEPHEN A. RESNICK, 36 LINCKLAEN STREET, CAZENOVIA, NY 13035. TN: (315) 655-2810. Private premises, appointment necessary. Small stock. Spec: paper Americana. Cata: general, 2-3 a year.

RESTON'S BOOKNOOK, 59 ROCKTON STREET, AMSTERDAM, NY 12010. Prop: Donna Reston. TN: (518) 843-1601. Est: 1965. Private premises; appointment necessary. Very small stock used; also oil paintings and prints, small antiques. Spec: New York State; fantasy and science fiction, especially Edgar Rice Burroughs.

MARY M. RICHTER, 170 BERKELEY STREET, ROCHESTER, NY 14609.

RIDGE BOOKS, P.O. BOX 58, STONE RIDGE, NY 12484. Prop: Peter E. Scott. Est: 1963. Private premises, mail order only. Very small stock used. Spec: Modern First Editions. Cata: 2 per year.

RIVEROW BOOKSHOP, 187 FRONT STREET, OWEGO, NY 13827. Prop: John D. Spencer. TN: (607) 687-4094. Est: 1976. Shop. Large stock. Spec: architecture and decorative arts. Cata: 2 per year. B: Owego National Bank. M: Ephemera Society, A.B.A.A.

RODGERS BOOK BARN, RODMAN ROAD, HILLSDALE, NY 12529. Prop: Maureen Rodgers. TN: (518) 325-3610. Est: 1964. Barn, open December through March, Saturday and Sunday 10.00 to 18.00; April through November, 10.00 to 18.00, Thursday to Monday. July and August open every day 10.00 to 18.00. Very large stock used, general.

CRAIG W. ROSS, P.O. BOX 148, MEDINA, NY 14103. (North Gravel Road.) TN: (716) 798-1493. Est: 1960. Private premises, appointment necessary. Small stock used. Spec: Americana. Cata: Americana and general, monthly.

WILLIAM SALLOCH, PINES BRIDGE ROAD, OSSINING, NY 10562. Prop: William & Marianne Salloch. TN: (914) 941-8363. Est: 1939. Private premises, appointment necessary. Large stock of rare books. Spec: Middle Ages, Renaissance, classics, music, history, literature, old and rare, scholarly. A.B.A.A. I.L.A.B.

SALMAGUNDI BOOKS LTD., 66 MAIN STREET, COLD SPRING, NY 10516. Prop: Caroline Krebs. TN: (914) 265-4058. Est: 1984. Shop, closed Mondays. Very small stock sec. and antiq. books. Spec: Hudson River.

KARL SCHICK, 180 EAST HARTSDALE AVENUE, HARTSDALE, NY 10530. TN: (914) 725-0408. Est: 1979. Private premises; appointment necessary. Very small stock old and rare books on philosophy, psychology, science and medicine. Cata: occasionally.

ANNEMARIE SCHNASE, P.O. BOX 119, 120 BROWN ROAD, SCARSDALE, NY 10583. TN: (914) 725-1284. Cables: Schnasbook. Est: 1950. Private premises, appointment necessary. Very large stock used. Spec: periodicals, academy publications, music, reprints. Cata: on foregoing, 6 a year. A.B.A.A. I.L.A.B.

SEABOOK SEARCH, CLINTON CORNERS, NY 12514. Prop: John de Graff Inc. TN: (914) 266-5800. Est: 1956. Storeroom; appointment necessary. Large stock used; also a few new books. Spec: nautical, pleasure boating, naval, marine, oceanography. Cata: nautical, 1 a year.

THOMAS W. SHAW, 11 ALBRIGHT AVENUE, ALBANY, NY 12203. TN: (518) 438-1078. Est: 1960. Private premises, appointment necessary. Small stock used. Spec: detective fiction. Cata: general, 2 a year.

HAROLD J. SHOEBRIDGE, MAPLE HILL, BERRY ROAD, LA FAYETTE, NY 13084. TN: (315) 677-3056. Est: 1980. Private premises, appointment necessary. Very small stock sec. and antiq. Spec: fine bindings, fore-edge paintings; hand-colored plates; New York State. Regular lists issued. Corresp. Français, Español. B: Key Bank of Central New York, Syracuse, NY.

MILTON SLATER, P.O. BOX 501, TARRYTOWN, NY 10591. Spec: manuscripts, documents, autographs. Cata: occasionally.

SLEEPY HOLLOW BOOKS, 45 MAIN STREET, TARRYTOWN, NY 10591.

NICHOLAS T. SMITH, P.O. BOX 66, BRONXVILLE, NY 10708. (51 Pondfield Road). TN: (914) 337-2794.

SYDNEY R. SMITH SPORTING BOOKS, R.F.D., CANAAN, NY 12029. Prop: Camilla P. Smith. TN: (518) 794-8998. Est: 1940. Private premises, appointment necessary. Large stock used, also new. Spec: horses, dogs, guns, fishing and allied subjects. Cata: on foregoing, 2 a year. A.B.A.A.

MADELEINE SWARTE, 122A SOUTH THIRD AVENUE, MOUNT VERNON, NY 10550. TN: (914) MOunt Vernon 7-2238. Est: 1950. Mail order only. Medium stock used, also research service and book search service.

SYLVESTER'S BOOK SERVICE, 4845 VELASKO ROAD, SYRACUSE, NY 13215. Prop: Richard M. Sylvester. TN: (315) 469-1413. Est: 1947. Appointment necessary. Small stock. Spec: Americana, New York State.

SYRACUSE BOOKSELLERS, 102 MANLIUS STREET, EAST SYRACUSE, NY 13057.

VICTOR TAMERLIS, 911 STUART AVENUE, MAMARONECK, NY 10543. TN: (914) 698-8950. Spec: Art, prints, early printing, illustrated. M: A.B.A.A.

THE THREE ARTS, 3 COLLEGEVIEW AVENUE, POUGHKEEPSIE, NY 12603.

THREE GEESE IN FLIGHT BOOKS, Box 454, Bearsville, NY 12409. TN: (914) 679-8787. Shop at 34 Mill Hill Road, Woodstock, NY. Spec: Celtic Mythology, Legend, Folklore.

TOTTERIDGE BOOK SHOP, RD1, 247a North Road, Amenia, NY.

TIMOTHY TRACE, 144 Red Mill Road, Peekskill, NY 10566. (R.F.D.1, P.O. Box 178). TN: (914) 528-4074. Shop, appointment necessary. Small stock used and selected new books. Spec: architecture, decorative arts. Cata: on foregoing. A.B.A.A.

BLANCHE E. TURNER, 8 Glendale Drive, Glens Falls, NY 12801.

ROBERT E. UNDERHILL, 85 Underhill Road, Poughkeepsie, NY 12765. Prop: C.E. Van Norman. TN: (914) 985-7482. Est: 1966. necessary. Very small stock used, some new. Spec: natural history, agriculture, horticulture. Also farming, wild animal dealer, fire-arms and sporting goods, nursery. A.B.A.

UNION VILLAGE BOOKS, Box 2, RD2, Greenwich, NY 12834.

VILLAGE BOOKSMITH, 223 Main Street, Hudson Falls, NY 12839. Prop: Clifford Bruce. TN: (518) 747-3261. Est: 1976. Shop open 10-5 Monday through Saturday and 1-5 on Sundays. Very large stock used.

R.M. WAFFLE, 226 West Monroe Street, Little Falls, NY 13365.

WANTAGH RARE BOOK COMPANY, P.O. Box 605, Neversink, NY 12765. Prop: C.E. Van Norman. TN: (914) 985-7482. Est: 1966. Private premises, appointment necessary. Medium stock used. Spec: Americana and American literature. Cata: Americana, 4 a year.

BERNICE WEISS, RARE BOOKS, 36 Tuckahoe Avenue, Eastchester, NY 10707. TN: (914) 793-6200. Est: 1966. Private premises, appointment necessary. Small stock used. Spec: literature, poetry, illus. bks., rare private press books, limited and signed editions. Cata: on foregoing, 5 a year. A.B.A.A.

WITH PIPE AND BOOK BRECK TURNER, 91 Main Street, Lake Placid, NY 12946. TN: (518) 523-9096. Shop, very large stock used. Spec: Adirondacks; Tobacco and pipes; Ice skating.

ANDREW WITTENBORN, 152 MOUNTAIN ROAD, PLEASANTVILLE, NY 10570. TN: (914) 941-2744. Spec: Automobiliana.

YANKEE PEDDLER BOOKSHOP, 3895 AT 104 WILLIAMSON, 14689 NY. Second shop at Village Gate Square, 274 North Goodman Street, Rochester, NY 14607. Prop: John, Janet & Douglas Westerberg. TN: (315) 589-2063 and (716) 271-5080. Est: 1970. Shops. Williamson, open Mon-Fri 10-5 and Sat and Sun 1-5; appointment preferable. Rochester, open Tues-Fri 11-5, Thurs till 9 pm, Sat 11-5, Sun 12-5. Very large stock used. Cata: Once a year. B: Key Bank. Acc. No: 065-110335-0. M: A.B.A.A. I.L.A.B. *Also mail order address at:* 11299 EAST LAKE ROAD, P.O. BOX 118, POULTNEYVILLE, NY 14538.

YELLOW HOUSE BOOKS, EAST CHATHAM, NY 12060.

YESTERDAY'S BOOKS 2130 BOSTON POST ROAD, LARCHMONT, NY 10538. TN: (914) 834-6630. Shop, open Mon-Sat, 12-6. Spec: archaeology, nature, animals, anthropology; art; hunting, fishing; military; poetry; drama.

ROY YOUNG, BOOKSELLER, INC., 145 PALISADES STREET, DOBBS FERRY, NY 10522. TN: (914) 693-6116. Spec: Art, architecture, illustrated books, books about books, western Americana. M: A.B.A.A.

MARGARET ZERVAS, P.O. BOX 562, MANHASSET, NY 11030. TN: (516) 767-0907. Private premises, appointment necessary. Spec: Americana, Autographs & manuscripts.

39. NORTH CAROLINA (NC.)

ASHEVILLE	HILLSBOROUGH
CHAPEL HILL	RALEIGH
CHARLOTTE	SANFORD
DURHAM	SHALLOTTE
ELIZABETH CITY	WAKE FOREST
FAIRMONT	WENDELL
FAYETTEVILLE	WEST DURHAM
GREENSBORO	WILSON
HIGHLANDS	WINSTON-SALEM

AUTOS & AUTOS, P.O. Box 280, 105 Pine Lake Drive, Elizabeth City, NC 27909. Prop: B.C. West, Jr. TN: (919) 335-1117. Est: 1973. Private house; appointment necessary. Small stock. Spec: Only Autographed books. Cata: 2-4 times per year. B: Peoples Bank. Acc. No: 170022165. M: Manuscript Society and Universal Autograph Collectors Club.

AVOCET BOOKS, 827 South Horner Boulevard, Sanford, NC 27330. Prop: John B. Cheesborough. TN: (919) 775-7928. Est: 1981. Private premises, appointment necessary. Small stock sec. and antiq. Spec: Natural history; travels and voyages; Americana; medical; sporting.

THE BOOK HOUSE, P.O. Box 1284, Chapel Hill, NC 27514. Spec: Southern states; Confederacy.

THE BOOK MART, P.O. Box 5094, Asheville, NC 28803. (7 Biltmore Plaza.) Prop: Nancy Brown. TN: (704) 274-2241. Est: 1947. Shop. Large stock used; also some new books, greetings cards and notepaper. Spec: North Carolina history.

THE BOOK TRADER, 304 South Main Street, P.O. Box 603, Fairmont, NC 28340. Prop: Billy Whitted. TN: (919) 628-0945. Est: 1965. Private premises; appointment necessary. Medium stock used; also new books. Spec: Caroliniana (North and South). Search service available.

BOONE'S ANTIQUES, INC., Highway 301 South, Wilson, NC 27893. Prop: Edgar I. Boone. TN: (919) 237-1508. Est: 1959. Very large stock used, also antiques. Cata: lists.

THE BROWSERY, 547 South Mendenhall Street, Greensboro, NC 27403. Prop: Ben O. Mathews & Charles G. Gibson. TN: (919) 273-7259. Est: 1976. Shop. Very large stock. B: Wachovia Bank & Trust, N.A. Acct: No: 0531 0952 3562 013940.

BROADFOOT'S BOOKMARK, Rt. 3, Box 318, Wendell, NC 27591. Prop: Thomas W. Broadfoot. TN: (919) 365-6963. Est: 1968. Shop. Very large stock. Spec: the Civil War; The South. Cata: American West; South; the Carolinas; maps and views; each 1 a year; Civil War, 8 a year.

THE CAPTAIN'S BOOKSHELF, INC., 26½ BATTERY PARK AVENUE, ASHVILLE, NC 28801. Prop: Chandler W. Gordon. TN: (704) 253-6631. Shop, closed Sundays and Mondays. Spec: 20th century first editions.

CAROLINA BOOKSHOP, 1601 EAST INDEPENDENCE BOULEVARD, CHARLOTTE, NC 28205. Prop: Gordon Briscoe, Jr. TN: (704) 375-7305. Est: 1975. Shop, closed Monday. Medium stock used. Spec: North Carolina history; South; American Civil War.

CYRANO'S BOOKSHOP, 765 MAIN STREET, HIGHLANDS, NC 28741. Prop: Randolph P. Schaffner. TN: (704) 526-5488. Est: 1978. Shop. Very small stock sec. and antiq. also new books. Corresp: Français, Deutsch. B: First Union National Bank, Highlands NC 28741.

DOLPHIN BOOKSHOP, LTD., P.O. DRAWER 5806, FAYETTEVILLE, NC 28303. (Eutaw Village). TN: (919) 484-5082. Est: 1966. A.B.A.

LOVETT & LOVETT, P.O. BOX 13, WINSTON-SALEM, NC 27102. TN: (919) 722-5499.

B.L. MEANS, 4200A, 5935 CREOLA ROAD, CHARLOTTE, NC 28226. Prop: Betty Means. TN: (704) 364-3117. By appointment only. Spec: Gardening and horticulture; illustrated books; children's.

JEREMY NORTH, P.O. BOX 6, SHALLOTTE, NC 28459. (Route 17 at Thomasboro, North Carolina.) Est: 1948. Shop, medium stock used. Spec: maritime, 19th century watercolours. Cata: on foregoing and old maps and prints, 3 a year. A.B.A.A.

OCTOBER FARM, ROUTE 2, BOX 183-C, RALEIGH, NC 27610. Prop: Barbara Cole. TN: (919) 772-0482. Est: 1976. Private premises; appointment necessary. Small stock used. Spec: horse books only (all aspects, including veterinary, shoeing, carriages etc.) Free lists 2 or 3 a year.

OLD BOOK CORNER, 137A EAST ROSEMARY STREET, CHAPEL HILL, NC 27514. Prop: Mrs. Paul Smith. TN: (919) 942-5178. Est: 1954. Shop. Medium stock used. Spec: Southern history, Civil War, Americana. Cata: 10 per year. B: N C National Bank.

OLD GALEN'S BOOKS, Box 3044, West Durham, NC 27705. Prop: G.S.T. Cavanagh. TN: (919) 489-6246. Private premises; appointment necessary. Medium stock used. Spec: medicine and science.

STEVENS BOOK SHOP, P.O. Box 71, Wake Forest, NC 27587. (Corner of North and Main Streets.) Prop: Richard L. Stevens. TN: (919) 556-3830. Est: 1954. Shop. Very large stock used, also new. Spec: religion, Baptist history, North Carolina history. Cata: on foregoing, monthly.

WENTWORTH AND LEGGETT BOOKS, 905 West Main Street, Brightleaf Square, Durham, NC 27701. Prop: Barbara & David Wentworth. Shop. General stock sec. and antiq. books. Spec: illustrated classic children's books and juvenile series.

C.B. WIMSEY, Box 1001, Hillsborough, NC 27278. Prop: C.B. & J.G. Gilbert. Private premises: postal business only. Small stock used. Spec: D.L. Sayers, C.S. Lewis; Detective fiction; Theology.

40.   NORTH DAKOTA (ND.)

DEVIL'S LAKE

HOWARD O. BERG, 317 Seventh Street, Devil's Lake, ND 58301. TN: (701) 662-2343. Est: 1951. Private premises; appointment necessary. Medium stock used; also new books to order. Spec: North Dakota.

41.   OHIO (OH.)

AKRON	ENGLEWOOD
ATHENS	FAIRBORN
BEACHWOOD	GREENSBURG
BLUFFTON	MANSFIELD
BOWLING GREEN	MIAMISBURG
CAREY	MOUNT VERNON
CHESAPEAKE	NORWALK
CINCINNATI	PARMA
CLEVELAND	POLAND
COLUMBUS	RAVENNA
DAYTON	SOUTH EUCLID
DELAWARE	SPRINGFIELD

TOLEDO	YELLOW SPRINGS
WESTLAKE	YOUNGSTOWN
WOOSTER	

A to Z BOOKFARE, 10-12 NORTH PHELPS STREET, YOUNGSTOWN, OH 44503.

ACRES OF BOOKS, INC., 633 MAIN STREET, CINCINNATI, OH 45202. Prop: John Coleman. TN: (513) 721-4214. Shop. Spec: science, technology, travel, history, literature. M: A.B.A.A.

BARBARA AGRANOFF, P.O. BOX 6501, CINCINNATI, OH 45206. (4025 Paddock Road, Rte 4). TN: (513) 281-5095. Medium stock sec. and antiq. Appointment advisable.

ALBERT BOOKS, P.O. BOX 19187, CORRYVILLE STATION, CINCINNATI, OH 45219. Prop: Stephen Albert. TN: (606) 261-0120. Est: 1980. Private premises: appointment necessary. Very small stock used. Spec: trade catalogues.

ALPHA-OMEGA BOOKS, 408 SOUTH MAIN STREET, POLAND, OH 44514.

ALZOFON BOOKS, 2662 GLENMARW AVENUE, COLUMBUS, OH 43202.

ANTIQUARIAN BOOKHOUSE, 718 HEIDELBERG ROAD, TOLEDO, OH 43615.

ARGUS BOOKS, P.O. BOX 3211, COLUMBUS, OH 43210. Prop: R.M. Weatherford. TN: (614) 262-5651. Est: 1974. Private premises; appointment necessary. Small stock used. Spec: North American Indians, Eskimos; Alaska and Arctic; travels and voyages in North America. Cata: on foregoing, 4 a year.

JACK D'AMBROSIO, 6510 FIR TREE CIRCUS, ENGLEWOOD, OH 45322. TN: (513) 836-6280. Est: 1950. Private premises; appointment necessary. Small stock used. Spec: Americana, unusual and obscure.

GLENN ARMITAGE, 108 FIFTH AVENUE, MIAMISBURG, OH 45342. TN: (513) 423-9569. Est: 1960. Private premises: mail order primarily. Medium stock used. Spec: 20th Century Literature, Criticism, Fine Arts, Paperback originals. Cata: Occasional lists. B: Franklin National Bank, Franklin, Ohio.

BACK ROW BOOK SHOP, 411 W. Main Street, Fairborn, OH 45324. Prop: Jerome A. Merkel. TN: (513) 879-2131. Est: 1973. Shop. Large stock available, also new books. B: 1st National Bank of Fairborn. Acc. No: 31-915-8.

BIBLIOPOLIS, 220 Williamson Buildings, Cleveland, OH 44114.

BOOKHAVEN, 739 North Limestone Street, Springfield, OH 45503.

BOOKLODE [PATRICK J. MOONEY], 1255 West First Avenue, Columbus, OH 43212.

BOOK LOVER'S, 6507 Britton, Cincinnati, OH 45227.

BOOKPHIL, P.O. Box 5628, 4110 North High, Columbus, OH 43221.

J. & E. BOOKSALES, 3042 De Camp Road, Youngstown, OH 44511.

THE BOOKSELLER INC., 521 West Exchange Street, Akron, OH 44302. Pres: Frank Klein. TN: (216) 762-3101. Est: 1948. Shop. Very large stock used; also some new books. Spec: Ohioiana, U.S. military aviation (lighter than air and Army); entertainment (movies and theatre); hand bookbinding, literature. Cata: 10 a year.

THE BOOK STOP, 2705 Far Hills Avenue, Dayton, OH 45419. Prop: Marilyn H. Bohlander. TN: (513) 293-2772. Est: 1978. Shop. Medium stock used. Spec: literature; history; military history.

THE BOOK STORE, 4258 North High Street, Columbus, OH. Prop: Roy & Tina Willis. TN: (614) 261-8550. Shop. Large sec. and antiq. stock.

GEORGE D. BROWN BOOKS, 7001 Bancroft Street, Toledo, OH 43617. Props: Alberta & George D. Brown. TN: (1-419) 841-4979. Est: 1967. Shop. Large stock used; antiquarian books. Spec: Great Lakes, Americana; art; archaeology; cookbooks; Bibles; railroad. Cata: occasionally. A.B.A.

BURLEY & BOOKS INC., 348 Franklin Park Mall, Toledo, OH 43623. Prop: Michael W. Lora. TN: (419) 472-0775. Est 1979. Shop. Very small stock sec. and antiq. Spec: bibliography; fine and limited editions; Malcolm Lowry, Thomas Puncheon. Corresp: Español. B: Ohio Citizens Bank, Franklin Park Mall, Toledo, OH 43623.

CAROL BUTCHER, 3955 NEW ROAD, YOUNGSTOWN, OH 44515.

ALBERT COHEN, 2343, SELMA AVENUE, YOUNGSTOWN, OH 44504.

CROISSANT & COMPANY, P.O. BOX 282, ATHENS, OH 45701.

BILL CURRY, 435 ROCKWOOD AVENUE, CHESAPEAKE, OH 45619.

DE ANIMA: BOOKS IN PSYCHOLOGY, 122 EAST EVERS, BOWLING GREEN, OH 43402. Prop: Ryan D. Tweney, Ph.d. TN: (419) 352-8533. Est: 1974. Private premises, appointment necessary. Small stock used. Spec: Psychology, Psychiatry, Philosophy. Cata: 1 or 2 times per year.

THE DRAGON'S LAIR, INC., 110 WEST FIFTH STREET, DAYTON, OH 45402. Prop: Richard E. Clear. TN: (513) 222-1479. Est: 1974. Shop; open Monday-Saturdays 10.00-18.45. Very large stock. B: Third National Bank of Dayton.

DUTTENHOFER'S BOOK TREASURES, 214 W. MCMILLAN, CINCINNATI, OH 45219. Prop: Stanley A. Duttenhofer. TN: (513) 381-1340. Est: 1975. Shop. Very large stock. Spec: Midwestern History, Illustrated Children's books. B: Fifth/Third Bank. Acc.No: 723-06914

BRUCE FERRINI, 933 WEST EXCHANGE STREET, AKRON, OH 44302. TN: (216) 867 2665 or (800) 321-3753. Spec: Western medieval illuminated manuscripts and manuscript leaves, prints, drawings. M: A.B.A.A.

KENDALL G. GAISSER, 1242 BROADWAY, TOLEDO, OH 43609. TN: (419) 243-7631. Est: 1937. Shop. Very large stock used. Spec: Americana, literature, history, art, first editions, rare. Also prints. A.B.A.A.

GENERAL MAGAZINE COMPANY OF PARMA, 7672 KOCH DRIVE, PARMA, OH 44134. Prop: K. Wolnik & J.T. Zubal. Est: 1970. Storeroom, appointment necessary. Very large stock of general magazines and trade journals.

GARRY E. GIBBONS, 823 THORNE, WOOSTER, OH 44691.

ARTHUR H. GILHAM, 26927 DETROIT ROAD, WESTLAKE, OH 44145.

J.A. GIOVAINNI, 58 ORGAN AVENUE, AKRON, OH 44319.

D. GRATZ, R.2, BOX 89, BLUFFTON, OH 45817. TN: (419) 358-7431. Est:
1952. Mail order only. Very small stock used, some new. Spec:
genealogy, family history. Cata: on foregoing, every 3 years.

GREAT LAKES BOOK STORE, P.O. BOX 4083 E, TOLEDO, OH 43609.
(347 Sumner Street.) Prop: Harry G. Shaffer. TN: (419) 243-0932.
Est: 1957. Storeroom, open normal business hours. Large stock used,
also new. Spec: hobby material in books. Cata: hobbies and general,
several a year.

ROBERT G. HAYMAN, 575 WEST STREET, P.O. BOX 188, CAREY, OH
43316. TN: (419) 396-6933. Est: 1959. House premises, open normal
business hours. Medium stock used, some new. Spec: Americana,
especially Midwestern Americana. Cata: Americana, 5 a year.
A.B.A.A.

SUSAN HELLER —BOOKSEARCH, P.O. BOX 22723, BEACHWOOD, OH
44122. TN: (216) 751-3311 (residence); 283-2665 (business). Est:
1974. Private premises, appointment necessary. Large stock used.
Spec: Fine (especially scholarly) out-of-print and rare signed copies.
Cata: Periodically. B: Shaker Savings. Acc.No: 205038247. Society
National Acc.No: 244-0888.

KAY'S BOOK & MAGAZINE SUPERMARKET, 620 PROSPECT AVENUE,
CLEVELAND, OH 44115. Prop: Michael Powell. TN: (216) 861-6783.
Est: 1946. Shop and warehouse. Stock of 1 million used, also new.
Spec: occult, technical, literature, biography, history, fiction.

KEISOGLOFF BOOK SHOP, 53 THE ARCADE, CLEVELAND, OH 44114.
Prop: Peter Keisogloff. TN: (216) 621-3094. Est: 1931. Shop. Medium
stock used, also new. Spec: limited editions, private press books, art.

KIDDS BOOKSTORE, 626 VINE STREET, CINCINNATI, OH 45202. Prop:
B. Baierschmidt. TN: (513) 621-0213. Est: 1846. Shop. Very small
stock used, also new. A.B.A.

MIRAN ART AND BOOKS, 2824 ELM AVENUE, COLUMBUS, OH 43209.
Prop: Marcia & Ivan Gilbert. TN: (614) 231-3707 or 236-0002. Est:
1974. Private premises, appointment necessary. Small stock used.
Spec: Illustrations, Photographs, Children's, General art and art books.

MORNINGSIDE BOOKSHOP, P.O. Box 1087, DAYTON, OH 45401. Prop: Robert J. & Mary E. Younger. TN: (513) 461-6736. Office hours 9-4, Mon to Fri, or by appointment.

MY BACK PAGES BOOKSTORE, 1896 NORTH HIGH STREET, COLUMBUS, OH 43201.

MYSTERIES FROM THE YARD, 101 CEMETERY, YELLOW SPRINGS, OH 45387. Prop: Mary Frost-Pierson. TN: (513) 767-2111. Est. 1979. Private premises, available afternoons Friday, Saturday and Sunday or by appointment. Medium stock sec. and antiq. Spec: detective fiction. Cata: occasionally. Corresp: Français, Arabic. B: Miami Bank, Yellow Springs, OII 45387.

MYTHISTORY, 819 QUINBY AVENUE, WOOSTER, OH 44697. TN: (216) 262-8581. Spec: Myths, Hero Tales.

PAUL H. NORTH, JR., 81 BULLITT PARK PLACE, COLUMBUS, OH 43209. TN: (614) 252-1826. Est: 1948. Private premises; appointment necessary. Medium stock used books, also art dealer and autographs. Spec: rare books, detective fiction, central and western Americana, Civil War, Confederacy. M: A.B.A.A., M.S.

OHIO BOOKHUNTER, 564 EAST TOWNVIEW CRESCENT, MANSFIELD, OH 44907. Prop: John Stark. TN: (419) 756-0655 or 526-1249. By appointment only. Spec: Ohio, general Americana. M: A.B.A.A.

THE OLD BOOK STORE, 210 E. CUYAHOGA FALL AVENUE, AKRON, OH 44310. Prop: Ron Antonucci. TN: 253-5025. Shop. Very large stock. Spec: Americana and science fiction and fantasy. Cata: 4 times per year. B: Bank Ohio. Acct.No: 2000-2684-2.

OWL CREEK BOOK SHOP, 309 W. VINE ST., MOUNT VERNON, OH 43050. Prop: B.K. Clinker. TN: (614) 397-9337. Est: 1969. Shop. Medium stock used. Cata: occasionally.

PAGES FOR SAGES, P.O. Box 22723, BEACHWOOD, OH 44122. Prop: Susan Heller. TN: (216) 283-2665. Spec: author and subject collections. M: A.B.A.A.

PAPER PEDDLERS, 4425 MAYFIELD ROAD, SOUTH EUCLID, CLEVELAND, OH 44121. Prop: Janet A. Blakeley & Carole M. Lazarus. TN: (216) 382-6383. Est: 1974. Shop, open on Sundays 10-6, and weekdays by appointment. Medium stock used, out-of-print, rare, ephemera.

THE PHOTO PLACE GALLERY & BOOKSHOP, 211 ARCADIA AVENUE, COLUMBUS, OH 43202. Prop: Tina & Ed. Hoffman. TN: (614) 267-0203. Shop, closed Mondays. Spec: photography.

PLOUGH'S WESTERN RESERVE, 467 SOUTH CHESTNUT STREET, RAVENNA, OH 44266. Prop: Cyrus T. Plough. TN: (216) 296-8720. Est: 1927. Private premises, appointment necessary. Very small stock used, also valuing and appraisals.

PROFESSIONAL BOOKS SERVICE, BOX 366, DAYTON, OH 45401. TN: (513) 223-3734. Cables PROBKS. Large stock sec. & also new books on law and medicine. San Francisco office: 55 Sutter Street (Suite 597) San Francisco, CA 94104. TN: (415) 788-1979.

RANDOLPH BOOKS, 475 SIXTH STREET, TOLEDO, OH 43605.

ROBERT RICHSHAFER, 1800 VINE STREET, CINCINNATI, OH 45210. TN: (513) 722-2052. Spec: Americana, (esp Ohio).

RON-DOT BOOKFINDERS, 4700 MASSILLON ROAD, GREENSBURG, OH 44232. Prop: Ron & Dot Clewell. TN: (216) 896-3482. Est: 1976. Shop, closed on Mondays and Tuesdays. Very large stock used. Cata: Occasionally. B: BancOhio National Bank. Acct.No: 3100-0382-3.

IRVING M. ROTH, 89 WHITTLESEY AVENUE, NORWALK, OH 44857. TN: (419) 668-2893. Est: 1946. Shop, but books seen by appointment only. Large stock used, also antiques and new books on antiques. Spec: freemasonry, Americana, old postcards and tradecards.

SHAW-BANFILL BOOKS, P.O. BOX 14850, COLUMBUS, OH 43214. Prop: Richard F. Shaw. TN: (614) 267-9022. Est: 1978. Private premises, appointment necessary. Small stock used. Spec: Science, Women's History.

J. STARK, 564 EAST TOWNVIEW CIRCLE, MANSFIELD, OH 44907. TN: (419) 756-0655. Shop, but appointment necessary. M: A.B.A.A.

SIGNIFICANT BOOKS, 4 WEST BENSON STREET, CINCINNATI, OH 45215. Prop: Bill & Carolyn Downing. TN: (513) 761-2694. Est: 1977. Shop: open noon Tuesday through Friday. Stock of 7,000 volumes. Spec: collectible and scholarly non-fiction.

BERTRAND SMITH'S ACRES OF BOOKS, INC., 633 MAIN STREET, CINCINNATI, OH 45202. Pres: Bert Smith, Jr. TN: (513) PArkway 1-4214. Est: 1924. Five floor building. Stock of about 300,000 volumes used, also new non-fiction. A.B.A.A. A.B.A. A.B.A. (G.B.)

KAREN WICKLIFF, 2579 NORTH HIGH STREET, COLUMBUS, OH 43002. TN: (614) 263-2903. Shop. Very large stock sec. and antiq.

MATHELLE G. WILLIAMS, 420 NORTH FRANKLIN STREET, DELAWARE, OH 43015. TN: (614) 369-1831. Private premises, appointment necessary. Very small stock used, also picture framing.

DAVID S. WOLOCH, BOX 5268, AKRON, OH 44313. TN: (216) 836-4494. Spec: Illuminated manuscripts pre-16th century.

JOHN T. ZUBAL, INC., 2969 WEST 25th STREET, CLEVELAND, OH 44113. TN: (216) 241-7640. Telex: 298256 ZUBAL UR. Est: 1964. Shop and storeroom. Very large stock. Spec: Back dated Periodicals, Out-of-print antiquarian, rare books in social sciences and humanities. B: Ameritrust Co Acc. No: 00555 2492.

42. OKLAHOMA (OK.)

EDMOND
OKLAHOMA CITY   STILLWATER

ALADDIN BOOK SHOPPE, 2037 NORTH WEST 23rd STREET, OKLAHOMA CITY, OK 73106. Prop: Miss Jerry Nelson. TN: (405) 528-0814. Est: 1930. Shop. Very large stock used. Spec: Oklahoma history. A.B.A.

RONALD BEVER, 320 TULLAHOMA DRIVE, EDMOND, OK 73034. TN: (405) 341-3590. Est: 1971. Mail order only. Small stock used. Spec: religion, speech, sermons, homelitics.

CARAVAN BOOKS (USED & RARE BOOKS DEPT.), P.O. Box 861, STILLWATER, OK 74076. Prop: John & Della Thomas. TN: (405) 372-6227. Est: 1978. Shop, closed Wednesdays. Medium stock sec. and antiq., and new books next door. Spec: Americana, Oklahoma; Children's; science fiction and fantasy. Cata: 2 or 3 a year. *Shop at* SOUTH KNOBLOCK, STILLWATER, OK 74074.

MELVIN MARCHER, BOOKSELLER, 6204 N. VERMONT, OKLAHOMA CITY, OK 73112. TN: (405) 946-6270. Est: 1969. Private premises, appointment necessary. Small stock used. Spec: Firearms, hunting, fishing, natural history. Cata: On foregoing—one on natural history and one sporting per year.

A POINTS NORTHE, 3630 N.W. 22, OKLAHOMA CITY, OK 2890. Prop: James Neill Northe. TN: (405) 949-0675. Est: 1940. Mail order and telephone only. Spec: Americana: (Oklahoma; Indian Territory). Also appraisals.

43.   OREGON (OR.)

BEAVERTON	MEDFORD
CORVALLIS	OREGON CITY
DUNDEE	PORTLAND
EUGENE	SALEM
GOLD HILL	SELMA
MCMINNVILLE	TROUT DALE

ACADEMIC BOOK RESERVE, P.O. Box 2041, SALEM, OR 97308.

APPLEGATE BOOKS, Box 541, MEDFORD, OR 97501. TN: (503) 772-8044. Private premises; postal business only.

ATLANTIS RISING BOOKSHOP, 7915 SOUTH EAST STARK STREET, PORTLAND, OR 97215. Prop: Frank J. Montagna. TN: (503) 253-4031. Est: 1970. Shop. Very large stock used, also new. Spec: metaphysics, astrology, science fiction, fantasy. Cata: metaphysics, astrology, every 2 years. Also posters, herbs, incense, occult supplies.

AUTHORS OF THE WEST, 191 DOFWOOD DRIVE, DUNDEE, OR 97115. Prop: Lee & Grayce Nash. TN: (503) 538-8132. Est: 1973. Private premises; appointment necessary. Small stock used; also new books. Spec: American literature; fiction; poetry; artistic factual writing on the West.

AVOCET USED BOOKSTORE, 614 SOUTH-WEST 3RD, CORVALLIS, OR. Prop: Howard & Sandra Mills. TN: (503) 753-4119. Est: 1979. Shop. Very large stock sec. and antiq. General stock.

BACKSTAGE BOOKS [HOWARD L. RAMEY], P.O. BOX 3676, EUGENE, OR 97403.

BARTLETT STREET BOOKSTORE, 16 SOUTH BARTLETT STREET, MEDFORD, OR 97501. TN: (503) 772-8049. Shop. Stock of 15,000 volumes used and rare.

DOUG BEARCE, P.O. BOX 7081, SALEM, OR 97303. Spec: all Boy Scout items prior to 1948.

BEAVER BOOK STORE, 1027 SOUTH WEST 5th AVENUE, PORTLAND, OR 97204. Prop: Frank L. Isbell. TN: (503) 223-7959. Est: 1956. Shop. Very large stock used. Spec: fiction and children's books (Victorian and modern).

B.L. BIBBY, BOOKS, 1225 SARDINE CREEK ROAD, GOLD HILL, OR 97525. Prop: George A. Bibby. TN: (503) 855-1621. Est: 1967. Mail order only. Small stock used. Spec: gardening, horticulture, natural history. Cata: on foregoing. A.B.A.A.

BOOK BROWSE, 922 NORTH WEST, 21st, PORTLAND, OR 97209.

BOOK CELLAR, 3640 SOUTH WEST 90th STREET, PORTLAND, OR 97225.

THE BOOK FAIR, 1409 OAK STREET, EUGENE, OR 97401. Prop: Jerry D. Leedy. TN: (503) 343-3033. Est: 1966. Shop. Very large stock including new books. B: Citizens Bank Acc. No: 00 822 191. M: A.B.A. Pacific Northwest Booksellers Assoc.

THE BOOK MANIFEST LIMITED, P.O. BOX 19806, PORTLAND, OR 97219. Prop: Christopher Skagen. TN: (503) 245-9096.

BOOK VAULT, 3125 S.W. CEDAR HILLS BOULEVARD, BEAVERTON, OR 97005.

CAMERON'S BOOK STORE, 336 SOUTH WEST 3RD AVENUE, PORTLAND, OR 97204. Prop: Fred J. Goetz. TN: (503) 228-2391. Est: 1940. Shop. Large stock used and out-of-print books and vintage magazines.

JIM COLANTINO, 1228 S.E. HARLOW, TROUT DALE, OR 97060.

ANDREA DRINARD, 1934 S.E. 37th AVENUE, PORTLAND, OR 97214.

GREEN DOLPHIN BOOKSHOP, 215 SOUTH WEST ANKENY STREET, PORTLAND, OR 97204. Prop: Wright Lewis. TN: (503) 224-3060. Est: 1965. Shop. Large stock used. Search Service. A.B.A.A.

LILLIAN KENNEDY, BOOKSELLER, P.O. BOX 19071, PORTLAND, OR 97219. TN: (503) 245-6187. Est: 1969. Private premises, appointment necessary. Very small stock used. Spec: Women, Pacific Northwest Americana, Religious history. Cata: 3 per year. B: 1st State Bank of Oregon.

MACLEAY COUNTRY STORE, 8342 MACLEAY ROAD, SE. SALEM, OR 97301. Prop: Dale C. Schmidt. TN: (503) 362-0282. Est: 1973. Shop. Very small stock used. Spec: Pacific Northwest Americana.

J. MICHAELS BOOKS, 160 EAST BROADWAY, EUGENE, OR 97401. Prop: Jeremy Nissel & Linda Ellis. TN: (503) 342-2002. Est: 1975. Shop. Very large stock used. Spec: art, architecture; photography literature; Western Americana.

V. MILKOWSKI, 8003 OLNEY SOUTH EAST, SALEM, OR 97301.

RICHARD MILLER [FINE ARTS BOOKSHOP], P.O. BOX 775, OREGON CITY, OR 97045.

NINETEENTH CENTURY PRINTS, 2732 S.E. WOODWARD STREET, PORTLAND, OR 97202. Prop: Elisabeth Burdon. TN: (503) 234-3538. Est: 1981. Private premises; appointment necessary. Very small stock used. Spec: old prints, maps and illustrated books. M: American Historical Print Collectors' Society.

OLD OREGON BOOK STORE, 525 SOUTH WEST 12TH, PORTLAND, OR 97205. Prop: Preston & Phyllis McMann. TN: (503) 227-2742. Est: 1949. Shop, open 11.00 to 17.00 (closed Sunday and Monday). Stock of over 125,000 volumes used and antiq., also some new books. Spec: Russia, Western Americana, anthropology, scholarly books. Cata: 2 a year. A.B.A.A.

PAPER MOON BOOKSTORE, 3538 S.E. HAWTHORNE BOULEVARD, PORTLAND, OR 97214.

PHILLIP J. PIRAGES, P.O. Box 504, 965 West 11th Street, McMinnville, OR 97128. TN: (616) 345-7220. Est: 1979. Private premises, appointment necessary. Small stock sec. and antiq. Spec: manuscripts, early printing, fine bindings, modern first editions and association copies. Cata: 2 a year. Corresp: Français, Deutsch.

JOSEPH SHECHTMAN, 11145 S.W. Cabot Street, Beaverton, OR 97005.

D.C. SCHMIDT, 610 Howell Pr. Road S.E., Salem, OR 97301.

M.L. STAFFORD, 2790 Country Lane, Eugene, OR 97401.

44. PENNSYLVANIA (PA.)

ALLENTOWN
ALTOONA
AMBLER
BARTONSVILLE
BEAVER FALLS
BEDFORD
BETHEL PARK
BETHLEHEM
BLOOMSBURG
BOYERTOWN
BRADFORD
BRYN MAWR
BUCKS COUNTY
CARLISLE
CASTLE SHANNON
CATAWISSA
CHADD'S FORD
CHALFONT
CHAMBERSBURG
CRAFTON
DENVER
DOYLESTOWN
EASTON
EPHRATA
ERIE
EXPORT
GETTYSBURG

GLEN ROCK
GWYNEDD VALLEY
HARRISBURG
HATFIELD
HARTSVILLE
HATBORO
HAVERTOWN
HOLTWOOD
HUNTINGDON VALLEY
INDIANA
JENKINTOWN
KING OF PRUSSIA
LANCASTER
LUMBERVILLE
MECHANICSBURG
MEDIA
MERCERSBERG
MOUNTJOY
NARBERTH
NEW HOPE
NEWTOWN SQUARE
NORTH EAST
NORTH HUNTINGDON
PAOLI
PITTSBURGH
PHILADELPHIA
POCONO PINES

POTTSTOWN	SWARTHMORE
READING	TRAFFORD
REVERE	VANDERGRIFT
RILLTON	WARREN
SAXTIB	WAYNE
SAYRE	WEST CHESTER
SELINSGROVE	WEST READING
SHIPPENSBURG	WILLIAMSPORT
SINKING SPRING	WYNNEWOOD
STRAFFORD WAYNE	WYOMING
STROUDSBURG	YARDLEY

ACORN b.c., 447 EAST PITT STREET, BEDFORD, PA 15522. Prop: Donald S. & Mary L. Jones. TN: (814) 623-9603. Est: 1959. Shop. Very large stock used. Spec: Americana, Pennsylvania.

MARGARET ALBURN, 929 SOUTH HIGH STREET, WEST CHESTER, PA 19380.

IRMA ALEXANDER, 155 WEST WASHINGTON LANE, JENKINTOWN, PA 19046. TN: (215) 884-9348.

WM. H. ALLEN, 2031 WALNUT STREET, PHILADELPHIA, PA 19103. Prop: George Allen. TN: (215) LOcust 3-3398. Est: 1918. Shop. Very large stock used. Spec: classics, English and American literature, Africa and the Orient, modern languages. Cata: on foregoing, 5 a year. A.B.A. (Int.).

THE AMERICANIST, 1525 SHENKEL ROAD, POTTSTOWN, PA 19464. Prop: Norman Kane. TN: (215) 323-5289. Est: 1960. Appointment advised. Large stock used and rare. Spec: American history and literature, manuscripts, first editions and auctioneers. Cata: on foregoing. 6-10 a year. A.B.A.A.

W. GRAHAM ARADER III, 1000 BOXWOOD COURT, KING OF PRUSSIA, PA 19406. Prop: Karen L. Nathan. TN: (215) 825-6570. Est: 1973. Shop, open Monday-Saturday 9 a.m. to 6 p.m., Sunday by appointment. Medium stock used. Spec: Rare maps, Americana, Travel, Color plate books, History of Cartography, Paper restoration. Cata: 6 times per year. B: First Pennsylvania Bank. Acc. No: 12l7-147-7. M: Institute of Paper Conservation.

G.H. ARROW COMPANY, P.O. Box 16558, 1133-39 North 4th Street, Philadelphia, PA 19123. Prop: Louis Kohn. TN: (215) 922-3211. Storeroom, open normal business hours. Large stock of back issue periodicals medical, scientific, technical and liberal arts.

JOHN K. BAKER, 17 South Carpenter Avenue, Indiana, PA 15701.

BALDWIN'S BOOK BARN, 865 Lenape Road, West Chester, PA 19380.

PHILIP E. BARACCA, 6017 Jenkins Arcade, 5th and Libery Avenues, Pittsburgh, PA 15222. Prop: Philip E. Baracca (the Biblio-Phil). TN: (412) 765-3231. Est: 1980. Shop in arcade. Small stock used.

CATHERINE BARNES, 2031 Walnut Street, (3rd Floor), Philadelphia, PA 19103. TN: (215) 854-0175.

FRANK BARRY, 707 South Warnock Street, Philadelphia, PA 19147. TN: (215) WA 3-4088. Private premises, appointment necessary. Very large stock used. Spec: circus, aviation, bull-fighting, show business, fiction, war, physical culture, nature.

ROBERT F. BATCHELDER, 1 West Butler Avenue, Ambler, PA 19002. TN: (215) 643-1430. Spec: Autograph letters, manuscripts and documents (American and European in all Fields), inscribed books. M: A.B.A.A.

BAUMAN RARE BOOKS, 1807 Chestnut Street, Philadelphia, PA 19103. TN: (215) 564-4274. Shop. Spec: Fine and rare books; maps; Americana; early English and American law; travel.

JAMES BEATTIE, 611 Arlyn Circle, Wayne, PA 19087.

BIKES AND BOOKS, 5952 Germantown Avenue, Philadelphia, PA. Prop: Art Carduner. TN: (215) 843-6071. Est: 1955. Shop; by appointment only. Very large stock sec. and antiq. books. Spec: Americana; poetry; fiction; military history. Cata: 4 a year. Corresp: Español.

THE BOOK EXCHANGE [OCCULT SCIENCES LIBRARY], 1429 LARDNER STREET, PHILADELPHIA, PA 19149. Prop: Israel Shotz. TN: (215) 744-5245. Est: 1944. Private premises; appointment necessary. Very small stock used, also new books. Spec: occult, spiritualism, metaphysics. Cata: general occulta, 2 a year.

THE BOOK HAVEN, 146 & 154 NORTH PRINCE STREET, LANCASTER, PA 17603. Prop: Kinsey Baker. TN: (717) 393-0920. Est: 1978. Shop. Stock of 20,000 used out of print and rare volumes. Spec: Children's and Illustrated books. B: Fulton Bank 011 340 096 7.

THE BOOK INN, 7116A RISING SUN AVENUE, PHILADELPHIA, PA 19111.

BOOK MARK, 2049 RITTENHOUSE SQUARE WEST, PHILADELPHIA, PA 19103. Prop: Robert C. Langmuir, Jr. TN: (215) 735-5546. Est: 1978. Shop. Medium stock used. Spec: Architecture, Illustrated books, Art, Literature. Cata: 2-3 per year. B: Fidelity, Acc. No: 758-802-3.

BOOKSOURCE, 7 SOUTH CHESTER ROAD, SWARTHMORE, PA 19081. TN: (215) 328-5083. Shop. Cata.

BRANDYWINE BOOKS, 715 SPRING STREET, SAXTON, PA 16678. Prop: William T. P. Shea. TN: (814) 635-2874. Est: 1963. Private premises; appointment necessary. Very large stock used. Spec: law; military; area studies.

JESSE H. BRUBACHER, R.D. 42, DENVER, PA 17517. TN: (215) 445-5966.

DON AND THERESA BUDD, 8738 PERCH LANE, PHILADELPHIA, PA 19103. TN: (215) MA-0629.

ANDREW CAHAN, BOX 30202, PHILADELPHIA, PA 19103. TN: (215) 557-7300. Private premises, appointment necessary. Spec: Americana; the arts.

CANTRELLS' BOOKS, 15 SOUTH PEARL STREET, NORTH EAST, PA 16428. Prop: Glenn W. Cantrell. TN: (814) 725-3681. Spec: American inland waterways. M: A.B.A.A.

ART CARDUNER, 6228 GREENE STREET, PHILADELPHIA, PA 19144. TN: (215) 843-6071. Search service, by appointment only.

BERNARD CONWELL CARLITZ, 1901 CHESTNUT STREET, PHILADELPHIA, PA 19103. TN: (215) 563-6608. Spec: old and rare books, maps, prints, art objects.

PAUL CAVA, 526 DELANCY STREET, PHILADELPHIA, PA 19106.

COINHUNTER, 1616 WALNUT STREET, PHILADELPHIA, PA 19103. Prop: C.E. Bullowa. TN: (215) PE5-5517. Est: 1946. Shop. Very small stock used; some new. Spec: numismatica. Cata: 2 a year. I.A.P.N. P.N.G. A.N.A. etc.

PATRICK COYNE BOOK SERVICE, P.O. BOX 10430, PITTSBURGH, PA 15234.

THOMAS S. DELONG, R.D. 6. BOX 336, SINKING SPRING, PA 19608. TN: (215) 777-7001.

DUBOIS AND BULLOCK, 940 QUEENS DRIVE, YARDLEY, PA 19067. TN: (215) 493-2047.

DOE RUN VALLEY BOOKS, P.O. BOX 255, CHADD'S FORD, PA. TN: (215) 593 6997.

EPISTEMOLOGIST SCHOLARLY BOOKS, 239 NORTH ROBERTS ROAD, BRYN MAWR, PA 19010. Prop: N. Lynn Wozniak. TN: (215) 527-1065. Est: 1972. Storeroom, appointment necessary. Small stock used. Spec: Psychology, Psychiatry, Philosophy. Cata: In foregoing subjects 3-4 times per year.

THE ERIE BOOK STORE, 717 FRENCH STREET, ERIE, PA 16501. Prop: Kathleen Cantrell. TN: (814) 452-3354. Est: 1921. Shop. Large stock used, also new. Spec: Western Pennsylvania, early Pennsylvania oil, Great Lakes. A.B.A.A. A.B.A.

D.J. ERNST, OLD BOOK STORE, 27 NORTH MARKET STREET, SELINSGROVE, PA 17870. TN: (717) 374-9461. Est: 1975. Shop. Small stock used.

THE FAMILY ALBUM, RD1, Box 42, Glen Rock, PA 17327. Prop: Ronald Lieberman. TN: (717) 235-2134. Est: 1969. Private premises, appointment necessary. Medium stock used. Spec: Americana, Pennsylvaniana, Photographica, Early imprints, Incunabula. Also appraisals. Cata: 3-4 per year. B: Hershey National Bank Acc. No: 526 607 2. M: A.B.A.A., Bibliographical Society of America, Library Company of Philadelphia.

DO FISHER BOOKS, 1631 Sheridan Street, Williamsport, PA 17701. Prop: Dolores and Robert Fisher. TN: (717) 494-1825. Est: 1965. Shop. Stock of more than 50,000 volumes. Spec: Pennsylvania histories; illustrated books. Cata: subject lists on application.

FRAN'S BOOKS, 6617 Lincoln Dr., Philadelphia, PA 19119. TN: (215) 438-2729.

FRIGATE BOOKSHOP, INC., 16 East Highland Avenue, Philadelphia, PA 19118.

DAVID GANELIN, 1708 7th Avenue, Beaver Falls, PA 15010. TN: (412) 847-2159. Est: 1979. Private premises; appointment necessary. Small stock used.

GAME BAG BOOKS, RD 2, Box 14-D, Holtwood, PA 17532. Prop: Henry S. Paul. TN: (717) 284-4391. Private premises; appointment necessary. Very small stock used. Spec: hunting, fishing and sporting dogs.

THE GATEWAY, Ferndale, Bucks County, PA 18921. Prop: J.U. Gorham. TN: (215) 847-5644. Est: 1931. Business by mail only. Large stock used; also new books. Spec: occultism, mysticism, self help. Occasional lists.

BRUCE GIMELSON AUTOGRAPHS, 96 South Limekiln Pike, Chalfont, PA 18914.

GRAEDON BOOKS INC., R.D.1, New Hope, PA 18938.

GRAVESEND BOOKS, P.O. Box 235, Pocono Pines, PA 18350. Prop: Enola Stewart. TN: (201) 891-5954. Est: 1969. Private premises; appointment necessary. Medium stock used; also new books. Spec: Sherlockiana, Doyle, Mystery fiction; Victorian military history. Cata on foregoing, 6 a year.

GWYNEDD VALLEY BOOK STORE, PLYMOUTH ROAD AT THE RAILROAD, GWYNEDD VALLEY, PA 19437. Prop: John & Alicia Goodolf. TN: (215) MI 6-0881. Est: 1967. Shop, open 09.00 to 23.00 hours, 365 days a year. Stock of over 100,000 volumes used books.

GEORGE HALL, JNR., 1441 LINCOLN WAY EAST, CHAMBERSBURG, PA 17201. TN: (717) 263-4388.

NATHAN O. HECKMAN, 3511 MERCERSBURG ROAD, MERCERSBURG, PA 17236. TN: (717) 328-3478, Shop, appointment advisable.

F. THOMAS HELLER. P.O. Box 356, SWARTHMORE, PA 19081. (435 RIVERVIEW ROAD). TN: (215) 543-3582. Cables: Tomehaller, Swarthmore. Spec: rare, early science and medicine, physchiatry, psycho-analysis. A.B.A.A.

THE HERMIT'S BOOK HOUSE, 34 MOUNT ZION ROAD, WYOMING, PA 18644. Prop: Stephen Casterlin. TN: (717) 696-1474. Est: 1978. Shop, appointment necessary. Medium stock used. B: Franklin First Federal Savings and Loan Assoc. Acc. No: 403540016. M: A.B.A.

HIVE OF INDUSTRY, P.O. Box 602, EASTON, PA 18042. Prop: Y. Mayer. TN: (215) 258-6663. Est: 1960. Storeroom; appointment necessary. Spec: history of technology, management, business studies, economics. Cata: 5 a year lists.

HOBSON'S CHOICE BOOKS, 511 RUNNYMEDE AVENUE, JENKINTOWN, PA 19046. TN: (215) 884-4853.

HOFFMAN RESEARCH SERVICES, P.O. Box 342, RILLTON, PA 15678. Prop: Ralph E. Hoffman. Est: 1965. Mail order and by appointment. Large stock used. Spec: scholarly, sports, Americana, crime, science and history of science. Search service. Cata: general, 2 a year.

THE HOUSE OF OLD BOOKS, MANHEIM and MAIN STREETS, MOUNT JOY, PA 17552. Prop: Neo American Church, Inc. TN: (717) 653-4328. Est: 1960. Shop. Very large stock used.

RALPH T. HOWEY, HAMPTON HOUSE—7G, HAGYS FORD, NARBERTH, PA 19072. TN: (215) MOhawk 4-3886. A.B.A.A.

JEAN'S BOOKSERVICE, P.O. Box 264, HATFIELD, PA 19440. TN: (215) 362-0732.

ROBERT J. KALANJA, 247 EAST FAIRMONT AVENUE, TRAFFORD, PA 15085. TN: (412) 372-8096. Private premises, not possible to see stock. Medium stock used. Spec: Natural history, non-fiction, all types of scrapbooks. Cata: Every month or two.

KASTENBAUM BOOKS, 333 WEST STATE STREET, MEDIA, PA 19063. Prop: Bernard Kastenbaum. TN: (215) LO 6-2400. Est: 1952. Shop. Medium stock used.

CESI KELLINGER, BOOKSELLER, 735 PHILA AVENUE, CHAMBERSBURG, PA 17201. TN: (717) 263-4474. Est: 1974. Private premises, appointment necessary. Large stock used. Spec: Art, Americana, First editions. Cata: Twice a year.

BONNIE KEYSER BOOKS, 328 W. MINER ST, WEST CHESTER, PA 19382. TN: (215) 436-4160.

KLEIN'S OLD BOOKS, 677 WOODWARD DRIVE, HUNTINGDON VALLEY, PA 19382. TN: (215) 947-2335.

WILLIAM V. KLINE, 2417 WARM SPRING ROAD, CHAMBERSBURG, PA 17201. TN: (717) 375-2575. Shop, appointment advisable.

MARY KOCH BOOKS, 128 W. HIGHLAND AVE., PHILADELPHIA, PA 19118. TN: (215) 247-4270.

KONIGSMARK BOOKS, 309 MIDLAND AVENUE, WAYNE, PA 19087. Prop: Jocelyn Konigsmark. TN: (215) 687-5965. Private premises, appointment necessary. Medium stock. sec. and antiq. Spec: first and fine editions; illustrated; children's; Jane Austen. (From June to August at Southwest Harbor Antiques Gallery, Southwest Harbor, ME 04679. Shop. TN: (207) 244-3162).

SAM LAIDACKER, P.O. BOX 416, BLOOMSBURG, PA 17815. (3 East 5th Street). TN: (717) 784-4912. Est: 1930. Shop. Medium stock used, also new books and antiques. Spec: American antiques and sale catalogues.

LAST HURRAH BOOKSHOP, 937 MEMORIAL AVENUE, WILLIAMSPORT, PA 17701. TN: (717) 327-9338.

LEGACY BOOKS, P.O. Box 494, Hatboro, PA 19040. (12 Meetinghouse Road.) Prop: Lillian Krelove. TN: (215) 675-6762. Est: 1958 as Folklore Associates. Private premises, appointment necessary. Very small stock, also new books. Spec: folklore (folksongs, tales, customs, folk art, dance, etc.). Cata: on foregoing, 1 a year. A.B.A.

PHILIP G. LEVAN, 2443 Liberty Street, Allentown, PA 18104.

THE LIBERTY BOOKSHOP, 2 Liberty Avenue, Carlisle, PA 17013. TN: (717) 245-2933. Shop.

LINCOLN WAY BOOKS, 136 Lincoln Way West, Chambersburg, PA 17201. TN: (717) 264-7120. Shop.

E. LINDH'S, 12060 McKee Road, North Huntingdon, PA 15642.

LITTLE BOOK SHOP, 54 East Main Street, Ephrata, PA 17522.

THOMAS MACALUSO, RARE AND FINE BOOKS, 111 South Union Street, Kennett Square, Philadelphia, PA 19348. TN: (215) 444-1063. Est: 1974. Shop open Wed-Sun, 12-5, or by appointment. Medium stock used. Spec: English and American literature, Americana, Art and Illustrated books, natural sciences, travel and exploration. Cata: Infrequently. B: Commonwealth Federal S & L, West Chester, PA.

BRUCE MCKITTRICK, RARE BOOKS, 2240 Fairmont Avenue, Philadelphia, PA 19130. TN: (215) 235-3209. By appointment only. Spec: 15-18th century continental books; Renaissance; humanism; science, medicine; history. M: A.B.A.A.

GEORGE S. MACMANUS COMPANY, 1317 Irving Street, Philadelphia, PA 19107. Prop: Clarence Wolf. TN: (215) 735-4456. Est: 1937. Shop. Very large stock used. Spec: Americana, English and American literature, Pennsylvania. Cata: frequently. A.B.A.A. I.L.A.B.

MAN OF ARAN BOOKS, 519 South Orange Street, Media, PA 19063.

MARCH HARE BOOK SHOP, 503 West Lancaster Avenue, Strafford-Wayne, PA 19087.

E.J. MATUSIAK, 113 FARRAGUT, VANDERGRIFT, PA 15690.

WILLIAM G. MAYER [THE LAMP], 204 AUBURN STREET, PITTSBURGH, PA 15206.

MEDICAL MANOR BOOKS, BENJAMIN FOX PAVILION, P.O. BOX 647, JENKINTOWN, PA 19046. TN: (215) 824-1476. Spec: scientific & medical first editions.

JOSEPH M. MITCHELL COMPANY, 5738 THOMAS AVENUE, PHILADELPHIA, PA 19143. TN: (215) SA 6-1101. Est: 1928. Law books.

E. MOORE, BOX 243, WYNNEWOOD, PA 19096. TN: (215) 649-1549. Est: 1965. Mail order only. Small stock used; also new books and prints and maps. Cata: Americana, autographs, documents, ephemera, memorabilia, 4 a year. A.B.A.A. I.L.A.B.

MUSEUM BOOKS AND PRINTS, 425 MUSEUM RD, WEST READING, PA 19611. TN: (215) 372-0642.

MYSTERY HOUSE, P.O. BOX 4235, READING, PA 19606. Prop: Robert C. Backer. TN: (215) 779-0903. Est: 1968. Private premises, appointment necessary. Medium stock used. Spec: Mystery—Detective only. Cata: Every 6 weeks.

MYSTERY MANOR BOOKS, P.O. BOX 135, HUNTINGDON VALLEY, PA 19006. Spec: First editions mystery & detective.

S & C NAJARIAN, 852 MILMAR ROAD, NEWTOWN SQUARE, PA 19073. TN: (215) 353-5165. Est: 1973. Private premises, appointment necessary. Very small stock used. Spec: Harper's Weekly and nineteenth century sheet music.

JOHN E. NORRIS, P.O. BOX 442, PAOLI, PA 19301. TN: (215) 644-5957. Est: 1975. Private premises; by appointment only. Very small stock sec. and antiq. books. Spec: poultry, cock-fighting, fancy pigeons and passenger pigeons. Cata: 4 a year.

OBSOLESCENCE, 24 CHAMBERSBURG STREET, GETTYSBURG, PA 17325. Prop: Donald R. Hinks. TN: (717) 334-8634. Est: 1972. Shop. Very large stock used. Spec: Brethren Church History, 18th Century books in German. Some new books on religion.

OLD BOOKSHED, 5910 CALIFORNIA AVENUE, ALTOONA, PA 16602.

ON THE ROAD BOOKS, P.O. BOX 334, SHIPPENSBURG, PA 17257. TN: (717) 532-4420. Shop, appointment advisable.

THE OWL, CORNER MORRIS AVENUE AND YARROW STREET, BRYN MAWR, PA 19010. Prop: Bryn Mawr College Alumnae Scholarship Fund. TN: (215) 525-6117. Est: 1971. Stock of over 50,000 used, out of print and rare books; also used records, music, periodicals.

PALINURUS ANTIQUARIAN BOOKS, P.O. BOX 15923, PHILADELPHIA, PA 19103. (2210 DELANCEY PLACE, PHILADELPHIA). Prop: John Hellebrand. TN: (215) 735-2970. Private premises; appointment necessary. Medium stock antiq. Spec: science; medicine; Americana; continental books before 1800. M: A.B.A.A.

WILLIAM B. PENNEBAKER, 1634 YORK ROAD, HARTSVILLE, PA 18974.

THE PETERSONS, 6324 LANGDON STREET, PHILADELPHIA, PA 19111.

R. PETRILLA, BOOKSELLER, P.O. BOX 65, DOYLESTOWN, PA 18901. TN: (215) 766-0233. Est: 1970. Medium stock used. Spec: out-of-print, rare. Cata: regularly. B: Bucks County Bank Trust Company. M: A.B.A.A., B.S.A., Philobiblon Club, Philadelphia.

PETROLEUM AMERICANA, P.O. BOX 1, WARREN, PA 16365. Prop: E. Miller. TN: (814) 726-2951. Est: 1950. Storeroom; appointment necessary. Small stock used. Spec: petroleum materials only.

THE PHILADELPHIA RARE BOOKS AND MANUSCRIPTS COMPANY, P.O. BOX 9536, PHILADELPHIA, PA 19124. Prop: David M. Szewczyk. TN: (215) 744-6734. Large stock sec. and antiq. Spec: Early printed books; Americana; Music; Law. Cata: occasionally. M: A.B.A.A.

WILLIAM H. POWERS, R.D.3, EXPORT, PA 15632. TN: (412) 327-6886. Est: 1969. Private premises, appointment necessary. Medium stock used, a few new. Spec: American Civil War, military history, Americana, Pennsylvania. Cata: on foregoing, 4 a year.

QUADRANT BOOK MART AND COFFEEHOUSE, 20 NORTH THIRD STREET, EASTON, PA 18042. Prop: Richard Epstein. TN: (215) 252-1188. Est: 1977. Shop. Very large stock used. Spec: local history; fiction.

QUIXOTE BOOKS, P.O. BOX 1991, 105 SOUTH 11th STREET, PHILADELPHIA, PA 19107. Prop: Lawrence MacKenzie. TN: (215) 925-6029. Est: 1969. Shop. Small stock used, also new. Spec: old and rare children's books. Cata: on foregoing, 1 a year. A.B.A.

ANTONIO RAIMO RARE BOOKS, 144 AMSTERDAM ROAD, LANCASTER, PA 17603. TN: (717) 285-3861. Private premises, appointment necessary. Spec: Bibliography.

D. RICHARDS, BOOKMAN, 314 BELLE ISLE AVENUE, PITTSBURGH, PA 15226. TN: (412) 531-0531.

RAY RILING ARMS BOOKS COMPANY, 6844 GORSTEN STREET, PHILADELPHIA, PA 19119. Prop: Joseph R. Riling. TN: (215) GE8-2456. Private premises; appointment necessary. Small stock used; also new books, and publishers of books on arms, etc. Spec: arms books, including gun collecting, shooting, hunting, military, Americana, Western lore. Brochures and listings sent by subscription. ($1.00). A.B.A.A. A.B.A.

RITTENHOUSE BOOK STORE, 1706 RITTENHOUSE SQUARE, PHILADELPHIA, PA 19103. Prop: Richard W. Foster. TN: (215) 545-6072. Est: 1946. Appointment helpful. Small stock rare and out-of-print, also new books. Spec: medicine. Cata: medicine, 4 a year (new books on medicine bi-monthly). A.B.A.A.

RIVERSIDE MAIL SERVICE, 204 GREEN STREET, DOYLESTOWN, PA 18901. Prop: Elranor Zwerdling. TN: (215) 345-7356. Est: 1967. Private premises; appointment necessary. Medium stock used. Spec: sociology, women, psychology. Cata: 2 a year.

VAL D. ROBBINS—BOOKS, P.O. BOX 44, BARTONSVILLE, PA 18321 (Rimrock Drive). TN: (717) 629-2360. Est: 1951. Shop; appointment preferable. Medium stock used; also antiques.

FRANKLIN M. ROSHON, 378 BUCHERT ROAD, POTTSTOWN, PA 19464.

ARTHUR SCHARF, 5040 CAROLYN DRIVE, PITTSBURGH, PA 15236. TN: (412) 653-4402. Est: 1968. Private premises, appointment necessary. Large stock used. Spec: travel books, U.S. WPA Writers guidebooks, Central Asia, South America, Africa. Cata: occasionally.

MICHAEL SHILLING, 283 KAUFFMAN STREET, CHAMBERSBURG, PA 17201. TN: (717) 375-2545. Shop, appointment advisable.

BETTY SCHMID CIRCUSIANA, 485 SLEEPY HOLLOW ROAD, PITTSBURGH, PA 15228. TN: (412) 341-4597. Est: 1966. Private premises, appointment necessary. Very small stock used. Spec: circus. Cata: lists on circus.

SCHOLARLY PUBLICATIONS CENTER, P.O. Box 528, STROUDSBURG, PA 18360. (737 Bryant Street.) Prop: Johannes L. Kagie. TN: (717) 424-5052. Est: 1972. Storeroom; appointment necessary. Medium stock used. Spec: humanities, social sciences. Cata: Slavic books, 5 or 6 times a year. Also periodical backfiles, mainly European.

SCHOYER'S BOOKS, 1404 SOUTH NEGLEY AVENUE, PITTSBURGH, PA 15217. Prop: Maxine A. Schoyer. TN: (412) 521-8464. Est: 1952. Shop. Very large stock used. Spec: Americana; first editions; ephemera. Cata: 2 a year.

JOHN EZRA SCHULMAN, 2238 MURRAY AVENUE, PITTSBURGH, PA 15217.

SCHUYKILL BOOK & CURIO SHOP, 873 BELMONT AVENUE, PHILADELPHIA, PA 19104. Prop: Samuel F. Kleinman. TN: (215) 473-4769. Spec: Graphic arts, autographs and manuscripts, collector's items. M: A.B.A.A.

ALEX SCHWARTZ BOOK SCOUT, 166 SUMMER STREET, BRADFORD, PA 16701. TN: (814) 368-4824. Est: 1969. Private premises; mail order business only. Medium stock used.

CHARLES SESSLER, INC., 1308 WALNUT STREET, PHILADELPHIA, PA 19107. TN: (215) 735-1086. Cables: Pickwick, Philadelphia. Est: 1882. Shop. Small stock rare, also new books, prints, framing, paintings, autographs. Cata: Illustrated issued frequently. A.B.A.A., A.B.A.(Int).

44. PENNSYLVANIA (PA.)

CHARLES SHEPHERD, 1020 MILTON ROAD, CASTLE SHANNON, PA 15234.

F.W. SKLEDER, 240 FORBES AVENUE, PITTSBURGH, PA 15222. TN: (412) 261-1890. Est: 1961. Storeroom, open normal business hours. Medium stock used; also new books. A.B.A.

OLGA SNYDER, 1107 FEDERAL STREET, PITTSBURGH, PA 15212. TN: (412) 231-6564. Est: 1940. Shop. Very small stock used; also new books on specialties, magazines, back-issues and paperbacks.

WILLIAM B. SPINELLI, 32 ELMWOOD, CRAFTON, PA 15205.

DALE W. STARRY, Sr., BOOKSELLER, 115 NORTH WASHINGTON STREET, SHIPPENSBURG, PA 17257. TN: (717) 532-2690. Est: 1965. Private premises, appointment necessary. Large stock used. Spec: Americana, Illustrated, Non-fiction.

H.F. STEEL BOOKSHOP, ROOM 201, BAILEY BUILDINGS, 1218 CHESTNUT STREET, PHILADELPHIA, PA 19107.

GEOFFREY STEELE, LUMBERVILLE, PA 18933. TN: (215) 297-5187. Est: 1941. Private premises, appointment necessary. Medium stock used. Spec: art and architecture, scholarly. A.B.A.A. I.L.A.B.

G.G. STOCTAY, P.O. BOX 5054, HARRISBURG, PA 17104. (226 South 19th Street.) Prop: Neo American Church, Inc. TN: (717) 238-8539 and 238-6441. Est: 1968. Shop, appointment necessary. Small stock used. Spec: erotica, occult. Cata: occasionally.

SUSQUEHANNA HOUSE, 203 MAIN STREET, CATAWISSA, PA 17820. Prop: John S. Laidacker. TN: (717) 356-7381. Est: 1960. Shop. Small stock used, also new. Spec: firearms, accoutrements, history, art. Also antique firearms, antiques, English campaign medals.

DAVID M. SZEWCZYK, 1633 HAWORTH STREET, PHILADELPHIA, PA 19124.

TAMERLANE BOOK SHOP, P.O. BOX C, HAVERTOWN, PA 19083. Prop: John & Elizabeth Freas. TN: (215) 449-4400. Est: 1970. Shop. Small stock used. Spec: Colour plate, sporting, natural history, travel, Illustrated. Fine Sets. Cata: Annually. M: Mainline Antique Dealers Assoc., Philobiblon Club, Philadelphia.

TECHNICAL AND SCIENTIFIC BOOK CENTER, 6640 LANDVIEW ROAD, PITTSBURG, PA 15217. TN: (412) 521-3267 and 241-3939. Spec: all areas of pure and applied science and technology.

WILLIAM H. THOMAS, 210 WEST MARBLE STREET, MECHANICSBURG, PA 17055. TN: (215) 766-7778. Est: 1960. Private premises, appointment necessary. Small stock used. Spec: Pennsylvania history.

THE TUCKERS, 2236 MURRAY AVENUE, PITTSBURGH, PA 15217. Prop: Mrs. Esther J. Tucker. TN: (412) 521-0249. Est: 1972. Shop, open 13.00-17.00 hours Mondays, Tuesdays, Wednesdays, Thursday, Friadays; 10.00-17.00 hours Saturdays. Other times by appointment. Medium stock used. Spec: Select general scarce and out-of-print stock. Cata: Lists issued occasionally.

CARMEN D. VALENTINO, 2956 RICHMOND STREET, PHILADELPHIA, PA 19134. TN: (215) 739-6056. Est: 1978. Private premises, appointment necessary. Small stock sec. and antiq. Spec: Pictorial Art, manuscripts; newspapers; documents. Corresp: Deutsch; Romanian.

VALLEY BOOKS, 111 SOUTH ELMER AVENUE, SAYRE, PA 18840. TN: (717) 888-9785.

WALNUT BOOK STORE, 900 WALNUT STREET, PHILADELPHIA, PA 19107. Prop: Joseph Rappaport. TN: (215) WA 3-1436. Est: 1930. Spec: antiquarian, color-plate, Americana, fine bindings.

JOHN F. WARREN, 124 SOUTH 19TH STREET, PHILADELPHIA, PA 19103. TN: (215) 561-6422.

DALE WEISS, 68 EAST BROAD STREET, BETHLEHEM, PA 18018.

S. WEST, 3 NARBROOK PARK, NARBERTH, PA 19072.

WHITE HOUSE BOOKS, 49 EAST PHILADELPHIA AVENUE, BOYERTOWN, PA 19512.

J. HOWARD WOOLMER, MARIENSTEIN ROAD, REVERE, PA 18953. TN: (215) 847-5074. Est: 1961. Private premises, appointment necessary. Small stock used. Spec: 20th century literature, rare and out-of-print. A.B.A., A.B.A.A., I.L.A.B.

C.B. YOHE, 4870 CRISS ROAD, BETHEL PARK, PA 15102. TN: (412) 835-4279. Est: 1945. Private premises, appointment necessary. Very small stock used, also novelties. Spec: magic, conjuring and related subjects. Cata: on foregoing.

45. RHODE ISLAND (RI.)

CRANSTON	NEWPORT
CHARLESTOWN	PEACE DALE
ESMOND	PROVIDENCE
HOPE VALLEY	WARWICK
JAMESTON	WATCH HILL

ANCHOR AND DOLPHIN BOOKS, 20 FRANKLIN STREET, P.O. BOX 823, NEWPORT, RI 02840. Prop: Ann Marie Wall and James A. Hinck. TN: (401) 846-6890. Est: 1977. Shop, but appointment advisable. Small stock used. Spec: landscape architecture and garden history; architecture and design, town and city planning. M: A.B.A.A.

ARNOLD ART STORE, 210 THAMES STREET, NEWPORT, RI 02840.

THE BOOK AND TACKLE SHOP, 7 BAY STREET, WATCH HILL, RI 02891. Prop: Bernard Ludwig Gordon. TN: (401) 596-0700. Est: 1953. Shop, summer only. Large stock. Spec: Science; medicine; natural history; Americana; fish and fishing; sailing. Cata: occasionally. M: A.B.A.A. (Winter residence in Massachusetts).

JACK CLINTON NAUTICAL BOOKS, HIGH STREET, HOPE VALLEY, RI 02832.

PATRICK T. CONLEY BOOKS, 43 WINDSOR ROAD, CRANSTON, RI 02905. TN: (401) 785-0169. Est: 1963. Shop, appointment necessary. Small stock used. Spec: Regional Americana (South and West), Law, Rhode Island, Civil War, American History. Cata: 8 per year. B: Citizen Bank, Providence, R.I. Acc.No: 14-100-3. M: Massachusetts and Rhode Island Booksellers Assoc.

W.L. CONLEY COMPANY, 273-275 THAYER STREET, PROVIDENCE, RI 02906. TN: (401) 621-9700. Est: 1969. Shop. Very large stock used, also new. Spec: rare books, fine bindings, Americana. Cata: general, 3-4 a year. Also antiques and jewelry.

CORNER BOOK SHOP, 418 SPRING STREET, NEWPORT, RI 02840. Prop: Rita V. Whitford. TN: (401) 846-8406. Est: 1962. Shop. Small stock used. Spec: History. Illustrated and rare.

EDWARD J. CRAIG, P.O. BOX 189, JAMESTOWN, RI 02840. TN: (401) 847-6498. Est: 1969. Private premises; appointment necessary. Spec: 18th Century Manuscripts of America and Stampless folded letters. Cata: Every month. B: Rhode Island Hospital Trust National Bank. 022995. M: Manuscript Society, American Philatelic Society, Sons of Revolution, Universal Autograph Collectors Club.

FORTUNATE FINDS BOOKSTORE, 16 WEST NATICK ROAD, WARWICK, RI 02886. Prop: Mildred E. Santille (Longo). TN: (401) 737-8160. Shop, open Fridays and Saturdays, or by appointment. Medium stock used; also some new books. Spec: Rhode Island; explorations (journals, logs, documents, letters).

S. CLYDE KING, Jr., P.O. BOX 2036, EDGEWOOD STATION, PROVIDENCE, RI 02905. TN: (401) 781-0837. Est: 1936. Private premises, appointment necessary. Large stock used. Spec: whaling, American literature, detective and mystery fiction/English literature, fantasy fiction.

LINCOLN BOOK SHOPPE, INC., LOG ROAD, RFD 3, ESMOND, RI 02917. Prop: Harold S. Ephraim. TN: (401) 231-6920. Est: 1917. Storeroom, appointment necessary or mail order. Very large stock used. Spec: scholarly books in all fields, library specialists, search service.

MERLIN'S CLOSET INC., 166 VALLEY STREET, PROVIDENCE, RI 02909. (On lower level facing South Water Street). Prop: Mrs. Gail Eastwood-Stokes, Miss Faye Ringel, Ph.D., Elliot Shorter. TN: (401) 351-9272. Est: 1979. Shop, closed Mondays. Large stock used; also new local and specialty books. Spec: H.P.Lovecraft; Fantasy and science fiction; children's; illustrated; Arthurian, mediaeval and Renaissance culture and history; occult.

METACOMET BOOKS, P.O. BOX 2479, 143 ELTON STREET, PROVIDENCE, RI 02906. Prop: James Sanford. TN: (401) 861-7182. Est: 1979. Private premises, appointment necessary. Small stock sec. and antiq. Spec: science and technology, Americana, women, labour. Cata: 6 a year. Corresp: Français, Deutsch. B: Citizens Bank, Providence, RI and Lloyds Bank, Southampton Row, London. M: Massachusetts and Rhode Island Antiquarian Booksellers.

ALVIN V. ROBINSON, 34 HART STREET, PROVIDENCE, RI 02906. TN: 751-2069. Private premises; appointment necessary. Medium stock, general.

RULON-MILLER BOOKS, P.O. BOX 2536, PROVIDENCE, RI 02906. Prop: Barbara Walzer. TN: (401) 253-7824. Est: 1959. Appointment necessary. Medium stock used. Spec: nautical, voyages and travel. M: A.B.A.A., Manuscript Society, Grolier Club.

THE SCRIBE'S PERCH, 62-64 THAMES ST., NEWPORT, RI 02840.

SEWARDS' FOLLY BOOKS, 139 BROOK STREET, PROVIDENCE, RI 02906. Prop: Schuyler & Peterkin Seward. TN: (401) 272-4454. Est: 1976. Shop, may be closed on Mondays and Tuesdays and therefore make appointment. Large stock used.

SIGN OF THE UNICORN BOOKSHOP, 604 KINGSTOWN ROAD, BOX 297, PEACE DALE, RI 02883. Prop: Mary Jo Munroe and John Romano. TN: (401) 789-8912. Est: 1978. Shop, closed Mondays and Tuesdays. Large stock used. Spec: Fritz Eichenberg illustrations; vintage paperbacks, but mainly general stock.

TYSON'S OLD AND RARE BOOKS, 334 WESTMINSTER MALL, PROVIDENCE, RI 02903. Prop: Mariette Bedard. TN: (401) 421-3939. Spec: Americana, Rhode Island.

WAYSIDE BOOKSHOP, P.O. BOX 261, CHARLESTOWN, RI 02879. Prop: James & Bernadine O'Donnell. TN: 1 (401) 783-7594. Est: 1974. Shop, open Mondays to Fridays or by appointment. Small stock used. Spec: Modern first editions, collector's mysteries, Americana and science fiction. Cata: 5 times per year. B: Westerly Credit Union. Washington Trust, Acc.No 648080.

CHARLES B. WOOD III, INC., P.O. BOX 2516, PROVIDENCE, RI 02906. TN: (401) 751-3140. Est: 1968. Private premises; appointment necessary.

46. SOUTH CAROLINA (SC.)

ABBEVILLE	HODGES
BEAUFORT	MURRELL'S INLET
CHARLESTON	MYRTLE BEACH
COLUMBIA	NEWBERRY
GREENVILLE	ROCK HILL
GREENWOOD	SPARTANBURG

ARCH BRIDGE BOOKS, 1410 POINSETT HIGHWAY, GREENVILLE, SC 29609.

THE ATTIC INC., BOX 128, HODGES, SC 29653. Pres: Donald Hawthorne. TN: (803) 374-3013. Est: 1961. Shop, open Saturdays, other times by appointment. Very large stock used. Spec: agriculture, South Carolina, Americana. Cata: general, occasional.

BEAUFORT BOOK COMPANY, P.O. BOX 1127, BEAUFORT, SC 29902. Prop: Martin & Isabel Hoogenboom. TN: (803) 524-5172. Shop. Publishers. Cata: Annually. B: Bankers Trust of South Carolina. Acc.No: 05320159-0044000989. M: A.B.A., Association of American Publishers.

BOOK BASEMENT, 243 KING STREET, CHARLESTON, SC 29401.

NORM BURLESTON, 104 FIRST AVENUE, SPARTANBURG, SC 29302. Prop: Norman L. Burleston. TN: (803) 583-8845. Est: 1979. Private premises; appointment necessary. Small stock used. Spec: Christian Theology.

HAMPTON BOOKS, ROUTE 1, BOX 202, NEWBERRY, SC 29108. Prop: Ben & Muriel Price Hamilton. TN: (803) 276-6870. Est: 1946. Shop. Over 100,000 volumes used, some new. Spec: cinema, television, photographica, aerospace, South Carolina. Cata: on foregoing, 1 a year, charged $1. A.B.A.A. I.L.A.B.

KITEMAUG BOOKS, 229 MOHAWK DRIVE, SPARTANBURG, SC 29301. Prop: Frank J. Anderson. TN: (803) 576-3338. Est: 1959. Private premises. Very small stock. Spec: submarine literature, ships and the sea. Also small private press (miniature books). Cata: annually.

JOEL MYERSON, 5869 WOODVINE ROAD, COLUMBIA, SC 29206.

NOAH'S ARK, 301 WASHINGTON STREET, ABBEVILLE, SC 29620. Prop: J.C. Wiley. TN: (803) 459-4126. Est: 1941. Shop. Large stock used; also antiques.

NOAH'S ARK BOOK ATTIC, STONY POINT, ROUTE 2, GREENWOOD, SC 29646. Prop: Donald Hawthorne. TN: (803) 374-3013. Est: 1954. Shop, open Saturdays, other days by appointment. Very large stock used; also some new. Spec: theology. Cata: 8 a year. A.B.A.

JAMES S. PIPKIN, OLD AND RARE BOOKS, 2322-B ROSEWOOD DRIVE, ROCK HILL, SC 29730. TN: (1-803) 366-3839. Est: 1969. Private premises; appointment necessary. Medium stock used. Spec: South Caroliniana, Greek and Latin Classics. B: Rock Hill National Bank. A/c no: 002217376.

BRANIMIR M. RIEGER, 936 SUNSET DRIVE, GREENWOOD, SC .29646. TN: (803) 223-7977. Private premises; business by mail only. Medium stock used. Spec: General, travel, British topography and travel, travel guides; English and American literature; Byron; Croatian and Yugoslavian Literature; History. Cata: Occasionally.

ROBBINS' RARITIES, 2038C LAURENS ROAD, GREENVILLE, SC 20607. Prop: LeRoy Robbins. Shop. Spec: prints and illustrated books; first editions; 16th and 17th century English and French history; British heraldry from early 1700's.

TEMPEST GALLERY, KINGS HIGHWAY AT GARDEN CITY, MURRELLS INLET, SC 29576. Prop: Lew Lysle Harr. TN: 263-2703. Shop. Medium stock used, a few new books and antiques, pictures, prints, maps.

LETTY WILDER BOOKS, 212 HIGHLAND BOULEVARD, MYRTLE BEACH, SC 29577. Prop: Letty Wilder. TN: (1-803) 449 3466. By appointment. Small stock used. Spec: material about South Carolina, North Carolina, birds. B: Bankers Trust, Myrtle Beach, SC. M: A.B.A.A.

47.   SOUTH DAKOTA (SD.)

WEBSTER

H.P. CHILSON [DAKOTA BOOKS], 505 MAIN STREET, WEBSTER, SD 57274.

48. TENNESSEE (TN.)

BRENTWOOD
CLEVELAND
CHATTANOOGA
KINGSPORT
KNOXVILLE

MADISON
MEMPHIS
NASHVILLE
RIPLEY

R.R. ALLEN, 5300 BLUEFIELD ROAD, KNOXVILLE, TN 37921. TN: (615) 584-4487. Est: 1962. Private premises, appointment necessary. Medium stock used. Spec: Tennessee books; Tenn. imprints prior to 1850. Cata: on foregoing, 3-4 a year.

ANDOVER SQUARE BOOKS, 805 NORGATE ROAD, KNOXVILLE, TN 37919. Prop: Marjorie & G. Allan Yeomans. TN: (615) 693-8984. Est: 1978. Private premises and a booth in Knoxville Antique Mall which is open 7 days a week from 10 a.m. to 7 p.m. Spec: Americana.

THE BOOK SHELF, 3765 HILLSDALE DRIVE N.E., CLEVELAND, TN 37311. Prop: William R. Snell. TN: (615) 472-8408. Est: 1974. Private premises, appointment necessary. Very small stock used. Spec: Tennessee history and authors. Cata: 4 times per year. B: First Citizens Bank, Cleveland, TN 37311.

BURKE'S BOOK STORE, INC., 634 POPLAR AVENUE, MEMPHIS, TN 38105. Prop: Harriette M. Beeson. TN: (901) 527-7484. Est: 1875. Shop. Spec: Local history: the South, Civil War; a wide range of literature and non-fiction. M: A.B.A.A.

ELDER'S BOOK STORE, 2115 ELLISTON PLACE, NASHVILLE, TN 37203. Prop: Charles Elder. TN: (615) 327-1867. Est: 1949. Shop. Large stock used; also new books. Spec: Southern Americana; Civil War; Tennesseana.

ENTERPRISE BOOKS, P.O. DRAWER 289, RIPLEY, TN 38063. (145 East Jackson Street.) Prop: William A. Klutts. TN: (901) 635-1771. Est: 1955. Appointment necessary. Medium stock used, also new. Spec: book arts, bibliography, printing. Cata: on foregoing.

JOHN HEFLIN, 5708 BRENTWOOD TERRACE, BRENTWOOD, TN 37027. TN: (615) 373-2917. Spec: Civil War and the Confederacy, Southern Americana.

48. TENNESSEE (TN.)

F.M. HILL, P.O. Box 1037, KINGSPORT, TN 37662. TN: (615) 247-8704. Est: 1958. Spec: Tennessee and Southern Americana.

MILESTONE PRESS, P.O. Box 12502, MEMPHIS, TN 38112. (4263 Montrose Drive.) Prop: Charlotte Edmondson Elam. TN: (901) 685-6975. Est: 1968. Private premises; appointment necessary. Very small stock used; and own publications new. Spec: genealogical records. Cata: 1 a year.

R.M. MILLS, BOOKSTORES, 1817 21ST AVENUE S., NASHVILLE, TN 37212.

OLD BOOK STORE, 1420 NEELY'S BEND ROAD, MADISON, TN 37115. Prop: Mrs. R.B. Fox. TN: 868-2078. Shop. Small stock used. Spec: Tennessee books. Also antiques.

OLD SOUTH BOOKS, 4639 PEPPERTREE LANE, MEMPHIS, TN 38117.

OLLIE'S BOOKS, 3218 BOXDALE STREET, MEMPHIS, TN 38118. Prop: Ollie McGarrh. TN: (901) 363-1996. Est: 1966. Private premises; appointment necessary. Medium stock sec. and some new.

READ MORE BOOKS, 727C MANSION CIRCLE, CHATTANOOGA, TN 37405.

49. **TEXAS (TX.)**

AMARILLO	GALVESTON
ABILENE	GLEN ROSE
ALPINE	HOUSTON
AUSTIN	LAMESA
BRYAN	LUBBOCK
CANUTILLO	MCALLEN
CORPUS CHRISTI	SAN ANTONIO
DALLAS	TEMPLE
DICKINSON	TYLER
EAGLE PASS	VICTORIA
EULESS	WACO
FORT WORTH	WAXAHACHIE

THE ALDREDGE BOOK STORE, 2909 1A MAPLE AVENUE, DALLAS, TX 75201. Prop: Billie Lyn Rhodes. TN: (214) 871-3333. Est: 1947. Shop. Medium stock used. Cata: occasionally.

316

TEXAS (TX.)   49.

AMERICAN SOUTH-WEST BOOKS, P.O. Box 148, Amarillo, TX 79105. Prop: R.D., J.R. & R.R. Hollingworth. TN: (806) 372-3444.

ANTIQUARIAN BOOK MART, 3127 Broadway, San Antonio, TX 78209. Prop: Frank Kellel, Jr. TN: (512) 828-7433/4885. Shop. Spec: Texas, south-western USA, military history, Civil War, general Americana. M: A.B.A.A.

W. GRAHAM ARADER III, 2800 Virginia Street, Houston, TX 77098. TN: (713) 529-8055. *Also in* Pennsylvania And New York City, q.v.

ARJAY BOOKS, 2500 River Hills Road, Austin, TX 78746. TN: (512) 263-2957. Book search service.

BARBER'S BOOK STORE, 215 West 8th Street, Fort Worth, TX 76102. Prop: B.A. Perkins. TN: (817) 335-5469. Est: 1925. Shop. Medium stock used, also new. A.B.A.

BARKER, CONWAY: AUTOGRAPH DEALER, P.O. Box 670625, Dallas, TX 75367-0625. TN: (214) 358-3786. Spec: Autographs and historical manuscripts.

BOEK STOAR, 1111 Colcord Avenue, Waco, TX 76707. Prop: Festus von Blon, Jr. Est: 1971. Shop. Medium stock used; also new books. Spec: railroadiana (U.S.); Texiana; military.

L.V. BOLING, 3413 Tiger Lane, Corpus Christi, TX 78415. TN: (512) UL 2-1131. Est: 1964. Private premises, appointment necessary. Very small stock used, also new. Spec: Texas, Southwest, Mexico. Cata: on foregoing, 6 a year.

A BOOK BUYERS SHOP, 711 Studewood, Houston, TX 077007. TN: (713) 868-3910. Store. Large stock used. Spec: Texas; bibliography.

THE BOOKCASE, 2419 South Shepherd, Houston, TX 77019.

BOOKED UP, 2611 Worthington Street, Dallas, TX 75204. Prop: W.R. Gilliland. TN: (214) 826-3339. Shop, open 11-5, six days a week. *Also in* Washington D.C.

BOOKETERIA, 3323 Fredericksborg Road, San Antonio, TX 78201.

BOOKFRONT, P.O. Box 5545, WEST AUSTIN STATION, AUSTIN, TX 78763.

THE BOOKIE, 2727 SOUTH STREET (SUITE D), DALLAS, TX 75201.

BOOKSEARCH OF WALDENBOOKS, WALDENBOOKS 496, 216 GULFGATE MALL, HOUSTON, TX 77087. Manager: Gay O'Connor. TN: 1 (713) 649-5563. Est: 1976. Storeroom, stock cannot be seen. Very small stock. Spec: Special book-finding for the Waldenbook's chain of stores. B: Greenspoint Bank. Account No: 00 2017 6.

THE BOOKSHELF, 1207 CULLEN BOULEVARD, HOUSTON, TX 77023. Prop: Mr. & Mrs. John O'Dowd. TN: (713) CA 4738. Shop, open 08.30 to 17.30 hours. Medium stock used, also new. Spec: religion and law.

THE BOOKWORM, 2610 SALEM, LUBBOCK, TX 79410.

CAMELOT BOOKS, P.O. Box 1647, ALPINE, TX 79831. (1701 West Highway 90). TN: (915) 837-2170. Spec: Texas.

THE CAROUSEL, BOOKSELLERS, 2920 FRY AVENUE, TYLER, TX 75701. Prop: Mike A. & Ann Hatchell. TN: (214) 597-9202. Est: 1978. Private premises; appointment necessary. Very small stock used. Spec: German Expressionism; prints and printmakers; Egypt and Egyptology.

COBLER BOOK STORES, 1716 POST OAK AT SAN FELIPE, HOUSTON, TX 77056.

COLLEEN'S BOOKS, 6880 TELEPHONE ROAD, HOUSTON, TX 77061. Prop: Colleen Urbanek. TN: (713) 641-1753. Est: 1971. Shop. Closed on Thursdays. Very large stock. Spec: American Wars, Texas, southwest US.

CRANDALL'S CORNER, 5608 PINEMONT DRIVE, HOUSTON, TX 77092. TN: (713) 680-1870. Shop. Spec: Modern First editions; Biography; cookery.

CULTURA MUSIC AND MUSICAL LITERATURE, P.O. Box 30630A, T.C.U. STATION, FORT WORTH, TX 76129. Prop: Martha Ligeti. TN: (817) 926-6543. Est: 1962. Private premises; appointment necessary. Stock of 6,000 volumes used; also new books. Spec: out-of-print music, rare musical literature. Cata: 3 or 4 a year.

DETERING BOOK GALLERY, 2311 Bissonnet, Houston, TX 77005.
Prop: Herman E. Detering, III. TN: (713) 526-6974. Spec: Fine
Editions, Rare Books, Out-of-print, illustrated books, press books.
A.B.A.A.

EVERGREEN BOOKS, 1500 West Magnolia Avenue, Fort Worth,
TX 76104.

ELIZABETH FOWLER, 2290 West Holcombe, Houston, TX 77030.

FRONTIER AMERICA CORP, P.O. Box 3698, Bryan, TX 77805. (200
West Brookside Drive). Prop: Fred White, Jr. TN: (409) 846-4462.
Est: 1967. Private premises, appointment necessary. Large stock rare
and out of print books. Spec: western Americana, Texas, railroads,
explorations. Cata: on foregoing, 2 a year. M: A.B.A.A.

DAVID GROSSBLATT, BOOKSELLER, P.O. Box 670001, Dallas, TX
75367. TN: (214) 373-0218. Est: 1973. Business by mail order or by
appointment only. Large stock. Spec: Western Americana, Texas, Civil
War. Also manuscripts, photographia, maps and fine books. Cata: 4-5
a year.

MICHAEL D. HEASTON COMPANY, 5614 Wagon Train Road,
Austin, TX 78749. TN: (512) 892-3730. By appointment only. Spec:
Western and General Americana; maps; atlases; manuscripts;
photography.

TEXAS AND THE AMERICAN WEST
IN BOOKS, PAMPHLETS, MAPS, PRINTS, MANUSCRIPTS

member ABAA, ILAB

FRONTIER AMERICA CORPORATION
Box 3698, BRYAN, TX 77805, U.S.A.

HI BOOKS, P.O. Box 1409, CANUTILLO, TX 79835. TN: (915) 581-8188. Shop at 6016 Doniphan Drive Building G-2, El Paso, TX 79932, open Friday, Saturday, Sunday. Spec: Americana, Military, Mystery fiction.

Doc. HILDRETH, P.O. Box 58852, HOUSTON, TX 77058. Prop: W.W. Hildreth, Ph.D. TN: (713) 333-2721. Est: 1973. Private premises; appointment necessary. Very small stock used. Spec: meteorology, geology, oceanography, history. Cata: on foregoing, 1 a year.

THE J.H. JENKINS COMPANY, P.O. Box 2085, AUSTIN, TX 78768. (7111 SOUTH INTERREGIONAL HIGHWAY.) TN: (512) 444-6616. Est: 1963. Shop. Very large stock used, also new. Spec: Americana, literature, rare books, Civil War, incunabula, manuscripts, Texana. Cata: general, monthly. A.B.A. A.B.A.A.

JONES AND JONES, 2100 SOUTH 10th, McALLEN, TX 78501.

BONNIE JUSTIN, BOOKSELLER, 1633 BABCOCK, SUITE 435, SAN ANTONIO, TX 28229.

KINGSTON BOOK STORE, 118 SAYLES BLVD., ABILENE, TX 79605. Prop: Ben R. & Mary M. Ezzell. TN: (915) 672-8261. Est: 1972. Shop. Small stock used.

MAGGIE LAMBETH, 136 PRINCESS PASS, SAN ANTONIO, TX 78205. TN: (512) 226-6049. Est: 1980. Private premises; appointment necessary. Small stock used. Spec: Texana, Mexico: Southwestern Culture.

THE LAMESA BOOKSELLERS INC., P.O. Box 1128, LAMESA, TX 79331. TN: (806) 872-2743. Est: 1967. Private premises; appointment necessary. Very small stock used. Spec: 18th century literature. Cata: 4 a year.

LIMESTONE HILLS BOOK SHOP, Box 1125, GLEN ROSE, TX 76043. Prop: Aubyn Kendall & Lyle Harris Kendall Jr. TN: (817) 897-4991. Est: 1975. Private premises; appointment necessary. Medium stock old and rare. Spec: 18th to 20th century literature; books about books; crime fiction; M: A.B.A.A.

LITTLE PETEY—UNCLE WICKER, P.O. Box 1189, TEMPLE, TX 76501.

LOCUS LIBRI, P.O. Box 674, AUSTIN, TX 78767. Prop: Judith Ramey. TN: (512) 474-5075. Est: 1979. Private premises. Very small stock. Spec: Classical, Medieval, Renaissance Studies, European cultural life 1880-1930. B: City National Bank. Acc.No: 10252085.

JOHN R. MARA LAW BOOKS, 5628 RICHMOND AVENUE, DALLAS, TX 75206.

MONTROSE BOOK SHOP, P.O. Box 66265, HOUSTON, TX 77006. Prop: Richard C. Palmer. TN: (713) 522-1713. Est: 1965. Private premises; appointment necessary. Small stock used. Spec: rare English and American literature. Cata: general, 1 a year.

THE OLD BOOKSHELF, 2125 39th STREET, GALVESTON, TX 77550. TN: (713) 763-8652. Est: 1967. Shop. Small stock used, a few new. Spec: Texas, railroads, sea.

JOE PETTY—BOOKS, 1704 PARK AVENUE, VICTORIA, TX 77901. Prop: J.W. Petty, Jr. TN: (512) 573-3320. Est: 1940. Private premises; appointment necessary. Small stock used. Spec: Texana; books about books.

BEN E. PINGENOT, P.O. Box 848, EAGLE PASS, TX 78852. (357 Main Street.) TN: (512) 773-2339. Est: 1961. Shop, very small stock second-hand, also new books. Spec: Texas, New Mexico, Mexico, Southwest. Cata: infrequently.

WALTER REUBEN, INC., SUITE 910, AMERICAN BANK TOWER, AUSTIN, TX 78701. TN: (512) 478-3338. TA: Reuben, Austin, Texas. Shop, appointment necessary. Small stock used. Spec: Americana (North & South), Antiquarian Maps, Music, Literature, History of Thought. Cata: 2-4 annually. B: American Bank, 221 West 6th, Austin, Texas. Acc.No: 063-241-4. M: A.B.A.A.

SCHROEDER'S BOOKHAVEN, RT.1, BOX 2820, DICKINSON, TX 77539. TN: (713) 337-1002. Est: 1968. Storeroom: appointment necessary. Very large stock sec. also new books. Spec: Texana. A.B.A.

DOROTHY SLOAN, P.O. Box 49670, AUSTIN, TX 78765-9670. TN: (512) 477-8442. Spec: general Americana, Texas, Latin Americana, south-west U.S.; women's history. M: A.B.A.A.

BETTY SMEDLEY, RARE BOOKS, 2509 HARRIS BOULEVARD, AUSTIN, TX 78703. TN: (512) 477-5013. Est: 1967. Private premises; appointment necessary. Small stock used. Spec: out of print Texana, Southwest; range life, cattle cowboys. Cata: on foregoing, 4 a year.

STATE HOUSE BOOKS, 1604 S. CONGRESS AVENUE, AUSTIN, TX 78704. Prop: Thomas A. Munnerlyn. TN: (512) 448-0700. Spec: Western Americana, Civil War and Confederacy; military; outlaws, rangers, shooting, firearms. M: A.B.A.A.

THE STEVENSONS, 316 SAGE LANE, EULESS, TX 76039. Prop: James G. Stevenson. TN: (817) 354-8903. Est: 1972. Private house, appointment necessary. Very small stock. Spec: boy scouting; Ernest Thompson Seton. Cata: 10 per year. B: Interfirst Bank Las Colinas N.A., Irving, TX 11-5190-1.

W. THOMAS TAYLOR, 708 COLORADO, SUITE 704, AUSTIN, TX 78701. TN: (512) 478-7628. Est: 1972. Shop. Small stock. Spec: English and American literature; early printing; voyages; printing arts. Cata: on foregoing, 4 a year. M: A.B.A.A.

TEXAS GALLERIES, 601 RIO GRANDE STREET, AUSTIN, TX 78701. Prop: Walter Reuben. TN: (512) 478-3338. Est: 1970. Shop. Medium stock. Spec: rare maps and atlases, topography, city views. Cata: on foregoing, 4 a year.

TRACKSIDE BOOKS, 8819 MOBUD DRIVE, HOUSTON, TX 77036. Prop: Lawrence E. Madole. TN: (713) 772-8107. Est: 1964. Storeroom; appointment necessary. Medium stock used; also some new books. Spec: railroadiana; Texana; transportation. Cata: on foregoing, at least 4 a year.

VON BLON'S BOOK STOAR, P.O. BOX 6422, WACO, TX 76707. (1111 Colcord Avenue.) Prop: H. Von Blon. Shop. Small stock used, a few new. Spec: railroads, Southwest, autos, printers' type catalogues, Texas Rangers, W.C. Brann.

WALDEN BOOK STORE, 465 GREENSPOINT MALL, HOUSTON, TX 77060.

RAY S. WALTON, 11504 QUEENS WAY, AUSTIN, TX 78759. TN: (512) 256-5416. Private premises; appointment necessary. Small stock used. Spec: Texana, Western Americana, Civil War. Cata: on foregoing and limited editions, 5 a year. A.B.A.A.

WILSON BOOKSHOP, 3005 FAIRMOUNT STREET, DALLAS, TX 75201. Prop: Mr. & Mrs. Robert A. Wilson. TN: (214) 747-5804. Est: 1965. Shop. Medium stock used. Spec: Texas and Southwestern Americana; fine sets. Cata: on foregoing, semi-annually. A.B.A.A.

MRS. CLARK WRIGHT, 409 ROYAL STREET, WAXAHACHIE, TX 75165. TN: (214) 937-3300. Appointment necessary. Medium stock used, some new. Spec: Southwestern and Western Americana, Mexicana and Latin Americana. Cata: on foregoing.

50. UTAH (UT.)

LAYTON	SALT LAKE CITY
LOGAN	

BOOK SHOPPE, 268 SOUTH STATE STREET, SALT LAKE CITY, UT 84111. Prop: Bonnie Burt. TN: (801) 532-8520 and 278-7139. Est: 1962. Shop. Small stock used; also original ceramic jewelry. Spec: books on Latter Day Saints (Mormonism), Utah, Anti-Mormon Americana.

BRENNAN BOOKS, P.O. Box 9002, SALT LAKE CITY, UT 84109-0002. Prop: Ed. and Anna Brennan. TN: (801) 278-7946. Est: 1978. Private premises; appointment necessary. Large stock used. Spec: Trans-Mississippi West Development.

BOOKS OF YESTERDAY, 36 WEST CENTER, LOGAN, UT 84321.

RON FAERBER BOOKS, 45 EAST GENTILE STREET, LAYTON, UT 84041.

SCALLAWAGIANA BOOKS, P.O. Box 2441, SALT LAKE CITY, UT 84110. Prop: Kent Walgren. TN: (801) 467-3011. Est: 1979. Bookshop at 1511 South 1500 East, Salt Lake City. Medium stock used. Spec: Utah and the Mormons; Western Americana; Vardis Fisher; freemasonry.

ZION'S BOOKSTORE, 254 SOUTH MAIN STREET, SALT LAKE CITY, UT. Prop: Sam Weller. TN: 328-2586. Est: 1929. Shop. Very large stock used, also new. Spec: Utah, Western States, Mormon. A.B.A.

51.   VERMONT (VT.)

BENNINGTON	NORTH POMFRET
BRATTLEBORO	NORWICH
BURLINGTON	PAWLET
CUTTINGSVILLE	PLAINFIELD
HARTFORD	READING
LUDLOW	RICHFORD
MANCHESTER CENTER	RUTLAND
MIDDLEBURG	WEST BRATTLEBORO
NEWPORT	WINDSOR
NORTH BENNINGTON	WOODSTOCK

RICHARD H. ADELSON, ANTIQUARIAN BOOKSELLERS. NORTH POMFRET, VT 05053. Prop: Richard & Jane Adelson. TN: (802) 457-2608. Est: 1971. Private premises; appointment necessary. Small stock used. Spec: voyages, (Pacific, Africa, North and South America), children's books. Cata: on foregoing, 2 a year. Corresp: Français, Italian. A.B.A.A., I.L.A.B., Vermont A.B.A.

THE ALLEGORY BOOKSHOP, 20 CENTRAL STREET, P.O. BOX 252, WOODSTOCK, VT 05091. Prop: Bruse Hartman. TN: (802) 457-3023, and (802) 763-8084. Est: 1981. Shop, closed Mondays during the winter. Small stock used. Spec: Music (Mozart, Haydn and their contemporaries; jazz and jazz musicians); history; literature; first editions.

THE BEAR BOOKSHOP, RD 4, BOX 219, WEST BRATTLEBORO, VT 05301. Prop: John Greenberg. TN: (802) 464-2260. Est: 1975. Private premises, open any time in business hours. Very large stock used. Spec: General Line, Academic Orientation. M: Vermont Antiquarian Booksellers Assoc.

THE BOOK CELLAR, 120 MAIN STREET, BRATTLEBORO, VT 05301. Prop: Stephen Greene. TN: (802) 254-6026. Est: 1948. Shop. Very small stock used, also new books and publishing. Spec: Vermontiana, covered bridge books, cards. Cata: out-of-print Vermontiana and Stephen Greene Press Books, once or twice a year. A.B.A. A.B.P.C.

BRADFORD BOOKS, WEST ROAD, BENNINGTON, VT 05201. Prop: Brad & Margot Craig. TN: (802) 447-0387. Est: 1973. Shop, closed from December-April, then closed on Mondays & Tuesdays. Medium stock used. B: Chittenden Trust Co. Acc.No: 14-46-0242-0. M: Vermont Antiquarian Booksellers Assoc.

BURNHAM'S OLD AND RARE BOOKS, BAILEY'S MILLS ROAD, READING, VT 05062. TN: (802) 484-7837. Shop, open May to October, by appointment November to April. Large stock sec. and antiq.

BYGONE BOOKS, 91 COLLEGE STREET, BURLINGTON, VT 05401.

THE COUNTRY BOOKSHOP, BOX 33, RFD 2, PLAINFIELD, VT 05667. Prop: Alexandra & Benjamin Koenig.

DAGUERREIAN ERA, MAPLE STREET, PAWLET, VT 05761. Prop: Thomas H. Burnside. TN: (802) 325-3360. Est: 1960. Private premises, appointment necessary. Spec: history of photography only. Cata: photography. Also reprints of photographic texts.

MICHAEL DUNN, BOOKS. P.O. BOX 436, NEWPORT, VT 05855. TN: (802) 334-2768. Private premises; appointment necessary. Small stock used. Spec: Americana, Canadiana, Vermontiana; hunting and fishing.

FRASER PUBLISHING, P.O. BOX 494, BURLINGTON, VT 05402. (309 South Willard.) Prop: James L. Fraser. TN: (802) 658-0322. Est: 1962. House premises; appointment necessary. Large stock used; also new books and publisher of business newsletters and investment counselling. Spec: financial history, stockmarket, Wall Street, speculation, business, economics. Cata: on foregoing, 1 to 3 a year. A.B.A.A.

DANIEL GROVER, 11 ELM AVENUE, RICHFORD, VT 05476.

HAUNTED MANSION BOOKSHOP, CUTTINGSVILLE, VT 05738. Prop: Clinton & Lucille Fiske. TN: (802) 492-3337/3462 Est: 1965. Private premises, open normal business hours and by appointment. Medium stock used, a few new. Spec: Americana, Vermont. Also old bottles. Closed Nov. to mid-May.

JOHN JOHNSON, NATURAL HISTORY BOOKS, R.F.D.2, NORTH BENNINGTON, VT 05257. Prop: John & Betty Johnson. TN: (802) 442-6738. Est: 1949. Private premises, appointment necessary. Large stock used. Spec: Botany, Birds, Animals, Fish, Reptiles, Insects, Invertebrates and naturalists' travels. Cata: 4 per year. M: A.B.A.A. I.L.A.B.

KNEEDEEP IN BOOKS, ELM STREET, (P.O. BOX 1314), MANCHESTER CENTER, VT 05255. Prop: Pat Estey. TN: (802) 362-3663 and 867-4495. Est: 1977. Shop, closed Mondays. Medium stock used; also book binding service. M: Vermont Antiquarian Book Association.

G.B. MANASEK, INC., P.O. BOX 705, NORWICH, VERMONT. Prop: F.J. Manasek. TN: (802) 649-3962. Private premises, appointment necessary. Small stock sec. and antiq. Spec: maps (esp Japanese), manuscripts, prints, old and rare science, cartography. Cata: occasionally. Corresp: Deutsch, Español, Japanese. M: A.B.A.A., ILAB.

NIGHT FLIGHT BOOKSTORE [RICHARD WEINER], 127 MAIN STREET, BRATTLEBORO', VT 05301.

STANLEY BOOKS, 104 MAPLE STREET, HARTFORD, VT 05147.

TUTTLE ANTIQUARIAN BOOKS INC., 28-30 SOUTH MAIN STREET, P.O. BOX 541, RUTLAND, VT 05701. Prop: Charles E. Tuttle TN: (802) 773-8930. Cables: Tuttbooks Rutland. Shop. Stock of 150,000 volumes used, also own publications. Spec: Americana, Orientalia, genealogy. M: A.B.A.A., A.B.A., A.B.A. (Int.)

VERMONT BOOK SHOP, 38 MAIN STREET, MIDDLEBURG, VT 05753.

MICHAEL ZUROY, DRAWER N, 5-7 HIGH STREET, LUDLOW, VT 05149. TN: (802) 228-5075. Est: 1968. Private premises and storeroom. Medium stock used. Spec: Books on Writing, Publishing, Biographies of authors. Cata: Occasional lists. B: Vermont National Bank, Ludlow, VT 05149.

52.   VIRGINIA (VA.)

ALEXANDRIA	NORFOLK
ARLINGTON	PETERSBURG
BERRYVILLE	PORTSMOUTH
CHARLOTTESVILLE	RESTON
CHESAPEAKE	RICHMOND
FALLS CHURCH	ROANOKE
GLOUCESTER	SPRINGFIELD
LANCASTER	VIENNA
LYNCHBURG	WARRENTON
LYNDHURST	WAYNESBORO
MANASSAS	WILLIAMSBURG
NEW CANTON	WINCHESTER
NEWPORT NEWS	WYTHEVILLE

TERRY ALFORD, MANUSCRIPTS, P.O. BOX 1151, SPRINGFIELD, VA 22151. Prop: Dr. Terry Alford. TN: (703) 256-6748. Est: 1974. Private house; appointment necessary. Spec: manuscript letters, diaries, collections of letters, travel journals, shiplogs. Cata: twice yearly. M: The Manuscript Society; U.A.C.C.

KARL ALTAU, 800 WARWICK, WAYNESBORO, VA 22980. TN: (703) 949-8867.

APPLELAND BOOKS, P.O. BOX 966, WINCHESTER, VA 22601. Prop: Gene Miller. TN: (703) 662-1980. Est: 1967. Mail order only. Very small stock used. Spec: Virginiana. Cata: monthly lists, Virginiana and Americana.

THE ASSOCIATES, P.O. Box 4214, FALLS CHURCH, VA 22044. Prop: R. William Selander. TN: (703) 578 3810. Shop. Spec: Modern first editions, Vietnam War literature. M: A.B.A.A.

R.W. BEATTY, LTD., P.O. Box 26, ARLINGTON, VA 22210. Prop: Richard W. Beatty. TN: (703) 524-4888. Est: 1960. Shop. Very large stock used and antiq., also new. Also publishing, editing and printing. Cata: general.

BIRD-IN-HAND BOOKSTORE AND GALLERY, 107 NORTH 17TH STREET, P.O. Box 8046, RICHMOND, VA 23223. Prop: Christopher Ackerman, M.D. TN: (804) 788-6898. Est: 1983. Open Sat and Sun 10-6, and by appointment. Medium stock used and small press. Spec: Virginiana; art and architecture. Free search service for out-of-print books. Send titles required or mention areas of specific interest.

BLOOMSBURY BOOKS, 104-C, SOUTH ALFRED, ALEXANDRIA, VA 22314.

NELSON BOND, 4724 EASTHILL DRIVE, ROANOKE, VA 24018. TN: (703) 774-2674. Est: 1967. Private premises; appointment preferable. Large stock used. Spec: fine first editions, signed books; James Branch Cabell. Cata: 6 a year. A.B.A.A. I.L.A.B.

THE BOOK BROKER, 114 BOLLINGWOOD ROAD, CHARLOTTESVILLE, VA. Prop: Vesta Lee Gordon. TN: (804) 295-5586 Est: 1984. Private premises, appointment necessary. Very small stock sec. and antiq. Spec: Southern Americana, Virginiana, Children's, the illustrated book. Cata: occasionally. Corresp: Français.

BOOK ENDS, 2710 WASHINGTON BOULEVARD, ARLINGTON, VA 22201. Prop: Janet & Mike Deatherage. TN: (703) 524-4976. Est: 1979. Shop, closed Tuesday, Wednesday and Thursday, open other days including Sunday. Very large stock used.

THE BOOKPRESS, LTD., Box KP, WILLIAMSBURG, VA 23187. Prop: John Robert Curtis, Jr, John & Emily Ballinger TN: (804) 229-1260. Est: 1973. Shop. Medium Stock. Spec: History of Printing, books about books; Americana; Travel and Voyages; Art and Architecture. B: United Virginia Bank. M: A.B.A.A.

BOOKS ETC., 4615 DUKE STREET, (Box 1502), ALEXANDRIA, VA.

THE BOOK HOUSE, 421A PRINCE GEORGE STREET, WILLIAMSBURG, VA
23185. Prop: M.L. Chapman. TN: (804) 229-3603. Est: 1977. Shop,
open Mon. through Sat. 10-5.

BOOK SEARCH, 1741 FAIRFAX STREET, PETERSBURG, VA 23805. Prop:
Joan T. Black. TN: (703) 451-4055. Est: 1976. Private premises, not
possible to see stock. Very small stock used. Spec: Book Search. B:
Continental Bank & Trust Co., Springfield, VA 22152. Acc.No:
10-0093-4.

BOOKWORM AND SILVERFISH, P.O. BOX 639, WYTHEVILLE, VA
24382. Prop: J.S. Presgraves. TN: (703) 686-5813. Est: 1953. Shop,
business hours 09.00 to 17.00. Saturdays by appointment only.
Medium stock used. Spec: Industrial technology; Appalachia;
American Civil War. Cata: old and scarce and out-of-print, about 10 a
year, A.B.A.A.

BUCKINGHAM BOOKS, RT. 1, P.O. BOX 186, NEW CANTON, VA 23123.

CAMELOT BOOKS, 7603 MULBERRY BOTTOM LANE, SPRINGFIELD, VA
22153. TN: (703) 455-9540.

COLLECTORS' OLD BOOK SHOP, 13 SOUTH 5TH STREET, RICHMOND,
VA 23219. Prop: Mary Clark Roane. TN: (804) 644-2097. Est: 1946.
Shop. Very large stock used; also new books. Spec: Virginia;
Confederacy.

MILDRED ROYALL COUSINS, 5113 INGLEWOOD ROAD, LYNCHBURG,
VA 24503. TN: (703) 384-1934. Est: 1970. Private premises,
appointment necessary. Very small stock used.

DAEDALUS BOOKSHOP, 121-123 FOURTH STREET N.E.,
CHARLOTTESVILLE, VA 22901. TN: (804) 293-7595.

FIRST EDITIONS BOOKSHOP, 4040 MACARTHUR AVENUE, RICHMOND,
VA 23227. Prop: Damon E. Persiani. TN: (804) 264 7276. Est: 1972.
Shop, open noon to 6. (24 hour answering service). Spec: modern first
editions; book arts; detective fiction. Cata: 2 a year. B: Bank of
Virginia.

THE FOREST BOOKSHOP, P.O. BOX 5206, CHARLOTTESVILLE, VA 22905-0206. Prop: Mary Hosmer Lupton. TN: (804) 296-3824. Est: 1955. Private premises. Small stock used. Spec: nature, birds, trees, Buddhism, mysticism, Virginiana.

FROM OUT OF THE PAST, 6440 RICHMOND HIGHWAY, ALEXANDRIA, VA 22306. TN: (703) 768-7827.

FRANKLIN GILLIAM: RARE BOOKS, 112 FOURTH STREET, NORTH-EAST, CHARLOTTESVILLE, VA 22901. TN: (804) 979-2512. Spec: southern and western Americana; bibliography. M: A.B.A.A.

GREAT BRIDGE BOOKS INC., 404 WOODFORD DRIVE, CHESAPEAKE, VA 23320. TN: 482-1666.

HAMILTON'S BOOK STORE, RT. 14 EAST, P.O. BOX 1001, GLOUCESTER, VA 23061. Prop: Jack D. Hamilton. TN: (804) 693-2005. Shop. Medium stock sec. and antiq. Spec: Old Rare; fine bindings.

HEARTWOOD BOOKS, 5 & 9 ELLIEWOOD AVENUE, CHARLOTTESVILLE, VA 22903. Prop: Paul Collinge. TN: (804) 295-7083. Est: 1975. Shop, open Mon-Sat, 11.00-18.00. Large stock. Spec: Americana and Thomas Jefferson. Cata: 3 a year. M: A.B.A.A.

HILTON VILLAGE BOOK SHOP, 10375 WARWICK BOULEVARD, NEWPORT NEWS, VA 23601. Prop: Jack D. Hamilton. Manager: Jim Hamilton. TN: (804) 595-5866. Shop. Medium sec. and antiq. stock. Spec: Old and rare; fine bindings.

OTTO KIRCHNER-DEAN, 10606 MANOR COURT, MANASSAS, VA 22110.

ALEXANDER LAUBERTS, 1073 WEST BROAD, FALLS CHURCH, VA 22046.

M.A. LEPLEY, 233 SOUTH SAINT ASAPH STREET, ALEXANDRIA, VA 22314.

PHYLLIS M. LUMB, 409 GLYNDON STREET, VIENNA, VA 22180.

METAPHYSICAL BOOK STORE, 1805 HIGH STREET, PORTSMOUTH, VA 23704. Prop: Jay Taylor. TN: (804) 397-4295. Est: 1972. Shop. Small stock. Spec: Religion, Philosophy, Technical and scholarly books on all subjects. B: Fidelity American N.A. Acc. No: 01-6-136. M: A.B.A.A.

Col. WILLIAM B. O'NEILL, 11609 HUNTERS GREEN COURT, RESTON, VA 22091. TN: (703) 860-0782. Est: 1952. Private premises; appointment necessary. Medium stock used. Spec: modern Greece, Cyprus, Turkey, Armenia, early travel, Baedeker guides. Rare books on other subjects. Cata: 1 or 2 per year.

PLANTATION BOOKS, 1511 PALMYRA AVENUE, RICHMOND, VA 23227. Prop: James Baylor Blackford. Storeroom, appointment necessary. Medium stock used, and manuscripts. Spec: Virginiana, American history, manuscripts.

JO-ANN REISLER LIMITED, 360 GLYNDON STREET NORTH EAST, VIENNA, VA 22180. TN: (703) 938-2967. Est: 1972. Private premises; appointment necessary. Small stock used. Spec: juveniles (children's and illustrated books). Cata: on foregoing, 2 a year.

THE RICHMOND BOOK SHOP, 808 WEST BROAD STREET, RICHMOND, VA 23220. Prop: V.T. Gilligan. Est: 1957. Shop. Large stock used, also new.

IRENE ROUSE, 1004 PRINCE STREET, ALEXANDRIA, VA 22314.

RULE BOOK SHOP, BOONSBORO SHIPPING CENTER, LYNCHBURG, VA 24503.

SAILOR'S BOOKSHOP, 4208 SOUTH 16th STREET, ARLINGTON, VA 22204.

SECOND STORY BOOKS, 816 No. FAIRFAX STREET, ALEXANDRIA, VA 22314. Prop: Allan J. Stypeck, Jr. TN: (703) 548-4373. Spec: Washingtonia; travel, exploration. M: A.B.A.A.

SEMINARY BOOK SERVICE, QUAKER LANE, ALEXANDRIA, VA 22304.

JERRY N. SHOWACTER, PINEWOOD, RT.1, LYNDHURST, VA 22901.

HENRY STEVENS, SON AND STILES, P.O. BOX 1299, WILLIAMSBURG, VA 23185, Prop: Thomas P. MacDonnell. TN: (804) 220-0925. Spec: General Americana, early travel, books and maps. M: A.B.A.A.

PAUL ROBERTS STONEY, ROUTE 2, BOX 521, LANCASTER, VA 22503.

MICHAEL TOTH, 6038 RICHMOND HIGHWAY, ALEXANDRIA, VA 22303.

LLOYD C. TUBBS, 520 WINCHESTER STREET, WARRENTON, VA 22186.

PAUL B. VICTORIUS, 1413 WEST MAIN STREET, CHARLOTTESVILLE, VA 22903. TN: (703) 293-3342. Est: 1923. A.B.A.A.

VIRGINIA BOOK COMPANY, 114 SOUTH CHURCH STREET, VA 22611, TN: (703) 955-1428. Est: 1947. Mail order only. Out-of-print and new books. Spec: Virginia. Cata: 4 a year.

SAMUEL YUDKIN AND ASSOCIATES, 1125 KING STREET, ALEXANDRIA, VA 22314. Prop: Samuel Yudkin. TN: (703) 549-9330 and 549-2950. Est: 1969. Shop. Very large stock used, and a few remainders new. Monthly book and print auctions.

53. WASHINGTON (WA.)

ANDERSON ISLAND	MERCER ISLAND
AUBURN	MONROE
BAINBRIDGE ISLAND	OLYMPIA
BLAINE	OPPORTUNITY
CAMAS	PORT TOWNSEND
CENTRALIA	RICHLAND
CLARKSTON	SEATTLE
ISSAQUAH	SPOKANE
LONGVIEW	TACOMA
LOPEZ	VANCOUVER
MABTON	VASHON ISLAND

BEACHCOMBER BOOKSHOP, 7824 BIRCH BAY DRIVE, BLAINE, WA 98230. Prop: Paul Gaudette. TN: (206) 332-8395. Est: 1960. Shop; appointment preferable. Small stock used; also new books. Spec: aviation books. Cata: World War II, aviation, lighter than air machines; the Third Reich.

BEATTY BOOK STORE, 1925 3RD AVENUE, SEATTLE, WA 98101. Prop: Mrs. Herbert T. Beatty. TN: (206) 624-2366. Est: 1964. Shop. Very large stock used, also new. Spec: Americana, literature, publishers' overstocks.

BIBELOTS AND BOOKS, 112 EAST LYNNE STREET, SEATTLE, WA 98102. TN: (206) 329-6676.

BOOKS PLUS, 602 N.E. 3rd, CAMAS, WA 98607.

BOOK STORE, 108 EAST 4TH AVENUE, OLYMPIA, WA 98501. TN: (206) 754 7470.

BOOKWORM, 1908-D GEORGE WASHINGTON WAY, RICHLAND, WA 99352.

M. TAYLOR BOWIE, 2613 FIFTH AVENUE, SEATTLE, WA 98101. TN: (206) 682-5363. Spec: 20th century literary First Editions; literary criticism and reference; travel and exploration; north-west Americana. M: A.B.A.A.

BROWSERS' BOOK SHOP, 107 NORTH CAPITOL WAY, OLYMPIA, WA 98501. Prop: Mrs. Ilene Yates Grimes, TN: (206) 357-7462. Est: 1970. Shop. Medium stock used, a few new.

CARL'S BOOK STORE, 925 BROADWAY, TACOMA, WA 98402. Prop: Jerry Culpepper. TN: (206) 272-8827. Est: 1954. Shop. Large stock used, some new. Spec: Northwest Americana, American first editions. Cata: general, 1 a year.

CLARK'S OLD BOOK STORE, 318 WEST SPRAGUE, SPOKANE, WA 99204. Prop: James & Irene Simon. TN: (509) 624-1846. Est: 1910. Shop. Very large stock used, also new on Western Americana. Spec: Western Americana.

COMSTOCK'S BINDERY & BOOKSHOP, 257 EAST MAIN STREET, AUBURN, WA 98002. Prop: David G. and Anita Comstock. TN: (206) 939-8770. Est: 1968. Shop. Medium stock used. Spec: military, naval, aviation, Northwest history. Also hand bookbinding and restoration. A.B.A.

PAUL COOK, 2943 NORTH EAST 178TH STREET, SEATTLE, WA 98155. TN: (206) 364-6429.

CRANDALL'S BOOKS, 103½ SOUTH TOWER, CENTRALIA, WA 98531. Prop: Mrs. Vivian M. Crandall. TN: (206) 736-6309. Est: 1956. Shop. Small stock used and some special new books. Spec: North West America.

R.E. De WEESE, 1919 LAWRENCE, PORT TOWNSEND, WA 98368.

53. WASHINGTON (WA.)

A DIFFERENT DRUMMER INC., 420 BROADWAY EAST, SEATTLE, WA 98102.

EAGLE HARBOUR BOOK COMPANY, 440 WAY EAST, BAINBRIDGE ISLAND, WA 98110.

GARY L. ESTABROOK—BOOKS, P.O. BOX 61453, VANCOUVER, WA 98666. TN: (206) 699-5454. Est: 1974. Private premises, appointment necessary. Small stock used. Spec: Fishing, Hunting, Derrydale Press. Cata: Quarterly.

BOB FINCH BOOKS, P.O. BOX 11254, BAINBRIDGE ISLAND, WA 98110. TN: (206) 842 0202. Est: 1977. Private premises, appointment necessary. Small stock used. Spec: Maritime and nautical, voyages, Polar exploration. Cata: 3 per year. B: First State Bank of So. California.

FLORA & FAUNA BOOKS, SEATTLE BOOK CENTER, 2231 SECOND AVENUE, SEATTLE, WA 98121. TN: (206) 625 1533.

FOX BOOK COMPANY, 1140 BROADWAY, TACOMA, WA 98402. Prop: Barbara Fox. TN: (206) 627-2223. Est: 1941. Shop. Very large stock used and antiq. Spec: rare and Northwest Americana. Cata: 2 to 4 a year.

FRANSEN'S BOOKS & PRINTS, ANDERSON ISLAND, WA 98303.

GOLDEN BOUGH BOOKSTORE, 2460B, 74th AVENUE S.E., MERCER ISLAND, WA 98040.

HOPFENGARTEN GALLERY AND BOOKSHOP, P.O. BOX 335, MABTON, WA 98935. (Indian Reservation Boundary Road.) Prop: L.O. Gannon & Sons Inc., Manager; Miss R.M. Anderson. TN: (509) 894-4383. Est: 1952. Shop; appointment preferable. Small stock used; also new books and art gallery. Spec: Chapbooks and songsters; ethnology, primitive arts; fine arts; Western Americana. Cata: on foregoing, 1 a year. A.B.A.

HORIZON BOOKS, 425 15th AVENUE EAST, SEATTLE, WA 98112. Prop: Donald A. Glover. TN: (206) 329-3586. Est: 1971. Shop. Small stock used, a few new. Spec: Alaska, Arctic, Western, science fiction, Victorian literature.

INLAND BOOK STORE, WEST 411, FIRST AVENUE, SPOKANE, WA 99204. Prop: Dean Gilbert. TN: MA4-9064. Est: 1955. Shop. Large stock used; also many new including paper editions. Spec: literature, history, fine bindings, art, philosophy.

ISLAND BOOKS, 3014 78TH AVENUE S.E., MERCER ISLAND, WA 98040.

KNUTSON'S FINE ARTS INC., 611 TOWER BUILDING, 7th AVENUE, AND OLIVE WAY, SEATTLE, WA 98101.

GEORGE E. LINTHICUM, P.O. BOX 98762, TACOMA, WA 98762. TN: (206) 584-7123. Private premises; appointment necessary. Very small stock: only signed limited editions of 20th century literature.

McDUFFIE'S BOOKS, NORTH 618 MONROE STREET, P.O. BOX 14557, OPPORTUNITY, WA 99214-4557. Prop: McDuffie Owen. TN: day, (509) 325-9022; evening, (509) 928-3623. Est: 1953. Spec: Western Americana; art; medicine; science; psychiatry, psychology; photography; technology, geology, mining. Cata: occasionally.

ROBERT W. MATTILA, BOOKSELLER, 119 FOREST AVENUE SOUTH, LOWER LEVEL, SEATTLE, WA 98104. TN: (206) 622-9455. Est: 1976. Private premises, appointment necessary. Small stock used. Spec: Alaska, Arctic, Antarctic, North West History (Washington, Oregon, Idaho, Montana). Cata: Quarterly lists.

MOUNTAINBOOKS, P.O. BOX 25589, SEATTLE, WA 98125. Prop: John Pollock. TN: (206) 365-9192. Est: 1976. Private premises; appointment necessary. Very small stock used; also a few new books. Spec: mountaineering; fiction; journals. Cata: 4 a year.

MOYE AND POLLEY BOOKS, 2231 SECOND AVENUE, SEATTLE, WA 98121. TN: (206) 625-1533.

EDWARD D. NUDELMAN, P.O. BOX 20704, BROADWAY STATION, SEATTLE, WA 98102. TN: (206) 782-2930. Est: 1980. Private premises; appointment necessary. Very small stock used. Spec: early juveniles; fine color-plate illustrated books.

THE OLD BOOK HOME, P.O. BOX 18777, ROSEWOOD STATION, SPOKANE, WA 99208. (2311 West 16th, Suite 222). Prop: Jerry D. Simpson. TN: (509) 838-6017. Est: 1954. Private premises, appointment necessary. Small stock used, a few new. Spec: Western Americana and books on, about or dealing with, fine printing, book binding, limited editions, bibliography.

O'LEARY'S BOOKS, 21021 100TH ST SW, TACOMA, WA 98499. TN: (206) 588 2503.

OOKKEE'S BOOKSHOP, 929 SOUTH BAY ROAD, OLYMPIA, WA 98506. Prop: David H. Schlottmann. TN: (206) 352-8622. Est: 1967. Private premises, appointment necessary. Medium stock. Spec: Jack London. Cata: general, irregularly.

SIMON OTTENBERG, P.O. BOX 15509, WEDGEWOOD STATION, SEATTLE, WA 98115. (717 Peke Street). TN: (206) 322-5398. Est. 1968. Shop. Small stock sec. and antiq. Spec: Africa south of the Sahara; Primitive and folk art. Cata: 1 or 2 a year. Corresp: Français. ABAA.

PEGASUS BOOKS, P.O. BOX 1350, VASHON ISLAND, WA 98070. Prop: J.R. Le Fontaine. TN: (206) 567-5224, Est: 1980. Shop: appointment on weekday preferred. Large stock sec. and antiq. also new books. Spec: books about books and authors; Western Americana; mystery, detective, fantasy and science fiction. M: A.B.A.

PEGGATTY BOOKS INC., 609 MAPLE STREET, CLARKSTON, WA 99403.

DICK PERIER, P.O. BOX 1, VANCOUVER, WA 98666.

SAMPLE BOOKSHOP, 506 EAST PINE STREET, SEATTLE, WA 98122.

SHAMROCK BOOKS, 1164½ COMMERCE, SUITE 6, LONGVIEW, WA 98632.

R. L. SHEP, P.O. BOX C-20, LOPEZ, WA 98261. TN: (206) 468-2023. Spec: Fine and Rare; performing arts; textile. Publisher of "The Textile Booklist".

JOHN W. SHLEPPEY, 4530 SHERIDAN WEST, SEATTLE, WA 98199. TN: (206) ATwater 4-4188. Est: 1930. A.B.A.A.

THE SHOREY BOOK STORE, 110 UNION STREET, SEATTLE, WA 98101. Prop: John W. Todd, Jr. TN: (206) MA 4-0222. Est: 1890. Stock of over 1 million volumes used in two Seattle stores, also new. Spec: Alaska, Northwest American History, Western Americana, geology, maritime, Natural history, Indians, history, biography, angling, American first editions. Cata: on foregoing, several yearly, occasionally changed. Also Indian artifacts, maps, prints, manuscripts, etc. also Shorey Publications, facsimile reprints of old rare books and pamphlets on N.W. History, American Indians, lost arts and skills and prospecting. A.B.A.A. A.B.A.

GEORGE H. TWENEY, 16660 MARINE VIEW DRIVE SOUTH WEST, SEATTLE, WA 98166. Prop: Maxine R. Tweney. TN: (206) 243-8243. Appointment necessary. Spec: Western Americana, Alaska and Canada, fine books, first editions, maps, manuscripts. Cata. A.B.A.A. I.L.A.B.

TYEE BOOK STORE, 4305 UNIVERSITY WAY NORTH EAST, SEATTLE, WA 98105. Prop: Miss Ludmila Kuvshinoff. TN: 632-6800. Est: 1950. Shop. Very large stock used; also some new books, paintings and prints. Spec: art; history, political economy, philosophy, foreign language books.

R. M. WEATHERFORD, 10902 WOODS CREEK ROAD, MONROE, WA 98272. TN: (206) 794-4318. Est: 1972. Private premises; appointment necessary. Small stock used; also some new books. Spec: North Americana, Indians, Northwest coast and Alaska. M: A.B.A., Appraisers Association of America.

WESSEX BOOKS, P.O. BOX 318, ISSAQUAH, WA 98027. (15 North West Alder Place.) Prop: Derek Lowe. TN: (206) 392-2333. Est: 1973. Shop. Medium stock used; also new books.

WORLD MOUNTAIN BOOKS, P.O. BOX 11174, TACOMA, WA 98411-0174. Spec: mountaineering.

54. WEST VIRGINIA (WV.)

BERKELEY SPRINGS	PARKERSBURG
BLUEFIELD	RICHWOOD
BRUCETON MILLS	SHEPHERDSTOWN
CHARLESTON	WHEELING
MORGANTOWN	

APPALACHIAN BOOKSHOP, ROUTE 2, BOX 442, BLUEFIELD, WV 24701. Prop: Arnold Porterfield. TN: (304) 325-3082. Est: 1972. Shop. Very large stock used. Spec: West Virginia, Appalachian Mountains. B: Princeton Bank & Trust Co., Princeton, WV.

THE BISHOP OF BOOKS, LTD, 1223 MARKET STREET, WHEELING, WV 26003. Prop: Roger Bertoria and Charles Bishop, Jr. TN: (304) 232-0057. Est: 1977. Shop. Stock 40,000 plus. Open Mon 10-9, Tues-Fri, 10-7, Sat 9-5. Spec: West Virginiana and Western Americana, Alcoholism, Autographs. Cata: 6 a year.

COMPASS BOOKSHOP, RT. 2, BOX 89, BERKELEY SPRINGS, WV 25411.

EMILY DRISCOLL, P.O. BOX 834, SHEPHERDSTOWN, WV 25443. TN: (304) 876-2202. Spec: autographs and manuscripts; also drawings and illustrations. A.B.A.A.

HILLBILLY BOOKSHOP, RICHWOOD, WV 26261.

INLAND RIVER BOOKS, 4408 PACKARD ST., PARKERSBURG, WV 26101. Prop: C.R. Williams. TN: (304) 428-4948. Est: 1970. Private premises, appointment necessary. Small stock used. Spec: Americana-West Virginia, Upper Ohio Valley. Cata: Two or three times per year.

MAJOR'S BOOK STORE, INC., 221 HALE STREET, CHARLESTON, WV 25301. Prop: Floyd C. Major. TN: (304) 344-3504. Est: 1921. Small stock used, also new. Spec: West Virginia. A.B.A.

STILWELL BOOKSHOP, 150 PLEASANT STREET, MORGANTOWN, WV 26505.

STROUD THEOLOGICAL BOOKSELLERS, STAR ROUTE, BOX 94, WILLIAMSBURG, WV 27991. Prop: John Nathan Stroud. TN: (304) 645-7169. Spec: Theology, church history, missions, methodism, American church history. M: A.B.A.A.

UNICORN LIMITED, INC., P.O. BOX 397, BRUCETON MILLS, WV 26525. Prop: Dr. W.R. McLeod. TN: (304) 379-8803. Est: 1979. By mail order only. Stock may be seen at time of Scottish Games. Very small stock sec. and antiq. books. Spec: Scottish, Celtic, Viking, Pictish books. Cata: 6 a year. Corresp: Français, Deutsch.

55. WISCONSIN (WI.)

APPLETON	MARSHFIELD
BIG BEND	MADISON
DELAVAN	MIDDLETON
DEPERE	MILWAUKEE
EAU CLAIRE	PLATTEVILLE
ELM GROVE	STEVENS POINT
GRAFTON	WATERTOWN
LAKE DELTON	

THE ANTIQUARIAN SHOP, P.O. BOX L, STEVENS POINT, WI 54481. (1329 Strongs Avenue.) Prop: Ellen Specht. TN: (715) 341-3351. Est: 1970. Shop. Medium stock used; also some specialized new books, antiques and art gallery. Spec: American history, literature; antiques.

55. WISCONSIN (WI.)

ARABEST BOOK SHOP, W224S, 6800 GUTHRIE ROAD, BIG BEND, WI 53103.

BAPTIST BOOK BOURSE, 745 WEST MAIN STREET, WATERTOWN, WI 53094. Prop: Dr. Richard C. Weeks. TN: (414) 261-0885. Est: 1963. Storeroom, appointment necessary. Very small stock used. Spec: bible commentaries, general theology, Baptist history, doctrine and biography.

BOB'S BOOK SHOP, 231A EAST COLLEGE AVENUE, APPLETON, WI 54911.

BOOKS, THEN AND NOW, 2137 UNIVERSITY AVENUE, MADISON, WI 53705. Prop: Joseph & Jayne Marek. TN: (1-608) 233-7030. Est: 1975. Shop, closed on Sundays. Medium stock used. Spec: History, mathematics, sciences. B: First Wisconsin Bank. Acc. No: 312 188.

BOOKSHOP AT STONECROFT, 1 DEANS WALK, GRAFTON, WI 53024.

DAN'S BOOKS, 111 SOUTH APPLETON STREET, APPLETON, WI 54911. Prop: Daniel K. Shenandoah. TN: (414) 739-6118 Est: 1978. Small stock used. B: Security Bank, Menasha. Account No: 132-492.

DESFORGES BOOKSELLERS, 400 EAST WISCONSIN AVENUE, MILWAUKEE, WI 53202,

RAYMOND DWORCZYK, 2114 10 ROGERS STREET, MILWAUKEE, WI 53204.

W. BRUCE FYE ANTIQUARIAN MEDICAL BOOKS, 1607 NORTH WOOD AVENUE, MARSHFIELD, WI 54449. TN: (1-715) 384-8128. Est: 1973. Private premises, Mail order only. Medium stock used. Spec: Medicine—old, rare and out of print, Medical history and bibliography. Cata: 4 per year. B: M and I Central Bank, Marshfield, WI; Acc. No: 00820148.

JAY T. JOHNSON, 3 WOODCREST HIGHLANDS, EAU CLAIRE, WI 54701.

MEYERS BOOKS, P.O. BOX 50, MILWAUKEE, WI 53201. Prop: Frank Meyers. Est: 1964. Storeroom, appointment necessary. Small stock used, a few new. Spec: politics, social science.

OLD DELAVAN BOOK COMPANY, 67 EAST WALWORTH AVENUE, DELAVAN, WI 53115. TN: (414) 728-6988.

PAPER MOUNTAIN, 85 North Hickory Street, Platteville, WI 53818.

RENAISSANCE BOOK SHOP INC., 834 North Plankinton, Milwaukee, WI 53203. TN: (414) 271-6850. Very large stock sec. and antiq.

SADLON'S, 109 North Broadway, DePere, WI 54115. TN: (414) 336-6665. Gallery. Spec: prints. Cata.

SCHROEDERS BOOKS & RECORDS, 636 West Wisconsin Avenue, Milwaukee, WI 53203. Prop: William E. Schroeder. TN: (414) 272-0583. Est: 1957. Shop. Very large stock used, also new. A.B.A.

T.S. VANDOROS RARE BOOKS, 5827 Highland Terrace, Middleton, WI 53562. TN: (608) 836-8254. Private premises, appointment necessary. Spec: 19th and 20th century English literary first editions, presentation copies, fine bindings. M: A.B.A.A.

WEST'S BOOKING AGENCY, P.O. Box 406, Elm Grove, WI 53122. Prop: Richard P. West. TN: (414) 786-7084. Est: 1977. Private premises; postal business only. Small stock used. Spec: detective, mystery fiction.

WISE OWL BOOKSHOP, P.O. Box 377, Lake Delton, WI 53940.

56. WYOMING (WY.)

CASPER   CHEYENNE

HAL JENSEN, P.O. Box 1587, Cheyenne, WY 82001.

LANGE'S BOOKSHOP, 136 SOUTH WOLCOTT, CASPER, WY 82601.

57. UNITED STATES EXTERNAL TERRITORIES

U.S. VIRGIN ISLANDS

JELTRUPS' BOOKS, 51 ABC COMPANY STREET, CHRISTIANSTED, SAINT CROIX, U.S. VIRGIN ISLANDS, VI 00820. Prop: Mrs Dorothy McKenzie Jeltrup. TN: (809) 773-1018. Spec: Virgin Islands and Caribbean books. M: A.B.A.A.

RULON-MILLER BOOKS, 8-5 A DECK POINT ROAD, RED HOOK, P.O. BOX 41, SAINT THOMAS, U.S. VIRGIN ISLANDS, VI 00802. Prop: Robert Rulon-Miller, Sr. TN: (809) 775-6308. Spec: U.S. Virgin Islands; books, maps, prints, manuscripts; Caribbean; Central and South America. M: A.B.A.A.

58. OTHER COUNTRIES

ARGENTINA	GUATEMALA
BERMUDA	MEXICO
BRAZIL	UNITED KINGDOM
COLOMBIA	VENEZUELA

ATLANTIS LIVROS LTDA., CAIXA POSTAL 21.206, 04698 SAO PAULO, BRAZIL. Prop: G.F. & Lucia Ehlers. TN: 011/542 4377. TA: Heydecker. Est: 1966. Storeroom, appointment necessary. Medium stock used. Spec: Brazil and works by Brazilian authors. Cata: on foregoing, approx. every month.

GUILLERMO BARAYA & CIA., AP. AEREO 5493, BOGOTA 1, COLOMBIA. Prop: Guillermo Baraya Borda. TN: 345746. Cables: Stechafner. Est: 1946. Storeroom; appointment necessary. Large stock used; also new books and laboratory equipment. Spec: Latin America; maps.

THE BOOKMART, P.O. BOX 826, HAMILTON 5, BERMUDA. (Reid Street.) Prop: Bermuda Drug Company. TN: (809) 295-1647. Cables: Youngsolo. Est: 1965. Very small stock used; also new books and picture framing. Spec: Bermudiana.

CASA EL CARMEN, 3-A AVENIDA NORTE 8, ANTIGUA, GUATEMALA, C.A. Prop: Paul F. Glynn. TN: 0320207. Est: 1980. Private premises; appointment necessary. Small stock used. Spec: Central America and Panama.

CHRISTMAS ARCHIVES, "Wassail House", 64 Severn Road, Cardiff, CF1 9EA, South Wales, United Kingdom. Prop: Countess Maria von Staufer. TN: Cardiff 41120. Est: 1978. Private premises; postal trade only. Large stock. Spec: Christmas; juvenile; art; aviation; cookery. Cata: occasionally.

LIBRERIA ANTICUARIA EDGARDO HENSCHEL, Reconquista 533 (Psip 1), 1003 Buenos Aires, Argentina.

LIBRERIA DE ANTANO, S. de Bustamante 1876, Buenos Aires, Argentina.

LIVRARIA PARTHENON LTD., Rua Barao De Itapetininga 140/1, Sao Paulo-Zpi, Brazil. Prop: A. & M. Bittencourt. TN: 35-0765 and 37-2623. Est: 1946. Storeroom, open normal business hours. Very large stock used, also new. Spec: Braziliana, English and French literature, bibliography, fine arts, music, old and rare, bindings. Cata: on foregoing, monthly lists. Associacao Brasileira de Livreiros Antiquarios.

LOLA (LITERATURE OF LATIN AMERICA), Rodriguez Pena 115 (7 Piso), 1020 Buenos Aires, Argentina. Prop: Colin & Maria Sharp. TN: (451) 45-0518. Spec: Latin American Natural History, Patagonia, Antarctica.

MOISES EPSTEIN, Casilla de Correos 2318, Buenos Aires, Argentina.

SANTO VANASIA, 1410 Cangallo, Buenos Aires, Argentina. TN: 40.3937. Specialist in Antiquarian books, reviews and rare periodicals. Can obtain books and periodicals quickly.

SANTO VANASIA, 26 P. DELA FACULTADES, MEXICO 20 D.F. TN: 48-01-05. Specialist in Antiquarian books, reviews and periodicals. Can obtain books and periodicals quickly.

SHAWCROSS BOOK SERVICE, A.P. 343, ANTIGUA, GUATEMALA, C.A. Prop: Michael S. Shawcross. Office, appointment necessary. Small stock sec. and antiq. Spec: Guatemalan imprints, southern Mexico. Central America. Corresp: Français, Español. B: Lloyds Bank California, 601 Clement Street, San Francisco, CA 94118, U.S.A.

SIRE & ESTEBAN, CASILLA CORREO CENTRAL 5295, BUENOS AIRES, ARGENTINA. Prop: Abraham B. Sire. Spec: Latin Americana, voyages, maps, colored plate books, drawings, paintings.

SOBERBIA, C.A., EDIFICIO DILLON-LOCAL 4, PUENTA YANEZ A TRACABORDO, CARACAS, 1010 VENEZUELA. TN: 561-90-38. TA: Soberbia Caracas. Shop. Large stock used, also new books, maps, etchings, documents. Spec: Venezuela, Latin America. Cata: general (except technical).

ALPHABETICAL INDEX

to the Geographical Directory of Dealers

The index numbers refer to the sections in the Geographical List

A

349

B

351

C

E

F

G

381

I

K

389

M

393

395

N

O

P

P.M. Bookshop, 321 Park Avenue, Plainfield, NJ 07060 34
Pacific Book House, Kilohana Square, 1016-G Kapahulu Avenue, Honolulu, HI 96816 15
Pacific Book Supply Company, P.O. Box 337, Farmersville, CA 93223 . . . 8
Pacific Books, 1135 Lonsdale, North Vancouver, B.C. V7M 2H4, Canada . . 3
Pageant Book and Print Shop, 109 East 9th Street, New York, NY 10003 . . 36
Pages for Sages, P.O. Box 22723, Beachwood, OH 44122 41
Pages of Yesteryear (The), Old Hawleyville Road, Newtown, CT 06470 . . 10
Paideia Books, 313 South State Street, Ann Arbor, MI 48104 26
Palenque Books, R.R.1, Box 12, Milton, NY 12547 38
Palinurus Antiquarian Books, P.O. Box 15923, Philadelphia, PA 19103. . . 44
Palma Book Service, P.O. Box 602, 120 West 19th Street, Wilmington, DE 19899 11
Palmer (Richard C.)=Montrose Book Shop, Houston, TX 77006 49
Pan American Books=John C. Huckans, Books, Cazenovia, NY 13035 . . . 38
Pangloss Bookshop, 65 Mount Auburn Street, Cambridge, MA 02138 . . . 25
Panos (Ellie), 402 Bedford Street, Whitman, MA 02382 25
Papantinas (Nicholas), 303 Stockley Street, Rehoboth Beach, DE 19971 . . 11
Paper and Ink Bookshop, 44 Beech Avenue, Berkeley Heights, NJ 07922 . . 34
Paper Moon Bookstore, 3538 S.E. Hawthorne Boulevard, Portland, OR 97214 43
Paper Mountain, 85 North Hickory Street, Platteville, WI 53818 55
Paper Peddlers, 4425 Mayfield Road, South Euclid, Cleveland, OH 44121 . 41
Paperback Alley Used Books, 5840 Hollister Avenue, Goleta, CA 93101 . . 8
Paperback Place, 1994 Cliff Drive, Santa Barbara, CA 93101 8
Paragon Book Gallery Limited, 2130 Broadway, New York, NY 10023 . . . 36
Parker Books of the West, 300 Lomita, Santa Fe, NM 87501 35
Parkers Books, 1465 Main Street, Sarasota, FL 33577 13
Parnassus Book Service, Box 33, Route 6A, Yarmouth Port, MA 02675 . . 25
Parnassus Book Shop, 26 Montgomery Street, Rhinebeck, NY 12572 . . . 38
Partridge Bookstore, 6739 Hollywood Boulevard, Hollywood, CA 90028 . . 8
Pass (Randall), 159 Jason Street, Arlington, MA 02174 25
Passaic Book Center, 594 Main Avenue, Passaic, NJ 07055 34
Past History, 136 Parkview Terrace, Lincroft, NJ 07738 34
Pastimes Paper Collectibles, 369 Oak Avenue, Cedarhurst, NY 11516 . . . 37
Patchogue Book Shop, 116 West Main Street, Patchogue, NY 11772 37
Patchy Fog (The), 142 West Main, El Cajon, CA 92020 8
Patterson (Joe)=Joe's Books, Tucson, AZ 85716 6
Patrick Books (Joseph), 1600 Bloor Street West, Toronto, Ont. M6P 1A7, Canada 2
Patterson (Eric Holmes)=Tom Davies Bookshop, Alburquerque, NM 87101 . 35
Paul (Christopher)=Christophers, Worcester, MA 25
Paul (Henry S.)=Game Bag Books, Holtwood, PA 17532 44
Paulson (Robert and Barbara), Allen Coit Road, Huntington, MA 01050 . . 25
Pavlov (N. & N.), 37 Oakdale Drive, Dobbs Ferry, NY 10522 38
Payson Hall Bookshop, 80 Trapelo Road, Belmont MA 02178 25
Peabody (Velton), 4548 Main Street, Buffalo, NY 14226 38
Peachtree Books Inc., P.O. Box 54501, Atlanta, GA 30308. 14
Pearson (J.E.), P.O. Box 446, Chicago, IL 60690 17
Pegasus Books, P.O. Box 1350, Vashon Island, WA 98070 53
Peggatty Books Inc., 609 Maple Street, Clarkston, WA 99403 53

411

413

414

415

T

417

U

V

421

X

Y

Z

SPECIALITY INDEX

to the Geographical Directory of Dealers

Specialities are arranged under the following heads:

AGRICULTURE which includes horticulture and gardening.

AUTOGRAPHS AND MANUSCRIPTS.

BIBLIOGRAPHY which includes all books about books.

BIOGRAPHY which includes autobiographies.

COLLECTING.

CRAFTS AND USEFUL ARTS such as cookery and photography.

ENTERTAINMENTS.

FICTION which includes fantasy, weird and witchcraft.

FINE AND RARE EDITIONS which includes all books sought because they are old, first or limited editions, private press books, fine printing and binding, miniature books, incunabula, etc.

FOREIGN which includes all books in languages other than English.

HISTORY which includes archaeology, folklore, genealogy.

JUVENILE.

LAW AND CRIMINOLOGY.

MEDICINE AND PUBLIC HEALTH.

MUSIC which includes scores and books about music.

NATURAL HISTORY which includes botany, entomology, ornithology and zoology.

PERIODICALS.

PICTORIAL ART which includes all books about or illustrative of the pictorial arts, color plates, fine illustrations and prints.

POETRY.

RELIGION (1) AND PHILOSOPHY which includes general religious literature, theology, psychology, rationalism and freethought, philosophy.

RELIGION (2) which includes astrology, occult and psychic.

SCIENCE.

SOCIOLOGY which includes political and social movements, freemasonry, political economy, government.

SPORTS AND PASTIMES.

TECHNICAL, INDUSTRIAL AND COMMERCIAL which includes engineering, journalism, manufacturing, military and naval, transport.

TEXT BOOKS AND OTHER EDUCATIONAL WORKS.
TOPOGRAPHY (AMERICANA).
TOPOGRAPHY AND TRAVEL (GENERAL) which includes foreign.

LIST OF DEALERS, GROUPED ALPHABETICALLY BY SPECIALITY

The index numbers refer to sections in the Geographical List

AGRICULTURE

includes HORTICULTURE, GARDENING

AUTOGRAPHS AND MANUSCRIPTS

BIBLIOGRAPHY

BOOKS ABOUT BOOKS

BIOGRAPHY
includes AUTOBIOGRAPHIES

COLLECTING

ENTERTAINMENTS

FICTION

includes FANTASY, WEIRD, WITCHCRAFT

FINE AND RARE EDITIONS

includes ALL BOOKS SOUGHT BECAUSE THEY ARE OLD, FIRST OR LIMITED EDITIONS, PRIVATE PRESS BOOKS, FINE PRINTING AND BINDING, MINIATURE BOOKS, INCUNABULA, etc.

FOREIGN

includes ALL BOOKS IN LANGUAGES OTHER THAN ENGLISH

HISTORY

includes ARCHAEOLOGY, FOLKLORE, GENEALOGY

JUVENILE

LAW AND CRIMINOLOGY

MEDICINE AND PUBLIC HEALTH

MUSIC

includes SCORES AND BOOKS ABOUT MUSIC

NATURAL HISTORY

includes BOTANY, ENTOMOLOGY, ORNITHOLOGY, ZOOLOGY

PERIODICALS

PICTORIAL ART

includes ALL BOOKS ABOUT OR ILLUSTRATIVE OF THE PICTORIAL
ARTS, COLOR PLATES, FINE ILLUSTRATIONS AND PRINTS

POETRY

RELIGION (1) AND PHILOSOPHY

includes GENERAL RELIGIOUS LITERATURE, THEOLOGY, PSY-
 CHOLOGY, RATIONALISM AND FREE THOUGHT, PHILOS-
 OPHY

RELIGION (2)

includes ASTROLOGY, OCCULT, PSYCHIC

SCIENCE

SOCIOLOGY

includes POLITICAL AND SOCIAL MOVEMENTS, FREEMASONRY,
POLITICAL ECONOMY, GOVERNMENT

SPORTS AND PASTIMES

TECHNICAL, INDUSTRIAL AND COMMERCIAL

includes ENGINEERING, JOURNALISM, MANUFACTURING, MILITARY
AND NAVAL, TRANSPORT

487

TEXT BOOKS AND OTHER EDUCATIONAL WORKS

TOPOGRAPHY (AMERICANA)

TOPOGRAPHY AND TRAVEL (GENERAL)

includes FOREIGN

SPECIALITY INDEX

DISPLAYED ADVERTISEMENTS

Index of Advertisers